CURRENCY AND COERCION

CURRENCY AND COERCION

THE POLITICAL ECONOMY OF
INTERNATIONAL MONETARY POWER

Jonathan Kirshner

PRINCETON UNIVERSITY PRESS PRINCETON, NEW JERSEY

Library of Congress Cataloging-in-Publication Data

Kirshner, Jonathan.
Currency and coercion : the political economy of international
monetary power / Jonathan Kirshner.
p. cm.
Includes index.
ISBN 0-691-03768-X
ISBN 0-691-01626-7 (pbk.)
1. Money. 2. International economic relations. 3. World politics.
4. Power (Social sciences) I. Title.
HG220.A2K66 1995
332.4—dc20   95-13294

For My Parents

Contents

List of Figures   ix

List of Tables   xi

Acknowledgments   xiii

PART I: THE THEORY OF MONETARY POWER

1. The Nature of Monetary Power   3

2. The Viability of Monetary Power   21

PART II: THE PRACTICE OF MONETARY POWER

3. Currency Manipulation   45

4. Monetary Dependence   115

5. Systemic Disruption   170

PART III: THE POTENTIAL OF MONETARY POWER

6. The Opportunity for Monetary Power   219

7. Monetary Power and International Relations   263

Index   283

Figures

3.1 Monetary Reserves and Imports of the Combatants   78

4.1 The Forms of Monetary Dependence   119

4.2 The Opportunity for Monetary Dependence   121

4.3 Simple Balanced Bilateral Clearing   125

4.4 Bilateral Clearing under Unbalanced Trade   127

5.1 Net Change in Gold Reserves, Britain, France, and Germany, July 1928 to December 1931   184

5.2 Net Gold Imports into Britain, Monthly, January 1927 to June 1928   185

5.3 General Trend in Gold Reserves, Britain, France, and Germany, Year's End, 1925–1932   186

5.4 French Gold Holdings, 1960–1970   200

6.1 The Market Value of the Lira in Milan, 1946   240

6.2 The Market Value of the Lira in Milan, 1947   241

Tables

2.1 Economic Instruments of Power   31

3.1 The Four Basic Forms of Currency Manipulation   46

3.2 U.S. Purchases of Chinese Silver, 1934–1941   55

3.3 The Monetary Position of the Combatants   77

3.4 Oil as a Percentage of Total Energy Consumption   80

3.5 The Practice of Currency Manipulation   108

4.1 The Sterling Balances   145

4.2 The Practice of Monetary Dependence   166

5.1 The Practice of Systemic Disruption   213

6.1 Britain, South Africa, and Gold, 1920–1925   250

6.2 Missed Opportunities   261

Acknowledgments

THIS BOOK makes bold claims to originality and innovation. Still, and of course, that which follows has clear intellectual debts and traditions, which are easily observed. It owes much to previous work, especially by economists whose interests led them to explore politics, but also by other scholars of international relations and international political economy. It would be impossible to recognize them all here. Rather, I would like to thank Charles Kindleberger, an intellectual hero of mine whom I have never met, as a representative of these men and women.

Most of the research for this book was conducted over a two-year period at the Center For International Affairs at Harvard University, first under a Ford Foundation Dissertation Fellowship in European Society and Western Security, and then under a John M. Olin Dissertation Fellowship in National Security. Further progress was facilitated by the Center for International Studies at the University of Southern California. Additional funding was provided by the Center of International Studies at Princeton through the Sumitomo Bank Fund Dissertation Fellowship, and the Institute for the Study of World Politics. I would like to thank Richard Eichenberg, Sam Huntington, Steve Rosen, John Odell, and Henry Bienen at these institutions, for their support of this work.

This project has benefited greatly from the comments and criticisms of other scholars. These included Tom Christensen, Alan Drimmer, George Downs, Aaron Friedberg, John Garofano, Robert Gilpin, Joanne Gowa, John Ikenberry, Peter Katzenstein, Robert Keohane, Beth Kier, Charles Kupchan, Peter Liberman, Joe Nye, Ken Oye, Mark Spaulding, and Shibley Telhami. I would also like to thank Malcolm DeBevoise at Princeton University Press, as well as Eileen Pratt, Karel Sedlacek, and Mildred Kalmus.

Special thanks go to my advisor, Michael Doyle, for his guidance and support. Karl Mueller and Beth Simmons provided remarkably detailed and invaluable comments, which have greatly improved this book. Finally, my greatest debt is to Esty, for covering the waterfront.

Part I

THE THEORY OF MONETARY POWER

1

The Nature of Monetary Power

Money Doesn't Talk, It Swears.
—Bob Dylan

Introduction

States and their leaders are very sensitive about the sanctity of their money. In England in 1350, counterfeiting the king's gold or silver coinage was declared a crime of high treason punishable by death. In seventh-century China, not only were counterfeiters subject to the death penalty, but their families and neighbors faced a similar fate. In the 1960s, balance-of-payments problems "remained a constant worry" to John F. Kennedy, then president of the largest and wealthiest economy the world had ever known. "What really matters . . . is the strength of the currency," he once said, in a lighthearted putdown of the importance of nuclear weapons. "Britain has nuclear weapons, but the pound is weak, so everyone pushes it around."[1]

This book is about the international political consequences of these concerns. It examines how states can and have used international monetary relations as an instrument of coercive power. "International monetary relations" refers to arrangements and actions that affect the value, uses, stability, and other attributes of national currencies issued by states. "Coercive power" refers to the manipulation of these relations by states in order to influence the preferences or behavior of other states. One example of this was the ability of the United States to exploit the weakness of the pound in order to force British withdrawal during the Suez crisis of 1956.[2]

International monetary diplomacy (which will also be called "monetary diplomacy," "monetary power," and "currency power") is a neglected area of study. Scholars of international monetary relations have focused principally on questions of efficiency, cooperation, and distribution. Students of eco-

[1] Arthur M. Schlesinger, Jr., *A Thousand Days: John F. Kennedy in the White House* (Boston: Houghton Mifflin, 1965), p. 654. On China, see D. C. Twitchett, *Financial Administration under the T'ang Dynasty* (Cambridge: Cambridge University Press, 1970), p. 74.

[2] This definition explicitly excludes interstate transfer of "money" for purposes traditionally defined as "aid." Also excluded is traditional financial diplomacy, such as the manipulation of lending by national and international institutions in order to reward friends and punish enemies or to promote various other values.

nomic statecraft have emphasized trade, aid, and financial relations. This work explores the intersection between these two fields of study.

The general goal of this book is to isolate and examine monetary power. This is not to deny (or ignore) the interrelationships between monetary and other forms of economic diplomacy. Additionally, this study will focus exclusively on the use of monetary power to advance security-related or other noneconomic goals. This specifically excludes those attempts to deploy monetary power taken by states that are dominated by concerns for increases in relative or absolute wealth. Once again, there are overlaps here, most obviously in the fact that in the long run it becomes increasingly difficult to distinguish between the pursuit of wealth and the pursuit of power.[3] However, this focus on noneconomic goals does not require that explicit lines of demarcation be identified, or even that they exist. It simply emphasizes one end of the spectrum, where noneconomic goals are dominant. In most cases, the principal concern is clear. For example, in international trade, the same type of economic sanction can be used to advance either primarily security or primarily economic goals. In the first case, an export embargo might be aimed at destabilizing or overthrowing a government, while in the second, it might be used in an attempt to force open foreign markets.

The point of restricting the analysis to cases involving noneconomic goals is to help isolate monetary power. With the focus on security, the variable of interest has a distinctness that would be lost in a tangle of interdependent variables under the more complex settings of international economic bargaining. The emphasis on security also serves the author's view that issues of power and security should be more explicitly integrated into the study of international political economy.

The specific goals of this book are to demonstrate the existence of monetary power and to understand how it works. This involves three major tasks. First is understanding the theory of monetary power: what forms it can take, and how and why it could be effective. Following the establishment of a theoretical framework for analysis, the second task is to establish the existence of monetary power by examining cases where it was employed. These cases will be drawn from episodes involving states from all parts of the world, throughout the twentieth century.[4] Finally, having established the theoretical viability

---

[3] Jacob Viner, "Power vs. Plenty as Objectives of Foreign Policy in the Seventeenth and Eighteenth Centuries," *World Politics* 1, no. 1:1–29 (1948).

[4] It was possible to practice monetary diplomacy before this century. Britain, for example, attempted to undermine the American continental currency during the Revolutionary War. See Lynn Glazer, *Counterfeiting in America* (Clarkson N. Potter, 1968), pp. 37–51; and Kenneth Scott, *Counterfeiting in Colonial America* (New York: Oxford University Press, 1957), pp. 253–63. One very early episode of monetary diplomacy may have occurred during the Peloponnesian War. In that conflict, Athens was forced to suspend the issue of silver coins, after Sparta facilitated the escape of slaves working in the Laurium silver mines. See Paul Einzig, *The History of*

of monetary power and demonstrated its existence, the third task is to understand the nature of monetary power. This inquiry will be pursued along a number of lines, including the ways various forms of monetary power are affected by different international monetary environments (such as fixed versus flexible exchange rates), the sources of the "success" and "failure" of the implementation of monetary power, and the factors that lead states to attempt these techniques.

International Monetary Relations and Economic Diplomacy

As noted above, international monetary power lies at the intersection of international monetary relations and economic diplomacy. While it is a distinct issue area, monetary diplomacy draws substantially from both of these fields. With regard to the former, monetary power draws indirectly from the lessons associated with the study of efficiency, cooperation, and distribution. It remains quite distinct from issues of efficiency or cooperation. Efficiency issues have primarily been examined by economists. Here, the main issue is which type of international monetary system is superior by the standards of economists: which maximizes global welfare, has the lowest dead weight loss, interferes least in the smooth functioning of trading markets, and so on.[5] While the monetary regime will affect the practice of monetary power, the issue of efficiency itself is blind to the concept of power. Similarly, the question of cooperation in monetary relations often involves issues of power, but deals primarily with how the distribution of power can affect the monetary system, and does not consider the converse.[6]

Foreign Exchange (London: Macmillan, 1962), p. 30; and Thucydides, *History of the Peloponnesian War* (c.410B.C.; reprint, New York: Penguin Books, 1972), pp. 156, 469. On the importance of the Laurium mines, see Alexander del Mar, *A History of Precious Metals* (1902; reprint New York: Augustus M. Kelley, 1969), pp. 44–46. However, such early cases are relatively few and isolated, and represent the "prehistory" of monetary power. As will be discussed in Chapter 2, monetary power is more likely to thrive in the context of a relatively modern, integrated, international economy.

[5] For representative arguments concerning efficiency, see Jacques Rueff, *The Monetary Sin of the West* (New York: Macmillan, 1972) (gold standard); Milton Friedman, "The Case for Flexible Exchange Rates," in Friedman, *Essays in Positive Economics* (Chicago: University of Chicago Press, 1953); Charles P. Kindleberger, "The Price of Gold and the N-1 Problem,', in Kindleberger, *International Money* (London: George Allen and Unwin, 1981) (key currency); Robert Triffin, *Gold and the Dollar Crisis* (New Haven: Yale University Press, 1960) (international asset).

[6] Good starting points for more on cooperation include the following: Richard N. Cooper, "Prolegomena to the Choice of an International Monetary System," *International Organization* 29, no. 1:69–98 (1975); Benjamin J. Cohen, *Organizing the World's Money* (New York: Basic Books, 1977); Barry Eichengreen, "Hegemonic Stability Theories of the International Monetary System," in Richard N. Cooper et al., *Can Nations Agree?* (Washington D.C.: Brookings Institu-

Distribution effects, on the other hand, do overlap with monetary power. Different monetary regimes have distinct distributional consequences. To the extent that states can use the wealth provided by a given monetary system to advance security-related goals, the consequences of distribution are relevant to the study of monetary power. In practice, this issue has been principally associated with gold-exchange standard systems.[7] In both of the modern gold-exchange standard systems, the issuer of the key currency did take advantage of its ability to create wealth by printing currency, which accumulated, basically inconvertible, in the reserves of member countries. During World War II, Egypt and India accumulated substantial sterling balances, and in the mid- to late 1960s, several European countries, especially Germany, accumulated dollars.[8] For this to be of concern for students of monetary power, it must be clear that the wealth was being used to finance security operations and, importantly, that power flowed from the monetary system to the dominant state.[9]

Thus, while studies of international monetary relations have not systematically considered monetary power, it can be noted that any consideration of such power necessarily draws on this field. Additionally, the choice of regime, the robustness of cooperation, and the distributional consequences of those interactions will shape the practice of monetary diplomacy.

---

tion, 1989); Benjamin J. Rowland, *Balance of Power or Hegemony: The Interwar Monetary System* (New York: New York University Press, 1976); Charles P. Kindleberger, *The World in Depression*, rev. ed. (Berkeley: University of California Press, 1986), esp. p. 289; Kenneth Oye, "The Sterling-Dollar-Franc Triangle: Monetary Policy 1929–1937," in Oye, ed., *Cooperation under Anarchy* (Princeton: Princeton University Press, 1986).

[7] Such a monetary regime, which is usually exclusively associated with the twentieth century, was first proposed by Plato as a domestic mechanism for controlling the distribution of wealth. Plato, *The Laws* (c.350 B.C.; reprint, London: Penguin Books, 1970), pp. 211–214.

[8] Fred Hirsch, Michael Doyle, and Edwin Morse, *Alternatives to Monetary Disorder* (New York: McGraw Hill, 1977), p. 27. For an analysis of how such a position can come to be a burden on the dominant state, see Susan Strange, *Sterling and British Policy* (London: Oxford University Press, 1971), and "The Politics of International Currencies," *World Politics* 32, no. 2:215–31 (1971). On the special role of India in the sterling system, see Marcello de Cecco, *Money and Empire* (Totowa, N.J.: Rowman and Littlefield, 1975). On Egypt and war finance, see Chapter 4.

[9] By these criteria, the 1960s case is a less clear example of monetary power because political pressure was used to hold the monetary system together. When the United States threatened to withdraw troops from West Germany if that country exchanged its dollars for gold, this represented the use of political power to continue economic extraction, which is distinct from the more implicit use of the monetary system as a means to finance power. In the latter mechanism, more clearly present in the British case, power is clearly the objective and economic structure is the instrument by which the objective is obtained. Both cases are considered below, from different perspectives.

It should be noted that the magnitude of seigniorage (the difference between the cost of producing a currency and its purchasing power, which accrues to the issuer) is subject to debate: many mainstream economists minimize its importance. See W. Max Corden, *Inflation, Exchange*

The exercise of currency power takes place in the space of international monetary relations. This is the source of the relationship between the two. Currency power is also an instrument of economic statecraft: this in turn is the source of the relationship between monetary diplomacy and that broader field of study. However, this particular instrument of coercion has been largely ignored. David Baldwin, for example, in his excellent book, *Economic Statecraft*, gives examples of seventeen negative and eleven positive types of sanctions, none of which have anything to do with monetary relations or affairs.[10] The influential study of Gary Clyde Hufbauer and Jeffrey J. Schott, *Economic Sanctions Reconsidered*, provides an in-depth analysis of 106 cases, of which 74 involve what the authors categorize as "financial" (as opposed to trade) sanctions. The bulk of these involve the suspension of aid and the freezing of assets; in fact, only three episodes involve any reference to monetary power, and in each case, the importance of monetary power is qualified. Little attention is paid to how monetary power is exercised or how important a contributing factor it was in these or other episodes.[11]

Occasional exceptions can be found to the silence of the economic statecraft literature on monetary power. Klaus Knorr, in *The Power of Nations*, observes that economic coercion can occur if "A acts to put B's international currency position under pressure." He also notes that "a weak reserve position will curtail a government's capacity to engage in warfare at home or abroad." He does not consider, though, how other governments could act to manipulate reserve positions in order to affect power capabilities.[12] Yuan-Li Wu's *Economic Warfare* offers an early and more focused discussion of monetary power. Wu's emphasis is principally on wartime operations, but the techniques he discusses are relevant during nominal peace as well. In a section entitled "Methods of Stimulating Price Inflation and the Dissipation of Enemy Reserves," Wu argues that "deliberately selling the enemy's currency on such unofficial markets or free exchange markets maintained in adjacent neutral countries at increasingly lower rates" will promote those goals, as well as stimulating capital flight from the target.[13] Wu's analysis points toward a more systematic integration of monetary diplomacy into overall national strategy, but even his more detailed attention to monetary power only begins to

---

Rates, and the World Economy (Oxford: Clarendon Press, 1977), ch. 6; and C. Fred Bergsten, *The Dilemmas of the Dollar* (New York: New York University Press, 1975), pt. 2 and p. 32. The economic costs and benefits of issuing the key currency are considered in Chapter 5.

[10] Princeton: Princeton University Press, 1985. Baldwin does mention the potential for monetary power in passing.

[11] Washington, D.C.: Institute for International Economics, 1985. Brief references to currency matters can be found on pp. 37, 276, and 653.

[12] New York: Basic Books, 1973, pp. 83, 88.

[13] New York: Prentice Hall, 1952, p. 142.

draw attention to the existence and potential of this instrument. A detailed and systematic analysis of such power is needed.

International Monetary Power

International monetary power can be exercised in three ways: through the practice of *currency manipulation*, the fostering and exploitation of *monetary dependence*, and the exercise of *systemic disruption*. "Currency manipulation" refers to actions taken to affect the stability and value of target currencies. This can be used, for example, to punish or coerce: the sanctioning (or "home") country can fail to support the target currency, or attack it outright. Monetary dependence can create a sphere of influence: a bloc of countries that use the home currency as their own, are pegged to it, or use it in international transactions provide the home country with power. With regard to the target countries, the home country gains an important degree of control over their economic destiny. With regard to third parties, the home country can gain trading advantages, which can insulate it from the policies of those outsiders, and may be able to exploit its sphere of influence to mobilize resources for war. "Systemic disruption" refers to attempts to exercise monetary power that are directed at specific international monetary systems or subsystems, as opposed to particular currencies.

Currency Manipulation

Currency manipulation is the simplest instrument of monetary power, and has the widest number of applications. Currency manipulation can be used either for short-term coercive power, that is, to change a target state's preferences or actions over a specific issue, or to provide general long-term support for an ally. This instrument has a great degree of flexibility: it can be used with varying degrees of intensity, ranging from mild signaling to the destabilization of national regimes.

In order for currency manipulation to be useful, target states must prefer that their currencies not be manipulated against their wishes (or must appreciate positive manipulation). There are a variety of reasons why this is the case. Some of these depend on the type of international monetary system in place. For example, under a system where states are obliged to defend fixed exchange rates, pressure on a currency automatically forces the drawing down of reserves and often results in balance-of-payments crises. Other reasons why states are sensitive to currency manipulation are more general. They have to do with specific economic interests, the psychology of currency values, and the legitimacy of governance.

Negative currency manipulations by definition move a currency away from the value preferred by the issuing government. Such a move can have a variety of unpleasant economic consequences. An unwelcome depreciation, for example, can cause increased inflation, capital flight, difficulty in attracting new foreign investment, an increased real debt burden, and a reduction in real living standards.[14] In general, wide swings in the value of the domestic money are likely to anger two groups: consumers of tradable goods, whose purchasing power would be reduced, and major exporters, who depend on a stable currency in order to participate in the international economy.[15] Major fluctuations in currency values can also interfere with development plans, which are dependent on consistent and predictable levels of foreign exchange receipts.[16] But even in the absence of an explicit national economic strategy, it should be clear that rapid and significant changes in the value of the currency would wreak havoc on the domestic economy, with the potential for major economic and political ramifications. The power of a large-scale, short-term predatory attack designed simply to promote chaos in the target country seems a strikingly simple and potent instrument of monetary power, especially against relatively weak or vulnerable targets.

Although they would not be required to do so under all circumstances, most nations would move to defend their currencies in the international market.[17] Obviously, states would defend their currencies in order to avoid the economic

[14] Currency manipulation could also bring about an undesired currency appreciation: appreciation hurts import competing and export industries and may cause unemployment. Moreover, nations may support an undervalued exchange rate in order to promote an export-oriented growth strategy or in the service of a more general mercantilist strategy of accumulation. Here, the economic strategy is vulnerable to excessive support for the currency, which would drive it up on the world market and undermine the strategy. This direction of pressure would probably be more difficult; assuming some effort to defend the currency, a country facing depreciation would be under more pressure than would one facing appreciation. The former would eventually run out of defenses, such as reserves, and ultimately even the ability to borrow additional reserves, while the latter could conceivably pile up foreign exchange assets indefinitely. On asymmetrical vulnerability of depreciators and appreciators, see Charles P. Kindleberger, *Power and Money* (New York: Basic Books, 1970), p. 198; see also Bergsten, *Dilemmas*, p. 12.

[15] This suggests that governments that serve at the pleasure of such groups would be particularly vulnerable to currency manipulation, or for that matter, monetary power in general. Democracies, for example, should therefore be relatively vulnerable, as should those military or authoritarian regimes whose power base comes from the support of a few dominant oligarchic economic interests. A country ruled by a relatively self-sustaining military establishment, on the other hand, should be less susceptible to monetary power.

[16] David Wall, *The Charity of Nations* (New York: Basic Books, 1973), p. 111.

[17] Under a system of floating exchange rates, states would not need to intervene in the market; in fact they would not technically need reserves at all, if they were willing to accept the "market" price for their currencies. Under fixed rates, participating states are legally bound to intervene. See Susan Strange, *International Monetary Relations*, vol. 2 of Andrew Shonfield, ed., *International Economic Relations of the Western World 1959–1971* (London: Oxford University Press, 1976), p. 2.

and political problems associated with the shifting of currency value away from the desired range. States under all kinds of international monetary systems during "normal" periods intervene almost continuously to manage the level of their currencies. It is logical to assume that they would defend their currencies whether the pressure they were under was the result of "natural economic" forces, speculation, or coercive monetary power.

The problem with currency defense is that it can be quite costly itself. For example, it may involve the drawing down of national reserves, which states dislike doing. According to Bergsten, "Countries usually resist any reserve losses, since losses are widely regarded as indicating a basic weakness in their currency and thus may accumulate."[18] Therefore, defending the currency can indirectly put it under even more pressure. One official described watching reserves fall as akin to seeing "a child bleeding to death and being unable to stop it." Winston Churchill, reacting to an ultimately inconsequential reserve loss in 1952, stated, "I know the financial position is desperate . . . the country has lost its way."[19] Countries are also reluctant to part with reserves because they represent international purchasing power, which can become especially important in times of crisis or war.[20] Finally, running reserves down too far can result in a balance-of-payments crisis, forcing a curtailment of imports. Thus, even a "successful" defense of the currency, which can mitigate the direct effects of the original pressure, may have other costs, with an attendant set of problems.

Beyond the direct economic costs that can be associated with negative currency manipulation, which can certainly be substantial, there is the underlying fear of currency collapse. This is a consequence of the unique psychology of money. Common to all (monetized) societies are the political implications of currency instability, which have no historical or geographical boundary. The monetary crisis in Poland in the seventeenth century, for example, which saw the Polish penny fall to 40 percent of its traditional value, became in the eyes of the populace there "the apocalyptic symbol of the misfortunes of the age, the apparent cause of all their worries and torments in the eyes of contemporaries." Some of the consequences of this included increased xenophobia, anti-Semitism, and class hatred, all casualties of the search for those responsible. In the words of one historian, the situation in Poland was "reminiscent of the psychopathic states to which a society falls victim in times of great scourges or epidemics."[21]

---

[18] Bergsten, *Dilemmas*, p. 532.

[19] Chancellor of the Exchequer Dalton, quoted in J.C.R. Dow, *The Management of the British Economy 1945–1960* (Cambridge: Cambridge University Press, 1970), p. 27; Churchill, quoted in S. Brittan, *Steering the Economy* (New York: Library Press, 1971), p. 197.

[20] Janet Kelly, "The International Monetary System and National Security," in Knorr and Trager, eds., *Economic Issues and National Security* (Lawrence: Allen Press, 1977), p. 236.

[21] Maria Bogucka, "The Monetary Crisis of the XVIIth Century and Its Social and Psychologi-

The Polish crisis was the result of a general European monetary crisis and international events, such as the Cossack uprisings and the Swedish invasion, not currency manipulation.[22] Nor can it be assumed that predatory manipulation will always have such far-reaching consequences. But the influence of monetary psychology is pervasive and can exacerbate the "real" economic consequences of an initial incident. According to Wu, "A general depreciation of the domestic currency may be associated in the public's mind with monetary inflation and the instability of the currency system."[23] This can lead to general economic pessimism, reduced investment, capital flight, and increasing downward pressure on the currency. The psychology of exchange rates can intimidate even the most experienced central bankers. When the large capitalist countries acted to depreciate a highly overvalued dollar in the mid-1980s, Paul Volcker, the U.S. Federal Reserve Board chairman, expressed repeated concerns over the pace and extent of the decline, fearing a "free fall" of the dollar.[24]

Finally, there is the issue of prestige and the legitimacy of governance. President Franklin D. Roosevelt, rejecting a proposed act of currency manipulation, stated, "Killing is all right, and you can attack religion with some impunity, but you were threatening something dearer than life to many people."[25] Essentially, at a more practical level, monetary stability is of great domestic political importance. The government is the manager of the currency, and signs of egregious mismanagement will put that government under pressure from a number of potent quarters. Thus the government will be particularly sensitive to the fact that a fall in the value of the currency might not be limited, but could gather momentum and lead to collapse.

The intimately related issue of prestige should not be underestimated with regard to exchange rate values. According to Kindleberger, "A country's exchange rate is more than a number. It is an emblem of its importance to the world, a sort of international status symbol."[26] Many nations and their leaders have demonstrated that they maintain this belief. The British restoration of the pound after World War I to its prewar value is perhaps the best known of the striking commitments to par values of currencies for cosmetic purposes, even at the expense of economic interests. Premier Poincaré in France also felt that national honor called for a restoration of the prewar value of the franc, and

---

cal Consequences in Poland," *Journal of European Economic History* 4, no. 1:137–52 (1975), p. 149 (1975)(first quote); ibid., pp. 150, 152 (second quote).

[22] Ibid., p. 141.

[23] Wu, *Economic Warfare*, p. 124.

[24] Yoichi Funabashi, *Managing the Dollar: From the Plaza to the Louvre* (Washington, D.C.: Institute for International Economics, 1988), p. 49.

[25] Quoted in John Steinbeck, "The Secret Weapon They Were AFRAID to Use," *Colliers*, January 10, 1953, p. 10.

[26] Kindleberger, *Power and Money*, p. 198.

was only prevented from establishing the franc at that value by the threatened resignation of the governor of the Bank of France. And in 1926, Mussolini swore to defend the lira to the "last drop of blood" and ordered that this commitment be etched in stone.[27]

The importance of national honor is not simply a disease of the 1920s. According to one scholar, under the gold standard system (1873–1914), "to go off gold was then thought of as an unmitigated disaster, although no one was clear why," Nor was this without its political implications: in 1911, business leaders pressured the German government to resolve the Agadir crisis peacefully in order to end a growing financial panic there and stem the outflow of gold.[28] In another era, Prime Minister Wilson of Great Britain, upon assuming office in October 1964, made an "irrevocable decision" not to devalue in response to the brewing economic crisis, viewing the implications of such a move as politically disastrous.[29] Nor, apparently, are states simply paranoid when they worry about how currency prestige looks to outsiders; it has been reported that President Lyndon B. Johnson expressed his admiration for France's staunch defense of the value of the franc, contrasting French strength with apparent British weakness in the need to devalue.[30]

It is clear, then, that states would find successful negative currency manipulation very costly, and thus positive currency manipulation highly attractive. Aside from the direct economic costs and the possible costs associated with defense, threats to currency stability are particularly subversive to existing governments. This is due to the unique psychology of this particular sphere of economics, where value depends explicitly on confidence, and because monetary stability is so closely associated with the legitimacy of governance.

Monetary Dependence

The second type of monetary power is the fostering and exploitation of monetary dependence. Any study of dependence begins with Albert O. Hirschman, and his book *National Power and the Structure of Foreign Trade*.[31] Dependence results from asymmetric benefits associated with interstate relations. It

[27] Leyland Yeager, *International Monetary Relations: Theory, History, and Policy* (New York: Harper and Row, 1976), p. 329 (France); ibid., p. 390 ("Last drop of blood").

[28] P. J. Wiles, *Communist International Economics* (Oxford: Basil Blackwell, 1968), p. 471. For more on Agadir, see also Chapter 3.

[29] Yeager, *International Monetary Relations*, p. 455.

[30] Johnson's views are discussed in Bergsten, *Dilemmas*, p. 438. Commenting in his memoirs on the British devaluation of 1967, Johnson reflected: "We had been forewarned, of course, but it was still like hearing that an old friend who had been ill has to undergo a serious operation. However much you expect it, the news is still a heavy blow." L. B. Johnson, *The Vantage Point* (New York: Holt, Rinehart and Wilson, 1971), p. 315.

[31] 1945; reprint, Berkeley: University of California Press, 1980.

should be noted that the term "dependence" used by Hirschman in his study and in this book is quite different from the concept of dependence used in dependency theory. In this book, as in Hirschman, " dependence" refers to an economic vulnerability—the economic future of the target state is dependent on moves or conditions in the home state. This vulnerability can then be exploited by the home state politically to dominate the target states. In dependency theory, " dependency" implies economic exploitation and the maintenance (against the will of the target state) of a trading relationship that locks the target into a long-term position of low economic growth. Here, power is used by the home state to force and perpetuate economic domination of the vulnerable states. The important difference is that dependence, in the sense used by Hirschman and adopted here, is primarily a power relationship (in fact the target state can gain, even relatively, in an economic sense). Dependency, on the other hand, is primarily a relationship of economic exploitation: that of a transfer of current and future wealth from target to home country. Many of the issues raised by Hirschman in his investigation of trade dependence carry over to the sphere of monetary relations; in fact, as will be discussed in Chapter 4, the introduction of monetary power was an essential element of the German trade strategy examined by Hirschman.

Dependence, in the context of monetary relations, is usually manifested through the creation of formal or informal currency zones, "areas," or "blocs." At various times, Britain, France, Germany, and the United States have each headed such currency areas. Here, the source of power is both internal and external to the zone. Against the outside world, the area can provide insulation as well as the potential for the mobilization and coordination of resources. Internally, power accrues to leader states both directly and indirectly. Directly, area leaders can coerce member states through manipulation of resources within the framework of the arrangement, with coordinated "punishment" by the leader and other states against a particular state. Most dramatically, coercion can be exercised through the threat of expulsion. Just as significant is the indirect power that accrues to the core state. This comes from the fact that participation in a monetary system or other international economic agreements transforms the interests of states. Participation in such organizations shifts the preferences of the target state toward harmony with those of the home state, and strengthens those actors in the target state's society who prefer close ties to the home state.

In order for dependence to have the potential for power, though, target states must be vulnerable: most obviously, they must fear the ultimate threat of expulsion. This consideration involves a more complex analysis than seen with regard to currency manipulation. Power accrues to the home state not simply from the threat of expulsion, but from the transformation of target interests as well. Thus, it is not simply that states fear expulsion, but that, over time, they become willing to engage in behaviors that are increasingly beneficial to the home state. To simplify the discussion, the consideration of the indirect power accruing from monetary dependence will be postponed, in favor of an analysis of the direct source of influence, the threat of expulsion.

Three interrelated considerations are paramount with regard to entry and exit for a member in a currency area: threats to currency stability, elimination of protection, and loss of privileges. Membership in a currency area enhances the stability of the exchange rates of members, especially the smaller ones, which are the most vulnerable to unwanted fluctuations. There are two sources of this stability. First, each member state is able to piggyback on the stability, credibility, and prestige of the system as a whole. Automatic convertibility into the key currency of the core state diverts market attention away from the currency of the peripheral state. Second, currency arrangements usually involve expanded access to reserves or other mechanisms that allow states to finance temporary balance-of-payments deficits. For the purposes of demonstration, the analysis will consider the effect of pooled reserves, which offers the greatest ease of measurement. This does not preclude the possibility that reputational effects or access to other forms of financing are more important in preserving stability.

For small states, pooled reserves greatly reduce the threat of frequent and immediate balance-of-payments crises. This is because the relatively massive pooled reserves of a currency area will dramatically expand the ability of small member states to weather temporary economic storms without drying up reserves and facing a payments crisis. Additionally, the arrangements of the currency area usually provide a mechanism for dealing with more structural disequilibria.

What is important to note here is the Hirschmanesque mechanism at work: a given member country might provide 2 percent of a currency area's pooled resources while the dominant country might provide 75 percent.[32] The small country is thus much more vulnerable to dissolution than the dominant country. In some ways, the dependence is even greater than in trade. This is because the importance of reserves has to do with their relationship to imports, not simply their absolute size. Small states gain more not only in terms of absolute reserves, but in the number of import days those reserves ultimately cover. Since small states import absolutely less than large states, the same amount of reserves is more valuable to them. For example, adding $1 billion to reserves adds a fifty-day cushion to a state that imports $20 million worth of goods a day, while the addition of the same amount of reserves adds only a ten-day cushion to a state that imports $100 million worth of goods a day. Dependence is therefore even more asymmetric than the simple percentages of reserves contributed implies. Given a two-state currency area, where country 1 provides $1 billion of reserves and imports $100 million a day; and

---

[32] This asymmetry carries over into the spheres of reputation and finance as well.

country 2 provides $10 billion in reserves and imports $200 million worth per
day, the magnitude of the asymmetry is actually twenty to one, not ten to one.
If the area breaks up, country 1 loses a cushion of one hundred days, whereas
country 2 loses a cushion of five days. Additionally, states seem more vulnerable to monetary dependence for another reason. With regard to currency
areas, the technique of diversification (suggested by Hirschman with regard to
exports and imports) is less feasible; you are either in a currency area or you
are not, and memberships are almost always mutually exclusive, or, if not,
hierarchical.

Good examples of the stabilizing effects of currency areas can be found in
the U.S. case. In Laos, the exchange rate was stable at 505 kip to the dollar
for eight years (1963–1971). This is a remarkable degree of stability for any
country, and Laos was a poor nation with a weak and war-torn economy. The
stability of the exchange rate was possible because Laos was a de facto member of a dollar zone. Through the Foreign Exchange Operations Fund, contributors (the United States and its allies) were willing to supply foreign exchange
indefinitely at the rate of 505 kip to the dollar. This removed excess kip from
the economy, which would have been a source of pressure and instability
under other circumstances.[33]

Another important stabilizing effect is the one that comes from the coordination of economic policies. Members in a currency area must coordinate
their economic policies, at the very least those policies that would affect reserve positions, but usually more. This coordination helps reduce the possibility that states will pursue contradictory economic policies, which can
export problems instead of solving them, or cancel out the intended effects of
domestic economic measures. Given that currency area members are usually
one another's most important trading partners, this coordination is especially
important.[34]

Exit from a currency area almost certainly includes the loss of a variety of
additional privileges, which are typically associated with monetary areas.
When Britain left gold in 1931, it restricted overseas lending, doing so again
in 1934 and 1936. Although originally many countries pegged their currencies
to sterling in order to protect themselves from reversals in the terms of trade
associated with the 1931 devaluation of the pound, "preferential access to the
British capital market became an additional reason for maintaining the link
with sterling."[35] As the sterling area evolved, preferential trade relations and

[33] Cheryl Payer, *The Debt Trap: The International Monetary Fund and the Third World* (New
York: Monthly Review Press, 1974), pp. 96–98. Payer also discusses similar U.S. monetary
relationships with the Philippines (pp. 50–53) and Cambodia (pp 110–112).

[34] Coordination also often involves the sharing of information and expertise, which can be of
considerable importance to relatively backward members.

[35] Yeager, *International Monetary Relations*, p. 349. According to Kindleberger, twenty-five
countries linked to sterling and followed it down, avoiding the strong deflationary pressures that

limited restrictions on the flow of capital within the zone, along with access to pooled reserves ("automatic" access to the U.K. exchange equalization account) meant that membership did in fact have its privileges.[36]

Finally, exit involves the loss of protection. As a member, each state enjoys the insulation that a currency area can provide from the world economy, such as guaranteed access to markets, even in a recession. Membership makes states less susceptible to currency manipulation from powerful states outside the zone. (And as a nonmember or, especially, as a former member, a state would be vulnerable to manipulation by the bloc leader itself.) Given huge intraarea trade, reliance on the capital of the dominant state, and the advantages of access to pooled reserves, exit is a hazardous option for member states. Before leaving the area, a member state would have to consider how its economy would fare in every important economic dimension: currency stability, maintenance of market share, and access to finance.

In summary, exit from a monetary area poses challenges to former members. For a number of good reasons, the target currency's reputation will diminish as a result of its new independence. Previously, the stability of the currency derived from the size and reputation of the bloc and the stability of the bloc leader's currency; after exit, it stands alone. The leader's currency not only guaranteed the target's rate of exchange, but also diverted market attention away from it. Had pressure resulted in the devaluation of the bloc's key currency, for example, member states would probably have matched the devaluation, mitigating its costs. Thus, when the target was a member of the system, involuntary devaluation was both less likely and less costly.[37] Additionally, the reputation of the target currency would be further suspect after exit because its economic policies would no longer be subject to any rules or supervision associated with the system. Therefore, compared to other similarly situated currencies, newly independent currencies would be subject to greater exchange problems, such as capital flight and speculation designed to test the state's ability to defend its par value.

Certain tests will pose particular challenges to former members, as they will have just lost the benefits of membership, leaving them particularly vulnerable: a reduction in international purchasing power as a result of diminished aid, an increase in interest paid on new international loans, and a reduction in

---

affected outsiders. See Charles P. Kindleberger, *A Financial History of Western Europe* (London: George Allen and Unwin, 1984), p. 380.

[36] Judd Polk, *Sterling, Its Meaning in World Finance* (New York: Harper and Row, 1956), p. 43. Membership may actually involve a general collection of perks, which become apparent only upon exit. When Guinea left the franc zone, French aid to that country "ceased abruptly." Wall, *Charity of Nations*, p. 48.

[37] Member states' economic relations are usually closest with other area participants, especially the leader. If all of the currencies of the area match the depreciation of the leader, internal economic relations are basically unaffected.

the terms of trade from the loss of area preferences. Should any of these result in unwanted devaluation (or possible collapse), it would result in the same costs of exit that are associated with negative currency manipulation. Alternately, the former member may attempt to accumulate the reserves necessary to defend its existing exchange rate. In this case, the cost of exit would be the cost of accumulating the reserves necessary to defend the exchange rate, which, given the challenges discussed above, could prove substantial.[38]

It is difficult to measure what represents an "adequate" amount of reserves. Such assets have a number of functions. Primarily, they must be able to defend the value of the currency, without imposing new restrictions on imports. (Any such measures would represent an additional cost of exit. It is easier to measure the cost simply by measuring the reserves necessary to prevent new import restrictions.) The reserves must be sufficient to cover significant seasonal variations in earnings, changes in the volume and prices of exports and imports, speculative attacks, and other exogenous shocks. Additional reserves are needed in the form of "precautionary balances," as insurance in case of war or natural disaster.[39]

The accumulation of reserves represents a significant cost. As an International Monetary Fund study noted:

> It must not be overlooked that reserves are real resources from the point of view of the countries holding them, and the holding of reserves is only one of the possible uses competing for the limited amount of resources at the disposal of each country. . . . In a poor country . . . the maintenance of an adequate reserve position may be at the expense of urgently needed industrial or agricultural equipment, or may even entail some hardship due to shortages of food or of other consumer goods which might have been imported by using a portion of its reserves.[40]

Thus monetary dependence can provide considerable political benefits for core states. Externally, the area provides increased autonomy and insulation, as well as new mechanisms through which resources can be mobilized. Internally, the underlying threat of expulsion in the context of a series of asymmetric relationships transfers power from periphery to core. Additionally, through mechanisms that will be more fully explored in Part II, the simple act of participation in the system over time tends to shift the preferences of member states toward those of the core state.

---

[38] The differences between these two choices should not be overemphasized. There is a positive correlation between the magnitude of the undesired depreciation and the amount of reserves required to support the preexisting exchange rate.

[39] On these issues, see M. June Flanders, *The Demand for International Reserves*, Princeton Studies in International Finance, no. 27 (Princeton University, 1971); and IMF, "The Adequacy of Monetary Reserves," *IMF Staff Papers* 8, no. 2:181–227 (1953).

[40] IMF, "Adequacy", p. 195.

Systemic Disruption

Systemic disruption is the threatened or actual disruption of monetary arrangements, designed either to destroy the system or to extract some other benefits.[41] Short of destruction, the goals of disruption can be to redistribute the privileges agents believe the system unfairly awards (either through the prestige the system provides as a result of its hierarchical structure or through some security link mechanism) or to extract side payments from those who are most dependent on the smooth running of the system. Two types of states seem most vulnerable to disruption. First, small members not only benefit from special arrangements (as discussed above), but have a stake in the stability of the system in general (given that the condition of the external economy is likely to be especially important to smaller states). They are thus vulnerable to extortion. Secondly, the dominant state in the system values the political rewards of leadership. It may also find itself vulnerable: in many arrangements, for example, the key currency must run balance-of-payments deficits to provide liquidity. Surplus countries can be in a position to threaten to dump their accumulated reserves and destabilize the system.[42]

Systemic disruption is most likely to be exercised by mid-sized states, who have sufficient power but not a dominant stake in the current system.[43] A good example of this type of monetary power is the French crusade against the dollar exchange standard in the 1960s. Disruption is usually a tricky proposition, for a number of reasons. When challenging the key currency, the home country is "aiming-up": the target may be vulnerable, but it is probably more powerful than the home state in an overall sense. This is unusual in economic coercion. The home state might actually be dependent on the target in a number of other areas; and as a mid-sized power, it does retain some stake in the smooth functioning of the system.

The costs of successful disruption to target states can be substantial. Obviously, the leader of the former system would lose the political benefits of leadership. All participants would bear specific economic costs as well. At the extreme, the effect of subversive disruption would be effectively to demonetize the international economy. Until an alternate international payments system emerged, trade would have to take place through barter arrangements. In

---

[41] If the goal is simply to destroy the system, this would be an application of "brute force" as opposed to coercion.

[42] Kelly, "International Monetary System," p. 239. The dominant country is also the most likely target of strategic disruption because it has both a large stake in the system and the resources to provide side payments.

[43] Charles Kindleberger, "The International Monetary Politics of a Near Great Power: Two French Episodes, 1926–1936 and 1960–1970" (1972; reprinted in Kindleberger, *Keynesianism vs. Monetarism* [London: George Allen and Unwin, 1985]).

this dramatic example, the economic cost of monetary power would be the difference in international trade with monetization and trade under barter. In the short run, the difference would be quite considerable and yield pervasive effects throughout both the local and the world economy, as various import- and export-sensitive industries collapsed, introducing negative multipliers. The strength of such action is that it would affect every state in the system, to a degree determined by the relative significance of the international sector to their individual economies. Its weakness is that such effects would likely be temporary, fading out as a new payments system was established.

Even "unsuccessful" disruption could prove quite costly to the target, however, as a consequence of the costs of defense: those actions the core state must take to ensure the survival of the system given the disruption. Such defense would involve ensuring the attractiveness of the key currency of the system relative to other possible reserve and transactions assets. Other things being equal, an increase in the interest rate will make the key currency more attractive. Additionally, the lower the rate of inflation (which measures the rate of the decay of the currency's purchasing power), the more attractive the key currency is as a reserve asset. Therefore, to maintain confidence in the key currency, the core state would likely adjust its fiscal and monetary policy, raising interest rates, reducing the money supply, raising taxes, and cutting government spending. The result would be to shift key economic variables, such as growth, unemployment, and inflation, in undesired directions.[44]

Thus, systemic disruption is another potentially potent type of monetary power. In its most dramatic expression, it can upset the gains associated with monetary areas: core states lose political power and member states lose economic benefits. Artfully timed, it can also direct a decisive episode of economic chaos at an adversary. Even without such catastrophic consequences, disruption offers an opportunity for mid-sized states to extract concessions on a variety of issues from larger states, against whom there may be few other forms of leverage available.

Plan of the Book

This chapter has introduced the concept of monetary power, discussed the various forms that this instrument of economic coercion could take, and demonstrated why they should be effective tools of influence when successfully implemented. Chapter Two addresses the technical viability of monetary diplomacy, that is, the question of whether or not monetary power can be successfully implemented. There are a number of challenges to its viability, the

---

[44] As with previous analyses, initial levels are assumed to be optimal; otherwise the act would not represent monetary coercion, but would in effect be a positive sanction.

most important of which questions whether the hypothetically constructed techniques of monetary power would be useful in the "real world." For example, one challenge to viability is that naturally occurring countervailing market forces would prevent monetary sanctions from being effective. Chapter Two establishes viability in two ways. The first section of the chapter compares monetary power with other instruments of economic diplomacy, in order to define the features of monetary power and to explore its expected relative utility as an instrument of economic coercion. The second section considers specific technical and theoretical economic challenges to the successful practice of each type of monetary power.

Having established the theoretical viability of monetary power, the rest of the book focuses on the tasks of demonstration and comprehension. The three chapters comprising Part II consider currency manipulation, monetary dependence, and systemic disruption; each chapter reintroduces and expands on the theory of one specific type of power, and examines a number of twentieth-century cases. These historical cases demonstrate the existence of monetary power, and the accompanying discussion begins the more thorough analysis of how it works. Each chapter in Part II concludes with a section that evaluates the lessons of the episodes (for the theory and practice of monetary power) in order to uncover patterns and generalizable tendencies. Analysis at this stage includes a first cut at the underlying reasons for the success or failure of attempts to introduce monetary power.

The two chapters in Part III focus on the potential for monetary power. At this stage, the analysis builds on the findings that emerged from the middle chapters. Chapter 6 looks exclusively at a number of "missed opportunities": occasions when the practice of monetary diplomacy appeared to be the logical move, but was not introduced. This will increase the understanding of when and why states choose to employ such tactics, which will fill in details relating to a number of questions raised in Part II.

Finally, Chapter 7 summarizes the theoretical and historical analysis in order to establish a general framework regarding the nature of monetary power, how it works, and when it will be successful. This chapter also considers the role of monetary power in the contemporary world, briefly addressing how recent changes in the international system suggest that monetary power will become increasingly important in international relations in the years to come.

2

The Viability of Monetary Power

The Relative Utility of Monetary Power

This section compares the nature, limits, and utility of monetary power with the properties of other instruments of economic coercion: aid, trade, and finance. This will involve a number of comparisons. The initial analysis serves to establish the way in which the cast of characters (and the shape of the stage itself) change with each type of power play. This not only reveals how monetary power is different from other instruments of economic diplomacy, but also begins the process of establishing expectations about the practice of monetary diplomacy in general.

For each component of economic power, the first question must be: Who are the agents (or "home" states) and who are the targets of each particular form of economic coercion? Players are considered in terms of their potential for effective use of economic coercion; Togo, for example, could deny economic aid and technical assistance to Germany, but this would not be a significant exercise of economic power. An awareness of the relative position of the players is vital for the evaluation of either utility or viability for any form of coercion.

In general, in the practice of economic statecraft, large states are home states, and small states are the targets.[1] The Hufbauer study suggests that a gross national product (GNP) ratio of ten to one (home to target) is the minimum feasible for sanctions to have a reasonable chance to work.[2] However, beyond this, different types of states are especially vulnerable to certain types of coercion, and some states are better situated than others as agents of power. With regard to aid, for example, a simple large/small dimension does not hold up.[3] Obviously, large, rich states are endowed with a pool of resources from

[1] "Large" and "small' in this study refer to economic size, unless otherwise noted.

[2] Gary Clyde Hufbauer and Jeffrey J. Schott, *Economic Sanctions Reconsidered* (Washington, D.C.: Institute for International Economics, 1985), p. 51. Obviously, David Baldwin (*Economic Statecraft* [Princeton: Princeton University Press, 1985]) would disagree with the narrow definition of the concept of work used here.

[3] On the politics of aid, see George Liska, *The New Statecraft* (Chicago: University of Chicago Press, 1960); David Wall, *The Charity of Nations* (New York: Basic Books, 1973); John D. Montgomery, *The Politics of Foreign Aid* (New York: Praeger, 1962); John D. Montgomery, *Foreign Aid in International Politics* (Englewood Cliffs, N.J.: Prentice Hall, 1967); Jacob J. Kaplan, *The Challenge of Foreign Aid* (New York: Praeger, 1967); Sidney Weintraub, ed., *Economic Coercion and U.S. Foreign Policy* (Boulder, Colo.: Westview, 1982).

which to operate, and small, poor states have a demand for aid, but the issue is more complicated. Small, rich states, such as Sweden, can become important donors, and so can large, poor states, such as China. Hence, many types of mid-sized actors (in an economic sense) can join the large states as agents of aid power.

Identifying the most vulnerable targets of aid power also goes beyond simple considerations of size. Here, degree of vulnerability is to a certain extent a state choice. States can allow themselves to become heavily dependent on continued aid. In some cases, aid can become vital for a particular government's operating budget, or provide necessary foreign exchange to pay for imports. Thus while most states would court aid and prefer its continuation, aid can either complement development plans, providing lubrication, or it can substitute for a development plan, and be used to maximize current wealth. In the latter case, targets are especially vulnerable.

An analysis of trade power also begins at the dimension of large and small, but once again only as a starting point. Small "specialists" can be effective agents of trading power (for example, those states that control important natural resources and raw materials). Contrapositively, large states can have specific dependencies that make them vulnerable. The most obvious example here is the pattern of the endowment of and dependence on oil. Secondly, absolute size is not as important as degree of dependence on trade, measured by the ratio of exports and imports to GNP. Small states that do not trade very much are insulated to some extent from the use of trade power. They may be less influenced by its utilization than much larger but trade-dependent powers. States that are large enough to have a high degree of absolute trade but a low trade/GNP ratio are the best situated in the arena of trade power, because they are at once powerful yet insulated.

Financial diplomacy differs from trade in that it affords less opportunity for specialization: large states are the important source of finance, and thus best able to control its distribution.[4] Small states, especially developing ones, are

---

[4] On the politics of financial diplomacy, see Herbert Feis, *Europe the World's Banker* (1930; reprint, New Haven: Yale University Press, 1964), and Jacob Viner, *International Economics* (1928; reprint, Glencoe: Ill.: Free Press, 1951). Typically, strategies of financial diplomacy have focused on diverting access away from adversaries and toward allies. See, for example, Feis, pp. 123, 211, 286; Viner, p. 82. For a broader and more modern perspective, see Benjamin J. Cohen, *In Whose Interest? International Banking and American Foreign Policy* (New Haven: Yale University Press, 1986).

In general, finance as a tool of state power has been examined less than has either trade or aid. Finance has a long history as an important *underlying component* of state power, but this is distinct from its use as an instrument of state power. See K. Rasler and W. Thompson, "Global Wars, Public Debts, and the Long Cycle," *World Politics* 35, no. 4:489–516, on the importance of access to cheap and plentiful credit as vital to winning major wars throughout modern history. The importance of finance for war has been recognized for quite some time. One early statement is by the eminent economist A. C. Pigou, in *The Political Economy of War* (London: Macmillan, 1921).

vulnerable because of their need for access to loans to finance development. There are important qualifications here, however. Large states can also become dependent on international loans, as the United States has been in the 1980s and 1990s. Additionally, sheer economic size does not necessarily translate into the ability to practice financial diplomacy. Some large states, such as Germany before each of the world wars, are limited in their capacity as agents, since they have little available capital for foreign lending.

The agents of monetary power are very large states: the great and near-great powers. This is because money is naturally hierarchical—as Kindleberger has observed, a single money is as natural as a single language for getting things done.[5] Further, there are no "small specialists" here: currency markets are like a world in which only one good is traded. Thus in the international monetary system, the issuer of the key currency is the most important player at any given time. An important qualification to this is that crucial supporters and major holders of the key currency can also wield power, either through their secondary (though still powerful) currencies, or because they are best placed to practice systemic disruption. Additionally, while hierarchy anticipates that there be a single system leader, a number of currency areas can coexist; consequently, there can be a number of bloc leaders, each with substantial monetary power.

A broad cross-section of countries are vulnerable to the exercise of monetary power. There is less likelihood of "natural insulation," which makes some countries less vulnerable to trade power, for example. Any country with a monetized economy can potentially be a target.[6] While small, open states, with their limited reserves and external dependence, are obviously prime candidates as targets of monetary power, other factors are also important. For instance, inflation-conscious countries are especially vulnerable to currency manipulation.[7] Formerly important monetary powers in decline are also vulnerable, because a variety of countries hold sizable balances of their currencies. Britain's economic problems in the 1970s were exacerbated by the volatility of foreign holdings of sterling.[8] One implication of the decline in the

---

[5] Charles P. Kindleberger, *The Politics of International Money and World Language*, Essays in International Finance, no. 61 (Princeton University, 1967).

[6] Very open economies would seem to be the most vulnerable, but relative closure and even inconvertibility do not guarantee protection: nominally inconvertible currencies are usually traded in third, unofficial, and black markets; these outlets can provide opportunities for manipulation. Further, external (or nondiscriminatory) convertibility is not a necessary prerequisite for the exercise of monetary power; in some cases inconvertibility can provide even greater opportunities for coercion, especially with regard to monetary dependence.

[7] Yuan-Li Wu, *Economic Warfare* (New York: Prentice Hall, 1952), p. 143. Of course, Wu does not employ the specific terminology "currency manipulation."

[8] Janet Kelly, "The International Monetary System and National Security," in Klaus Knorr and Frank N. Trager, eds., *Economic Issues and National Security* (Lawrence, Kans.: Allen Press, 1977), p. 95. The implications of the postwar "sterling overhang" are also central to Strange's pioneering work.

power of a once great currency is that it can provide a window of opportunity
that broadens the number of agents of monetary power:mid-sized powers can
reverse the potential flow of coercion as a once dominant currency becomes a
burden instead of a prop.[9] Still, in general, there are fewer natural agents of
monetary power (although at least as many targets) than for the other instruments of economic coercion. Thus it seems likely that in general there will be
fewer opportunities productively to practice monetary diplomacy than to employ the statecraft of aid and trade. While acknowledging this, the comparison
below evaluates the four instruments of economic coercion under those circumstances that afford the opportunity for each. Similarly, the prevailing international economic environment also affects the opportunity to practice
economic coercion.

That is, economic instruments of coercion can be compared along the dimension of economic prerequisites, focusing on the degree to which a modern, somewhat integrated, international market economy (henceforth referred
to as a global economy) is necessary for the transmission of a given type of
economic power. Aid as a form of power is not very dependent on a global
economy. Aid can take the form of physical goods or technical expertise, and
therefore could exist in the absence of trade relations or even money. Aid
needs no international infrastructure or established norms; in fact, it is usually
distributed in a bilateral and ad hoc fashion. Obviously, the existence of monetized economies makes aid more fungible, and to that extent a global economy can enhance aid power, but aid is not dependent on its existence.

Trade power is more dependent on a global economy than aid, but its dependence is still only moderate. State trading can take place in the absence of
free markets. Additionally, the creation of a dependent trade relationship often
involves the fostering of bilateralism as opposed to multilateralism. This
means that increases in multilateral relations could actually undermine trade
power under some circumstances. On the other hand, the global economy
would make trade a relatively more important and widespread element of
most national economies, and would therefore make states more vulnerable to
the manipulation of trade relations.

The practice of financial diplomacy is more dependent than trade on the
existence of a global economy. It is inherently a market phenomenon. Beyond
this fundamental point, financial relationships represent economic "flows,"

---

[9] Thus, large holders of sterling, which became less attractive than it once was, found themselves in a position to exercise monetary power. Libya was able to use monetary power for
signaling purposes, when, as an important holder of sterling, it dropped out of the sterling area in
1971, "primarily for political reasons." Leyland Yeager, *International Monetary Relations: Theory, History, and Policy* (New York: Harper and Row, 1976), p. 162. In 1967, several Middle
Eastern countries sold sterling to punish Britain for supporting Israel. C. Fred Bergsten, *The
Dilemmas of the Dollar* (New York: New York University Press, 1975), p. 239.

which, unlike "stocks," cannot easily be bartered. Finance also requires exchange mechanisms for introducing or repatriating funds. Further, financial relations themselves expand interdependence, and must be reasonably extensive in order to provide opportunities for manipulation.

Monetary power is also highly dependent on the global economy, though not completely so. As mentioned in Chapter 1, scattered opportunities for the practice of monetary power have existed throughout recorded history. Nonmarket or isolated countries can still be vulnerable to operations that interfere with the international monetary economy, on black and other unofficial markets, or through a policy of denial of hard currencies used in international transactions. Still, of the four instruments, monetary power and financial relations are clearly more dependent on an integrated world economy than aid or trade.

To reiterate, the four instruments of monetary power will be compared in the context of the general environment each can thrive in. This is not a comparison of the size of the universe of cases for each component, but rather a comparison of representative elements from each universe. In this respect, the relatively high dependence of monetary power on a global economy is inconsequential. Recall that this study is limited to the twentieth century, in part because of this dependence. Even if closure in the international economy were to increase, the condition of modernity would still hold, and there would still be a number of interdependent subsystems within and between which monetary power will remain relevant.

The issues of agents and global economy define the playing fields, but do not directly enable comparison of the instruments of economic power within those fields. This question of relative utility can be measured along two broad dimensions: the limitations on the usefulness and the relative efficiency of each component.

Limits

The limitations on economic instruments of power come in three overlapping forms: feedback, circumvention, and defense. Feedback effects cause self-limitation on the part of home states, resulting from the fear that the use of a particular type of economic power to change a target's behavior may undermine other policy goals. Circumvention comprises methods by which target states can avoid the negative effect of a sanction. Defense comprises techniques by which target states protect themselves from the potential use of sanctions.

The manipulation of aid is especially vulnerable to limitations from feedback. As one author notes: "If [a state] punishes by withholding aid, it risks defeating the purpose for which the aid was originally offered."[10] Further, the greater the absolute aid and thus the power potential, the greater the threat of feedback is likely to be. States can circumvent aid cutoffs by replacing the home state with another benefactor, probably an adversary of the home state. Defense, through threats of replacing the home state with its adversary, is even more powerful than circumvention. This is because competitors would likely be more receptive to a state offering to switch patrons than to a state, already abandoned, coming with hat in hand.

Commercial power is also vulnerable to feedback, but much less so than aid. Export restrictions against important customers (such as the U.S. grain embargo against the Soviet Union) can hurt domestic producers, and import restrictions hurt local consumers and producers, but in most cases involving established players and vulnerable targets, the pain will be sufficiently asymmetric (or at least absolutely small in the home country) to minimize its importance. The weak link in trade sanctions comes in the circumvention stage. This problem exists because there is profit in circumventing trade sanctions, and private networks that divert and direct trade through third parties will spring up spontaneously as a result of natural market forces. Opportunities for defense also exist through the diversification of export and import markets wherever possible, though in practice this strategy is usually dominated by the goal of maximizing welfare.

Financial measures are also only moderately vulnerable to feedback effects, though, as in trade, they do impose some costs on the home country. But they are also vulnerable to circumvention, because the profit motive exists in this case as well, so when one agent pulls out, another will be tempted to replace it. Circumvention is not as easy as with trade, however, because lending usually has to go through formal and official channels. Hence the supporters of the target state must stand up and be counted, and therefore the potential for control is greater. With this component, however, defense can be a major problem. The best form of defense with regard to financial sanctions is the

---

[10] Montgomery, *Foreign Aid*, p. 64. Others concur. The paradox of foreign aid is that the greater the potential for influence, the less likely the home state is to use it. States tend to direct aid to states which they consider important. On the United States, see Kaplan, *Challenge*, p. 49. More generally, Liska distinguishes between "acquisitive" and "creative" aid. "Acquisitive aid" refers to aid that is tied implicitly or explicitly to benefits for the home state, which would be lost should aid cease. Liska, *New Statecraft*, pp. 33–35. Most aid appears to be acquisitive, and this might explain why Knorr finds success in only two of the twenty-five cases of aid coercion he examines. Klaus Knorr, *The Power of Nations* (New York: Basic Books, 1973), p. 81. Liska also discusses a number of other problems with aid that tend to increase the costs relative to the benefits of this instrument of influence, including the need to continue sending aid in order to protect the sunk investment, getting involved in aid races with hostile states that border the target state and their benefactors, and the need to keep similarly situated allies content that they are getting as much as one another. Liska, *New Statecraft*, p. 49. For a more optimistic view, see Weintraub, *Economic Coercion*.

threat of default. If a nation already owes money to foreigners, threats of financial sanctions can be met with threats of default, the ability to do so being entirely within the control of the target state. This of course leaves economically "responsible" nations with less defense, but such states would generally be less dependent on finance, and should find finance easier to replace. Basically, a similar paradox, as in the aid case, is at work here: the big borrowers are at once the most vulnerable to and the best able to defend against financial sanctions.

Monetary power is the least subject to feedback effects of all of the forms of economic power.[11] Every other form of economic power is subject to the central feedback paradox: the more important the relationship, the greater the potential for power, but also the greater the logic of self-restraint. Finance and trade are less affected by this than aid, because there are greater opportunities for asymmetry of interest, but the paradox still exists there to varying degrees. A's ability to manipulate B's currency, however, is neither determined nor inhibited by the degree of interdependence between them. Further, monetary warfare may require real resources, such as foreign exchange assets, but not the forgoing of economic opportunities or the loss of markets (which is the case for trade and financial sanctions). Some types of monetary power do involve feedback effects, but more in terms of establishing an optimal degree of pressure as opposed to inhibiting the practice of power. For example, the exploitation of monetary dependence is limited by the desire of the home state to preserve the currency bloc, and therefore exploitation must not be so great as to make targets prefer to exit. Systemic disruption can also be limited when the home state and the target state are participants in the same system; when one is involved in boat rocking, one is ultimately inhibited by fears of capsizing.

Monetary sanctions are very difficult to circumvent, short of declaring one's currency inconvertible, or purposefully demonetizing one's own economy, both costly and dramatic measures.[12] Monetary power is exercised more in the manner of an attack, as opposed to interference or displacement, which could be circumvented by replacement and rerouting. Defense is also problematic. One method would be to find a protector (if one were available), but the attractiveness of this option is diminished by the fact that it would trade vulnerability to one state for dependence on another.

Efficiency

Economic instruments of power also vary in efficiency. "Efficiency" refers to the ability of the home state to wield the instrument skillfully and to direct it

---

[11] Of course, this does not mean that feedback effects are necessarily absent in the context of monetary diplomacy. Such feedback will be evaluated in the chapters below.

[12] Such a strategy would be akin to committing (monetary) suicide in order to escape murder.

specifically at the target government. Three main questions determine the relative efficiency of the components of economic power. First, how independent is the central government of the home state with regard to the use of the instrument? This is a crucial consideration. Without such independence states cannot wield economic power systematically against others. Second, how public are the various components? Publicity can be important for signaling third parties. However, publicity can also undermine sanctions by making compliance more difficult because of the potential for "loss of face" both nationally and internationally, and can inspire nationalism, strengthening the will of the target to resist.[13] Since public sanctions cannot be made private, while private ones can be made public (or at least others can be made aware of them), economic components of power that can be exercised privately are more efficient than those that can only be exercised publicly. Third, how focused is the coercion on the target? Economic sanctions are often most effective when they can contribute to the destabilization and overthrow of a recalcitrant government, followed by a new government that changes the offending policies.[14] Thus the ability of different components to focus discomfort in a way that is most likely to destabilize the target government is an important measure of their relative efficiency.

By these three measures, trade is an inefficient instrument of state power. Trade is usually dominated by domestic policy concerns. In the United States, Congress has not hesitated to become involved in trade policy to support local interests or in order to advance its own foreign policy agenda.[15] Trade is also in most cases functionally outside of government management (state trading being the exception) and thus the state's hands are not on the levers of control. Trade sanctions usually must be legislated, and are thus public. Finally, with possible exceptions, such as strategic minerals, trade sanctions influence the target economy in a broad and general way, reducing overall wealth and perhaps sowing discontent, but not directly undermining the government. As Hufbauer and Schott note, "[Financial sanctions] can disrupt government plans whereas shortages can usually be spread around the nation."[16]

Aid is somewhat more efficient than trade as a coercive lever. For the most part, it suffers from the same problems with central government autonomy as does trade. In the United States, for example, Liska notes that "Congress is jealous of its role in the foreign aid field: there are not many areas in which the

[13] Baldwin, *Economic Statecraft*, p. 108.

[14] On the sequence and relationship of destabilization leading to overthrow leading to accommodation, see Richard Stuart Olson, "Economic Coercion in World Politics: With a Focus on North-South Relations," *World Politics* 31, no. 4:471–94 (1979).

[15] Stephen Krasner, "Domestic Constraints on International Leverage," in Knorr and Trager, *Economic Issues*, p. 173.

[16] Hufbauer and Schott, *Economic Sanctions*, p. 3.

power of the purse so directly impinges on foreign policy."[17] Aid is also publicly determined. However, its disbursement is entirely within government control, and its effects are more directly focused on the target government. This is most likely when aid accounts for a large percentage of government revenue, or finances a large percentage of a country's imports.[18]

Financial diplomacy is about as efficient as aid. The central government is somewhat more autonomous than with aid, but is still subject to pressures. The government is also an important (though certainly not the exclusive) provider of finance, and although general financial cutoffs would have to be public, there is more room for informal maneuvering in finance than in trade. This is because of the concentration of banking interests as well as the typically close ties among the central bank, the treasury or finance ministry, and the private banking system as a whole. Finally, such sanctions have the potential to cause a financial or general economic crisis in the target country and thus can be effective destabilizers.

Monetary power is a remarkably efficient component of state power. While most governments are not usually in the trading business, they are, in the domestic economy, always the exclusive producers of currency, with complete control over its output and autonomous with regard to its manipulation.[19] Further, domestic pressures (and those filtered through the legislative body) are minimal, or at least muted. The U.S. case provides a good and representative example. According to one scholar, "[T]he monetary system does not bring to mind any particular group whose vital interests are at stake," in contrast to trade issues, which most average citizens are likely to be aware of and many even directly affected by.[20] Monetary issues are more mysterious to the layperson. A New York Times/CBS poll, taken in the mid-eighties,

[17] Liska, *New Statecraft*, p. 65.

[18] On focus, see Montgomery, *Politics*, p. 218; Montgomery, *Foreign Aid*, p. 23.

[19] The state's currency monopoly has been recognized throughout modern history as an aspect of sovereignty. Some libertarian economists, however, consider this monopoly to be an unnecessary and inherent source of inefficiency. See, for example, F. A. Hayek, *Denationalization of Money* (London: Institute of Economic Affairs, 1976). For a discussion of these issues, see Vera C. Smith, *The Rationale of Central Banking and the Free Banking Alternative* (1936; reprint, Indianapolis: Liberty Press, 1990), and Lawrence H. White, *Competition and Currency: Essays on Free Banking and Money* (New York: New York University Press, 1989).

[20] Kelly,"International Monetary System," p. 240. Obviously, international bankers and investors will have an interest in the monetary system, but this will usually be manifested in support of broad, general goals, such as "stability." Further, these interests are likely to converge on the issue of the stability of the *home* currency, which should not be threatened by the practice of monetary power.

Joanne Gowa offers a public goods argument in support of the view that central governments have relatively high autonomy with regard to exchange rate policy. See "Public Goods and Political Institutions: Trade and Monetary Policy Processes in the United States," *International Organization* 42, no. 1:15–32 (1988).

when the dollar was very high, found that 60 percent of the respondents thought that the strong dollar was "good for U.S. trade," while only 25 percent thought it was bad.[21] Congress also remains aloof from monetary affairs. The dramatic swings of the dollar in the 1980s eventually gained some congressional attention, but in the words of one senator:

> I don't think the Senate was thinking so much of the overvalued dollar as they were the trade deficit and what they regarded as unfair practices by some of our trading competitors. Congress regards itself as in a position to pass trade legislation, good or bad, and taxes, up or down, But we don't think of ourselves often as the group that should try to realign world currencies.[22]

Thus, the executive branch, through the Treasury Department and the Federal Reserve, is in a position to dictate currency manipulation. [23] And if Congress will not intervene when the dollar-yen relationship swings wildly, it certainly will not respond to a run on some relatively obscure foreign currency.[24]

Monetary power can also be exercised quite privately. It requires no legislation—in fact, many in the home country might not even notice what is going on. If it were so inclined, the home country would not even have to tell the target country that it, the home country, was the source of the monetary trouble. Finally, monetary sanctions are remarkably focused, aimed at one of the foundations of governance and sovereignty, the issuance of legal tender. One obvious example of this is the introduction of currency manipulation to promote or exacerbate a dramatic currency run, something that traditionally destabilizes governments.

Table 2.1 summarizes the comparison of the four components of economic power. Broad measures—"low," "moderate," and "high"—are used. Such descriptors are sufficient for the goals of this exercise: a first look at the distinct attributes of monetary power, and the construction of a set of expectations about its utility.

The implications of the preceding discussion are striking. Given a reasonably integrated international market economy, monetary power, *in theory*,

---

[21] I. M. Destler and C. Randall Henning, *Dollar Politics: Exchange Rate Policymaking in the United States* (Washington, D.C.: Institute for International Economics, 1989), p. 104.

[22] Senator R. Packwood, quoted in Yoichi Funabashi, *Managing the Dollar: From the Plaza to the Louvre* (Washington, D.C.: Institute for International Economics, 1988), p. 75. Indeed, Robert Pastor's comprehensive *Congress and the Politics of U.S. Foreign Economic Policy* (Berkeley: University of California Press, 1980) discusses trade, aid, and finance, but does not address issues associated with monetary power. As that astute politician Richard Nixon noted while president, there were "no votes" in dealing with the problems of the Italian lira.

[23] Central government independence at the highest levels with regard to monetary power is common in the advanced capitalist countries. See Funabashi, *Managing the Dollar*, passim.

[24] Destler and Henning note that the yen/dollar rate went from 203 in December 1980 to 278 in November 1982, and from 263 in February 1985 to 120 in May 1989. *Dollar Politics*, p. 1. They examine the Treasury/Fed relationship in chapter 5, and Congress in chapter 6.

TABLE 2.1

Economic Instruments of Power

	Aid	*Trade*	*Finance*	*Money*
Number of actors	Moderate	High	Low	Low
Independence from global economy	High	Moderate	Low	Low
Limits	High	Moderate	Moderate	Low
Efficiency	Moderate	Low	Moderate	High

Note: The number of actors is defined as the typical number of states capable of effectively practicing each instrument of economic power at any given time.

should be the most potent instrument of economic coercion available to states in a position to exercise it. While the comparison has been made at a high level of generality, monetary power appears to be both the least inhibited and most efficient instrument. Despite the impressive performance of monetary diplomacy in this comparison, however, the absolute *power* of monetary sanctions has not yet been sufficiently explored. They have been shown potentially to be an easy and accurate blow to deliver, but the extent to which the force of that blow is mitigated by intervening forces has not been determined.

The Theoretical Viability of Monetary Power

The fundamental challenge to the concept of monetary power is that, while states can attempt to employ its various techniques, those practices developed in the laboratory will fail to perform in the real world. Just as edifices constructed in the zero-gravity environment of outer space would collapse if they were transported to earth, this criticism maintains, so will monetary power collapse under the weight of market forces.

Currency Manipulation

Currency manipulation is subject to the most straightforward challenge: Can currencies be manipulated? Or will actions that attempt to push the target currency from point a to point b be met by natural countervailing forces that push the currency back towards point a, almost like water seeking its own level?[25] This depends to a large extent on whether point a is a stable, unique

[25] In discussing market forces, there is the danger of anthropomorphization, as well as the

equilibrium. Currency manipulation can take place under a number of monetary regimes, and can be practiced in both positive and negative forms. The issue of equilibrium and how it affects the opportunity for this type of monetary power must be considered from all of these perspectives.

There are a large variety of international monetary regimes, but there is one particularly applicable dichotomy for this analysis: all monetary regimes involve either fixed or floating exchange rates.[26] With fixed exchange rate regimes, the challenge to currency manipulation falls well short of the mark. The values associated with pegged rates do not represent equilibria, except momentarily and by chance. Additionally, some natural market forces actively destabilize such regimes. Thus, in these cases, the market would be more likely to assist than to stymie currency manipulation.

Par values are usually not chosen by rigorous economic reasoning, but rather by instinct, precedent, and circumstance. This was the method by which the gold price for the dollar was chosen in the 1930s. In this instance,

[w]hile Roosevelt ate his eggs and drank his coffee, the group discussed what the day's price would be. The precise figure each day was less important than the encouragement of a general upward trend. One day Morgenthau came in, more worried than usual, and suggested an increase from 19 to 22 cents. Roosevelt took one look at Morgenthau's anxious face and proposed twenty-one cents. "It's a lucky number," he said with a laugh, "because it's three times seven."[27]

The eventual gold price, $35 per ounce, was the result of a number of factors, prominent among which was the timing of the congressional passage of the Gold Reserve Act of 1934.[28]

---

danger of relying too heavily on analogies from the physical sciences. The actions and imperatives of "the market" are actually the result of countless individual actors in pursuit of their own interests. Arising from these individual decisions is Adam Smith's "invisible hand" of the market, a powerful force in restless and relentless pursuit of the zero-profit equilibrium.

[26] On the variety of regimes, see, for example, Peter Wickham, "The Choice of Exchange Rate Regime in Developing Countries: A Survey of the Literature," *IMF Staff Papers* 32, no. 2:248–88 (1985); Victor Argy and Paul de Grauwe, eds., *Choosing an Exchange Rate Regime: The Challenge for Smaller Industrial Countries* (Washington, D.C.: International Monetary Fund, 1990); and H. Robert Heller, "Choosing an Exchange Rate System," *Finance and Development* 14, no. 2:23–27 (1977).Specific practices are detailed in International Monetary Fund, *Exchange Arrangements and Exchange Restrictions* (Washington, D.C.: IMF, annual editions). For the evaluation of the viability of currency manipulation, however, the simple dichotomy of fixed versus flexible captures the fundamental theoretical challenges.

[27] Arthur M. Schlesinger, Jr., *The Age of Roosevelt: The Coming of the New Deal* (Boston: Houghton Mifflin, 1958), p. 241.

[28] Others argued for an even greater devaluation, such as $41.34 per ounce. Joseph E. Reeve, *Monetary Reform Movements: A Survey of Recent Plans and Panaceas* (Washington, D.C.: American Council on Public Affairs, 1943), pp. 56, 59; see also Schlesinger, Coming of New Deal, p. 246. There was no obvious choice for the new value of the dollar, which frustrated those left in the dark. When Roosevelt was told that a definite price "must be set," he responded: "Poppycock–the bankers want to know everything beforehand, and I've told them to go to hell" (p. 235).

It is vital to recognize that even if the par value happens to represent a stable equilibrium when it is established, it almost certainly drifts from this equilibrium over time[29], as a number of economic variables shift. For example, $35 per ounce, the U.S. gold price in 1937, 1947, 1957, and 1967 (and all the years in between), was probably the only economic variable that did not change significantly over that period. As one economist noted:

> It is clear that a fixed rate of exchange between any two freely vendable currencies cannot for any lengthy period be maintained unless, by accident or design, congruent monetary policies are pursued in the two countries concerned, and their price levels are kept in substantially constant relationship with one another. In the absence of these conditions a relatively less desired convertible currency is certain to be successfully raided and its exchange rate broken.[30]

Because of the natural drift of equilibrium, or as the result of economic policies or exogenous shocks, the par value of a given state's currency tends to come under pressure from time to time. Governments can defend their currencies through the use of open market operations, intervention in the forward exchange market, or through the direct manipulation of foreign exchange assets. However, there is a limit to the government's ability to resist this pressure, especially when outside forces are pushing down the value of the currency.[31]

Compounding this problem is the fact that under fixed exchange rates, there is an incentive for speculators to test the limits of the government's ability to defend its par value. Betting that there will be depreciation offers great rewards and no risk outside of transactions costs. If the exchange rate is five dollars to the pound ($5/£), speculators expecting dollar devaluation sell their dollars for pounds. If devaluation occurs (which they will have helped bring about) and the new rate is set at $10/£, those actors can sell their pounds for dollars and double their money. If there is no devaluation, they simply sell their pounds at the old rate, and break even (less transactions costs). Consequently, once a government's reserves are thought to reach some threshold level, speculators will touch off a flight from the currency, which will virtually force devaluation.[32] In these cases, market forces focus and magnify an initial

[29] It is more accurate to say that the equilibrium rate of exchange drifts away from the par value, since the par is fixed while the equilibrium changes.

[30] Frank D. Graham, "Achilles' Heels in Monetary Standards," *American Economic Review* 30, no. 1:16–32 (1940), p. 25.

[31] Paul Krugman, "A Model of Balance-of-Payments Crises," *Journal of Money, Credit, and Banking* 11, no. 3: 311–25 (1979), p. 11; Joan Robinson, *Essays in the Theory of Employment* (New York: Macmillan, 1937), p. 184 fn. 1.

[32] Krugman, "Payments Crises," p. 312. Adapting the work of Stephen Salant, Krugman compares the flight to foreign currency as government reserves dwindle to the holding of a commodity when the government's buffer stock (used to stabilize the price of that commodity) runs down. He concludes that "balance-of-payments crises are a natural outcome of maximizing behavior by investors." Ibid., p. 324. Robert P. Flood and Peter M. Garber attempt to calculate the "threshold

attempt at currency manipulation. At times, then, the market will be a powerful ally of the agent of monetary power.

Currency manipulation is clearly viable, therefore, with any form of fixed exchange rate. These findings do not necessarily carry over to floating exchange rates, however. A pure float, with the market determining the exchange rate, avoids the problems mentioned above. Still, the challenge to the viability of currency manipulation boils down to whether or not a unique, stable equilibrium for currency values exists. Three conditions must hold: First, there must be an equilibrium for the market to search out and rest at. Second, the equilibrium must be stable; otherwise any action that could nudge currency value from that point would send it reeling out of control. Third, the equilibrium must be unique. Otherwise, successful currency manipulation could knock the currency from one equilibrium to a less desired one.[33]

The first attempt to uncover unique stable equilibria in the foreign exchange market was by the Swedish economist Gustav Cassel, whose work on what he called purchasing power parity (PPP) remains significant to this day. Although it evolved into a collection of interrelated theories, all of them centered around the idea that exchange rates are determined by the variations in inflation rates from state to state. All other factors, such as "confidence," or the balance of trade, "have only a quite secondary and temporary importance."[34]

Although it was a major breakthrough in economics, is still used to make technical conversions, and remains popular in some circles, the PPP doctrine failed to find the holy grail of the perfect equilibrium. Cassel himself found the need to qualify his theory repeatedly, ultimately urging its use as a policy

---

point" at which speculation will suddenly cause exchange rate collapse, in "Collapsing Exchange Rate Regimes: Some Linear Examples," *Journal of International Economics* 17, no. 2:1–13 (1984). See also Maurice Obstfeld, "Rational and Self-Fulfilling Balance-of-Payments Crises," *American Economic Review* 76, no. 1:72–81 (1986).

[33] It should be noted that even if these three conditions held, the opportunity for currency manipulation, even with a pure float, would not be completely eliminated. The act of the manipulation itself would bring new information to the market, which would influence the determination of exchange rates. Additionally, in many cases, the market for a particular currency will be rather small, and the force of a powerful agent's manipulations could completely overwhelm that market.

[34] Gustav Cassel, "The Present Situation in the Foreign Exchanges," *Economic Journal* 26, no. 101:62–65 (March 1916), p. 64; Cassel, "The Present Situation in the Foreign Exchanges," *Economic Journal* 26, no. 103:319–23 (September 1916); Cassel, "The Depreciation of Gold," *Economic Journal* 27, no. 107:346–54 (1917); Cassel, "Abnormal Deviations in International Exchanges," *Economic Journal* 28, no. 112:413–15 (1918); Cassel, "The Depreciation of the German Mark," *Economic Journal* 29, no. 116:492–96 (1919); Cassel, *Money and Foreign Exchange* after 1914 (1924; reprint, New York: Macmillan, 1930). See also E. C. Van Dorp, "The Deviation of Exchanges," *Economic Journal* 29, no. 116:497–503 (1919); Eric Lundberg, "The Influence of Gustav Cassel on Economic Doctrine and Policy," *Skandinaviska Banken Quarterly Review*, no. 1:1–6 (1967); and Lawrence H. Officer, "The Purchasing-Power-Parity Theory of Exchange Rates: A Review Article," *IMF Staff Papers* 23, no. 1:1–60 (1976).

guide rather than a model of a natural force.[35] Despite its shortcomings, the theory of purchasing power parity provides, under normal circumstances, a good estimate of exchange rates over the long run, especially when large inflations have occurred. The theory explains reasonably well, for example, the fluctuations of the 1920s. However, as one scholar noted, its performance for the 1970s is "dismal."[36] This poor performance continues through the 1980s, even if exchange rates are retrospectively adjusted for changes in relative productivity between states.[37]

Clearly, despite its continued usefulness, especially for technical conversions, the PPP theory has not uncovered the source of a unique stable equilibrium. This focus on purchasing power parity does not exhaust the possible explanations of exchange rate determination. However, it is of special significance. It is the oldest and most thoroughly examined theory, and has been used as a guide for policy throughout the twentieth century. Finally, the theory has remained popular to this day among many politicians and business leaders.[38]

There are a number of other attempts to explain exchange rate determination, which, if correct, could satisfy the three conditions. These approaches include (to name a few) the monetary view, the portfolio balance approach, and a "fundamental equilibrium exchange rate" argument.[39] That so many competing approaches coexist underscores the fact that the solution remains elusive. Instead of critiquing each of these theories in turn, the analysis here instead challenges the existence of a single, unique equilibrium as a concept.

The idea of such an equilibrium actually makes little economic sense. As the eminent economist Joan Robinson once observed with regard to the foreign exchanges: "The idea of a position of equilibrium, to be maintained, or restored after it has been lost, is merely an economist's version of the myth of

---

[35] Cassel, *Present Situation* (March 1916), p. 64; Cassel, *Present Situation* (September 1916), pp. 321–22; Cassel, *Abnormal Deviations*, p. 413; Cassel, *Depreciation*, p. 492, p. 496.

[36] "Dismal": Jacob A. Frenkel, "The Collapse of Purchasing Power Parities during the 1970s," *European Economic Review* 16, no. 1:145–65 (1985), p. 145; "normal conditions": Officer, "Purchasing-Power-Parity Theory," p. 25. For more on PPP, see "Purchasing Power Parity: A Symposium," *Journal of International Economics* 8, no. 2: 157–339 (1978).

[37] Paul De Grauwe, *International Money: Post-War Theories and Trends* (Oxford: Clarendon Press, 1989), pp. 62–64. For the dramatic divergences between PPP values and market values of the dollar/yen rate during 1973–1993, see Federal Reserve Bank of Cleveland, *Economic Trends*, September 1993, p. 15.

[38] Officer, "Purchasing-Power-Parity Theory," pp. 27–8, 51.

[39] For more on the various theories of exchange rate determination, see De Grauwe, *International Money*; Paul Hallwood and Ronald MacDonald, *International Money: Theory, Evidence and Institutions* (Oxford: Basil Blackwell, 1986); Richard Baillie and Patrick McMahon, *The Foreign Exchange Market: Theory and Econometric Evidence* (Cambridge: Cambridge University Press, 1989); John Williamson, *The Exchange Rate System* (Washington, D.C.: Institute for International Economics, 1985); Ronald MacDonald and Mark P. Taylor, "Exchange Rate Economics: A Survey," *IMF Staff Papers* 39, no. 1:1–57 (1992).

the golden age."[40] Indeed, Robinson's view is increasingly shared by economists, more of whom are finding exchange rate movements "random and unpredictable," with "sustained deviations" from anticipated levels.[41] This certainly seems to be the case of the yen/dollar exchange rate in the 1980s, which went from 203 in December 1980 to 278 in November 1982, and then from 263 in February 1985 to 120 in May 1989.[42] These figures, of the relationship between the world's two largest economies, suggest that any (or every?) "equilibrium" that might have existed was of little real significance. The market is not an omniscient, omnipotent diviner of truth. Rather, in the absence of a clearly identifiable equilibrium, the market is like an elephant in the dark, lumbering about with an insatiable hunger, in this case for new information.

This is why flexible exchange rate schemes have often been considered *more* susceptible to disruptive "arbitrary speculative behavior" than fixed-rate schemes.[43] The question, then, reduces to, How will the market respond to currency manipulation?[44] Since currency manipulation can be done secretly, it

[40] Joan Robinson, "Exchange Equilibrium," *Collected Economic Papers*, vol. 1 (1950; reprint, Oxford: Basil Blackwell, 1966), p. 215. Roy F. Harrod offered a similar view when he stated: "The government may wash its hands of the matter and declare that it will let the exchange find its natural level; but there is no natural level! There are an infinite number of possible levels". Quoted in M. June Flanders, *International Monetary Economics 1870–1960* (Cambridge: Cambridge University Press, 1989), pp. 266–67.

In fact, were such an equilibrium to exist, in theory, it might well be "self-denying" in that the general comprehension of its existence would add new information, changing behavior patterns.

[41] Neil Wallace states plainly: "For fiat currencies, there are no inherent fundamentals that determine equilibrium exchange rates." "Why Markets in Foreign Exchange Are Different from Other Markets," *Federal Reserve Bank of Minneapolis Quarterly Review* 3, no. 4:1–7 (1979), p. 1. See also Michael L. Mussa, Exchange Rates in Theory and Reality, Essays in International Finance, no. 179 (Princeton University, December 1990), esp. pp. 2 (1st quote), 7, 14–15; Sebastian Edwards, *Real Exchange Rates, Devaluation and Adjustment* (Cambridge: MIT Press, 1989), esp. pp. 8 (2d quote), 56, 100; De Grauwe, *International Money*, "equilibrium values of exchange rates cannot be known with much precision" (p. 160), also pp. 60, 75, 99, 179; Hallwood and MacDonald, International Money, "most of the changes in exchange rates are wholly unanticipated" (p. 134), also pp. 130, 145; Baillie and McMahon, *Foreign Exchange Markets*, "omnipresent disequilibrium in exchange rates" (p. 8), also p. 236.

[42] Destler and Henning, *Dollar Politics*, p.1.

[43] "Arbitrary speculative behavior" is from Flood and Garber, "Collapsing," pp. 6–7. It is indicative of floating regimes' reputation for instability that the authors were asserting in this case that fixed-rate regimes were just as vulnerable as flexible ones to this sort of problem. The view that flexible exchange rate systems are fundamentally vulnerable to destabilizing speculation was a central thesis of Rangar Nurkse's influential study of interwar monetary relations. Nurkse, *International Currency Experience: Lessons of the Interwar Period* (Princeton: League of Nations, 1944).

[44] Given the large size of contemporary foreign exchange markets, the ability of states to affect exchange rates is often called into question. Recent work has argued that central bank intervention can influence the exchange rate, moving it in the opposite direction from natural market forces. See Kathryn M. Dominguez and Jeffrey A. Frankel, *Does Exchange Intervention Work?* (Washington, D.C.: Institute for International Economics, 1993). See also Hali J. Edison, *The*

can be assumed that the agent will make its actions public in those instances when the market would complement the policy. However important the issue of publicity, though, it remains a force multiplier, not an initial source of power.[45] The more narrow question is how the market would react to the new information of apparent pressure on a given currency, from sources unknown.

In economic terms, an exchange rate movement caused by currency manipulation would be either self-limiting or self-inflammatory. In the former case, speculators expect the deviation to be temporary, and "lean against the wind." In the latter, the movement is seen as a first step toward further movement in the same direction. It is interesting to note that the German exchange rate from 1920 to 1924 experienced first a self-limiting phase, and then a self-inflammatory one. In retrospect, the market was "wrong" both times, that is, too optimistic in the first phase and too pessimistic in the second one. Up or down, self-inflammatory movements appear to be especially strong under floating regimes.[46]

The question, in political terms, is whether the market will balance against or bandwagon with the currency manipulation.[47] Unfortunately, there is no one answer. As Robinson notes, speculation can be equilibrating, but "if speculators read a slight fall as a sign that a further fall is to be expected," then the exchange rate can be "sent hurtling towards zero."[48]

What factors affect the relative likelihood of balancing and bandwagoning? Essentially, the information available to the market. There are two primary types of information: information about the magnitude of the pressure (or support—positive sanctions should not be forgotten), and information about the target state. The first type is rather straightforward: other things being equal, the stronger the pressure, the more likely it will be recognized as a

---

Effectiveness of Central Bank Intervention: A Survey of the Literature after 1982, Special Papers in International Economics, no. 18 (International Finance Section, Department of Economics, Princeton University, July 1993). However, focusing on movements of the dollar contributes to a false controversy. An overwhelming majority of exchange transactions involve the U.S. dollar. The mark and the yen also account for considerable shares. Add the two or four other most widely traded currencies, and the remaining foreign exchange market looks relatively minuscule. If, for the purpose of argument, one were to eliminate the prospect of manipulating the seven largest currencies given the current size of (and liberal regulations governing) financial markets, that would still leave over 150 currencies vulnerable to manipulation. As discussed below (see note 50 in Chapter 3 and Part III), changes in market size, regime nature, and regulatory structure affect the nature, but not the viability, of currency manipulation.

[45] The distinct technique of "rhetoric" is an independent source of power.

[46] Frank D. Graham, "Self-Limiting and Self-Inflammatory Movements in Exchange Rates: Germany," *Quarterly Journal of Economics* 43, no. 2:221–49 (1929), pp. 221, 227.

[47] Balancing and bandwagoning are, of course, terms used to describe alliance formation. See Stephen M. Walt, *The Origins of Alliances* (Ithaca, N.Y.: Cornell University Press, 1987).

[48] Robinson, *Essays*, pp. 200–201. Graham concurs, noting that while representing a possible bargain for speculators, "[a] heavy fall in the exchange . . . can frighten away those who would otherwise be disposed to buy." "Self-Limiting," p. 230.

significant trend. Thus, in a somewhat similar fashion to political alliance formation, the market will bandwagon with overwhelming force, but be more likely to balance against less convincing displays of power.

The second type of information is more complex. In considering its response, the market will evaluate the current and historical economic policies of the target, its current political standing, and traditional characteristics of the target currency. In other words, the slippery and difficult-to-measure concept of prestige, so often disdained, has an element that can be rehabilitated as the concept of *reputation*. This characteristic both lends itself to clearer definition and is easier to measure.[49] Thus two important considerations, the strength of the manipulation and the reputation of the target, will determine the likelihood of whether the market will act as a force inhibitor or a force multiplier, and more generally when currency manipulation will have a greater chance of success. The importance of reputation raises yet another reason why states prefer not to have their currencies manipulated against their wishes: such movements can be self-fulfilling. A currency that suffers repeated attacks could get a reputation for instability; on the other hand, support for currencies (through positive manipulation) can allow them time to establish reputations for stability, and ultimately to thrive independently of support.

Clearly, then, currency manipulation will not always "work." Nor will it have the same effect across different settings. As with other instruments of state power, its effectiveness will be shaped by a set of exogenous factors, which will have specific consequences from case to case. But there remains no reason to challenge the theoretical viability of currency manipulation. Rather, there are good reasons to have confidence that there will be occasions when it should be an effective tool of statecraft.[50]

---

[49] In contrast to balancing and bandwagoning, the security analogy in this case is a less perfect fit. In military confrontation, the extent to which reputation is an important aspect in determining the success of deterrence is not clear; rather, issue-specific interests appear to have the most explanatory power. With monetary power, reputation counts: it provides implicit deterrence against market-based support of currency manipulation.

[50] It should be noted that the nature and scope of this effectiveness can change given the prevailing monetary regime. The preceding discussion has established the viability of currency manipulation. However, regime change may alter some of the characteristics of manipulation. It has already been accepted as axiomatic in the general discussion of economic diplomacy above that large states are (in general) both more powerful and less vulnerable with regard to economic coercion. With a pure float, large states may enjoy even greater relative power and security. With no legal requirement of intervention, such states need not engage in costly defense against currency manipulation, but can choose to allow the market to determine the outcome. The theoretical discussion above suggests that such large states would be protected by three crucial factors: As large actors, the relatively large natural trading market in their currency would mean that any manipulation would provide a correspondingly small percentage of the new information about the currency, which determines market reaction. Second, bigger states are likely to have better currency reputations, or at a minimum, a reputation for relatively stable rates of change, inhibiting market bandwagoning with large sudden swings. Finally, large states may be less influenced by

Monetary Dependence

The exploitation of dependence does not face the same type of challenge to its technical viability as currency manipulation did. Obviously, system leaders have the ability to expel members. In considering viability, however, it is worthwhile to consider the market reaction to unwelcome expulsions from a monetary area. There are good reasons to expect market forces to bandwagon against the newly isolated currency. (That is, monetary diplomacy would unleash complementary, as opposed to countervailing, market forces.) The greater the expectations of this bandwagoning, the stronger the position of the core in dealing with members.

The market is likely to test a new fixed exchange rate, while some initial depreciation from the membership value should be expected in the event of a float. Assume that the membership rate represents the "optimum" value of the currency. The optimum rate is defined as that level from which any decline would raise the price of imports relative to exports, representing a reduction in the target's real income.[51] Under such circumstances, market forces should put pressure on the target currency. This is because

[i]f the exchange rate stands at the optimum level, any chance fall will precipitate a progressive decline, for each fall in the rate reduces the trade balance and promotes a further fall. In the absence of control, the ex-rate is stable only so long as it stands above the optimum level.[52]

Even in the absence of this phenomenon, pressures on newly isolated currencies easily mount and snowball. Given the uncertainty of the new situation, traders (not merely speculators) will take steps to defend their positions, actions that will put even greater pressure on the currency, for example, by depleting reserves. Any reasonable fear of devaluation or depreciation would lead such actors to stockpile essential imports in order to lock in a supply of those goods at current prices. Similarly, paying for imports immediately while delaying incoming payments will also minimize any losses associated with

---

changes in their exchange rates, given a smaller external sector. A devaluation would be more politically salient than a similarly sized depreciation under floating rates. However, these same factors suggest that the vulnerability of small states to currency manipulation increases under a float. Since big states were relatively safe all along, there is no reason to believe that there should be fewer net opportunities to practice currency manipulation under a flexible exchange rate regime.

[51] Robinson, *Essays*, p. 198. Of course, this may not be the case. But then the consequences of expulsion may not have been "unwelcome," For the purpose of measuring monetary power, the assumption that actions are taken that result in *undesired* pressures is retained.

[52] Ibid., p. 199. Further, if export markets are saturated, the tendency for a lower currency value to expand exports would be reduced, exacerbating this problem. C. Murdock, "Economic Factors as Objects of Security." in Knorr and Trager, *Economic Issues*, p. 94; see also Cheryl Payer, *The Debt Trap* (New York: Monthly Review Press, 1974), p. 18.

devaluation. However, all of these actions represent a flight from domestic to foreign currency, and would exacerbate any balance-of-payments crisis.[53] Using reserve levels as an illustration of one way in which this pressure could be manifested, the implication of this is that

> [a] reserve run-down which would have amounted to only $500 million if reserves had been, say $1 billion, may result in a serious exchange crisis if reserves are only $500 million. Thus, reserves must be larger than any allowable current account deficit in order to maintain confidence.[54]

More generally, Kenen pointed out that "[w]e must remember that an enormous flight of capital can be touched off by . . . a threat of decline or a rumor of devaluation."[55] Thus, not only is the exploitation of monetary dependence technically viable, but for a number of reasons, it is expected that market forces would naturally and automatically bandwagon with any pressure placed on a target currency as a result of expulsion. This finding would remain significant even if two challenges to the exploitation of monetary dependence held. The first challenge is that monetary arrangements are "neutral," or yield symmetrical rewards, eliminating the potential for leverage. (Thus, instead of dependence, there is interdependence.) As discussed in Chapter 1, though, while system leaders may greatly value the survival of the regime, each individual member gains more from the system than the leader gains from the participation of that particular member. The second challenge is that while there may not be free entry, there is "free exit" from the system. That is, since membership is voluntary, a state may leave at any time. While it would be an overstatement to call such a state of affairs "frictionless," "free exit" does accurately describe the options available to member states. Any time the costs of membership exceed the price of exit, states will be expected to leave.[56] This places a limit on the amount of coercion that can be exercised through the mechanism of a monetary system. But this truism does not undermine the viability of monetary dependence as a component of monetary diplomacy. It simply places an unspecified and theoretical limit on how much power can be extracted through the use of techniques that exploit dependence. The magnitude of a number of potential costs faced by target states, which will vary from situation to situation, determines the extent of this power. Clearly, under

[53] IMF, "The Adequacy of Monetary Reserves," *IMF Staff Papers* 8, no. 2:181–227 (1953), p. 191.

[54] Ibid., pp. 191–92.

[55] Peter B. Kenen, *British Monetary Policy and the Balance of Payments 1951–1957* (Cambridge: Harvard University Press, 1960), p. 16.

[56] The preferences of member states are changed by their participation in a currency area, through a process defined as "entrapment" (see Chapter 4). This shift raises the costs of exit above what they would appear to be at the moment of entry. Thus entry and exit with regard to monetary systems do not satisfy the condition of "frictionlessness."

a number of circumstances, the opportunity to exploit monetary dependence is theoretically viable.

Strategic Disruption

The main challenge to the viability of systemic disruption is market based: that is, the techniques introduced to practice disruption would be overwhelmed by market forces. This type of criticism has already been addressed with regard to currency manipulation, and was not found to be of consequence. However, the issue of disruption gives added weight to these challenges, for two reasons. First, targets in these cases will typically be much larger than the target in a typical attempt at currency manipulation. Second, the agents will conversely be relatively smaller. This suggests that those market mechanisms that do inhibit monetary diplomacy will be potentially greater obstacles to this type of monetary power. It is therefore likely that there will be fewer opportunities to practice disruption than manipulation. Some possibilities will remain, though. Additionally, some techniques of disruption are not market based, and would therefore not be subject to such challenges. Rather than reassess earlier findings with regard to the market in this context, the theoretical viability of systemic disruption can be demonstrated by revealing opportunities for its practice which clearly should remain.

In fact, disruption, while certainly the most difficult of the three types of monetary power to practice, is a viable instrument of power. There are three principal avenues, which occasionally intersect, through which disruption can be implemented: exploitation of the rules, manipulation of the key currency, and interference with base commodities.

Each monetary system must have rules; it is the sum of those rules that distinguishes insiders from outsiders. This provides two opportunities for disruption. The first comes from the nature of these rules. It should be recognized that these rules are designed to circumvent the will of the market. If the market provided the same results as the rules did, there would be no need for the rules. As a result, disrupters may be able to parlay this leverage in an attempt to unleash market forces that might put pressure on the smooth functioning of the rules-based system. Second, in most cases, those rules assign rights and responsibilities to member states. Here, members can practice disruption either through failing to fulfill their responsibilities or by gratuitously exercising their rights at inopportune moments. An example of the former is a state's failing to contribute its foreign exchange earnings to the pool of such reserves. The latter can involve the encashment of key currency for other assets, such as gold. This type of action, taken publicly, can be effective. It is akin to stimulating a run on a bank, which in some cases can force solvent institutions into bankruptcy.

Manipulation of the key currency is another avenue of disruption. Many such techniques would be limited by the relative market power of the potential agent and target in this instance (though the declining reputation of a particular system leader might mitigate this). Some techniques, though, would not be subject to market constraints. The most obvious example is the massive forging of the key currency.

Interference with base commodities can also be an effective technique of disruption. Monetary standards can be based on any commodity. Producers of such a base commodity, either from within the system or without, are especially well placed to manipulate its supply. Other actors might find manipulating the commodity market to be easier than manipulating the key currency, providing a back door to disruption.

As with all of the types of monetary power, the practice of disruption is affected by a number of international-level variables. For example, a global economy characterized by several monetary subsystems will provide greater opportunities for disruption than will a global economy characterized by one system. With several systems, each will be smaller and have less market power than would one comprehensive system. Under such circumstances the possibility of lateral (subsystem versus subsystem) disruption also exists. Additionally, with the existence of several systems, important nonmarket techniques, such as encouraging members to defect from one bloc to another, become increasingly viable.

While disruption is typically the most difficult weapon of monetary power to deploy, neither the constraint of the market nor target size is sufficient to eliminate the ability to practice disruption. Under the right conditions, monetary systems can be threatened with disintegration. Given that every system leader in history has valued the survival of its regime, opportunities to use disruption as a coercive tool should arise.

Part II

THE PRACTICE OF MONETARY POWER

3

Currency Manipulation

Introduction

This chapter is the first of three chapters that make up Part II of the book. These chapters consider currency manipulation, monetary dependence, and systemic disruption. As stated in Part I, the goals of this book are to establish the theoretical viability, demonstrate the existence of the practice, understand the mechanisms, and explore the potential of monetary power. Part I addressed the issue of theoretical viability. The chapters in Part II focus on mechanics and demonstration.

Demonstrating the existence of monetary power involves introducing a sufficient number of cases to show that states have practiced monetary diplomacy in the past. Not only must the exercise of monetary power have taken place, but the states involved must have done it consciously. This can be successfully shown by one demonstration case. However, in order to understand the mechanics of monetary power, and to be able to generate theories with regard to its practice and likely outcomes, a number of cases are required.

To properly address the issue of existence and to enhance the understanding of the nuances of monetary power, a focal case strategy is adopted. Each chapter considers a focal case in depth, and then considers a number of illustrative cases. With currency manipulation, the analysis includes two focal cases, in order to consider carefully cases involving both flexible and fixed exchange rates. All of the cases could be examined as focal cases, but for considerations of space and clarity. The focal cases chosen not only represent particularly consequential episodes of monetary diplomacy, but each offers a distinct perspective on the broader issue under consideration. Illustrative cases are important demonstration cases, but are even more useful in understanding how different forms of monetary diplomacy work, and what they can and cannot do. The cases selected do not represent an exhaustive list of examples of the practice of monetary diplomacy. Rather, they were chosen in order to highlight some novel aspect of the instruments, which may not have been clear previously or which had been considered only as a theoretical possibility. Each chapter in Part II concludes with a consideration of the lessons from all of the episodes in order to develop general conclusions, and to understand the strengths, weaknesses, and constraints on each form of monetary power. These lessons are reintroduced and further expanded upon in Part III, where the focus is on the potential of monetary power.

TABLE 3.1
The Four Basic Forms of Currency Manipulation

	Motive	
Technique	*Positive*	*Negative*
Intervention	Protective	Predatory
Disengagement	Permissive	Passive

The Theory of Currency Manipulation

There are four basic forms[1] of currency manipulation: two positive forms (protective and permissive) and two negative forms (predatory and passive). "Positive" and "negative" refer to whether the action is designed to support or punish the target; the distinction has nothing to do with whether the policy increases or decreases the value of any particular currency.[2] Beyond the positive/negative dimension, there is the dimension of intervention/disengagement. Permissive and passive actions are attempts at manipulation that result from states' refraining from, as opposed to introducing, certain types of behavior. These four possibilities are summarized in Table 3.1.

Protective currency manipulation involves intervention by the home state to bolster the currency position of the target state. In its purest form this would involve the purchase of the target state's currency on the open market. This can either be a short-term intervention or part of a long-standing policy of support. There are numerous techniques of protection, however, beyond this primary example. It should be recalled that *the definition of all of the forms of currency manipulation is ends-oriented*. In this case, therefore, protective manipulation includes all actions taken to bolster the target currency in support of security goals.[3] No currency need be bought or sold. For example, if the agent

---

[1] Monetary power is an instrument of economic influence. Other such instruments available to states include trade, aid, and finance. There are three types of monetary power: currency manipulation, monetary dependence, and systemic disruption. Predatory currency manipulation is a form of currency manipulation; there are different forms of all of the types of monetary power. Finally, for each form there is more than one technique; basically the form represents the policy and the technique the method of its execution. Thus, dumping target currency is one technique of predatory currency manipulation.

[2] As discussed in Chapter 1, states may prefer that their currencies maintain a low, or even a falling, value. Driving up the value of such a currency with the intent to coerce such a state would be a "negative" act. In the interwar period, states often attempted to reduce their currency values relative to other states; similar practices can be observed in the postwar era with regard to countries engaging in export-oriented growth strategies.

[3] Once again, it should be pointed out that this study is concerned with the exercise of monetary power in the pursuit of noneconomic goals.

(or "sender") state purchases assets of the target state in order to bolster the foreign exchange reserves of the target (which, for example, needs those reserves to defend its currency from a predatory attack), this qualifies as protection. In fact, protective currency manipulation can be engaged in without the involvement of a second state. In these instances, the agent and the target are the same, and the manipulation is considered one of "self-protection." An example of this would be the coordinated purchase of one's own currency with the goal of driving up its value (as opposed to driving down the value of another currency).

Permissive currency manipulation occurs when the agent forgoes actions that would be in its own economic interest but be deleterious to the target country. This can take the form of tolerance for a target's manipulation of its own currency, such as one that undervalues that currency and gives the target a trading advantage relative to the agent. Perhaps even more overtly permissively, the agent can hold on to target currency that it would be otherwise inclined to sell. Any action not taken that would otherwise be done except for the fact that it would undermine the currency position of the target falls into the category of permissive currency manipulation.

Predatory currency manipulation involves actions taken to undermine the currency position of the target state. A pure form of this would involve the dumping of the target currency on the world market. Once again, though, there are a number of ways in which predatory manipulation can be exercised. In fact, if a state mobilizes its armed forces in order to force a countermobilization that will require devaluation, if the goal was to force unwanted devaluation, then predatory currency manipulation has been exercised.[4] This would be a rather dramatic technique. On the other hand, predatory manipulation can be entirely rhetorical. A careful campaign of rumormongering, designed to foster a run on a currency perceived to be weak, could be an effective form of predatory manipulation.

Passive currency manipulation involves the withdrawal of protective or permissive support in order to coerce the target state. If the relationship between agent and target was one of protection, then passive manipulation would involve the end of such support. Here, the agent can choose to switch to permissive manipulation, or disengage completely, and act without reference to target interests. If the positive relationship was permissive initially, then passive manipulation simply involves a resumption of maximizing behavior on the part of the agent without reference to target interests. Passive manipula-

---

[4] A variation on this is the possibility that the first state mobilizes in order to gain a bargaining advantage. It believes that this advantage can be secured because the target state will not mobilize because that mobilization would force devaluation. This is not currency manipulation, but it is the exploitation of currency weakness. This issue will be explored further in Part III, on the potential for monetary power.

tion does not include a shift by the agent toward policies that discriminate against the target. Such acts would fall into the category of predatory manipulation. But passive manipulation can take the form of failing to be forthcoming with aid if any assistance is requested. This will be considered passive even if the aid would have been costless to the sender.

Currency Manipulation and the Monetary System

The four basic forms of currency manipulation are not employed in a vacuum. How they can be employed, how their effects are manifested, and the prospects for their success or failure are greatly influenced by the economic environment, or the type of international monetary system, under which they are introduced. While there are a large number of possible systems, one key defining characteristic is whether they involve fixed or flexible exchange rates.

FIXED EXCHANGE RATES

There are a number of possible exchange rate systems involving fixed exchange rates. Two of the most popular have been a commodity standard and commodity-exchange standards, where "key currencies" are used as reserves to supplement the commodity base. "Commodity standard" refers to a monetary system backed by a particular commodity, traditionally but not necessarily gold or silver. Bimetallic systems have also been practiced, but these often are de facto unimetallic because of the functioning of Gresham's law.[5]

For currency manipulation under a fixed exchange rate regime, the key variable is the level of reserves of the target state. The focus of the threat is forced suspension of convertibility and the associated unwelcome depreciation. The concurrent short-term threat is the pain associated with the measures taken by the target government to protect the reserves under attack.[6] Producers of base commodities, and issuers of key currencies, are better placed to practice currency manipulation than other states. Such producers can acquire

[5] Gresham's law, that bad money drives good out of circulation, was observed by Aristophanes in his play *The Frogs* (405 B.C.; reprint, London: Penguin Books, 1964), pp. 182–83]. Aristophanes was referring to the effects of the Peloponnesian War on the Athenian coinage. By the time of this play, even the gold and silver objects in the temples had been melted down to provide emergency coinage, currency that was quickly "pounced upon" by hoarders, while silver-plated copper coins were used for transactions. (p. 150).

For more on Gresham, whose sixteenth-century activities represent one of the earliest attempts at currency manipulation (though for wealth effects), see H. Buckley, "Sir Thomas Gresham and the Foreign Exchanges," *Economic Journal* 34:589–601 (1924); and Raymond DeRoover, *Gresham on Foreign Exchange* (Cambridge: Harvard University Press, 1949).

[6] Obviously, positive sanctions aim to maintain convertibility and ease the pain of defense.

reserves and dispose of them more easily, particularly in the short term, than can nonproducing states.

The most obvious form of protection under fixed rates is the sale of reserves, such as gold, from the agent state to the target state in exchange for target currency, at good rates and in guaranteed, sizable volume. Of course, outright gifts or loans of reserves would also fall into this category. Actions can also be taken to support the value of the currency in the open market. As always, rhetorical support is possible. Permissive support could take the form of postponing encashment of accumulated balances of the target currency.

Predatory moves focus on challenging the viability of the currency and faith in its continued convertibility. This involves encashment of the target's notes, and in the cases of pure commodity standards, goes beyond that to reach the domestic banks of the target. Any moves that threaten the solvency of the target's banks challenge a commodity standard. Thus the predator may withdraw its own funds, or engage in other actions designed to weaken the target banks. The failure or increased public fear of failure of one or more of those banks can trigger a run by the depositors, who will tend to convert their paper holdings into the base commodity. This can be especially destabilizing in the likely event that there is a fractional reserve system in effect (here, with regard to both the banks and the currency). Passive manipulation would involve the withdrawal of positive support of any form, with the intent to coerce. It can also take the form of refusing new sales of precious metals to the target. (Suspending existing sales, of course, would be a predatory act.)

FLEXIBLE EXCHANGE RATES

Under floating exchange rates, currencies have no fixed value, are not backed by any commodity, and are not "redeemable" on demand. Their price is determined in markets all over the world by the supply and demand for a given currency relative to the others. Governments need not hold reserves or intervene in the market to support exchange rates (though they usually do). Floating exchange rates are also relevant for the manipulation of nominally inconvertible currencies. With inconvertibility, there is no legal mechanism for exchanging the national currency of a given state for other currencies or commodities. This is often a temporary situation, the result of an economic crisis or a tactic introduced by one or more of the belligerents during wartime to protect gold and foreign exchange reserves and to maintain control over the disposition of private financial resources. Although the exchange rate is "fixed"—permitted exchange transactions are highly regulated—this hybrid system involves floating exchange rates in both domestic black markets and international exchange centers.

With floating rates, the key variable to watch with regard to currency manipulation shifts from the reserve position of the target to the value of the target's currency relative to other currencies. Protective power under this regime can be exercised through currency purchases in the free markets, rhetorical support, or the purchase of assets of the target to enable the target to undertake self-protective purchases. Currency support can also be offered through stabilization loans or even outright grants. Permissive power can occur when an agent state accumulates the currency balances of the target, when under normal circumstances it would prefer to exchange them with the target government or sell them on the open market. Predatory power can also be exercised through actions in international markets, and here, rhetorical "acts" can be used to complement the currency manipulation. Passive manipulation, as usual, is the hostile cessation of protective or permissive actions.

Inconvertibility adds a number of additional wrinkles to this story. Here, of great concern is the difference between the "official" rate of exchange and the rate in free markets. The greater the divergence, the more serious the situation is for the target state. Confidence may be undermined in the currency or in the government in general, and local citizens, other states, and institutions may become increasingly unwilling to hold the target currency. Different techniques become available, such as the permissive act of engaging in formal transactions at that official rate of exchange, or predatory operations directed at local black markets. Currency manipulation also works differently in this context: with inconvertibility, activity in the free market affects the target economy indirectly, especially with regard to those actions taken to affect confidence in the viability of the "official" rate and the willingness of foreign governments and institutions to engage in transactions at the official rate. Under a regime of floating exchange rates, the changes in the value of the currency influence the real economy directly, as do the measures taken by the home government to influence its exchange rate.

While there are recurring themes with regard to how monetary regimes affect the various instruments of currency manipulation, there have also been some striking differences. One example of this is that under a gold standard, an agent state can protect a target by selling that state gold in exchange for the target's currency. This bolsters the target currency on world markets and adds to the ability of the target to protect itself by increasing its reserve "war chest." On the other hand, under floating rates, an agent wishing to protect a target would buy gold from the target in exchange for the agent's currency. This would provide the target with the foreign exchange reserves necessary to intervene in the market and support its currency. These types of differences can be important, in fact, decisive, with regard to the ability of states to practice currency manipulation. In the example above, it might be that because of political or domestic economic imperatives, the agent state would be willing to sell gold but unwilling to buy it, or vice versa. Thus the regime has the potential to determine whether a given manipulation will be undertaken at all. Further, once the manipulation has been implemented, the regime can be important in determining how successful that action will ultimately be.

Focal Case: China and Monetary Warfare, 1935–1941

The case of China during the Japanese invasion and occupation from 1931 to 1945 is perhaps the richest of all episodes for the examination of currency manipulation. This was a case of open currency warfare, involving a variety of protective and predatory techniques employed by a number of states. The battleground was China, and in addition to that country, the participants were the United States and the United Kingdom, engaging in protection of the Chinese currency, with Japan as the predator. In 1931, Japan invaded China and seized the northern provinces (Manchuria), initiating a war, which lasted until 1945. The war was of a relatively small scale and scope until July 7, 1937, when the bombing of the Marco Polo Bridge by Japan signaled the beginning of its new, intense effort to conquer all of China.[7]

China was traditionally on a silver standard. Consequentially, in 1934, the American Silver Purchase Act, initiated for purely domestic political reasons, put tremendous pressure on China's monetary system. The rise in the price of silver encouraged people in China to convert currency notes into silver, and silver into gold, resulting in a chronic scarcity of currency with attendant serious deflationary effects.[8] As a result of this pressure, China abandoned the silver standard on November 3, 1935. Silver was nationalized, and a managed currency, consisting entirely of unbacked paper notes, was introduced. The managed currency was kept fixed in terms of foreign exchange. The Chinese did not peg their currency to any other specific issue, but rather balanced the Chinese dollar between par values associated with both the U.S. dollar and the British pound. This was possible because of the stability between those two issues that existed at the time.[9] The Chinese currency during the period under consideration was therefore a managed floating currency.

---

[7] A. N. Young, *China's Wartime Finance and Inflation 1937–1945* (Cambridge: Harvard University Press, 1965), p. 3.

[8] Chang Kia-ngau, "Toward Modernization of China's Currency and Banking, 1927–1937," in Paul K. T. Sin, ed., *The Strenuous Decade: China's Nation Building Efforts, 1927–1937* (New York: St. John's University Press, 1970), p. 156; see also D. H. Leavens, *Silver Money* (Bloomington, Ind.: Principia Press, 1939), ch. 5. The American purchases contributed to a reversal in the sustained fall of the price of silver, which had been insulating silver-using economies from the global deflation. See H. M. Bratter, "Silver—Some Fundamentals," *Journal of Political Economy* 39, no. 3:321–68 (1931); Frank D. Graham, "The Fall in the Value of Silver and Its Consequences," *Journal of Political Economy* 39, no. 4:425–70 (1931); Maxwell S. Stewart, "Silver— Its International Aspects," *Foreign Policy Reports* 7, no. 13:241–58 (1931); and T. E. Gregory, *The Silver Situation* (Manchester, England: Manchester University Press, 1932).

[9] T. A. Bisson, *American Foreign Policy in the Far East, 1931–1941* (New York: Institute of Pacific Relations, 1941), p. 28; Leavens, *Silver Money*, p. 315.

The United States and Silver Purchases, 1935–1938

From the end of 1935 to the end of 1938, the primary form of protective currency manipulation was U.S. purchases of China's silver. These large purchases of China's silver, which began when China was still one of the world's largest holders of silver (in 1933 the country had by far the world's largest stocks of the metal[10]) and ended when the Chinese reserves ran dry, provided the foreign exchange resources that kept China's currency afloat. Without this assistance, the Chinese dollar would have collapsed in the face of Japanese pressure, and China probably would not have held out against Japanese aggression.

When China was forced off the silver standard and opted for a free, but managed, currency, a stabilization fund was required for intervention to regulate the value of the newly floating legal tender. Finance Minister H. H. Kung thought that a stable exchange rate and a sound and uniform currency throughout China would provide an important stabilizing influence on the political situation in his highly regionalized country. The sale of China's huge silver reserves appeared to be the only way to raise the exchange necessary to operate such a fund. This could be carried out with any reasonable degree of success only through the sale of silver to a foreign government. Free markets were unpredictable, and worse, sales of such large quantities of silver would reduce the price, successively lowering the returns on each large sale.[11] Late in October 1935, Chinese Ambassador Sao-ke Alfred Sze approached Washington about the possibility of selling the United States 100 million to 200 million ounces of Chinese silver. Treasury Secretary Henry Morgenthau, Jr., was receptive, under certain conditions, and offered the following five-point plan:

1. The United States would buy 100 million ounces, and more if both sides were satisfied.

2. The proceeds of the sale would be used exclusively for the purpose of currency stabilization.

3. China would set up a stabilization committee to oversee stabilization operations. The committee of three would include two Americans.

4. Proceeds from the sale would be kept in New York.

5. The New Chinese currency would be tied to the U.S. dollar.

The Chinese ambassador agreed to all of the points except the fifth.[12] Instead, he offered trade concessions, which the United States did not accept. To tide

---

[10] Leavens, *Silver Money*, p. 164.

[11] On Kung, see A. S. Everest, *Morgenthau, the New Deal, and Silver* (New York: King's Crown Press, 1950), p. 114. On the market, see A. N. Young, *China and the Helping Hand 1937–1945* (Cambridge: Harvard University Press, 1963), p. 31.

[12] The U.S. negotiating position raises an important theoretical issue, which will be discussed more fully below. All three nations involved in currency manipulation, the United States, Britain,

the Chinese over while negotiations continued, the United States immediately purchased 20 million ounces of Chinese silver.[13]

While the United States continued negotiations with China, the Yokohama Specie Bank of Japan raided the Chinese exchange fund on November 11, 1935. This was a serious attack, and few attacks of that magnitude could be withstood by China's fledgling reserve fund. This was just a part of Japan's effort, which included raids and propaganda campaigns, to undermine confidence in China's currency. This act, though, influenced U.S. opinion, and the United States immediately agreed to buy 50 million ounces of Chinese silver, provided the funds were used exclusively for currency support, the money was left in New York, and the United States was consulted on the operations of the fund. The purchase price was at 65.625 cents per ounce, which was well over the market price. (Subsequent purchases would be at 45, or even 43 per ounce.) These conditions were accepted by China.[14]

Despite this initial purchase, in December 1935, when Japanese banks again raided the Chinese exchange fund, the United States was not forthcoming with new purchases of silver. Morgenthau was distrustful of China, fearing that agents within the government there were engaging in silver speculation for private gain.[15] Continued Japanese aggression eventually overwhelmed these concerns, and on April 8, 1936, the United States agreed to purchase 75 million ounces of Chinese silver, 12 million in June, and 9 million each month after that until January 1937. As with the previous sale, the United States would pay in gold or U.S. dollars, which would be deposited in New York and used only for currency stabilization.[16]

From November of 1935 to the middle of 1937, the United States bought 125 million ounces of silver for $67 million. But there was still a great deal of silver in China, and the Chinese government was anxious to move it out not only for currency stability, but also to avoid its capture by the Japanese. Liter-

---

and Japan, wanted China to peg its currency to theirs. China resisted in each case. But this resistance became more difficult when one of the nations, Japan, became increasingly aggressive in its predatory acts. Turning to one of the competing states for assistance gave that state enhanced bargaining power. China faced, as many nations presumably face, a trade-off between protection and dependence. The Chinese were able to hold firm on this point, probably because the agent and the target (the United States and China) saw a harmony of interest in U.S. protection. This undercut U.S. bargaining power, and made it worthwhile for the United States to provide protection even in the absence of concessions.

[13] Everest, *New Deal and Silver*, pp. 111–12.

[14] A. N. Young, *China's Nation Building Effort 1927–1937: The Financial and Economic Record* (Stanford: Hoover Institute Press, 1971), p. 236; Everest, *New Deal and Silver*, p. 112.

[15] J. M. Blum, *From the Morgenthau Diaries* (Boston: Houghton Mifflin Co., 1959), vol. 1, p. 218. Morgenthau's distrust of China grew as the years passed and corruption there increased. In 1944, he privately stated: "I will do business with Chen, because he will keep his word, but the rest of them are just a bunch of crooks." U.S. Congress, *Morgenthau Diary (China)*, vol. 1 (Washington, D.C.: U.S. Government Printing Office, 1965), p. 133.

[16] Everest, *New Deal and Silver*, p. 116.

ally on the eve of the Marco Polo Bridge bombing and the widening of the war, the United States agreed to buy 62 million additional ounces through the end of 1937. But the start of a wider war led to panic selling of the national currency in China. In the five weeks following the outbreak of the wider war, the central bank spent $42 million to support the Chinese dollar. Even this was not sufficient to stabilize the currency, as fighting at Shanghai heightened public fears. The government was forced to declare a bank holiday in August, and this combined with domestic deflationary measures and some progress on the military front finally eased the currency situation.[17]

China still faced a critical problem. Reserves, still falling, were needed to support the currency, which was considered a symbol of China's unity and strength. In recognition of this, the United States continued to engage in protective currency manipulation, purchasing Chinese silver, including four blocks of 50 million ounces each in the form of biweekly purchases throughout 1938. These purchases were eventually extended into 1939 and beyond. Starting with the June 1937 purchase, the funds received by China were allowed to be used for purchases of military equipment. But the reserve situation was critical, as they continued to fall almost as quickly as they could be replaced. This was a matter of great concern: the Chinese government continued to view the currency war as at least as important in the overall struggle with Japan as the shooting war. Of the $379 million of Chinese reserves in mid-1937, in the first eight months of fighting $85 million went for war supplies, while $121 million went in the defense of the currency. Even with this effort, by 1939 the government was forced to introduce exchange rationing.[18]

China was going to need even greater assistance if it was to protect the currency and stay afloat, especially as the country ran out of silver. An internal State Department memo dated December 29, 1939, neatly summarized the situation:

> The Chinese government has upon several occasions called attention to the fact that its currency reserves are dwindling and has emphasized the extreme importance which it attaches to the maintenance of external and internal value of the Chinese currency. Dr. A. Young, American financial advisor to the Chinese government . . . is convinced of the necessity of maintaining the value of China's currency if China's resistance is to be continued. It is feared that during the coming months the Japanese will renew their offensive against the Chinese currency and that, given the present meagerness of Chinese reserves, the currency may collapse and prices get out of hand, with consequences injurious not only to China but to the U.S.[19]

[17] Young, *Helping Hand*, pp. 6, 30, 35–38.

[18] Ibid., pp. 39, 61, 63, 64. On the 1939 extension, U.S. Department of State, *Foreign Relations of the United States (FRUS)*, 1938, vol. 3 (Washington, D.C.: U.S. Government Printing Office, 1954), p. 588.

[19] *FRUS*, 1939, vol 3 (Washington, D.C.: U.S. Government Printing Office, 1955), p. 553.

TABLE 3.2
U.S. Purchases of Chinese Silver, 1934–1941

Year	Ounces	Cost
1934	19,506,000	$10,427,997
1935	50,115,000	32,166,303
1936	66,975,000	30,157,000
1937	130,026,000	58,512,000
1938	165,892,000	115,530,000
1939	33,341,000	13,787,000
1940	5,142,000	1,800,000
1941	805,000	282,000
Total	571,802,000	$262,662,300

Source: A. S. Everest, *Morgenthau, the New Deal, and Silver* (New York: King's Crown Press, 1950), p. 178.

By the time that memo was written, however, the most important form of protective currency manipulation afforded China had shifted from silver purchases (see Table 3.2) to direct financing of currency stabilization. This phase was initiated by the British, as China's silver stocks ran dry.

The U.S. protective currency manipulation, in the form of massive, regular purchases of Chinese silver was of great consequence. In 1937, Morgenthau "became profoundly convinced that this help in making China strong enough to resist Japan, would, in historical perspective, be the most important thing he did as Secretary of the Treasury." In providing this assistance, it should be noted that he had to overcome two important obstacles. One of these obstacles, U.S. neutrality legislation, shows the flexibility of monetary power. Through the purchase of silver, Morgenthau was able to circumvent the strict U.S. neutrality laws of February 1936 and May 1937. The second obstacle, on the other hand, was peculiar to monetary power: the opposition of the powerful silver lobby in the United States. In general, the silver interests were delighted when currency manipulation involved the sale of U.S. silver, but dismayed when the United States bought foreign silver. The protection of the Chinese currency, then, involved actions which were against the interests of the "silver senators." In this case, the domestic political situation was probably eased by the good relations between the silver states and the Roosevelt administration, dating back to the silver purchase act of 1934.[20]

[20] "profoundly convinced . . . ," Everest, *New Deal and Silver*, p. 118; neutrality legislation, Bisson, *American Foreign Policy*, p. 56; "silver senators," Young, *Helping Hand*, p. 33. The "silver senators" were fourteen senators from seven western states (Idaho, Utah, Montana, Colorado, Arizona, Nevada, and New Mexico) in which silver was mined. They combined with

While U.S. silver purchases were vital to China, and probably kept that country in the war, the United States hesitated to take the next step necessary to protect the Chinese currency, which was required when Chinese silver stocks were exhausted. At this point, the British took the initiative.

Great Britain and Currency Stabilization Boards

As early as January 6, 1938, the Chinese approached the British for a loan of 20 million pounds to support their currency. The British were informed that without such a loan, China "could not carry on with its currency much longer." The British were in favor of such a loan, but reluctant to move ahead without a similar American commitment, which would bring the level of the loan to about $100 million. Secretary of State Cordell Hull rejected the idea, arguing that it would alienate the Japanese. He noted that the support provided from U.S. silver purchases was significant, and would continue.[21]

The situation worsened in the summer of 1938. Sales of foreign exchange by the Chinese government supported the currency in the face of military defeats. In June of that year, China was assisted by some British banks in this task, as fear in Britain regarding the Chinese currency situation increased. By the end of July, however, reserves were almost exhausted. In September, Shanghai financier K. P. Chen, speaking on behalf of the Chinese government, approached the United States for additional assistance. While thanking the United States for its support with regard to silver purchases, "which made it possible for China to maintain its financial structure during the first year of fighting," Chen asked for an immediate credit for currency support. He was turned down. On November 21, the day Canton fell and four days before Hinshaw followed, Chen again requested currency support, "because even China's continuance in the war might depend on maintaining an orderly exchange market." The United States remained suspicious of direct currency support, and instead provided $25 million in commercial credits. China was able to hold the currency position with a supplementary sale of 15 million ounces of silver.[22]

As the war continued into 1939, the British became convinced that the key to the position in China was the currency situation. On January 6, the British embassy in Washington told the U.S. State Department that British and Amer-

---

midwestern senators, representing farming interests, to form a very powerful prosilver, proinflation voting bloc in the U.S. Senate. For more on the "silver senators," see Ray B. Westerfield, *Our Silver Debacle* (New York: Ronald Press Co., 1936); see also Neil Carothers, "Silver—a Senate Racket," *North American Review* 23, no. 3:4–15 (1932).

[21] *FRUS*, 1938, vol. 3; pp. 525, 533, 535, 537, see also 576.

[22] Young, *Helping Hand*, pp. 70–81.

ican interests in China "would be seriously threatened by a collapse of the Chinese currency," and urged joint assistance and encouragement. The United States was once again reluctant to go ahead with such a scheme. The British, viewing the situation as critical, made plans to move ahead on their own.[23]

On March 8, 1939, the formal announcement of the creation of a stabilization fund for China, underwritten by the British Treasury, was made. The agreement involved arrangements among the British government, the Chinese government, and four local or regional banks (the Bank of China, the Bank of Communications, the Hong Kong and Shanghai Bank, and the Bank of India, Australia and China). The banks agreed to provide the £10 million for the fund. The British accepted the responsibility of reimbursing each bank for any losses when the exchange fund was disbanded. The Chinese government agreed to pursue economic and monetary policies that would stabilize its dollar relative to the pound, and to use the appropriate banks for foreign exchange transactions. The fund would operate out of Hong Kong, and be administered by two bank representatives, along with one representative of the Chinese government, jointly chosen by the British and the Chinese.[24]

The official announcement of the currency credit plan was received with "unrestrained joy and gratification in Chunking." However, the respite was only temporary, for during the summer of 1939 the resources of the fund fell rapidly, and they ran completely dry on July 18. The result of the cessation of stabilization operations was a 50 percent drop in the exchange rate by August 11. This precipitous fall in China's exchange rate demonstrates the great extent to which outside protective currency manipulation was supporting the value of the Chinese national currency. Ironically, with the outbreak of a general European war on September 1, the exchange rate rebounded, as a result of the flight from European currencies. Through strategic selling of Chinese dollars at this time, the stabilization board was able to replenish its reserves, and was back in business.[25]

Within six months, however, the fund was once again in trouble, and it ceased operations from April to May 1940. The situation was again critical in October and November, but this time the United States unexpectedly and suddenly agreed to get involved in exchange operations. This change of heart came about after Young personally told Hull in mid-November that "China's weakest spot was probably finance."[26] This, combined with the course of the

---

[23] "key to the position," Young, *Helping Hand*, p. 157; British/U.S discussion, *FRUS*, 1939, vol. 3, pp. 640–44.

[24] *FRUS*, 1939, vol. 3, pp. 653–55.

[25] Young, *Finance and Inflation*, pp. 213–16, 222; also *FRUS*, vol. 3, 1939, pp. 685–86. For foreign exchange rates of the Chinese dollar, in pounds and U.S. dollars from 1920 to 1937, see Young, *Nation Building*, pp. 469–73; for the 935–1945 rates, see Young, *Finance and Inflation*, pp. 360–61.

[26] On the operations of the British stabilization fund and American reversal, see Young, *Help-*

European war and increasing tensions with Japan, probably tipped the balance in favor of U.S. action at this time.

The United States offered China a $100 million credit, half for purchases and half for currency stabilization. The British made a parallel offer of £5 million. A board of five was set up to run the fund—three from China, including the chair, along with one American and one Briton, both nominated by China. The United States, ever suspicious, wanted to limit the drawing to $5 million per month, but this was successfully opposed as threatening to the successful operation of the fund. After some delay, the agreement was signed on April 25, 1941. After this point, and into the U.S. participation in the war, U.S. support of China's currency, as well as the lend-lease of military equipment, became routine.[27]

The establishment of exchange stabilization boards underwritten by the agents of monetary diplomacy represented the second phase of protective currency manipulation. What is most notable was the impressive performance of the manipulation in terms of achieving important gains with limited means. Participants and observers alike came to this conclusion. Young argued that the British realized their support of the Chinese currency was the "surest means in the present circumstances of preserving British interests in the Far East." Similarly, the French foreign minister and other French officials thought in 1938 that "Chinese resistance could and would continue indefinitely provided China could obtain a loan for the purpose of maintaining Chinese currency in foreign exchange markets."[28] Protective monetary power was decisive in keeping China active in its war against Japan. This weakened and diverted the ultimate enemy of the states providing the support. But the United States and Britain were not unopposed in their endeavors. On the other side, Japan was engaged in a remarkable degree of predatory currency manipulation against China, which went far beyond the reserve raids discussed above.

Japan and Predatory Currency Manipulation

The Japanese currency efforts in China were actually the vanguard of a new wave of currency manipulation, which flowered during World War II. During the war, there was an expansion in the use and functions of military currencies. The original functions of paying troops and compensating owners of

---

ing Hand, pp. 165–72; On the Young-Hull conversation, see Young, *Finance and Inflation*, p. 227.

[27] Young, *Helping Hand*, pp. 171–73, 181. On the operations of the American stabilization board, see ibid., pp. 198–204. On the original U.S. plans and the November negotiations, see U.S. Congress, *Morgenthau Diary*, pp. 179, 243, 261.

[28] *FRUS*, 1939, vol. 3, pp. 658–59 (Young); *FRUS*, 1938, vol 3, p. 534 (France).

seized property were expanded to include the manipulation of the economy of the occupied territory. Military currencies were made legal tender, circulated widely, and protected from discrimination. They had considerable impact on the economies of the occupied countries, and became a vital aspect of occupation policy, for both Allied and Axis conquerors.[29] The new currency warfare included defensive as well as offensive measures. In areas threatened by occupation, the home state could mark its currency, facilitating repudiation should that currency fall into enemy hands. After Pearl Harbor, U.S. dollars in Hawaii were marked for this purpose.[30]

The Japanese predatory currency manipulation against China went far beyond the new functions associated with military currencies. More than to ease the cost of occupation, Japan's operations were designed to undermine the legitimacy of National Chinese rule, and break down that country into autonomous regions dependent on Japan. The currency battle began in earnest when Japan set up the Federated Reserve Bank of China in northern China on March 10, 1938. The goal of Japanese strategy was to oust Chinese national currency from the Japanese- occupied areas and to sway the loyalty of the citizens of the region. At first, this met with only limited success, since the pure fiat currency was unpopular, partly because it was not convertible into any foreign currency. The Japanese responded with even tighter monetary controls, and it became difficult to get National Chinese notes into the occupied areas.[31]

Japan's master plan involved the proliferation of puppet currencies—each different occupied region of China would have its own. The Japanese military also had its own currency, and to confuse matters, there was even currency issued independently by the Chinese Communists. The Federated Reserve Bank issued its dollars in the north (FRB$), and the Japanese-created Central Reserve Bank of Nanking did the same in central and southern China (CRB$). The puppet dollars and military yen were introduced at parity with the National Chinese dollar (NC$), but these currencies were discounted within a year or two to about 40 percent of their original value.[32]

---

[29] Vladimir Petrov, *Money and Conquest: Allied Occupation Currencies in World War II* (Baltimore: Johns Hopkins University Press, 1967), p. 16. For a discussion of the practical aspects of occupation currencies, including public reaction, convertibility, and legal responsibility, see F. A. Southard, Jr., *Some European Currency and Exchange Experiences: 1943–1946*, Essays in International Finance, no. 7 (Princeton University, 1946). For more on specific episodes of the introduction of such currencies, see Henry Simon Bloch and Bert F. Hoselitz, *Economics of Military Occupation* (Chicago: Foundation Press, 1944), chs. 2 and 3. On the difficulty in managing these issues, see Walter Rundell, Jr., *Black Market Money: The Collapse of U.S. Military Currency in World War II* (Baton Rouge: Louisiana State University Press, 1964).

[30] R. A. Lester, International Aspects of the Wartime Monetary Experience, Essays in International Finance, no. 3 (Princeton University, 1944), p. 2.

[31] Young, *Helping Hand*, pp. 65–67.

[32] Lester, *Wartime Monetary Experience*, p. 3; Young, *Finance and Inflation*, p. 184. For more on the various reserve banks, see Bank for International Settlements, *Eleventh Annual Report* (Basle: BIS, 1941), pp. 46–50.

Actually, the reduction in the value of these puppet currencies was a sign of how well the Japanese were employing them to extract wealth from China to support their war effort. By July 1943, the Japanese had acquired about NC$3 billion in exchange for their puppet currencies. Therefore, the National dollars increased in value because of their relative scarcity.[33] But Japan was not simply interested in profiting from occupation. Rather, the goal was to delegitimize the Chinese national rule and replace it with its own. To this end, steps were taken to remove national currency entirely from circulation. (If the motive had been profit or exploitation, Japanese interests would have been served best by a weakened but viable Chinese national currency.) Puppet and military currencies became the only way to pay taxes, buy train tickets, transact exports and imports, and pay utility bills, and were the units of account and deposit for all government and bank accounts in the occupied areas. Internationally, the Japanese tried to bolster the legitimacy of the puppet currencies. On December 1, 1938, they attempted to pressure the British and French to accept the FRB dollars as the legal tender of China. Not only were they turned down, but in fact the British helped China smuggle national currency notes into the northern regions.[34]

The Japanese, though, did not give up on their efforts to enhance the international legitimacy of the puppet currencies. In July of 1939, during Anglo-Japanese negotiations, Japan's demands included the surrender of Chinese silver under British control, and the nonrecognition of Chinese currency as legal tender. The British responded that they were already bound on both issues—the silver had been paid for and it was not legally possible for them to withdraw legal tender status from the currency of a recognized government.[35]

In fact, from as early as 1935, Japan engaged in predatory currency manipulation against China, as an integral part of its strategy to dominate that country. These actions taken by Japan were recognized as a serious threat by the both the United States and British governments. Both the U.S. Treasury Department and the State Department considered the manipulation dangerous and the situation serious. In a memo from monetary research director Harry White to Morgenthau dated July 10, 1939, the methods and returns of Japanese policy were reviewed:

Japanese currency war technique has varied, but the principle has been the same: that of forcibly substituting a fiat currency subject to strict exchange control for the Chinese currency which in practice is freely available. The Japanese through their currency maneuvers have already partly succeeded in (a) breaking down the stability

---

[33] Lester, *Wartime Monetary Experience*, p. 3. For more on the economic aspects, see Warren S. Hunsberger, "The Yen Bloc in Japan's Expansion Program, *Far Eastern Survey* 7, no. 22:251–58 (1938).

[34] Ibid., p. 4 (domestic measures); Young, *Helping Hand*, pp. 67–68 (international moves).

[35] *FRUS*, 1939, vol. 3, p. 694.

of the Chinese currency, and (b) obtaining a substantial trade advantage for their nationals. The Japanese substitute their fiat notes for Chinese notes and then buy foreign exchange with Chinese currency. This practice gives them a considerable amount of foreign exchange and weakens the Chinese currency. Japanese sales of Chinese currency are generally considered to have been a very important factor in driving down the Chinese currency from 29 cents to 16 cents during 1938; and from 16 cents to 12 cents in June of 1939.[36]

The State Department, in its analysis of Japanese practices in December 1939, noted a four-stage process of military and economic conquest: (1) military occupation of a region; (2) establishment of a puppet regime there; (3) creation of a puppet currency; and (4) driving out existing currencies and pegging the puppet currency to the yen. This fourth step was most crucial, for when coupled with import and export controls the region would be completely isolated, able to trade only with Japan and not with any other foreign country. In central China, the first three steps had been accomplished, but the resilience of the Chinese national currency was preventing the critical fourth step from being taken. Thus the continued existence and strength of the national currency was essential. The memo concluded that a collapse of the currency "would result in the lowering of Chinese morale and in disorganization which would tend to reduce the effectiveness of any assistance [which the U.S might extend]."[37]

In summary, the Japanese predatory currency manipulation in China demonstrates how effective such actions can be in contributing to the conquest of another state. The Japanese made significant economic and political gains in their drive to conquer China though currency manipulation. Had the British and the Americans not intervened with countervailing protective measures, the Chinese national currency would have collapsed. The puppet currencies would have flourished, tying each region closer to Japan and delegitimizing the national government. The degree of the threat to China from Japan's currency manipulation was put in perspective by China's Finance Minister Kung in 1939, when he stated that "Japan's endeavors to obtain control of China's currency . . . was just as serious a threat to China as military operations."[38]

Lessons from the Chinese Episode

A number of important lessons can be culled from this episode. The first is the impressive power of currency manipulation. In the opinion of an economist on the scene, Allied support of the Chinese currency, first through silver pur-

---

[36] U.S. Congress, *Morgenthau Diary*, p. 10.
[37] *FRUS*, 1939, vol. 3, p. 553.
[38] Ibid., p. 647

chases and then though direct exchange stabilization support, was "invaluable." Without such support, the Chinese currency would have collapsed, and China would have probably been knocked out of the war before Pearl Harbor.[39] Another remarkable aspect of this currency manipulation was its low cost. For the United States, the silver transactions were virtually costless, since it purchased silver of considerable value. The exchange stabilization operations did have a real cost in terms of (high-risk) loans, but this price for keeping China in the war was surely a bargain. As for the Japanese, they were actually able to create billions in wealth for the cost of printing puppet currency. Their currency manipulation effort, which was aimed at undermining the very legitimacy of their adversary in an ongoing military conflict, and which had the potential to succeed in creating dependent states within China, actually showed a profit.

The impressive performance of currency manipulation in significantly influencing the course and outcome of a major war, and at low cost, cannot be overemphasized. This particular episode also calls attention to two important issues regarding monetary power. First is the importance of a national currency, not just as a symbol, but as one of the fundamental elements of sovereignty. Had the Japanese actually been able to displace the national Chinese currency, it would not simply have been a demoralizing blow (as it surely would have), or a great step toward creating autonomous financial dependencies within China, but it would have been a fundamental displacement of Chinese sovereignty over those areas. The lesson here, which underscores the potential of monetary power, is that the establishment of a new currency need not follow conquest; the successful introduction of a new currency by outsiders can be the ultimate cause of conquest.

The second new wrinkle to appear in this episode is a result of competition. As discussed above, the existence of both potential predators and protectors can leave the target with a choice between hostile manipulation and unwanted dependence. More generally, competition also will make strategy (and the analysis of that strategy) more complex. The influence of countermoves and third-party reactions to attempts at monetary coercion must be considered in appropriate cases, as they may be decisive in explaining both the initiation and outcome of currency manipulation.

Finally, the flexibility of currency manipulation is highlighted in this episode. U.S. currency manipulation was able to evade restrictive neutrality laws in the United States and still play a pivotal role in a major foreign conflict. Additionally, protective currency manipulation by both the United States and Britain was more subtle than other actions that could have been taken to assist China and hurt the Japanese (such as direct military aid or strong punitive sanctions against Japan). This was important to those nations, which (espe-

[39] Young, *Helping Hand*, pp. 206, 210.

cially in the early stages) did not want to anger Japan unnecessarily and had not ruled out coming to an understanding with that country.

Focal Case: The Suez Crisis

The Suez crisis of 1956 is a rich, important, and enlightening episode for the study of international relations. The mechanics of the crisis—military and economic warfare, secret meetings, complex alliance relationships, international organization and bargaining behavior, and the role of the personalities and even the health of the decisionmakers involved—provides the raw material for a number of possible investigations. The crisis was also of great historical consequence, as it caused great strain on U.S.-European relationships, which would not soon be forgotten, affected international politics within the Middle East and between the Middle Eastern nations and the rest of the world, and had a profound effect on British politics, ending the career of Anthony Eden and elevating Harold Macmillan unexpectedly to the position of prime minister.

In the decade prior to the Suez incident, sterling endured numerous crises. Britain emerged from World War II, as did all the belligerent powers save the United States, with a currency whose convertibility was strictly regulated and controlled. Even within Europe itself, payments were bilateral, an extraordinarily inefficient system, which inhibited trade; this problem was somewhat relieved with the formation of the European Payments Union in June of 1950. Britain had the additional problem of large sterling balances held by Commonwealth countries, accumulated during the war as Britain attempted to finance its war effort and mobilize commonwealth resources.[40]

The United States, on the other hand, was interested at this time in establishing a multilateral payments network with free convertibility. The United States was motivated by its belief that trade and exchange controls had contributed to the cause of the war, and by a desire to eliminate imperial preferences which discriminated against U.S. goods. In accordance with this policy, the United States forced convertibility on Britain in 1947.[41] This move was premature, given the general economic conditions, and convertibility was suspended soon after it was introduced. The next monetary episode of note for Britain was the controversial 1949 devaluation, a measure taken in response to a drain on reserves and a concern for competitiveness, which lowered the value of the pound from $4.08 to $2.80.[42] Another exchange crisis occurred

[40] For more on the sterling system, see Chapter 4.

[41] On the 1947 crisis, see Randall Hinshaw, *Toward European Convertibility*, Essays in International Finance, no. 30 (Princeton University, 1958); J. C. R. Dow, *The Management of the British Economy 1945–1960* (Cambridge: Cambridge University Press, 1970).

[42] On the 1949 devaluation, see A. Cairncross and B. Eichengreen, *Sterling in Decline* (Ox-

in 1951, but this was weathered without incident.[43] After the Commonwealth Conference of December 1952, where it was confronted by angry sterling holders, Britain began to ease its exchange controls.[44] In February 1955, sterling was made convertible for nonresidents, and the Bank of England was permitted to support the rate of "transferable" sterling balances (this referred primarily to sterling balances accumulated since the war). Dollars could thereafter be obtained for transferrable sterling at the official rate.[45] The currency crisis associated with Suez was the most intense of four sterling crises of varying severity, which occurred in rapid succession during 1955–1957.[46]

Monetary Power and the Suez Crisis

When British and French forces attacked Egypt on October 31, 1956, with the stated goal of seizing the Suez Canal, it was not an unexpected bolt from the blue, but rather the boiling over of an animosity that had been brewing between those countries for more than one year. Egyptian president Gamal Abdel Nasser and the allies each saw the other as attempting to impose a hostile hegemonic rule throughout the Middle East. Nasser interpreted the Baghdad Pact of 1955, a defensive alliance among Britain, Pakistan, Iran, Iraq, and Turkey, as an anti-Egyptian organization created to promote British power in the Middle East (as opposed to an instrument of anti-Soviet containment). In response, he turned to the Soviet Union, signaling this shift with a purchase of Czechoslovakian arms.[47]

Both the United States and Britain were dismayed by this turn of events, and hoped to woo Egypt back away from the Soviets. Appeasement of Egypt dated at least back to 1954, when Britain agreed to withdraw its combat troops from the Suez Canal zone, which it subsequently did, on schedule, in June 1956. Now the West held out the promise of financing of a major Egyptian development project: a dam at Aswan. In December 1955, the United States

---

ford: Basil Blackwell, 1983); Roy F. Harrod, *The Pound Sterling*, Essays in International Finance, no. 13 (Princeton University, 1952); see also Dow.

[43] *The Economist* had several essays on this financial crisis, which together form an excellent on-the-scene narrative of the incident. See "Deep in the Red," October 6, 1951; "The Gold Drain," January 12, 1952; "Sterling since the Budget," March 29, 1952; "No Respite for Sterling," April 12, 1952; and "The Gold Loss Analyzed," July 5, 1952.

[44] Peter B. Kenen, *British Monetary Policy and the Balance of Payments 1951–1957* (Cambridge: Harvard University Press, 1960), p. 92.

[45] Dow, *Management of the British Economy*, p. 88.

[46] See Samuel I. Katz, *Sterling Speculation and European Convertibility: 1955–1958*, Essays in International Finance, no. 37 (Princeton University, 1961).

[47] R. A. (Lord) Butler, *The Art of the Possible* (memoirs) (Boston: Gambit, 1972), p. 185. Also note here that "the allies" referred to are Britain and France.

and Britain agreed to provide a $70 million loan, and to support a$200 million loan from the World Bank to finance construction of the dam.[48]

But Nasser was proving to be a difficult man to appease successfully. Under his orders, subversive groups operated in Libya, Jordan, Iraq, and Sudan. There and elsewhere, assassination attempts were also carried out, and the Cairo-based "Voice of Arabs" radio was vehemently anti-Western.[49] For Anthony Eden, the British prime minister, the last straw came in March of 1956 when a British general, Sir John Glubb, was relieved of his duties on the Jordanian general staff by the king of Jordan. Eden was convinced that the king had acted under pressure from Nasser and his anti-Western propaganda. Regarding Nasser, Eden raged, "I want him destroyed!"[50]

While actively in confrontation with British interests in the Middle East, Egypt's relationship with the United States was also deteriorating. The U.S. secretary of state, John Foster Dulles, lost his temper when he felt that the Egyptians were attempting to play the United States and the Soviets off each other. When the Egyptian ambassador told Dulles that the United States should not threaten to withdraw Aswan Dam financing because he had an alternate source of funding "in his pocket," Dulles angrily and suddenly withdrew the U.S. funds. He did this clumsily and "undiplomatically" on July 19 without consulting the British, who could not continue their involvement without American support.[51]

In response, Nasser nationalized the Suez Canal one week later, on July 26. This was done, it was claimed, to collect the tolls from its operation in order to finance the Aswan Dam. Nasser's expropriation speech seemed designed to be as combative and taunting as possible. The British were extremely concerned, since they saw Suez as a literal lifeline, and were alarmed at the prospect of that lifeline's being under Nasser's thumb.[52] The United Kingdom was the largest shareholder in the Suez Canal Company, owning 44 percent of

[48] Nigel Fisher, *Harold Macmillan* (London: Weidenfeld and Nicholson, 1982), p. 160.

[49] Anthony Eden, *The Suez Crisis of 1956* (excerpts from his memoirs, *Full Circle*) (Boston: Beacon Press, 1968), p. 48.

[50] Anthony Nutting, *No End of a Lesson, The Story of Suez* (New York: Clarkson N. Porter, 1967), p.34.

[51] Herman Finer, *Dulles over Suez* (Chicago: Quadrangle Books, 1964), p. 48. Finer reports the following exchange:

Ambassador Hussein: "Don't please say you are going to withdraw the offer, because . . . we have the Russian offer to finance the dam right here in my pocket."

Dulles: "Well as you have the money anyway, you don't need it from us. My offer is withdrawn!"

[52] On the expropriation, see R. H. Ferrell, ed., *The Eisenhower Diaries* (New York: W. W. Norton, 1981), p. 329. On the importance of Suez, Eden wrote in his memoirs that the "failure to keep the canal international would inevitably lead to the loss one by one of all of our interests and assets in the Middle East." Eden, *Suez Crisis*, p. 54.

its shares. Further, one-third of the 14,666 ships that passed through the canal in 1955 were owned by Britain, and the canal was both the most important route for Middle Eastern oil shipments to Western Europe and the conduit of British influence with friendly powers there. An "Egyptian committee" was immediately formed within the cabinet, and as early as August 2, the decision was made to use force if negotiations to internationalize the canal failed.[53]

The French also supported bold action. They were disposed against the Egyptians partly because of Egypt's aggressive policy toward Israel, whose survival France actively supported, and partly because of Egypt's support of the Algerian liberation movement. The United States, however, was much more pacific. It did not equate the expropriation with theft, and was less concerned with the implications of the change in the status quo. In fact, a minimalist interpretation of the significance of the expropriation was reasonable. Nasser had expropriated the Suez Canal Company, and promised compensation to its shareholders. He had not seized the canal, which Egypt already legally owned. The threat to close the canal was not new, since Egypt had always controlled the two cities on the terminal points of the canal, and therefore could have effectively closed the canal at any time without expropriation. Israeli ships were being excluded under Egyptian supervision, a violation of the treaty of 1888, but they were already being excluded before the expropriation.[54]

The United States was also in an election year, and Eisenhower was strongly interested in maintaining his image as a peacemaker. Further, the United States was not opposed to the decline of European influence in the oil-rich Middle East. If the United States had a concern, it was the ability of Egyptian pilots to successfully operate the canal, which was a widespread source of anxiety.[55]

Given the U.S. predisposition for a peaceful resolution and the fact that it was estimated that it would take at least six weeks before a military task force would be prepared, Britain initially pursued nonviolent avenues of conflict resolution. The first incarnation of this effort was the London conference, in which twenty-two powers met from August 16 to August 23. Even before the conference met, though, Harold Macmillan (then chancellor of the exchequer) had noted in his diary: "We must have (a) international control of canal; (b)

---

[53] Alastair Horne, *Macmillan: 1894–1956* (vol. 1 of the official biography) (London: Macmillan, 1988), pp. 395, 398.

[54] Chester L. Cooper, *The Lion's Last Roar: Suez 1956* (New York: Harper and Row, 1978), p. 107. For a discussion of the legal aspects of the Suez issue, from the perspectives of the Egyptians, the British, and the Americans, see Robert R Bowie, *Suez 1956: International Crises and the Role of Law* (New York: Oxford University Press, 1974).

[55] On the importance of U.S. domestic politics, see, for example, Selwyn Lloyd, *Suez 1956: A Personal Account* (London: Jonathan Cape, 1978), p. 80. Fears regarding the Egyptian ability to manage the canal were also widely retold. See, for example, Nutting, *No End*, p. 46.

humiliation or collapse of Nasser." The London conference adjourned with a majority of eighteen, representing over 95 percent of the traffic that passed through the canal, calling for its internationalization. As Egypt had not attended the conference, the prime minister of Australia, Sir Robert Menzies, was selected to go to Egypt, officially inform the Egyptian government of the conference resolutions, and negotiate with Nasser.[56]

Before he left for Cairo, Menzies agreed to sell £20 million pounds' worth of gold to the Bank of England in exchange for pounds in order to improve Britain's reserve position given the current international crisis.[57] This exercise of protective currency manipulation was the first use of monetary power in the crisis. And this action on September 2 was the most significant event to emerge from the Menzies mission, in which the Australian prime minister negotiated with the intransigent Egyptian leader.

Menzies' task was made even more difficult by repeated renunciations of force by both Dulles and Eisenhower.[58] But while the Americans were abandoning thoughts of force, the British certainly were not. On August 18, Macmillan wrote in his diary: "If Nasser 'gets away with it' we are done for. . . . It may well be the end of British influence and strength forever. So in the last resort, we must use force and defy opinion, here and overseas." Britain was not helped in this position, though, by the surprising ability of the Egyptians to run the canal, and their apparent intention not to close it.[59]

With the failure of the Menzies mission, the Suez Canal User's Association (SCUA) was formed at a second meeting in London convened September 19–21 in order to provide the canal's maritime customers with a united front. But as with the Menzies mission, the SCUA was undermined by Dulles's peace-mongering: Dulles would not discuss whether SCUA tankers could defend themselves, challenge blockades, or use or respond to threats in any way. When pressed, he referred to the option of steaming around the Cape of Good Hope. Obviously, a "no comment" in response to any of these questions could have strengthened the SCUA's bargaining power without committing the United States to any action.[60]

With the realization that SCUA was not the answer to their problems, Britain and France decided to go to the United Nations, primarily for the purpose

[56] "We must have . . ." Horne, *Macmillan*, p. 399. On the London conference, see Eden, *Suez Crisis*, pp. 80–82.

[57] Harold Macmillan, *Riding the Storm (Memoirs 1955–1959)*, (New York: Harper and Row, 1971), p. 117.

[58] These statements by Eisenhower and Dulles were particularly aggravating to the British principals. See Eden, *Suez Crisis*, p. 118; Lloyd, *Suez 1956*, p. 160; and Macmillan, *Riding the Storm*, p. 125.

[59] Horne, *Macmillan*, p. 393. *The Economist* reported that the canal was "running smoothly," in its September 29 issue.

[60] Finer, *Dulles over Suez*, ch. 11, passim, esp. pp. 282–83.

of establishing the argument that every possible peaceful avenue had been explored before force had been used. On October 14, Eden and his foreign secretary, Selwyn Lloyd, went to Paris to consult with their opposite numbers, the French prime minister, Guy Mollet, and foreign minister Christian Pineau. There they discussed plans for using force against Egypt, and the possibility of a joint operation with the Israelis, whose military involvement was considered essential. One week later, on October 22, the four men met again in Paris, this time with their Israeli counterparts, Prime Minister David Ben Gurion and Chief of Staff Moshe Dayan, in attendance.[61] Israel was interested in an opportunity to strike preventively against its increasingly aggressive and belligerent neighbor to the west, which was bent on Israel's destruction. France remained the most bellicose of the three powers, and the capture of the Egyptian yacht Athos on September 16, laden with 70 tons of arms for Algerian nationalists, added fuel to the French fire. A humiliation of Nasser and perhaps his overthrow could only help France's position in that conflict.[62]

At the two Paris meetings, the three nations formed their plan. Israel would attack Egypt if the allies would destroy the Egyptian air force. Given this outbreak of war in the region, Britain and France would issue an ultimatum demanding that the combatants cease fire and separate, in order to protect the canal. Of course, the Egyptians would reject this, and the British and French would move in, seize the canal, and destroy other Egyptian assets. It was expected that once the canal was taken, the humiliation would seriously weaken and ultimately result in the overthrow of Nasser.[63] The operation went off almost completely as planned, although the justification for allied intervention was somewhat undermined by the spectacular nature of the Israeli military successes. The only problem was the reaction of the United States, which both Eden and Macmillan had assumed would be at the very worst neutral. Instead, the United States led the rally against the British and the French, and took the issue to the UN. There, a vote demanding an immediate ceasefire and withdrawal was passed, 64–5, with France and Britain voting against the United States in the Security Council for the first time.[64]

The action at the UN, however, was only the tip of the iceberg. On November 5, the Federal Reserve Bank of New York, under orders from Treasury secretary George Humphrey, began to sell pounds. Nominally this was to avoid losses since sterling was under pressure, but that was a transparent cover story, as central banks do not manage their portfolios to maximize

[61] On the October 16 meeting, Horne, *Macmillan*, p. 431; on the October 22 meeting, Fisher, *Harold Macmillan*, p. 66.

[62] G. Barraclough, *Survey of International Affairs 1956–1958* (London: Oxford University Press, 1962), p. 47. As *The Economist* noted on August 11: "France looks at Suez through an Algerian Prism" (p. 621).

[63] Horne, *Macmillan*, p. 431.

[64] Eden, *Suez Crisis*, p. 55; Macmillan, *Riding the Storm*, p. 158.

profits. If anything, their interventions are countercyclical. The magnitude of the selling clearly revealed the act to be one of predatory currency manipulation. Macmillan noted: "Certainly the selling by the Federal Reserve Bank seemed far above what was necessary to protect the value of its own holdings."[65] And as if this was not enough, the Soviets began to make threatening noises regarding their own intervention.

Despite all of this, on November 6, at a cabinet meeting, Eden, Salisbury, Lloyd, and others decided to push onward. However, this was only because they did not realize the seriousness of the financial crisis. British reserves, which had fallen by $57 million in September and $84 million in October, had already fallen by $279 million in November, or 15% of the total. R. A. Butler, senior Eden adviser and former chancellor of the exchequer, and Macmillan, recognizing the seriousness of the situation, placed a call to Secretary Humphrey. When Humphrey returned their call, he told Butler, "Rab, the president cannot help you unless you conform to the UN resolution on withdrawal." Butler noted, "This was blackmail, but we were in no position to argue." Butler then explained to Macmillan that not only would the United States fail to provide help without a ceasefire and withdrawal, but it would block British access to its own International Monetary Fund reserves. But if Britain did comply with the U.S. demands, the United States would not block access to the IMF and would provide an additional $500 million export-import credit to ameliorate Britain's financial troubles. Macmillan considered this an "unforgivable" violation of the letter and spirit of the IMF, but agreed in principle with the deal.[66]

Macmillan then returned to the cabinet, and informed the ministers that a run on the pound, "viciously orchestrated" in Washington,[67] was extremely serious, and help would only be provided by the United States if a ceasefire was ordered by midnight that evening. All of the ministers who were involved

[65] Macmillan, *Riding the Storm*, p. 164. The United States was by far the most significant, but not the only, actor engaged in predatory currency manipulation at this time. Sales of sterling by China and some Middle Eastern nations were undertaken for political reasons, but these actions can best be described as signaling. Cooper, *Lion's Last Roar*, p. 191.

[66] On the cabinet meeting, see Horne, *Macmillan*, p. 440. For Butler's phone conversation with Humphrey, see Butler, *Art of the Possible*, p. 194; and for Macmillan's reaction, see Macmillan, *Riding the Storm*, p. 164.

[67] Some scholars have recently downplayed the relative importance of the sales of sterling by the United States. See Diane B. Kunz, *The Economic Diplomacy of the Suez Crisis* (Chapel Hill: University of North Carolina Press, 1991). On p. 205, Kunz reports that U.S. holdings of sterling stood at $84 million on September 30 and $72.8 million on December 31. This means that U.S. dumping of sterling was a minimum of $11.2 million and a maximum of $84 million (allowing for U.S. repurchases of sterling after its demands were met). While significant, these figures suggest that (1) market bandwagoning with the U.S. manipulation was substantial, and (2) the blocking of IMF access was probably as important a technique of predatory monetary warfare as the actual sales of sterling.

and later recorded their thoughts noted that Macmillan had shifted from the most aggressive hawk to the mildest dove with regard to Suez intervention. He impressed Eden, Lloyd, and the others, and at 5 P.M. on November 6, against the passionate protests of the French, who could not continue alone, a ceasefire was ordered.[68] Thus the United States, through a combination of predatory currency manipulation in the form of the sale of pounds by the New York Fed and the ability to block Britain's access to its IMF funds, coupled with the promise of protective support to bail Britain out of the financial mess the United States had created, was able to stop a military invasion in its tracks.[69] And Macmillan, who would "rather pawn the National Gallery than give in to Nasser,"[70] when actually faced with that type of choice, gave in.

Competing Explanations of the Suez Case

The Suez crisis ended with the abrupt halt and withdrawal from a major military operation by two highly motivated powers. The timing of the allied capitulation is important, since it was estimated that in two to five days the canal would have been secured and most of the goals of the mission accomplished. At that time, Britain and France would have been in a much stronger bargaining position. There are four alternate competing explanations for the outcome: in order of increasing significance, (1)mission accomplished; (2)Russian intervention; (3)domestic dissent; and (4)oil pressure.

MISSION ACCOMPLISHED

This explanation holds that the reason why Britain and France halted their operation was because their forces had accomplished the mission of separating the warring parties and protecting the canal. This was obviously not the case, but it must be considered because Prime Minister Eden, Foreign Minis-

---

[68] Butler, *Art of the Possible*, for example, noted:

Speculation against sterling . . . [had a profound effect on Macmillan,] who switched overnight from being the foremost protagonist of intervention to being the leading influence for disengagement—as well he might, for the loss of $279 million . . . represented about 15 percent of our total gold and dollar reserves. (p.199)

[69] The U.S. Government has remained silent on the nature of its currency manipulation during the Suez crisis. The State Department has since released over 1,300 pages of documents on the incident, with only one reference to the practice of monetary diplomacy. This is an editorial note, which carefully states that "[n]o documentation concerning the British request or the American response has been found in Department of State files. Matters relating to the International Monetary Fund fell within the jurisdiction of the United States Treasury. The United States at a later date approved repayment of Great Britain's first two tranches." U.S. Department of State, *Foreign Relations of the United States 1955–1957*, vol. 16, *Suez Crisis July 26–December 31, 1956* (Washington, D.C.: U.S. Government Printing Office, 1990), pp. 1012–13.

[70] Macmillan, quoted in Cooper, *Lion's Last Roar*, p. 78.

ter Lloyd, and Chancellor of the Exchequer Macmillan all gave this as the main reason for the cessation of the British action. Obviously, this was the party line, maintained for reasons of national security and personal reputation. The "mission accomplished" story covers up the Israeli connection and the real reason for the invasion, which was, of course, to regain the canal and destroy Nasser.

The Israeli connection was an extremely sensitive one. Macmillan, when discussing candidly the Israeli connection with his official biographer, said that he had even burned those portions of his diaries that referred to Israel in this affair. He related the cover story in his memoirs, he added, because that is what Eden had done, and Eden was still alive. In fact, Eden read and commented on the Suez chapter before publication.[71] It should also be noted that all of the participants had personal reasons for sticking to the cover story, as they all had repeatedly denied allegations challenging that story during and immediately after the crisis.[72]

Despite the intellectual bankruptcy of the "mission accomplished" explanation, its expression does provide support for the monetary interpretation. This is because each of these three men offered secondary explanations for their decision to end the mission. By default, it is logical to assume that these reasons were actually the most important. Foreign Secretary Lloyd gave two reasons for British action—success and the need to protect sterling from speculation, which Macmillan reported was being stimulated by the U.S. Treasury. Eden took a similar line: again, after the cover story, Eden stated that a run on the pound "at a speed which threatened disaster to our whole economic position" had developed in the American market. Macmillan delivered the figures, which were "gloomy and foreboding and could have been decisive within the next few days," to the cabinet.[73]

Macmillan's memoirs are trickier, because he felt the need to explain his role as the man who pulled the plug. In the end, he offers no explanation once the cover story is stripped away. He raises and rejects two possibilities, the first of which is money, which he discusses at great length. After reviewing the severity of the situation, the American pressure, and his anger at the U.S. action, Macmillan concludes that while the situation was serious it "would have not been decisive . . . We still could stand plenty of battering on this front." Macmillan then raises the oil issue, which he also rejects, arguing that "the oil position was indeed more dangerous, but not in the short term."[74] Thus nothing conclusive can be drawn from Macmillan's memoirs.

Macmillan's two most recent biographers, however, including his official biographer, are able to reach a specific conclusion. Fisher states it plainly:

[71] Horne, *Macmillan*, p. 429.

[72] On November 3, for example, *The Economist* editorialized that the motives of Prime Minister Eden "must be questioned." (p. 391).

[73] Lloyd, *Suez 1956*, pp. 210–11; Eden, *Suez Crisis*, pp. 201–2.

[74] Macmillan, *Riding the Storm*, p. 165.

"The real reason for the withdrawal was the run on the pound." Horne also states that the "pound was decisive," but couples this with the "shock [to the British] of American hostility."[75] One could speculate that Macmillan's reluctance to embrace the monetary explanation as fully as those around him (Eden, Lloyd, Butler, his biographers, and other officials) is related to the fact that he felt responsible for the value of the pound, which was critically threatened by circumstances that he (and every one else) had not anticipated. Regardless, what is clear is that "mission accomplished" was a frail cover story, and one which, on closer examination, actually yields strong support for the monetary explanation.

RUSSIAN INTERVENTION

The second competing explanation is that the Western powers backed down in the face of Soviet threats. On November 5, the Soviet premier, Nikolai Bulganin, sent threatening letters to London and Paris, discussing the use of Russian "rockets" and "volunteers." There are two ways in which these threats could have influenced the outcome of the crisis: by intimidating the United States, which would in turn rein in Britain and France, or through the direct intimidation of the two European countries themselves.

Finer, in his book *Dulles over Suez*, makes the former argument, stating that "unwilling to contend against Russian pressure, they forced Eden to capitulate."[76] This fits neatly into Finer's interpretation of the Suez crisis with Dulles as the chief villain who gets his just deserts: the brinksman is out brinked. But it is not supported by the facts. The Russian threats were "ambiguous and consisted only of diplomatic statements," and the Americans responded with a small-scale alert. Further, Eisenhower authorized his press secretary to state that if the Soviets acted against the Europeans, the United States would oppose them, and General Gruenther, commander of allied forces in Europe, stated that "if the Soviets attacked Britain or France, the USSR would be destroyed as surely as night follows day."[77]

In support of the second Russian explanation was *The Economist*, which, despite the fact that the Bulganin letter was quoted in *The Times* (London) on November 6 on the same page as a report of the U.S. promise to oppose any Soviet intervention, argued that the Soviet threats were decisive. The analysis of *The Economist*, though wrong, (later, by its own admission) once again points to the power of the monetary explanation. This is because *The Economist* seized on the Russian threats as an explanation because of the issue of timing:

[75] Fisher, *Harold Macmillan*, p. 169; Horne, *Macmillan*, p. 443.

[76] Finer, *Dulles over Suez*, p. 411.

[77] Richard K. Betts, *Nuclear Blackmail and Nuclear Balance* (Washington, D.C.: Brookings Institution, 1987), pp. 62–65.

Something changed the plan. Expressions of disquiet and dissent must have been coming in greater or less degree from many sources at home and abroad, but only from one was there any decisive new development on Monday that might explain Tuesday's decision to halt the adventure. The new development on Monday was Mr. Bulganin's threat to intervene with force[78]

The Economist seized on the key question—what was different on Tuesday than on Monday?—but at this early date, they got the wrong answer. They could not have been aware of the Tuesday cabinet meeting, discussed above, where the decision was initially made to press on even after the Russian threat was considered but before the new monetary news was presented. Nor could they have been aware that in the years to follow, the participants, their biographers, and most outside analysts would agree that the Russian threat was not an important factor.[79] At that time, they were not even aware of how serious the monetary situation had become, but this realization would change their interpretation of the resolution of the crisis when the facts became clear two months later:

> Any remaining illusions about what would have been sterling's fate if the chancellor had not been able to make his swift and grandiose mobilization of second line reserves must be finally shattered by the December gold figures. Without the drawing of $561.5 million from the IMF the reserves would have fallen by not short of $400 million; the extent of the loss without the knowledge that this and other major reinforcements were available defies imagination.[80]

Thus the "Russian intervention" explanation has little explanatory power of its own, but it, too, provides further evidence for the monetary interpretation.

DOMESTIC DISSENT

The argument that domestic dissent in Britain forced the early end to the Suez operation has two strands: dissatisfaction among the general public and dissension within the ranks of the Conservative party itself. One scholar argues that the "widening split in the party may have impressed ministers as much as the run on the pound."[81] The dissent argument must be taken seriously. The

---

[78] *The Economist*, November 3, 1956, p. 483.

[79] Nutting argued that the Russian threats were little more than a diversion from their crushing of the Hungarian revolution (*No End*, p. 149). Barraclough was also unimpressed by the Russian threats (*Survey*, p. 68). See also Eden, *Suez Crisis*, p. 200; Macmillan, *Riding the Storm*, p. 165; Horne, *Macmillan*, p. 442.

[80] *The Economist*, January 5, 1957, p. 56.

[81] Anthony Adawthwaite, "Suez Revisited," *International Affairs* 64, no. 3:449–64 (1988), p. 463.

British public was deeply and passionately divided over the Suez crisis. Within the ruling party, there was some outrage, manifested most plainly in the resignations of Anthony Nutting from the Foreign Office and Edward Boyle from the Treasury. However, as an explanation for the Suez outcome, it comes up short. There are three main problems with the dissent argument: it has little support in the memoirs and biographies, there are important problems with its internal logic, and most important, it is completely undermined by the issue of timing.

The memoirs and biographies do not dwell on the issue of internal dissension. Macmillan and Eden, in particular, dismiss such questions. Macmillan reported "full cabinet" support, and Eden stated that party politics and popularity "were not concerns." There are good reasons for the participants' lack of attention to the dissent issue. First, the Conservative party was united at the top. Eden, Macmillan, and Lloyd were strongly in favor of the operation. Butler was also in favor of the operation, according to Macmillan, though later Butler would distance himself from it.[82] Nutting and Boyle did resign, but they were junior ministers, and on the day Nutting resigned, Churchill himself came out publicly in support of the operation.

Not only was the Conservative party leadership united, but it is unclear why suddenly calling a halt to the operation would ease the problem of domestic dissent. Eden was under pressure from both the left and the right. When the ceasefire was announced, *The Economist* discussed whether there would be a revolt from within the party from the right by the "Suez group," and decided that such an occurrence was "quite conceivable."[83] Similarly, the public was passionately divided, not uniformly opposed to the attack. Any action would be bound to alienate one side or the other. This division introduces the most important challenge for the domestic dissent explanation. Not only does it fail to explain the particular timing of the sudden ceasefire, but the ceasefire itself came at the worst possible time if the main concern was domestic politics. Moving in with force and then withdrawing in failure satisfies neither the hawks nor the doves. Once the invasion was under way, the best thing to do would be to grit one's teeth and push on through the additional two to five days deemed necessary for success. That way, the political right flank would be secure, and any degree of success gained would mute criticism from the left. Once again, the puzzle is timing, and the timing makes sense with regard to the monetary explanation, but undermines the domestic level analysis.

OIL PRESSURE

The issue of oil is central to understanding the Suez crisis. An interpretation of the crisis using oil pressure as the key explanation has the most internal and

---

[82] On general support, see Macmillan, *Riding the Storm*, p. 165; Eden, *Suez Crisis*, p. 202. On Butler, *Art of the Possible*, see Horne, *Macmillan*, p. 433; see also Butler, *Art of the Possible*, passim.

[83] *The Economist*, November 3, 1956, p. 490.

external consistency of the four possible alternate competing explanations. It does not explain the timing, though, and even more important, when tests are constructed in which the monetary explanation and the oil theory would predict different results, history supports the former.

The oil pressure scenario holds that when the invasion closed the canal, and the trans-Arabian pipelines were also cut off, the Europeans faced the prospect of a serious oil shortage. The United States, with its vast oil reserves and production capability, could ease the shortage with increases in production and diversion of shipping to Europe. Alternatively, the United States could do nothing and let Europe bear the brunt of the shortage. The United States made it clear to the Europeans that no oil assistance would be forthcoming without an immediate ceasefire, forcing the invasion to a halt.[84]

Oil was one of the concerns that brought the British and the French forces to the canal zone in the first place. Macmillan noted in his diaries before the invasion that there was a dilemma with regard to the oil:"[I]f we act, we could lose it, if we fail to act, it could be nationalized, and we'd lose it that way."[85] The problem with oil as an explanation is that although everyone realized how critical it was, and it was discussed at length in planning sessions before the invasion, no participant or analyst at the time attributed the ceasefire to oil problems or pressures. Macmillan was the only major figure to mention the oil situation in his memoirs—-Butler, Eden, and Lloyd did not. Further, as mentioned earlier, although Macmillan considered the oil situation to be very serious, he considered it to be a longer-term problem. His concern for oil supplies did not influence the course of his views or recommendations on the hostilities.[86]

Even more surprising than the fact that no major figure considered oil to have played a major role in the outcome of the crisis is that *The Economist* never put forth such an argument. After all, that journal had published in its pages two lengthy analyses describing the importance of oil to the British and European economies, and the problems that the Suez invasion had raised in that regard. Yet *The Economist* did not consider oil to be the answer; it went from "Russian intervention" in November to "currency crisis" in January.[87]

Another problem for the oil explanation is that it does not stand up to direct competition with the monetary one. This analysis can be a relatively simple one, such as a test that compares preparedness. The argument is that, other

---

[84] Robert O. Keohane, *After Hegemony* (Princeton: Princeton University Press, 1984), pp. 170–73.

[85] Horne, *Macmillan*, pp. 410–11.

[86] During the fighting, when Macmillan heard a rumor that the United States might impose oil sanctions, he even exclaimed, "Oil sanctions—that finishes it," but that was the extent of his reaction; he did not contemplate nor suggest any policy shifts as a result of this development. Horne, *Macmillan*, p. 439.

[87] See "Oil Is Critical," *The Economist*, November 10, 1956, pp. 523–27; and "First Reckoning for Suez," *The Economist*, November 17, 1956, pp. 615–19.

things being equal, the unexpected problem will be more challenging than the expected problem. In this case, Britain was expecting oil trouble; contingency plans were made for various eventualities—the closing of the canal, the loss of the pipelines, and so on. But in consideration of the monetary front, only the strain of the costs of the operation was considered, and deemed acceptable; there was no expectation or contingency plan for a run on the pound. In this regard, the British were caught off guard.[88]

A more sophisticated and thorough test of the two explanations is even more damning to the oil interpretation. This test begins with the observation that while Britain was brought to its knees by outside pressure, France was pleading with Britain to continue with the operation, at least for a few more days, so that the results of the capture of the canal could be allowed to have an effect on the situation. In trying to understand the relative power of oil and money, a test can be created by comparing the steadfast and the coerced. Each state was facing a monetary crisis (French reserves were also falling rapidly) and an oil crisis. Two hypotheses thus emerge: (1) that monetary pressure explains the outcome, and (2) that oil pressure explains the outcome.

A test can be devised to evaluate these hypotheses, by comparing the relative vulnerabilities of the two countries. With regard to oil, either the French were more vulnerable or the British were. The same is true for money: France's vulnerability to monetary pressure was greater or less than Britain's. This yields four possible states of nature with regard to the relative vulnerabilities of the two countries to oil and money pressure.[89]

Two of these possible states of nature support specific hypotheses. The state where the French are more vulnerable to oil but less vulnerable to monetary pressure provides very strong support for the first hypothesis (that monetary power explains the outcome) and against the second hypothesis, because the oil-vulnerable power was urging action while the money-vulnerable power was surrendering, obviously suggesting that oil pressure was having little influence, while monetary power was decisive. Alternately, the state where the French are less vulnerable to oil but more vulnerable to money, would provide very strong support for the second hypothesis (that oil power best explains outcome) and against the first hypothesis, because the monetarily vulnerable power was urging action while the oil-vulnerable power was surrendering, suggesting that monetary pressure was ineffective while oil power forced retrenchment. The other two possible states of nature do not include variations with regard to relative vulnerability and are thus uninformative.

The task is to determine the state of nature and see how the hypotheses fare. First, with regard to monetary vulnerability, two variables are crucial, given

---

[88] See, for example, Eden, *Suez Crisis*, p. 201.

[89] Allowing for equality of vulnerability would yield nine states of nature. Adding these complicates the model without affecting its explanatory power.

TABLE 3.3
The Monetary Position of the Combatants

	France			Britain		
	Reserves	Change in Reserves	Percentage Change	Reserves	Change in Reserves	Percentage Change
8/57	1,645	—	—	2,276	—	—
9/57	1,655	+10	+0.1	2,328	+52	+2.3
10/57	1,638	−17	−1	2,244	−84	−3.6
11/57	1,500	−138	−8.4	1,965	−279	−12.43
12/57	1,416	−84	−5.6	1,572	−393	−20.00
9/57–11/57	—	−145	−8.81	—	−311	−13.66
9/57–12/57	—	−239	−14.47	—	−704	−30.93

Sources and notes: The Economist, various issues; Federal Reserve Bank of New York, *Federal Reserve Bulletin* (monthly), various issues. Reserves are at the end of the month and in millions of U.S. dollars. It should be noted that the increase in British reserves in September, which might be confusing given reports that British reserves fell in this month, is attributable to the sale of Trinidad oil for £63 million. Without this sale, engaged in to increase assets, British reserves would have fallen in that month.

the fixed-rate regime: the loss of reserves, and the number of import days the remaining reserves covered. The test will look at reserves for September, October, November, and December (see Table 3.3). The reserve loss through November represents the real situation the decisionmakers faced;[90] including December reserves shows the entire cost (monetarily) of the operation. The December figures will exclude the British $561 million IMF drawing, which was possible only after the operation was halted. (The French made no drawing in December.) This calculation shows the true extent of the operation on the reserves.

The figures show that Britain was facing a much more serious monetary crisis than was France, with reserves through November falling about 65 percent faster. Beyond this, the British must have realized that the situation was getting much worse. In December, even with the cessation of hostilities and the promise of American help (two things that would not have been the case if the operation had continued), British reserves fell even faster, and continued to fall much faster than did French reserves (real reserves leaving Britain almost four times as quickly as they left France.) Additionally, not only were British reserves falling faster and at an increasingly faster rate than were French reserves, but Britain was more vulnerable to a fall in reserves since its

---

[90] Kunz argues that British reserve losses in November were actually much larger than officially reported, $401 million as opposed to $279 million (*Economic Diplomacy*, p. 150). This test will use the published figures, which, if anything, biases it against the monetary explanation.

Import Days Covered

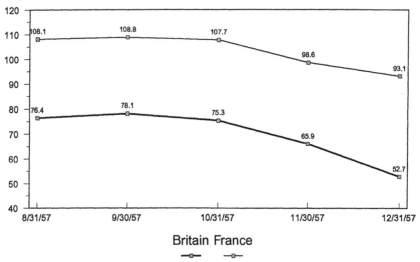

Figure 3.1 Monetary Reserves and Imports of the Combatants
Sources: See note 91, below.

reserves covered fewer import days than did France's. At the start of the crisis, France's reserves covered over 40 percent more import days than did Britain's (see Figure 3.1).[91] In fact, no country had smaller reserves relative to imports and more volatile reserves than did Britain.[92] Therefore, there can be no doubt that Britain was clearly more vulnerable with regard to the currency situation than was France.

Britain was much better placed with regard to the oil situation. Oil vulnerability can be measured by the extent of dependence and the state of reserves. Dependence is defined as the percentage of energy generated by oil in the economy. Reserves are measured by the number of import days that are covered by a nation's holdings. With regard to dependence, oil satisfied less than 15 percent of the total energy requirements in the United Kingdom, as compared with 20 percent for France. As for reserves, Lloyd stated that Britain had six weeks of oil supplies, and was "relatively better off than our neighbors."[93]

---

[91] Compiled from import data reported in *United Nations Yearbook of International Trade Statistics 1956*; *Great Britain Annual Statement of the Trade of the United Kingdom 1956*, vol. 16 (London: H.M. Stationery Office, 1958); *Annuare Statistique de La France 1957* (Paris: Institute Nacional De La Statistique, 1957).

[92] Kenen, *British Monetary Policy*, p. 14.

[93] On oil consumption in Britain, see *The Economist*, August 4, 1956, p. 420; on oil consumption in France, see *The Economist*, November 11/3/56, p. 712., On British reserves, see Lloyd, *Suez 1956*, p. 81.

Summarizing the findings on the state of nature with regard to the oil and monetary position at the time of the crisis, it appears that Britain was much more vulnerable to monetary pressure and less vulnerable to oil pressure, which, as noted initially, provides very strong support for the hypothesis that monetary power was decisive and against the hypothesis that oil power was important.

Aside from the inferences from the memoirs of the decisionmakers and retrospective analyses, and the results of the hypotheses testing, there is a third persuasive argument against the oil explanation and in favor of the monetary one. This has to do with the timing of the operation and the strategy of conflict in general. As has been mentioned before, the French urged that the operation go on, at least for a few days. Optimists estimated that the operation could be successfully completed within two days, though Eden argued that it would probably take five.[94] One advocate of the oil explanation has raised the question of why the Europeans did not call the Americans' bluff. That is, despite the threatened American oil sanctions, why did not the United Kingdom and France complete the Suez operation, and present the United States with a fait accompli?[95] This strategy makes perfect sense, drawing on Schelling's concept of "relinquishing the initiative."[96] This involves the purposeful shifting of the burden of escalating the conflict, and challenging the credibility of threats in general. Specifically, in this case, under the oil explanation, the U.S. goal was to stop the invasion and its threat was oil sanctions. But the oil sanctions would not have taken effect for weeks, probably months. Meanwhile, the British and the French could have ignored this threat and finished the job. The United States would then have been faced with the decision of whether or not to actually impose the sanctions. This decision would have rested on two considerations: would it still have been in the United States's best interest to engage the sanction even if it could not stop the invasion, and was the threat ever credible?

The answer to both of these interrelated questions is no. Eisenhower said that if Europe ever lost access to Middle Eastern oil production, its "sheer existence" would be threatened.[97] Given that fact, regardless of the Suez outcome, it would have been in the best interests of the United States to do as it did, increasing production and diverting that production to Europe. Additionally, the oil weapon was less credible than the monetary weapon because the oil weapon was indiscriminant. Because of the nature of the commodity, any pain or dislocation attendant on oil sanctions or any shortage of oil would be felt throughout Western Europe. Thus, in an attempt to punish the British

---

[94] Butler, *Art of the Possible*, p. 193; Eden, *Suez Crisis*, p. 204.

[95] Ethan Kapstein, *The Insecure Alliance: Energy Crises and Western Politics Since 1944* (New York: Oxford University Press, 1990), p. 117.

[96] Thomas Schelling, *Arms and Influence* (New Haven: Yale University Press, 1966). See esp. ch. 2.

[97] Kapstein, *Insecure Alliance*, p. 110.

TABLE 3.4
Oil as a Percentage of Total Energy Consumption

Britain:	<15	Denmark:	37	France:	20
Norway:	25	Belgium/Lux:	16	Sweden:	14
Netherlands:	26	Germany:	09	Italy:	33
Switzerland:	29	Turkey:	30		

Source: The Economist, November 24, 1956, p. 712.

and the French, the United States would be inflicting pain on all of its European allies, most of whom actually opposed the Suez adventure. In fact, most of the other European countries were more vulnerable to oil sanctions, as the the data in Table 3.4 show. Monetary power, on the other hand, could be directed specifically at the target states.

An analysis of the strategy of conflict of the Suez crisis under the oil explanation yields the conclusion that a serious blunder was made by the British. However, there is an alternate explanation, which explains the sequence of the moves completely. The monetary sanction imposed on the United Kingdom by the United States was an immediate, painful measure. There was no credibility problem—the action was under way. Further, the situation for the British, already critical, would automatically get worse, and probably at an ever-increasing rate, unless there were an immediate cessation of hostilities. On top of this, a credible promise of assistance was offered for compliance with U.S. demands.

Oil was important in the Suez case, but as a U.S. sanction it was a long-term threat of highly questionable credibility. The French, who were more oil-vulnerable, urged what was for them the correct strategic move—press for the fait accompli and challenge the United States to escalate with an incredible threat. The British, under tremendous immediate and short-term pressure, did not have this luxury. Monetary sanctions were decisive, and the monetary explanation is the only one to explain fully the critical issue of the timing of the moves of each state.[98]

[98] It is worth noting that not only were sanctions swift and effective, they were also quite powerful. This conclusion is reached in a study that compares the monetary crisis of 1956 with all of the monetary crises in Britain from 1931 to 1956: the quarter-century before Suez. The 1956 crisis was more severe in both its economic and its political potential than the crises of 1947, 1952, and 1955. In each of those three cases, leaders at the time viewed the situation as critical, and economic sacrifices were forced on the country to defend the currency.

More surprisingly, the 1956 crisis was much more severe than the 1949 crisis, which was viewed as a major economic crisis with fundamental political consequences. In fact, the only crisis more severe than the one during Suez was the 1931 crisis, and decisionmakers at the time knew that the 1956 crisis had the potential to get that bad. This was a daunting prospect as the 1931 crisis was part of a major international financial panic, which forced Britain off the gold standard in peacetime for the first time in two hundred years, and fundamentally transformed British politics.

Lessons from the Suez Case

The Suez case is not the story of one isolated attempt at the practice of monetary diplomacy, but rather is a part of a complete cycle of currency manipulation involving the United States and Britain. Before the crisis, the United States was engaging in permissive (and occasionally protective) manipulation, tolerating discrimination in order to allow the international monetary system time to mature. With the onset of the crisis, the United States engaged in two predatory techniques of currency manipulation and one passive one. The predatory acts were the sale of pounds and the blocking of access to the IMF. The passive technique was the refusal to guarantee new export-import loans, a request that would probably have been granted in the pre-Suez environment. Finally, both to encourage and as a result of British capitulation, the United States adopted a protective stance, providing the new export-import credits, and supporting the British request for a substantial IMF loan.

A great deal can be learned about currency manipulation from the Suez episode. First and foremost, this case demonstrates once again that predatory currency manipulation can be an extraordinarily effective coercive instrument of state power. In this instance, monetary diplomacy was exercised costlessly, privately, quickly, and with great success. It was costless in that it involved the sale of one currency in exchange for other currencies at a relatively fixed price—if anything, it was the efficient move if profit was the only concern. The blocking of access to the IMF was also cost free. (The second, protective phase of the operation was also relatively inexpensive: the withdrawal of interference with Britain's IMF transactions, and a $500 million export-import loan.) It was private, in that no one but the elites in the executive branch of the U.S. government and their opposite numbers in the British government were aware of what was going on. In fact, few others knew that monetary power had even been exercised for years after the incident. Comparing this with trade or aid sanctions underscores the relative privacy of monetary power.

The currency manipulation was also effective very quickly. It was able to inflict pain almost immediately after implementation. This may prove to be one of the most important aspects of monetary diplomacy in general. In this case, only a sanction that would be effective almost immediately could have been expected to satisfy the policy goal of stopping the invasion. Comparing monetary diplomacy to trade sanctions underscores the point. Even a credible and manageable boycott (two conditions that are rarely likely to exist in any case) can take months before any pain of the sanction is felt, as target coun-

---

Thus, predatory currency manipulation, exercised by the United States against Great Britain, was able to foster a currency crisis in Britain, which forced Britain to bow to U.S. demands. Not only was the manipulation the decisive factor, it worked: British leaders understood correctly the severity of the situation—British capitulation was not an error born of panic.

See Jonathan Kirshner, "Suez 1956: The Case for Monetary Power" (unpublished paper, 1992).

tries run down stockpiles, and continue to receive for some time imports from ships that left port before the embargo was implemented.

Finally, the currency manipulation was successful. It stopped a highly motivated military power from achieving goals that days earlier had seemed well within its reach. The issue of success, however, points to the fact that the preconditions of success must also be considered. France, for example, was not swayed by monetary pressure. While it is true that the French were apparently not explicit targets of predatory currency manipulation, they did suffer significant reserve losses. But Britain was more vulnerable to monetary pressure: the country had a currency that was widely held, had a low ratio of reserves to imports, and attached a higher than average degree of importance to the reputation and stability of its currency than did other states. These types of variables will remain important in any attempt to explain the relative success and failure of the practice of currency manipulation.

Another lesson concerns currency manipulation and the prevailing monetary regime. With fixed exchange rates, as discussed above, the target of the manipulation is the reserves, not the value of the currency. One result of this is that not only can the source of a nation's economic troubles be hidden with currency manipulation, but the general public's awareness of the existence of those troubles can be delayed. The length of the delay depends on how often reserve statistics are published.[99] In Britain during this period the statistics were published monthly. This led not only to *The Economist*'s missing the reason for withdrawal at first, but, more interestingly, led to *The Times* (London) reporting on November 2, 3, and 5, that sterling was either "steady" or "strong."[100] Finally, the particular players in the crisis are noteworthy: treasury secretaries and finance ministers played a large and decisive role in foreign affairs, in both agent and target countries.

Illustrative Cases

In the two focal episodes currency manipulation has proven to be an extraordinarily powerful tool of influence in international relations, under either fixed or flexible exchange rates. A greater understanding of the mechanics associated with the use of this instrument can be attained through a consideration of some additional cases.[101] Each case below features something different. The Agadir episode, for example, highlights the central role that domestic banks play in cases involving a commodity standard. The Mexican case showcases the evolution of currency manipulation through various stages, and also considers the domestic politics of currency manipulation. A comparison of the

[99] Because of this factor, targets under flexible exchange rate regimes may be under even greater immediate time pressure than would be the case with fixed rates.

[100] *The Times* (London), November 2, 3, 5, 1956.

[101] These cases are discussed in chronological order from the start of the influence attempt.

Nazi counterfeiting scheme with Japanese predatory measures against China demonstrates how different manipulative techniques can be used in the pursuit of similar goals.

The Agadir Crisis

The Agadir crisis of 1911 was a confrontation between France and Germany over the fate of Morocco. These two powers had tangled over the Moroccan question in 1905, and the issue had never been decisively settled. France had a long-standing desire to add Morocco to its African empire, and Germany wanted to match French influence there, or at least gain compensation should France come to dominate Morocco. The proximate cause of the crisis was the decision by France to send an expeditionary force into the capital of Fez in June 1911, nominally to quell unrest there and protect European lives and interests. However, this move was an extension of French jurisdiction beyond what was generally recognized, and it was viewed as a French move finally to establish a protectorate in Morocco.[102]

The German reaction was originally restrained: the German government stated that it would require compensation should France come to dominate Morocco. Talks on compensation were held, but positions quickly hardened on both sides. Tensions mounted in July, as both sides alluded to their willingness to fight over the issue. The situation was complicated one week later when the British firmly and publicly came to the support of the French. The British were not insensitive to the German position, but viewed the the German tactics as an attempt to undermine the Anglo-French entente.[103]

With the British intervention, the likelihood of immediate war receded, but negotiations, with the specter of war lurking behind them, continued through August. The talks appeared to break down on September 1, and this was followed by the onset of an economic crisis in Germany. On Monday, September 4, a panic hit the German stock exchange, with industrial and financial stocks falling as much as 10 percent in one hour and 30 percent in one day. Even more threatening was a run on German banks, with depositors desperately cashing in marks for gold.[104]

The French press bragged that the financial crisis in Germany was caused

---

[102] Brief chronologies of the 1905 crisis and the 1911 crisis can be found in Glenn H. Snyder and Paul Diesing, *Conflict Among Nations* (Princeton: Princeton University Press, 1977), pp. 534–37 and 541–45. The classic treatise on the Agadir crisis is I. C. Barlow, *The Agadir Crisis* (Chapel Hill: University of North Carolina Press, 1940); chapter 8 discusses the French march on Fez.

[103] On the July 15 negotiations, see Snyder and Diesing, *Conflict Among Nations*, p. 543; on the British reaction, see Barlow, *Agadir Crisis*, pp. 285, 301.

[104] On negotiations, see Barlow *Agadir Crisis*, 330–37, 350. On the economic crisis, see G. Barraclough, *From Agadir to Armageddon* (London: Weidonfield and Nicolson, 1982), p. 3.

by the withdrawal of French funds from German banks. These funds were substantial, and they were withdrawn for political reasons, but the extent to which the withdrawals caused the crisis is unclear. Regardless, the German government was able to check the market crash with a published announcement on September 5, which stated that negotiations had been resumed and they would probably progress on an "easier course [than] before their interruption."[105] On November 4, a treaty was signed recognizing Morocco as a French protectorate. The Germans were allowed "equal economic access" to Morocco, and also gained an unappealing slice of the French Congo. The settlement was viewed within Germany as a humiliating defeat.[106]

Some have suggested that German bankers, under the pressure of the drain of gold exacerbated by French withdrawals, forced the government to give in. Others argue that there is not one "shred of evidence" to support this. The consensus is that once Britain sided with France, German strategy failed and its position was doomed.[107] This conclusion is logical, but it does not explain the timing of the German decision to capitulate (well after the British involvement but on the heels of the financial crisis) or the degree to which economic factors influenced German strategy. An internal British review of the economics of the Agadir crisis suggests that a concern for monetary reserves was crucial to the German decision, but indirectly so. German bankers were greatly displeased with the political crisis, the uncertainty that surrounded it, and the drain of gold that accompanied it. In order to compensate for the withdrawal of British and French funds, interest rates had to be raised. The run on banks to convert marks into gold placed some smaller banks in jeopardy, and two of them failed.[108]

However, it does not appear that the German banking community insisted that the government capitulate in the crisis. It does appear, though, that the bankers insisted that the crisis be resolved, in one way or another, as soon as possible. The gold drain was simply intolerable. If the crisis ended in surrender, the outflow of gold would cease. If the crisis ended in war, the gold standard would be suspended, and the export of gold prohibited, and so in war

---

[105] Barlow, *Agadir Crisis*, p. 351.

[106] M. Kitchen, *The Political Economy of Germany, 1815–1914* (London: Croom Helm, 1978), p. 228; A. J. Ryder, *Twentieth Century Germany, From Bismark to Brandt* (New York: Columbia University Press, 1973), p. 104. Barlow notes that the French "won their prize" *Agadir Crisis* (p. 362).

[107] On the monetary explanation, see P. Wiles, *Communist International Economics* (Oxford: Basil Blackwell, 1968), p. 471. "[N]o shred of evidence," Barlow, *Agadir Crisis*, p. 355. On the importance of British intervention, Snyder and Diesing, *Conflict Among Nations*, p. 544; see also Luigi Albertini, *The Origins of the War of 1914* (Oxford: Oxford University Press, 1952), p. 330.

[108] See "The German Financial Crisis," report by F. Oppenheimer prepared for Foreign Secretary E. Gray, October 21, 1911, reprinted in G. D. Gooch and H. Temperley, eds., *British Documents on the Origins of the War 1898–1914*, vol. 7, *The Agadir Crisis* (London: H.M. Stationery Office, 1932), pp. 796–805.

as well the outflow of gold would cease. In early September, then, the banks did not dictate surrender; they simply demanded a resolution. Given the decisive presence of the British, the German government must have felt that it had no choice.

The Agadir crisis represents a minor episode of currency manipulation. The practice involved the withdrawal of French funds from Germany, which contributed to a financial crisis that threatened the solvency of the German currency; that crisis compelled Germany to bow to what was already likely once the British intervened. However, it represents an early step toward the more general practice of monetary diplomacy. For the parties themselves, it led to an increasing awareness of the potential of monetary power.[109] For an understanding of the mechanics of currency manipulation, there are three particularly important observations. First, this episode provides a good demonstration of the importance of encashment of currency notes by nationals under a commodity standard, a regime that features domestic banks as a source of reserve drain and economic vulnerability. Second is the observation that from the very start, private banks, central banks, and the relationship between governments and these banks is a crucial variable. Third, there is the realization of the fact that the stability of national currency and the reserve position will be of paramount concern to any nation engaged in not only open warfare but also crisis negotiation. With the onset of World War I, monetary warfare would become an instrument of state power more frequently, thoughtfully, and systematically employed.

Monetary Power and World War I

With the outbreak of World War I, all of the belligerent nations left the gold standard and suspended convertibility. Great Britain was an exception, but still successfully restricted convertibility through a web of daunting regulations.[110] Both the Allied and Central powers were highly concerned with the position of their currencies. Following the suspension of the gold standard, the international currency market bifurcated, featuring official controlled markets within the belligerent states, and free markets operating in the neutral ones. With the outbreak of the war, the franc fell by 8 percent, the lira by 17

---

[109] Oppenheimer noted, "Haute finance has chosen to some extent to force the hands of the government . . . it may some day be driven to do so from reasons of self-defense." Ibid., p. 805.

[110] On the European monetary system before the war, see A. I. Bloomfield, *Monetary Policy under the International Gold Standard 1880–1914* (New York: Arno Press, 1977); I. A. Drummond, *The Gold Standard and the International Monetary System, 1900–1939* (London: Macmillan, 1987); and Peter Lindert, *Key Currencies and Gold 1900–1913*, Princeton Studies in International Finance, no. 24 (Princeton University,1969).

percent, and the ruble by 28 percent. The pound was initially stronger, as it was supported by capital flight from the continent.[111]

The Western Allies, Britain and France, were sensitive to currency concerns but were reasonably secure. The franc stabilized, and Britain was able to engage in its traditional role as wartime banker to its allies, at least until the entry of the United States into the war. Even before that point, though, the Allies recognized that the dollar/pound rate was the linchpin of Western currency stability. Accordingly, in 1915, when large gold flows to the United States put pressure on the pound, Britain intervened in the New York market to prevent its currency from falling against the dollar.[112]

That British intervention was the first step in a coordinated policy of protective currency manipulation, which in this case was the self-protection of its own currency. In 1915 Britain pegged the pound to the dollar at $4.764/£. This rate was maintained by the J. P. Morgan Company, which acted as the agent for the British government. The funds for intervention were raised by loans floated in the New York market and the mandatory surrender of dollar assets by British investors.[113] The exchange issue became one of the most difficult problems facing the British government. The exchange rate overvalued the pound, putting pressure on that currency, but the British benefited from the arrangement, which guaranteed continuous access to relatively inexpensive dollars, which were vital to the war effort. The interventions necessary to maintain this stability ultimately cost the government £800 million.[114]

Shortly after the United States entered the war, the British faced a new exchange crisis. U.S. assistance was urgently needed. On June 28, 1917, officials in Britain noted:

> [T]he British agents in the United States now have enough money to keep the exchange up for only one day more. If exchange with England fall [sic] exchange with all European Allies also will immediately fall and there will be a general collapse. . . . Unless we come to their rescue we are all in danger of disaster.[115]

[111] G. Hardach, *The First World War 1914–1918* (Berkeley: University of California Press, 1977), p. 144, 147.

[112] Ibid., p. 144.

[113] Paul Einzig, *Exchange Controls* (London: Macmillan, 1931), p. 24; T. E. Gregory, *Foreign Exchange before, during, and after the War* (London: Oxford University Press, 1927), p. 70. On the Morgan Company and with Britain, see W. A. Brown, Jr., *England and the New Gold Standard 1919–1926* (New Haven: Yale University Press, 1929), p. 45.

[114] S. E. Harris, *Monetary Problems of the British Empire* (New York: Macmillan, 1937), p. 246; Kathleen Burk, "J. M. Keynes and the Exchange Rate Crisis of July 1917," *Economic History Review*, 2d ser., 32, no. 3:405–16 (1979) (benefits of peg); see also Einzig, *Exchange Controls*, p. 25 (£800 million).

[115] Kathleen Burk, *Britain, America, and the Sinews of War, 1914–18* (London: George Allen and Unwin, 1985), p. 199.

That same day, British foreign secretary Balfour cabled Wilson confidant Colonel House, stating, "[W]e seem to be on the edge of a financial disaster which would be worse than a defeat on the field."[116]

The United States came through with increased support, representing a new phase of monetary diplomacy, that of U.S. permissive currency manipulation. It was permissive in that the United States did not actively intervene itself. Rather, despite reservations in Washington, it allowed the British to use some of the assistance provided by the United States to fight the war to be employed to defend the pound.[117] The monetary power exercised by both the United States and Britain was consequential, at least in the eyes of many participants. John Maynard Keynes, then with the British treasury, felt that without U.S. support for the British exchange position, "the whole financial fabric of the alliance [would] collapse." He further argued that a forced float of the British currency would affect the outcome of the war:

> Turning to the psychological consequences, the results would be plainly disastrous. . . . Chief of all there is the effect on the mind of the enemy. . . . The encouragement and corroboration of their hopes which they discover in the abandonment of the exchanges would, therefore, be enormous. . . . It would be said that with the collapse of their exchanges the Allies cannot endure six months more. . . . We have constantly proclaimed to the world that it is the cornerstone of our policy. To point out the depreciation of the German exchanges and the stability of our own has been a favorite form of propaganda in all parts of the world.[118]

The stability of the pound did contrast dramatically with the experience of other European issues. Currency speculation had become an important feature of the conflict, and currency values came to be viewed as a way of gauging how each nation was faring in the war.[119] The German mark (which was floating at this time) and the Russian ruble (the most vulnerable of the Allied currencies) came to be the most volatile and observed barometers of the war. Though all of the European states took actions in support of their currencies, Germany was the most aggressive currency manipulator during the war. One of Germany's war aims was to achieve a separate peace with Russia. Pressure

---

[116] Ibid., p. 200.

[117] The United States did engage in acts of protection as well. In 1918, acting on a special plea from Clemenceau, the United States sold dollars to France for francs. For most of the war, the British intervened in the market to support the franc. Harris, *Monetary Problems*, pp. 259, 345; Einzig, *Exchange Controls*, p. 28).

[118] Elizabeth Johnson, ed., *The Collected Writings of John Maynard Keynes*, vol. 16, *Activities 1914–1919: The Treasury and Versailles* (London: Macmillan, 1971), pp. 255 (1st quote), 261 (block quote). See also "Memorandum on the Probable Consequences of Abandoning the Gold Standard" [January 17, 1917], ibid., pp. 215–22.

[119] Brendan Brown, *Monetary Chaos in Europe* (London: Croom Helm, 1988), pp. 37, 44.

on the sinking Russian currency would probably have been eased by Russia's withdrawal from the conflict. Thus, the more serious currency problems became, the more Russia had to gain from a separate peace.

The ruble was in serious trouble indeed. At the beginning of the war, the currency was almost completely backed by gold. By the time of the Russian Revolution, this backing had collapsed to 8 percent. The ruble continued to fall, spurred on by speculators who doubted Russia's ability to survive the war.[120] In 1916, while simultaneously pursuing a policy of negotiating a separate peace, the Germans gathered all the rubles that they could find in the territories that they occupied, and dumped them in the Stockholm market. This not only put increased pressure on the ruble, increasing the value of a separate peace, but increased German holdings of neutral currencies, which could be used to purchase supplies or engage in protective currency operations.[121] Germany would find a need for foreign exchange later on in order to engage in a major operation in support of its own currency. Toward the end of 1917 the German mark was coming under increasing speculative pressure. As noted above, all governments were concerned that the exchange rates of their currencies could become self-fulfilling prophecies with regard to the outcome of the war. In order to prevent defeatism at home, both Germany and Austria-Hungary made the publication of foreign exchange data illegal. On the international front at this time, the Germans intervened on neutral markets with "unheard of" levels of buying, purchasing marks and selling French francs and other currencies. This policy was able to lift the mark from 60 to 90 francs within a few months.[122]

German currency manipulation was not able to force Russia into a separate peace, nor did it win the war. But important lessons can be drawn from the German policies in this period, and the concerns of all of the belligerent states in general. The ruble-dumping episode is the first modern case of direct currency manipulation for political ends. Here, the growing awareness of the importance of currency values can be observed; and the issuance of new Rus-

[120] At first this speculation was driven by expectations of a German victory, but later by the possibility of internal collapse. Ultimately, it was the revolution that led to the withdrawal of the Russians from the war and rendered the Tsarist currency worthless. Boris Eliacheff, "Le Rouble pendant la guerre," *Revue d'Economie Politique* 33, no. 1:13–40 (1919), pp. 13–18, 26–29. On the ruble before the war, see I. M. Drummond, "The Russian Gold Standard 1897–1914," *Journal of Economic History* 36, no. 3:663–88 (1976).

[121] B. Brown, *Monetary Chaos*, pp. 54–55. The Russian currency experience in this period is worthy of further attention. In the last days of the Provisional Government, there were actually three Russian currencies circulating: the tsarist, or national, currency; the Kerensky ruble, issued by the Provisional Government in September of 1917; and the "Red," or Communist, currency, which was almost worthless. See Eliacheff, "Le Rouble," p. 29; see also B. Brown, *Monetary Chaos*, p. 75.

[122] Charles Blankhart, *Die Devisenploitik Während Des Weltkreges* (Zurich: Art. Institut Orell Füssli, 1919), p. 114; see also B. Brown, *Monetary Chaos*, pp. 57, 76.

sian currencies once again demonstrates the important link between currency viability and the concepts of sovereignty and legitimacy, which were seen to be so important in the China episode.

Both sides in the war engaged in active self-protective currency manipulation. Exercised successfully early in the war by the British, self-protective monetary power became an important weapon (or shield) for Germany, when it sacrificed precious foreign exchange in an operation designed solely to boost the value of the mark in order to affect international perceptions of the war. This underscores once again the extent to which currency stability is valued not simply for its economic consequences, but as a barometer of both the domestic and international position and competence of a nation and its government.

India and the Threat to Convertibility

At the beginning of World War I, the rupee was a silver-based currency, with silver coins circulating and paper notes, in larger denominations, fully convertible into silver. The rupee was pegged to the pound and intricately bound within the British international monetary network, and therefore also had some links to gold. But for the local government and economy, as well as traditional society, silver was the dominant metal.[123] With the outbreak of the war, India, like all the belligerents, moved to conserve gold. The effects of the outbreak of war on the financial position of the country were to be expected— a weakening of the rupee on the world market, withdrawals from saving banks within the country for the encashment of notes into silver, and an increased demand for gold—and all fell within tolerable levels. India was able to survive the first two years of the war without any major financial difficulty.[124]

At the end of 1916, though, an acute shortage of silver coupled with high wartime demand for the metal left the Indian government facing the prospect of inconvertibility of the rupee. Silver became scarce, as belligerents restricted its export, and the price of silver rose in the face of the high global demand. The situation was exacerbated by a rumor, spread by the Germans, that the paper rupees would soon be inconvertible. The government was also concerned that as the price of silver rose, rupee coins would disappear from circulation, negatively affecting domestic liquidity. Further, there was the fear

---

[123] For an analysis of the rupee before 1914, see B. E. Dadachanji, *The Monetary System of India* (Bombay: D. B. Taraporevala, n.d.) On the interwar period, see P. K. Goswami, *Indian Currency and Exchange 1835–1940* (New Delhi: Milind Publications, 1983).

[124] "Report of Committee on Indian Exchange and Currency, 1919" (Babington Smith Committee), in Government of India, *Reports of Currency Committees* (Calcutta: Government of India, 1931), pp. 240–42. See also C. J. Hamilton, "Recent Problems of Indian Currency and Exchange," *Bengal Economic Journal* 2, no. 1:1–21 (1918), pp. 5–6.

that silver rupees would even be melted down and shipped abroad for sale.[125]
The situation became critical in March and April of 1918, when unfavorable
war news caused a run on the Bombay currency office. On April 1, silver
reserves had fallen over 40 percent below what was considered a safe minimum. Within two months, reserves had fallen by another 60 percent, and
stood at 4 crores (10 million rupees' worth), or less than 25 percent of the 18.5
crores considered the safe minimum. The government took steps to limit the
silver drain through bureaucratic interference and the introduction of new
nickel coins, but the suspension of convertibility appeared inevitable.[126]

The suspension of the convertibility of the paper rupee would have had
great economic and political consequences within India, and would have affected the course, and possibly the outcome, of the war. On the economic
side, inconvertibility would have led to a run on the savings banks and possibly a general economic panic among the general public in India. It would
prevent a further expansion of the note issues, and cause a general inflation in
the paper currency, which would hamper India's ability to obtain war supplies
and export them to Europe. It would prevent the floating of any domestic
loans to support the war effort, and would be a blow to India's and thus the
Allies' prestige worldwide. Beyond the economic effects would have been far-
reaching and potentially more dangerous political ones. Inconvertibility
would have been exploited by anti-British politicians to stir up public sentiment against the British. The possibility of local revolt and disorder existed in
these circumstances, which, in the worst case, would affect Indian troops in
Europe and even divert British troops to India.[127]

Given these fears, the British ambassador to the United States approached
that government in an effort to procure some silver for India. This resulted in
the passage of the Pittman Act of 1918, which went through the U.S. Senate
quickly and quietly, and allowed India to buy over 200 million ounces of
silver from the United States at $1.015 an ounce. The act was passed on April
23, and the bulk of the sales took place between July 1918 and July 1919.[128]
In the words of the committee commissioned to study the Indian currency
position during the war,

> The timely help thus rendered by the United States Government in placing at India's
> disposal a supply of silver which represents considerably more than the world's

[125] Babington Smith Committee, "Indian Exchange," pp. 244–50; see also Hamilton, pp. 17–
19. The German attempt is mentioned in Everest, *New Deal and Silver*, pp. 5–6; and Westerfield,
Silver Debacle, p. 20.

[126] Babington Smith Committee, "Indian Exchange," pp. 254–255.

[127] Leavens, *Silver Money*, p. 170.

[128] Everest, *New Deal and Silver*, p. 6; Leavens, *Silver Money*, pp. 145–146. For a discussion
of complementary measures to ease India's currency crisis, see B. F. Madan, "Our Currency
Problems," *Bengal Economic Journal* 2, no. 2:120–61 (1918).

annual mine production since 1914 enabled the Government of India to tide over a very serious currency crisis and to maintain the convertibility of the note issue.[129]

U.S. protective currency manipulation was also able to assist India under similar circumstances in World War II, when financial difficulties, exacerbated by German broadcasts aimed at undermining faith in the paper currency, placed the rupee under new pressure. The stability of the Indian currency was again vital to the Allied war effort. India was still an essential cog in the British international monetary system, an important base of operations against the Japanese, and was an important source of raw materials for industrial and wartime needs. U.S. transfers of silver, initially in the form of secret loans in 1940, helped keep the Indian currency viable throughout the war.[130]

Both Indian cases featured a novel technique of monetary power: predatory currency manipulation of a purely rhetorical nature. German actions appear to have been successful in that they were able to contribute to instability and a loss of confidence in the rupee. Such a technique obviously depends on bandwagoning market forces. A limited instrument, it is, however, costless, and has the potential to do serious damage. American protective manipulation was also completely costless. The U.S. government sold its own silver to India, and then purchased replacement silver with the proceeds from the initial sale. This action prevented an allied power in wartime from facing a major economic and political crisis. Additionally, monetary power was essential—no other instrument of statecraft, regardless of speed or cost, would have likely been able to defuse the Indian situation.

An Interpretation of the Tripartite Monetary Agreement

On September 25, 1936, it was simultaneously announced in London, New York, and Paris, that the French franc would be devalued, there would be no retaliation from the other parties, and there would in the future be consultations between the three states on all monetary matters. This agreement, known as the Tripartite Monetary Agreement, was the first tangible sign of international monetary cooperation the world had seen since the international financial crisis of 1931, which had forced the British to abandon the gold standard. There has been some controversy with regard to the significance of

---

[129] Babington Smith Committee, "Indian Exchange," p. 252. While this was "[a] war measure, not . . . a monetary one," which aided "one of our allies in a very serious emergency" (Leavens, *Silver Money*, p. 150), in contrast to the Chinese case, it was supported by the U.S. silver interests, although they were somewhat disappointed with the price.

[130] Everest, *New Deal and Silver*, pp. 134, 152–55, 157; *FRUS*, 1944, vol. 5 (Washington, D.C.: U.S. Government Printing Office, 1965), pp. 248–85.

the agreement and the causes leading up to it.[131] It is argued here that the Tripartite Monetary Agreement was a mechanism designed to allow the United States and Great Britain to provide permissive currency manipulation of the French franc, toward two ends: first, a strengthening of the French economy and French resolve in the face of a growing fascist threat, and second, as a signal to the fascist powers of the unity of the democracies.

Before cooperation, however, there was chaos. In the previous half-decade, a series of devaluations and suspensions of convertibility had caused world trade and payments relationships to compartmentalize, with each bloc distrustful of the others. France, leading the orthodox gold bloc, criticized the monetary experiments of the others. The British were bitter over the American devaluation, and Britain in turn was accused of using the Exchange Equalization Account to manipulate, as opposed to stabilize, the value of the pound.[132] From 1934–1936, the French were able to defend the value of the franc, a goal on which they placed great value even though the currency was widely held to be overvalued. This overvaluation, combined with electoral instability and upheaval in the gold bloc (with the withdrawal of Belgium in 1935), caused periodic speculative pressures on the franc, which were combated with deflationary policies. Deflation was preferred by the government to devaluation.[133]

This preference ordering was to change in the wake of international developments. On Saturday, March 7, 1936, the Germans remilitarized the Rhineland, in violation of the Treaty of Locarno. On the following Monday, the franc came under some selling pressure, and the British intervened in the

[131] Kenneth Oye, in "The Sterling-Dollar-Franc Triangle: Monetary Policy 1929–1937," in Oye, ed., *Cooperation under Anarchy* (Princeton: Princeton University Press, 1986), views the agreement as a turning point, and a challenge to the "hegemonic stability theory"; M. Drummond, in *London, Washington, and the Management of the Franc, 1936–39*, Princeton Studies in International Finance, no. 48 (Princeton University, 1979), argues that little changed as a result of the pact.

[132] On competitive devaluation and compartmentalization, see Oye, "Sterling," pp. 176–91; Charles P. Kindleberger, *A Financial History of Western Europe* (London: George Allen and Unwin, 1984), pp. 391–92; and Chapter 5. On the equalization account, see Susan Howson, *Sterling's Managed Float: The Operations of the Exchange Equalization Account, 1932–39*, Princeton Studies in International Finance, no. 46 (1980); Bank of England, "The Exchange Equalization Account: Its Origins and Development," *Bank of England Quarterly Bulletin* 8:377–90 (1968), pp. 379–80; Lowell M. Pumphery, "The Exchange Equalization Account of Great Britain 1932–1939: Exchange Operations," *American Economic Review* 32, no. 4:803–16 (1942); and N. F. Hall, *The Exchange Equalization Account* (London: Macmillan, 1935), pp. 4, 23–25.

[133] David E. Kaiser, *Economic Diplomacy and the Origins of the Second World War* (Princeton: Princeton University Press, 1980), p. 203; M. Wolfe, *The French Franc between the Wars 1919–1939* (New York: Columbia University Press, 1951), p. 109. For background on the franc leading up to this period, see ibid.; and Eleanor L. Dulles, *The French Franc, 1914–1928* (New York: Macmillan, 1929).

market to prevent the franc from weakening beyond Fr75/£. The French, meanwhile, hinted that they might use force to remove the Germans. In reaction to this, the three-month discount on the franc jumped from 8 percent to 14 percent per anum. Shortly thereafter, the French made it clear that they would not use force, and the pressure on the franc eased.[134]

As early of 1934, some observers harshly criticized the "French fetish of monetary orthodoxy," arguing that with a growing German threat, "The French nation has to choose between the franc and France."[135] But the Rhineland incident provided the first indisputable signal to the French that their international security position and their currency position were inexorably linked. The intimacy of this relationship actually predated the Rhineland incident by several years. Among the deflationary measures introduced by the French government to protect the value of the franc was a reduction in public spending, from Fr55.7 billion in fiscal year 1931–1932 to about Fr50 billion in 1935. Almost all of these savings were from defense, which fell from Fr15.5 billion to Fr10.7 billion in this period, with most of the savings coming from reductions in the purchase of new weapons.[136] Until the middle of 1936, the French were more interested in defending the franc than in military spending, but France now wanted to rearm, and it was clear to French government officials that (1)an increase in military expenditures could not be undertaken without devaluation, and (2)without international cooperation and support, devaluation would not be effective, given that any devaluation could be matched by compensating devaluations from the dollar and sterling areas. French preferences, therefore, shifted to favor both devaluation and international cooperation.[137]

French officials visited both Britain and the United States, and painted a rather bleak picture of the military situation in Europe in order to gain support. The British, close as they were to the situation, were easier to impress. The United States was more reluctant, but two factors proved decisive. First was the continuing rise of the fascist threat. The March remilitarization of the Rhineland was followed in May by the Italian conquest of Ethiopia and in July by the beginning of the Spanish Civil War. These actions represented a disturbing pattern of aggressive behavior on the part of the fascist states. Second was the fact that the agreement would affect only the dollar/franc rate and not

[134] Brendan Brown, *The Flight of International Capital* (London: Routledge, 1987), p. 71.
[135] Paul Einzig, *France's Crisis* (London: Macmillan, 1934), pp. viii, ix (quotes); also pp. 110–11, passim.
[136] Kaiser, *Economic Diplomacy*, p. 203.
[137] R. Frankenstein, "The Decline of France and British Appeasement Policies," in W. J. Mommonsen and L. Kettenacher, eds., *The Fascist Challenge and the Policy of Appeasement* (London: George Allen and Unwin, 1983), p. 237; S.V.O. Clarke, *Exchange Rate Stabilization in the Mid-1930s: Negotiating the Tripartite Agreement*, Princeton Studies in International Finance, no. 41 (Princeton University, 1977), pp. 5, 8.

the dollar/pound rate. With regard to the pound, Morgenthau's concerns were dominated by economics, and especially by the price competitiveness of U.S. products. But Morgenthau's advisors told him that the franc/dollar exchange rate was not an important influence on American trade or on the country's ultimate recovery from recession.[138]

The U.S. secretary of the Treasury was now in a position, therefore, to carry out his "growing determination to use monetary policy to build a united, democratic front to resist Hitler." He believed that aiding the French devaluation would strengthen the French government in particular and the forces of democracy in Western Europe in general. Both the Americans and the British feared that the survival of France as a democracy was threatened from both within and without, and the Tripartite Monetary Agreement seemed a way of bolstering that democracy. And so in September of 1936, the agreement was signed. Morgenthau told the Soviet ambassador in the spring of 1937 that the agreement was "an instrument of peace."[139]

The tripartite pact allowed for the practice of permissive currency manipulation by Britain and the United States The two countries agreed to acquiesce in currency moves made by the target state that could hurt them economically and that they had the ability to counter. It was also used, as economic diplomacy often is, as a signal to potential enemies. The course of monetary relations in the following years among the principal tripartite players supports the argument that the agreement was designed for political, as opposed to economic, ends. A political interpretation of the agreement would find that for permissive purposes, the United States and Britain would accept some further French devaluation, and the three nations would keep the agreement alive even if it became economically irrelevant, lest the wrong signal be sent. A purely economic interpretation would expect the agreement to fall apart in the face of gross violations.

In the first six months of the agreement, the franc was stable. This distressed Morgenthau, who wanted the French to take advantage of the agreement and devalue a bit further in order to strengthen their economy. He feared that French weakness resulting from France's reluctance to devalue further might even tempt the Germans to invade. Finally, in April 1937, the French allowed the franc to fall from 105 to 112 to the pound. However, once the French started to devalue, they did not stop. Every month from April 1937 through December 1938, the franc averaged a lower value than it had the month before. This included a devaluation in June 1937, which caused the fall of the Blum government, and a further major devaluation in May 1938. With this last devaluation, French monetary dependence was underscored by the

---

[138] Clarke, "Tripartite Agreement," pp. 28–29; Drummond, "Management," pp. 3–4.

[139] "[G]rowing determination" and "instrument of peace," Blum, *Morgenthau Diary*, vol. 1, pp. 140, 471; On concerns for democracy, see Drummond, "Management," pp. 4, 32.

quotation of the value of the franc in pounds for the first time, instead of in gold.[140]

While the United States welcomed the April 1937 devaluation, it was dismayed by the continued rapid decline in the franc, which lost 43 percent of its value in the two years following the agreement. This clearly violated the spirit of the agreement, but, as one analyst noted, "The U.S. and the U.K. were prepared to swallow almost any French action rather than announce that the agreement was dead."[141] This was because the signal of unity would be replaced with one of discord amongst the democracies. Foremost in the Allies' minds was not stabilizing the franc, but helping France and sending a signal to the Axis powers. Without the Axis threat, the agreement probably would have fallen apart under the weight of repeated French devaluations.

Permissive currency manipulation requires a sacrifice of economic for political interests. In this case specifically it was the rise of security concerns, which came to dominate economic ones, that convinced the United States and Britain to act. France's experience also underscores once again the vital link between currency concerns and security interests.

Mexico: A Cycle of Manipulation

From 1935 to 1941, the United States engaged in both positive and negative manipulation of the Mexican currency, in an episode that featured both fixed and floating exchange rates. Four stages can be observed: two phases of protection, a shift to passive currency manipulation, and finally a resumption of protective assistance. Mexico in this period was on a de facto silver standard, and silver was an important part of that nation's economy. Not only was silver the basis for the Mexican currency, but it was an important export industry, rivaling oil as a source of foreign exchange, and was an important tax base for the national government. Like China, Mexico was rocked by the U.S. silver purchases, which began in 1934. The rise in the price of silver threatened the survival of the silver Mexican peso as a currency, as the price of silver passed the point at which it became profitable to melt pesos down and ship them abroad. Therefore, in May 1935 the government forced an exchange of the silver currency for paper notes.[142]

---

[140] Drummond, "Management," p. 14; Wolfe, *French Franc*, p. 213; and R. Girault, "The Impact of the Economic Situation on the Foreign Policy of France, 1936–1939," in Mommonsen and Kettenacher, p. 220. See Wolfe, *French Franc*, p. 213, for quotations of the franc/dollar rate, January 1919 to December 1939.

[141] Drummond "Management," pp. 32, 53 (quote); also Pumphery, "Exchange Equalization Account," p. 813.

[142] B. Wood, *The Making of the Good Neighbor Policy* (New York: Columbia University Press, 1961), p. 223; J. P. Paris, *Monetary Policies of the United States, 1932–1938* (New York:

Toward the end of 1935, though, silver prices began to fall, and the Mexican government became concerned about the move in this direction as well, which threatened to undermine confidence in the Mexican currency, since reserves were held primarily in silver. The Mexican currency troubles of 1935 afforded the United States an opportunity to engage in protective currency manipulation. In March, the United States sold 32,000 ounces of gold to Mexico to bolster reserves there; and in December, the United States agreed to buy from Mexico 5 million ounces of silver a month, to support the price and provide Mexico with needed dollar exchange.[143] This move gave the United States a chance to showcase its new "good neighbor" policy toward Latin America.

Relations between the United States and Mexico soured in 1937, however, as controversies over Mexican claims on U.S and European agricultural and oil holdings there arose. This had a negative effect on the value of the peso, and in November a Mexican delegation headed by Finance Minister Eduardo Suarez arrived in Washington seeking further support for the Mexican currency. The administration was divided over how to respond. The State Department viewed this as an opportunity to use American economic leverage to extract concessions from Mexico on the oil issue. Secretary of State Hull was supported by the oil interests as well as the silver interests, who were traditionally opposed to the purchase of foreign silver in general. The U.S. ambassador to Mexico, Josephus Daniels, and Treasury Secretary Morgenthau, on the other hand, were in favor of providing unconditional support. Their view was triumphant, and in December the United States announced new monthly purchases of a total of 35 million ounces of silver at 45 cents per ounce.[144]

The December 1937 purchase represented the second round of protective monetary power provided by the United States In the first round, protection was relatively uncontroversial and the motive was to enhance national reputation. In this second case, more specific security concerns won out over powerful and diverse economic interests. The oil and silver interests were in favor of pressure, not support. But at the beginning of 1938, the need to protect the western hemisphere from fascist political advances became paramount, especially in the mind of Morgenthau. He was convinced that the United States had to provide active support for the nations of Latin America, or they would become "a helpless field for political and economic exploitation by the aggressor nations." For this reason, he moved to support the Mexican currency in the face of strong domestic pressure. Morgenthau was active on other fronts as

---

Columbia University Press, 1938), p. 63; Westerfield, *Silver Debacle*, p. 145. Unlike China, as a producer as well as a consumer of silver, Mexico was also greatly hurt by the earlier fall in the price of silver. Bratter, "Silver," pp. 359–62; Stewart, "Silver," pp. 253–55.

[143] Leavens, *Silver Money*, p. 327; Everest, *New Deal and Silver*, pp. 80–83.

[144] E. D. Croon, *Josephus Daniels in Mexico* (Madison: University of Wisconsin Press, 1960), pp. 175–76.

well. In 1937, the United States engaged in reputation-enhancing protective currency manipulation in Brazil, supporting its currency by helping that country create a central bank and through the sale of up to $60 million of gold over five years to that nation. The United States also provided additional foreign exchange against the gold that Brazil would possess. Though Morgenthau personally disliked General Getulio Vargas, the political strongman of Brazil, U.S. protective monetary power helped to keep him a "loyal Pan-American."[145]

On March 13, 1938, though, the Mexican situation became complicated once again, as President Lazaro Cardenas unexpectedly expropriated the properties of Dutch, British, and U.S. oil companies. Secretary Hull was furious, and only through the self-interposition of Ambassador Daniels between Hull and the Mexican government was an open break of relations avoided. The pressure to impose sanctions on Mexico was tremendous. Morgenthau was reluctant, again because of his view that the primary concern of U.S. Latin American policy should be to "keep the Countries of North and South America from going fascist." However, this time, the pressure was too great, and Morgenthau announced the suspension of the December silver purchase agreement.[146]

What is especially interesting is that Morgenthau deliberately chose to exercise the sanction in a passive instead of a predatory way. If he could not stop the sanction, he could at least cushion the blow. The United States continued to buy Mexican silver on the world market. In effect, then, the punishment was not a boycott of Mexican silver (which many in the United States were demanding)—this would have been a predatory act. Instead, the sanction consisted of the loss of the predictability of the American purchases, as well as a drop in the purchase price, from the premium price the United States was paying to the world market price. This shift from protection to indifference is a classic example of passive currency manipulation.

This did not mean, however, that the passive sanctions did not have a considerable effect on the Mexican currency. In fact, even this passive action did have a significant effect, once again demonstrating the speed and effectiveness of monetary power. The American action resulted in a fall in the price of silver, from 45 cents per ounce to 44 and then 43 cents. This last price was the lowest quotation for silver in four years. The fall in the price of silver lowered the value of Mexican reserves and undermined confidence in the peso.[147] The result of this was a devaluation of the peso. Although the 1937 recession,

[145] Blum, *Morgenthau Diary*, vol. 2, p. 50; vol. 1, p. 498.

[146] On the expropriation, see Wood, *Good Neighbor Policy*, p. 203. On the Hull/Daniels note controversy and its effect on U.S.-Mexican relations, see Josephus Daniels, *Shirt-Sleeve Diplomat* (Memoirs) (Chapel Hill: University of North Carolina Press, 1947), p. 231. On Morgenthau's reaction and sanctions, see Croon, *Josephus Daniels*, pp. 177, 191.

[147] Leavens, *Silver Money*, p. 327.

capital flight in the wake of the expropriation, and a desire to improve the balance of trade all played a part, it was the currency situation that was the primary cause. As one analyst noted:

> At the time of the expropriation, the bank of Mexico possessed a metal reserve [which was] already very weak ($42.3 million), insufficient to satisfy the avalanche of demands . . . there was no other solution but to abandon the exchange rate to market forces.[148]

The peso was therefore allowed to float to a new equilibrium, bolstered by deflationary policies, and then defended by the Bank of Mexico. In 1939 the government intervened in the market to support the peso at 4.99 to the dollar, a devaluation of over 35 percent from the level of 3.60, where it was fixed before the crisis. In August 1939, the Mexican government was unable to support this rate, and the peso fell to 6 per dollar.[149] Passive currency manipulation was able to wreak havoc on the peso, but it did not force capitulation. The Mexicans preferred their currency troubles to conceding on the expropriations issue.[150] They were able to hold out while negotiations over compensation dragged on. In these negotiations time was on their side. The United States was becoming increasingly concerned with Axis advances in Latin America. In 1938 German and Japanese trade with Mexico increased, while Mexican-U.S. trade fell. The Axis powers were attempting to increase their influence throughout the region. Even Secretary of State Hull, a "hawk" on the Mexican issue, came to view Axis penetration in the hemisphere to be of paramount importance.[151]

Secretary Morgenthau continued to believe in the power of positive currency manipulation as an important and cost-effective tool of influence. He stated that U.S.–Latin American relations could be substantially improved by "an intelligent use of a small proportion of our enormous gold and silver

[148] R. Torres, *Un Siglo de Devaluationes del Peso Mexicano* (Mexico: Siglo Veintiuno, 1980), pp. 251–53.

[149] Ibid., pp. 253–54.

[150] This serves as a reminder that the success of all forms of economic statecraft depends not simply on the weight of the sanction, but on the value that the target attaches to the issue in question. The Mexican government preferred the potential gains in oil wealth and national prestige to currency stability. This marks an interesting contrast to the British in the Suez case, who would probably not have taken the first step if they had thought devaluation might result. On the other hand, the British were targets of predatory manipulation, whereas the Mexicans suffered only from passive action. Given the dislocation simple passive manipulation caused, it is reasonable to assume that predatory action in that case would have had the potential to completely destroy the Mexican peso. In that instance, it is less clear whether the Mexican government would have preferred obstinance to submission.

[151] On Hull and the Axis threat to the western hemisphere, see Cordell Hull, *The Memoirs of Cordell Hull*, vol. 1 (New York: Macmillan, 1948), pp. 495, 601, 692, 813. On Axis trade, see also Croon, *Josephus Daniels*, p. 234. For more on German economic penetration in Latin America, see Chapter 4.

holdings." In June 1940 the president ordered Hull to shore up relations to the south in the aftermath of the fall of France. In July, Hull tried his hand at monetary diplomacy, offering nations at the Havana conference U.S. loans or arrangements designed to strengthen the monetary systems and stabilize the currencies of those nations.[152]

Mexico was of necessity at the center of any policy to protect the hemisphere from Axis influence. The United States therefore came around to settling the issue of compensation in Mexico's favor, over the objections of the U.S. oil interests, accepting $40 million to be paid over nineteen years. (The oil companies had been seeking $500 million; a more accurate value for their losses was probably around $125 million.) In exchange for the Mexican compensation, the United States agreed to resume protective manipulation of the peso, providing a $40 million stabilization loan and promising to buy 6 million ounces of silver a month. These agreements, signed in November 1941, allowed the Mexicans to revalue the peso to 4.85 to the dollar, and ensured continental solidarity on the eve of Pearl Harbor.[153]

The four-layer Mexican case shows, among other things, that even passive currency manipulation can carry quite a punch. This form of monetary power is also costless: in fact, the United States saved money on its international silver purchases as a result. Despite the damage inflicted, however, it was not sufficient to alter the target's behavior. The related reluctance to engage in predatory acts in this case reveals that feedback, however relatively rare, can inhibit monetary power. The first round of currency manipulation was in support of the good neighbor policy. Subsequent actions,—protection, the decision to attack with passive, as opposed to predatory power, and the resumption of protection—were all determined by international security issues unrelated to the more specific U.S.-Mexican relationship and narrow economic conflict.

While monetary diplomacy in this case was limited by other policy concerns, domestic politics was not one of them. In fact, the independence of monetary power from domestic politics was remarkable in this case, even by the high standards of currency manipulation in general. Here, monetary diplomacy was, in the final three stages, working in fundamental opposition to powerful, organized economic interests within the United States, the silver and oil industries. These interests consistently wanted pressure when the United States was providing support, and when the United States finally exerted pressure, the technique of that coercion was designed to cushion the severity of the blow. In the end, U.S. oil interests were the big losers, with the silver interests left unsatisfied.

[152] Blum, *Morgenthau Diary*, p. 321.

[153] Wood, *Good Neighbor Policy*, p. 203; Everest, *New Deal and Silver*, p. 96; Croon, *Josephus Daniels*, pp. 250, 259, 268, 270, Torres, *Devaluationes del Peso*, p. 254; Daniels, *Shirt-Sleeve Diplomat*, p. 501.

The Nazi Counterfeiting Scheme

As noted in Chapter 2, if taken to an extreme, the logical culmination of predatory currency manipulation is to completely destroy the currency of the target state, that is, to literally take away its money, eliminating the monetary economy, causing tremendous dislocation in the real economy, humiliating the central government, and forcing international default and bankruptcy. In most instances a technique of predatory manipulation that, when successful, specifically brought about this result and this result only would be an inappropriate tactic. Except as a threat, it would represent a rather blunt instrument of brute force rather than a more flexible tool of coercion.[154] However, there are certain circumstances when annihilation is the goal. While the United States, for example, did not want to inflict any permanent damage on the pound during the Suez crisis, Japan, wanted specifically to destroy the Chinese national currency. One technique that could have been employed to meet this end for Japan, provided it had the capability to do so, would have been to forge great amounts of the Chinese currency and distribute it throughout the mainland. An operation of sufficient magnitude, aided perhaps by a panic triggered by these actions, would have rendered the currency worthless.

The Japanese did not attempt any such counterfeiting schemes during World War II, but the Germans did.[155] Reinhard Heydrich, deputy to SS chief Heinrich Himmler, came up with the idea of the Germans' forging massive numbers of pound notes, and distributing them in such a way as to cause national bankruptcy in Britain.[156] If the scheme had been successful, the results would have been devastating. But even without complete success, any doubt cast on the integrity of the pound would have had major international economic ramifications, given the fact that sterling was held in large amounts all over the world. Any crisis in confidence in the pound could have undermined the Allied cause and had a significant effect on the outcome of the war.[157]

The Germans created at least £150 million worth of remarkably good pound notes from 1942 to 1945. The question then became one of how to place them into circulation in a way that would do the most harm. The original plan was

---

[154] One of the characteristics that make monetary power particularly well suited for coercion is that it can often inflict considerable pain without leaving permanent damage.

[155] In fact, the Japanese annihilation attempt employed a technique that was the polar opposite of counterfeiting. Instead of flooding the target with its currency, Japan chose to drain the target of its legal tender. These two strikingly different techniques, which were used in support of similar goals, demonstrates once again the remarkable flexibility of currency manipulation in adapting to the opportunities provided by the specific situation.

[156] Petrov, *Money*, p. 36.

[157] G. J. McNally, "The Great Nazi Counterfeit Plot," *Reader's Digest*, July 1952, p. 26. McNally, a major in the U.S. Army, was involved in tracking counterfeit currency in Europe for the U.S. government.

to fly the notes over Britain and scatter them across the countryside. This option, which would have been the most direct method of introduction, was ruled out by the fact that by the time the notes were ready the British had won the Battle of Britain and now controlled the skies there.[158] The second method of introduction was to sell the notes in German-occupied Europe, which was a slower and more indirect method, but still formidable. This plan might have succeeded, but it was stopped voluntarily by the Germans themselves after a hundred thousand of the notes had been introduced in France, Greece, and Italy. Specifically, the German minister of economic affairs ordered that Operation Bernhard (as it was known) "was in no circumstances to operate in any part of Europe in German occupation," because it would undermine currencies in the areas he was attempting to stabilize.[159]

The cessation of the European plan, which ultimately doomed the entire forging operation[160], provides a striking example of feedback inhibiting the exercise of an otherwise potent form of monetary power. This is a distinct type of feedback: "environmental feedback," which could have prevented other episodes of currency manipulation from getting past the planning stage. In all cases of monetary diplomacy, then, attention must be paid to the fact that in an interconnected international economy, the movements of target currency can affect other currencies or international monetary arrangements. Theoretically, there should be many cases where the resort to monetary power would have to be ruled out, when these concerns will outweigh the potential gains from the specific goals of the manipulation itself.

Although ultimately a failure, the potential of the Nazi counterfeiting operation should not be underemphasized. Before the scheme wound down, the Nazis were producing about four hundred thousand notes a month, mostly British five-pound notes. And by 1944, they were producing good U.S. fifty- and hundred-dollar bills.[161] This episode also features a distinct and poten-

---

[158] W. Hoettl, *Hitler's Paper Weapon* (London: Rupert Hart-Davis, 1955), pp. 30, 32. Hoettl was a German officer involved in the operation. See also McNally, "Nazi Counterfeit Plot," p. 29.

[159] Hoettl, *Paper Weapon,* pp. 48–49; see also Anthony Pirie, *Operation Bernhard: The Greatest Forgery of All Time* (London: Cassell, 1961), p. 17. Managing the currencies in the occupied regions proved a formidable task. In Greece, the drachma had depreciated to such an extent that normal trade with Germany became impossible. The German authorities, however, did not adjust the rate for fear of upsetting the entire house of cards that was their occupation currency system. Bloch and Hoselitz, *Economies of Military Occupation,* p. 37.

[160] Plans to introduce the notes in Latin America also came to naught. See Hoettl, *Paper Weapon,* pp. 87, 91; Pirie, *Operation Bernhard,* pp. 75, 76, 80, 85. In the end, the pound notes were used in an ad hoc fashion, primarily to buy information and finance covert operations, including the Mussolini rescue operation. Hoettl, *Paper Weapon,* p. 77; McNally, "Nazi Counterfeit Plot," p. 31. On specific operations, see Hoettl and esp. Pirie.

[161] McNally, "Nazi Counterfeit Plot," pp. 29–30. The Nazi plot became a topic of discussion in the 1950s, during the cold war, when it was feared that the Soviets might embark on a similar plan. This apparently never came to fruition.

tially important form of feedback, as well as an act of currency manipulation designed to annihilate, rather than to coerce. Thus both the larger monetary setting and the goal of the manipulation must be considered when evaluating the technique and its likely long-term effect. Finally, the introduction of this new technique demonstrates once again the remarkable flexibility of currency manipulation with regard to its techniques, its applications, and the ability to practice it across a wide variety of periods, regions, forms of government, and monetary regimes.

The Nigerian Civil War, 1967–1970

From 1967 to 1970, Nigeria was engaged in a bloody civil war, between the federal government and the secessionist republic of Biafra, formerly Nigeria's eastern province. One of the most important and consequential measures taken by the ultimately victorious federal government during the war was a dramatic act of predatory currency manipulation.

As with many former African colonies, Nigeria was not a "nation" but a collection of nations captured arbitrarily in its borders. Some but not all of these distinctions were represented by the country's four provinces. For example, the huge northern province, with 45 percent of Nigeria's gross domestic product and 53.5 percent of its population, was predominantly Muslim, while the eastern province, dominated by the Ibo tribe, was more Christian.[162] Underlying tribal suspicions and hostility were punctuated by massacres and violent efforts to dominate the federal government. On May 28, 1967, Colonel Yakubu Gowon, head of the federal government, declared a state of emergency and announced that Nigeria was now composed of twelve regions, led by a powerful central government. This was the proximate cause of the declaration of independence announced by the local military governor, Lieutenant Colonel Chukwuemeka Odumegwu Ojukwu, on May 30, which stated that the entire former eastern province was now the independent state of Biafra.[163] The war that followed got off to a slow start, with the federal government content to impose economic sanctions and wait the Ibos out. Hostilities technically commenced on July 6, 1967, but the only significant action taken by the federal government was the seizure of the country's principal oil terminal. This was in service of the economic strategy, however, as the move was de-

[162] Sir Rex Niven, *The War of Nigerian Unity 1967–70* (Ibidan: Evans Brothers, 1970), pp. 11, 56; E. Wayne Nafziger, *The Economics of Political Instability: The Nigerian-Biafran War* (Boulder, Colo.: Westview Press, 1983), p. 107.

[163] Julian Critchley, ed., "The Nigerian Civil War: The Defeat of Biafra," Crisis Paper no. 7 (London: Atlantic Information Centre for Teachers, January 31, 1970), p. 5, 6–8; Niven, *War of Nigerian Unity*, p. 70, 77 90, 104. For biographical sketches of all of the principals, see Christian Chukwunedu Aguolu, *Nigerian Civil War, 1967–1970: An Annotated Bibliography* (Boston: G. K. Hall, 1973).

signed to make it impossible for the eastern province to support itself through the sale of its considerable oil reserves.[164] The military silence was broken by a dramatic invasion on August 9 of the midwestern province by eastern forces. This spurred the central government into action, and until Biafra's unconditional surrender on January 15, 1970, the federal government's army engaged in sustained military operations against the secessionists, punctuated only by two Biafran counteroffensives.[165] A major turning point in the war occurred in January 1968. In "one of the most effective federal moves of the conflict," Gowon announced that the Nigerian currency would be changed and the entire operation would be completed by January 22. Individuals could exchange up to N£30 each, while most businesses could exchange N£600.[166] In a mere nineteen days, the old Nigerian currency would be worthless. As the finance commissioner, Chief Obafemi Awolowo, suggested, the move was taken to prevent Biafra from using Nigerian currency to finance its war. Biafra had three significant sources of the old notes: its reserves, currency held by the population, and close to N£40 million taken from central banks overrun by the Biafran forces in the east and midwest.[167]

The Biafran government had been converting its Nigerian currency in order to raise foreign exchange, usually at less than one-half of the official rate of exchange. In order to prevent the black market rate from declining even further, these conversions were done gradually. With the announcement of the new currency, the eastern province was forced to engage in panic selling. The government there gathered all of the pounds it could, a process including mandatory surrender of the currency by the general population (in exchange for credits), and then dispatched agents to Europe with the money. The international currency markets were flooded with old Nigerian notes. One speculator was reported to have bought N£50,000 at U.S.$0.14/N£. The day after the exchange deadline, N£230,000 in old Nigerian notes was found in seven abandoned suitcases in a London airport. Months later, N£300,000 worth turned up in Rome.[168]

---

[164] John J. Stremlau, *The International Politics of the Nigerian Civil War* (Princeton: Princeton University Press, 1977), pp. 73, 76; also Critchley, "Defeat of Biafra," p. 8. The strategy was designed to isolate the eastern province from the rest of the world. Economic sanctions proscribed the import or export of Nigerian currency notes and bank transfers from the eastern region. (Niven, *War of Nigerian Unity*, p. 105).

[165] Zdenek Cervenka, *A History of the Nigerian Civil War 1967–70* (Ibidan: Onibonoje Press, 1972), p. 50

[166] At that point, both the Nigerian pound and the British pound were equivalent to $2.40

[167] John de St. Jorre, *The Brothers' War: Biafra and Nigeria* (Boston: Houghton Mifflin, 1972), p. 187 (quote); "Nigeria: Banknotes and Biafra," *West Africa*, January 6, 1968, p. 25; Niven, *War of Nigerian Unity*, p. 163.

[168] Niven, *War of Nigerian Unity*, pp. 163–64; de St. Jorre, *Brothers' War*, p. 187; Stremlau, *Nigerian Civil War*, p. 221; "After the Currency Change," *West Africa*, January 13, 1968, p. 53; and "Nigeria: Federal Forces Approach Onitsha," ibid., January 20, 1968, p. 82.

The federal note exchange "dealt a massive blow to [Biafra's] financial resources." At the outbreak of hostilities, accounts belonging to the former eastern province contained over $20 million (N£8.3 million) in foreign exchange reserves, but these were run down quickly at the start of the war. The Nigerian blockade effectively prevented Biafra from exporting oil. The Ojukwu government was able to raise considerable amounts of federal pounds through invasions and forced exchange, but these were now worthless. The most conservative estimates place the loss to Biafra from the currency conversion at N£30 million, but whatever the potential purchasing power lost, the conversion left the Ojukwu government virtually bankrupt.[169]

The thesis that the currency conversion was the major turning point in the war is supported by three principal arguments. First, the eventual outcome, federal victory and unconditional surrender, had not been the only likely resolution. Second, the much more limited reserves that the secessionists were able to raise sustained Biafra for some time. Third, both central decision-makers and outside observers considered the currency issue a crucial one.

At the start of the war, there was no reason to expect an easy Nigerian victory. Biafra had a number of logistical advantages: at 30,000 square miles it was about the size of South Carolina, and its population was among the largest in Africa. The federal government possessed an army of only seven thousand men, mostly northerners, some of whom had to be stationed in the west to maintain federal control there. That army was in poor shape, with little armor and no tanks. Perhaps even more important, between the coups and normal retirements, the federal army was left with only five of the fifty-seven officers who had been commissioned prior to independence in 1960. A report issued by the International Institute of Strategic Studies was pessimistic about the federal army's chances of mounting a successful military campaign in 1968, noting that "[t]he Nigerian army . . . was never intended as an instrument of invasion."[170]

Further, Nigeria could not afford a long war. Although its finances were certainly in better shape than Biafra's, the war was taking its toll. One report noted that an extension of the war past March 1968 would have "grave financial and economic consequences."[171] This suggests that any factor that affected Biafra's ability to prolong the war would be significant. The loss of (at least) N£30 million was a staggering blow to the Biafrans, and did undermine

---

[169] de St. Jorre, *Brothers' War*, p. 187 (quote); Stremlau, *Nigerian Civil War*, p. 220; Nafziger, *Nigerian-Biafran War*, p. 165. The forcible exchange of Nigerian notes alone netted the Biafran government N£41 million (Nafziger, *Nigerian-Biafran War*, p. 164), which is one reason why other estimates put the loss at over N£50 million.

[170] Stremlau, *Nigerian Civil War*, pp. 70, 72, 149 (quote).

[171] "The Cost of the War," *West Africa*, January 20, 1968, p. 57. For more on this issue, see "The War Budget," "The Economy and the War—1," and "The Economy and the War—2," *West Africa*, May 11, 1968, pp. 543–54; June 15, 1968, p. 683; and June 22, 1968, p. 718.

its ability to sustain the war effort. (The entire country of Nigeria spent only N£17.7 million on defense *and* internal security in 1966.) Precious foreign exchange was subsequently counted by the hundreds of thousands, not millions, of pounds. As Ojukwu later noted, "The only source of income available to us was the hard currency spent by the churches. . . . It wasn't much, but enough to sustain us." These expenditures provided Biafra with foreign exchange because of a legal mechanism created by the government. In order to spend money on goods and services in Biafra, one had to pay hard currency to an Ibo-controlled bank in London, which would then authorize the "release" of the "equivalent" amount of new local currency, issued by the Ojukwu regime. One observer estimated that of the £1,153,000 in foreign revenue Biafra was apparently able to earn from April to September 1968, about £613,000 was raised through this mechanism, by payments of hard currency from aid organizations and missionaries. (The rest came primarily from selling assets, such as jewelry.) During the course of the war, it was estimated that relief organizations provided Biafra with a minimum of £1.5 million and a maximum of £8.5 million in hard currency.[172]

The assessment of the participants confirms the logical conclusion of the preceding analysis: that the currency manipulation introduced by the Gowon regime was a devastating blow to the secessionists. Major General Alexander Madiebo, commander of the Biafran Army from September 1967 to the end of the war, stated:

> The Biafran financial disaster, if not a total collapse as a result of the change in currency by Nigeria in January 1968, was the most important single reason why we lost the war. At the end of the financial chaos which followed in Biafra, we had lost over 50 million pounds which could have made a world of difference in our favor. . . . As a result of that fantastic financial loss, Biafra found it difficult to support her army at war.[173]

Madiebo lays the blame for the disaster at the door of the political leadership, which he felt should have anticipated the Nigerian tactic and countered it. Ojukwu does not argue with this, admitting that his failure to issue Biafran currency and exchange Nigerian currency faster was "one of his greatest mis-

[172] On defense expenditures, Nafziger, *Nigerian-Biafran War*, p. 128. On the payments mechanism and the 1968 estimates, Kennedy Lindsay, "Financing Biafra's War," *West Africa*, October 19, 1968, pp. 1228–29; see also the correspondence relating to this essay, ibid., November 2, 23, 1968. Quote is from Stremlau, *Nigerian Civil War*, p. 239; minima and maxima are from de St. Jorre, *Brothers' War*, p. 250. Nafziger reports that relief agencies spent £3.5 million and mission agencies only £800,000. He also accounts for another million: £750,000 sent from Ibos abroad, £150,000 from "Aid Biafra" groups in the West, and £100,000 in new Nigerian currency from the four million Ibos still living in the other parts of Nigeria.

[173] Alexander A. Madiebo, *The Nigerian Revolution and the Biafran War* (Enugu: Fourth Dimension Publishers, 1980), pp. 381–82.

takes." (He does note, though, that "economic advisors" told him the federal government did not have the technical expertise necessary to effect a conversion of the currency.) From that point on, Ojukwu claimed, the Biafrans never had more than £1 million on hand at any time for military procurement.[174]

In summary, the federal government of Nigeria engaged in a highly successful act of predatory currency manipulation against the secessionist republic of Biafra. This action robbed Biafra of its international purchasing power and was one of the most important events in the war. The technique was virtually costless to the Nigerian government, and the effects of the manipulation were felt immediately.[175] The variations on the specific technique employed in this episode could be of potential use not only in civil wars, but also in cases involving shared monetary assets, large foreign exchange holdings, and currency substitution.[176]

3.5 The Theory and Practice of Currency Manipulation

The purpose of this chapter has been to explore the mechanics of currency manipulation and demonstrate that it has been practiced by states. The analysis shed some light on the strengths, weaknesses, and nuances associated with the exercise of this form of monetary power and began to explore the issue of success and failure.[177] The questions of existence and demonstration have been put to rest. Nine specific settings that featured currency manipulation have been introduced, involving sixteen different agents engaging in twenty-four distinct influence attempts.[178] These episodes featured the prac-

---

[174] Stremlau, *Nigerian Civil War*, p. 221. During the war, Ojukwu also noted that the currency crisis was the "biggest test of confidence" for the Biafran people. C. Odomegwu Ojukwu, *Biafra: Selected Speeches and Random Thoughts of C. Odomegwu Ojukwu* (New York: Harper and Row, 1969), p. 52. For a negative portrayal of Ojukwu, see Htieyong U. Akpan, *The Struggle for Secession, 1966–1970: A Personal Account of the Nigerian Civil War* (London: Frank Cass, 1972). The author was the chief secretary to the government and head of the civil service of "Eastern Nigeria," 1966–1970; Akpan, not a member of the inner circle, opposed the war but remained at his post, where he "worked for a peaceful settlement" (p. 62).

[175] Had the manipulation not occurred, it is still likely that Biafra would not have defeated the Nigerian army. But the Biafran strategy was not to conquer the rest of Nigeria but rather (at least after August 1967) to hold out until Nigeria became exhausted or abandoned the effort under the weight of world opinion. The manipulation was able to seriously undermine Biafra's effective staying power, and the price it could extract from the central government for victory. Thus the practice of monetary power determined the course and may have determined the outcome of the war. This is especially true with regard to the terms of the surrender (unconditional). A stronger Biafra might have been able to reach a more attractive negotiated settlement.

[176] For more on currency substitution, see Chapter 5.

[177] Many of the issues in this section also raise questions regarding the potential for the practice of currency manipulation. These issues will be explored more fully in Part III.

[178] This does not represent the universe of cases of currency manipulation, nor does it even

tice of all four forms of currency manipulation and numerous techniques of implementing each of those forms. Monetary power was exercised consciously, under a variety of fixed and flexible exchange regimes, in virtually every corner of the globe, throughout the twentieth century.

Table 3.5 catalogues the cases discussed in this chapter. The influence attempts are evaluated as "success," "failure," or "mixed." A mixed outcome has elements of both success and failure. For example, the Japanese manipulation against China was in some ways very successful: it cost the target a great deal, increased the possibility for Japan's victory in the war, and was very inexpensive (in fact it was highly profitable). But the manipulation was never able totally to destroy the Chinese currency, which was its primary goal.

The influence attempts are also categorized as "major" or "minor." The judgment that an influence attempt was in some way a minor effort usually is based on the action's explaining only a small amount of the outcome. The table shows sixteen successes (nine major), three failures (all major), and five mixed outcomes (three major). This provides support for the hypothesis that monetary diplomacy will be a highly effective tool for those states in a position to practice it. Each of the episodes contains lessons with regard to the practice of currency manipulation. The mixed cases should be especially informative, since they have elements of both success and failure captured within one influence attempt, providing the closest thing available to a controlled experiment. The nominal failures not only help define the limits of monetary power, but also, unexpectedly, further reinforce its theoretical viability. Even a failure such as the U.S. passive manipulation against the Mexican peso inflicted real economic damage, forcing devaluation of first 35 percent and then 60 percent; and this was in the absence of predatory acts.

The issue of the causes of success and failure is considered more systematically in Part III, but already some patterns have emerged, which will contribute to this analysis. One is that positive manipulation was in general more successful than its negative forms. This may be because such manipulation is easier to implement. Given this conclusion, there should be numerous opportunities for passive manipulation. On the other hand, it may be that this form of monetary power is vulnerable to feedback: that the withdrawal of support might undermine other goals. This did occur in the Mexican case, which was a source of the failure of monetary diplomacy in that episode. The study of non interventionist episodes in general is hampered by the fact that such episodes might prove elusive to the observer.

Finally, it was suggested in Chapter 2, and noted with regard to the Suez case, that the most effective attempts at manipulation would be those that

---

represent an exhaustive list of those episodes discussed in this book. Other chapters refer to episodes of monetary diplomacy in general and currency manipulation in particular, which are not necessarily examined as separate cases.

TABLE 3.5
The Practice of Currency Manipulation

Agent/Year	Target	Form	Technique	Evaluation	Major/Minor
France/1911	Germany	Predatory	Withdrawals	Mixed	Minor
Britain/1915–1917	Britain	Protective	Purchases	Success	Major
Germany/1916	Russia	Predatory	Sales	Failure	Major
U.S./1917–1918	Britain	Permissive	Diversion	Success	Major
Germany/1917	Germany	Protective	Purchases	Mixed	Major
U.S./1918	France	Protective	Purchases	Success	Minor
Germany/1918	India	Predatory	Rhetoric	Mixed	Minor
U.S./1918–1919	India	Protective	Sales	Success	Major
Japan/1935–1945	China	{ Predatory	Sales	Mixed	Major
		{ Predatory	Puppet issues	Mixed	Major
U.S./1935–1939	China	Protective	Purchases	Success	Major
Britain/1939–1940	China	Protective	Intervention	Mixed	Major
U.S.–Britain/1941–1945	China	Protective	Intervention	Success	Major

Case/Date	Country	Type	Action	Outcome	Stakes
U.S./1935–1937	Mexico	Protective	Purchases	Success	Major
		Protective	Sales (gold)	Success	Minor
U.S./1938–1939	Mexico	Passive	Suspension	Failure	Major
U.S./1940	Mexico	Protective	Purchases	Success	Minor
U.S./1937	Brazil	Protective	Sales	Success	Minor
U.S.–Britain/1936–1939	France	Permissive	Acquiescence	Success	Major
Germany/1942–1945	Britain	Predatory	Forfeiting	Failure	Major
U.S./1944	India	Protective	Transfers	Success	Minor
U.S./1944–1956	Britain	Permissive	Acquiescence	Success	Major
U.S./1956	Britain	Predatory	Sales	Success	Major
		Predatory	Block IMF	Success	Major
		Passive	Indifference	Success	Major
U.S./1956	Britain	Protective	New loans	Success	Major
Australia/1956	Britain	Protective	Purchases	Success	Minor
Nigeria/1968	Biafra	Predatory	New issue	Success	Major

worked with market forces. While this may be the case, a surprising number of successful attempts worked in direct contradiction to market forces, either because the manipulation added new information that mitigated those forces, or because the manipulation simply overwhelmed them. This was especially true in the protective cases.

Currency Manipulation and Economic Statecraft

Part I introduced a number of dimensions along which instruments of economic power can be evaluated. These dimensions can now be examined with regard to the practice as well as the theory of currency manipulation. One of these dimensions was feedback, or the possibility that the use of a certain instrument of power would undermine other goals. Feedback was observed in two of the episodes, the Mexican case and the Nazi counterfeiting case. While concerns for how the exercise of monetary diplomacy would affect other policy goals determined the extent to which and the methods by which monetary power was practiced in the Mexican case, few general conclusions can be drawn. This is because the source of the feedback was completely unrelated to the exercise of monetary power. Any other form of coercion would have been subject to the same type of feedback. The German counterfeiting case, though, introduced a form of feedback that is special to monetary power: the manipulation of one currency may affect other currencies or monetary arrangements in an undesired way. While this "environmental feedback" was not important in any of the other cases considered, the phenomenon does represent a generalizable limit to the freedom from feedback which currency manipulation enjoys. The nature of this limit is important for understanding the potential for monetary diplomacy, and this concept will also be revisited in Part III.

Other potential limits on the utility of economic coercion include defense and circumvention. In none of the cases was there the opportunity for circumvention. As expected, posing a direct attack, rather than an interruption, monetary sanctions cannot be outmaneuvered. In World War I, for example, embargos could be circumvented through a diversion of trade through third parties. Currency manipulation during the war, though, could be defended against, but not circumvented.[179]

Attempts at defense against currency manipulation were observed in a number of cases, and those attempts raise a number of interesting points. First, defense itself can be costly, as it usually involves painful deflationary measures and economic sacrifice in general. Second, defense may require finding

---

[179] Defense against an embargo would, for example, involve a shift to substitute products that were produced domestically.

a protector. This could mean that defense against manipulation may in some cases involve the voluntary establishment of a dependent relationship. The potential importance of benefactors also suggests that the success of currency manipulation might be dependent on the distribution of economic and military power in the international system. One possibility is that when power is concentrated, currency manipulation is more likely to succeed, while a system with more dispersed power might feature a greater number of dependent relationships.

Part I also introduced a number of concepts involving the "efficiency" of various forms of economic coercion. This consideration included the issues of publicity and freedom from domestic politics. The ability of the agent of currency manipulation to exercise that power privately or publicly depending on its preference, and the importance of this characteristic of currency manipulation, was revealed in a number of cases. The Nazi pound-forging scheme required utmost secrecy. On the other hand, the Tripartite Monetary Agreement was purposefully public. The Mexican case showed how public actions (the suspension of regular silver purchases) can be used for signaling, while quiet measures (the continued purchase of Mexican silver against the wishes of domestic silver and oil interests) can be used discreetly to calibrate (and in this case soften) the extent of the sanction. This example also highlights the relative independence that the central government has in exercising monetary power. In the Mexican case, the exercise of monetary power was continuously at odds with organized and powerful domestic interests. Often, currency manipulation can be exercised without challenging organized interests, or it can be engaged in without those groups even realizing their interests are being subverted. In the Suez case, only a handful of people in the U.S. government were even aware of what was going on. The other cases provide support for the argument that monetary issues simply have less domestic political ramifications than do trade or aid issues. Interestingly, powerful organized economic interests were not very successful in influencing monetary power even in those cases when public legislation was involved.

A number of other important general findings emerge from the episodes explored in this Chapter. They have to do with the speed, cost, flexibility, and weight of currency manipulation. The dramatic weight, or influence, of monetary power has already been reviewed above. The performance of currency manipulation along the three other dimensions has been similarly remarkable. In the Suez case, the speed of monetary power was decisive—the effect was almost instantaneous—and any form of coercion that would have taken more than just a few days to have effect would probably not have been successful. The speed of protective power in surmounting major economic crises was seen in the Indian and Chinese cases.

The low cost of most of the influence attempts involving monetary power is as striking as the speed of those efforts. In most of the cases examined, the manipulation was either costless or even profitable. In the cases that did involve cost, such as the establishment and guarantee of stabilization funds, the expenses were relatively low (especially relative to their returns). The low cost of currency manipulation does not mean that any state can practice it, however. In most cases, the costless transactions, such as the sale of silver to India or the purchase of silver from China, require large and ready resources: in the first case, an available store of silver, and in the second case, gold and currency with which to purchase silver. Even the completely costless rhetorical support or subversion of currency depends to some extent on the credibility and importance of the source.

The episodes of currency manipulation discussed above also reveal it to be a remarkably flexible instrument of state power. Different techniques of manipulation were employed in support of similar goals, depending on the prevailing circumstances. Currency manipulation can take the form of a speech made by a central banker at a press conference, sales of counterfeit currency in black markets by covert agents, or the simple refusal to step forward with vital aid. This instrument of coercion can also be used with varying degrees of intensity: the same technique can be used to offer a mild warning signal or represent a predatory act designed to annihilate the target currency. On the other hand, short of annihilation, a temporary monetary sanction leaves no scars. Public trade sanctions can disrupt private economic relationships permanently, and leave feelings of mistrust between states in their wake. Discreet monetary sanctions, however, can be employed without long-term disruptive or political implications. Thus currency manipulation might be an easier tool to use against traditionally friendly states than a suspension of trade or aid. Finally, and related to the issue of freedom from domestic politics, currency manipulation has been shown to be flexible in its ability to surmount obstacles that would prevent other forms of influence from being exercised. One example of this was the ability of the United States to provide vital support to China during its war with Japan, when most forms of support were barred by strict U.S. neutrality laws.

The Varieties of Currency Manipulation

The case studies have also added to the understanding of how the four basic forms (and their respective techniques) of manipulation differ from one another, and how different international regimes affect their practice. One observation is that negative currency manipulation will in general be less costly than positive manipulation. In fact, most of the cases considered actually involved profits for the predators, even though the goal of those operations was not profit maximization. Passive manipulation is by definition costless or profitable (relative to the status quo ante manipulation). With regard to positive manipulation, the surprising finding is that the cases considered above suggest that permissive actions are generally more expensive than protective ones. This is because protective actions often involve exchanges instead of grants. Permissive manipulation, on the other hand, requires the renunciation of specific economic steps that would benefit the home economy and normally be taken. These opportunity costs, though less obvious, can be substantial. Less surprisingly, interventionist measures will have a greater impact on the target than non-interventionist ones. What should be noted, however, is that this distinction does not necessarily hold across cases. That is, passive manipulation directed at one target may be more consequential than predatory manipulation directed at another.

The international regime was shown to have a profound effect on how currency manipulation is exercised.[180] Episodes involving commodity standards, for example, differ from other examples with regard to the domestic economy of the target. In cases such as the Agadir crisis and the first Indian case, encashment of notes for bullion by private citizens within the target country was more important than the loss of reserves from domestic to foreign control. Under a commodity standard, domestic banks become both a primary conduit for encashment (and reserve loss) as well as a potential source of instability in and of themselves when withdrawals threaten the solvency of individual banks. The potential of domestic flight from the local currency is shared to lesser extent by other monetary regimes.

Fixed exchange rate regimes in general have the distinction of being the least publicly vulnerable. That is, a state under one such regime could have its reserves come under tremendous pressure, but the extent of that pressure would be masked until reserve statistics were published.[181] As seen in newspaper reports during the Suez crisis, private agents can be completely unaware of major shifts in the reserve position. Therefore, states under fixed-rate regimes may have more time to act than those with floating currencies. Additionally, since the extent of the problem is shielded, at least temporarily, it is less likely that a run on the reserves under such a regime would be self-perpetuating or self-fulfilling, features of crises under the other monetary regimes that can be more damaging than the initial crisis itself. On the other hand, if states value their membership in a given international monetary system, then they might be compelled to take actions that increase the pressure from currency manipulation. For example, under a gold-exchange standard, states are required to defend the value of their currencies. Under a regime of floating exchange rates, states can choose not to intervene. They would not be bound to react to currency manipulation. Thus states under fixed-rate regimes,

[180] As discussed in Part I and in this chapter, the regime type also affects the distribution of capabilities and vulnerabilities in the system with regard to monetary power.

[181] It would be apparent that the currency was under selling pressure in the markets, but the extent of that pressure would not necessarily be obvious.

less vulnerable to self-inflammatory movements, may have fewer options with regard to the way they respond to coercion.

States usually do react, though, to the best of their abilities, as seen in the Mexican case. One of the findings from this chapter that should not be under-emphasized is the importance that states place on the stability and "strength" of their currencies, even under floating rates. Such attributes of the currency, which make up its reputation, are seen as reflecting the strength and stability of the issuing government as well. This is true whether markets are official, as in the China case, or in third markets, as they were during World War I. In all cases, governments' concern for the value and stability of their currencies reflected something much greater than the narrow economic consequences of those attributes, even though, as the cases above reveal, those consequences could be quite severe.

4

Monetary Dependence

Introduction

This chapter looks at monetary dependence, or, more specifically, the exploitation of such dependence. As discussed in Part I, such dependence results from three factors: (1) the asymmetric distribution of benefits of membership in an international monetary system[1], (2) the costs of exiting such a system, and (3) changes in the preferences of the target. Asymmetric benefits result from the fact that because of their economic size, small members gain relatively more from their association with the core state than the latter gains from its association with them. This issue has been explored with regard to trade by Hirschman[2], and, as shown earlier, holds true for international currency relations as well. To review briefly, small states individually provide relatively little to the system, but derive increased stability, protection, expertise, and significant privileges with regard to trade, access to finance, and more. The costs of exit involve the loss of these advantages, which can be aggregated as the one-time economic dislocations associated with the transition from membership to nonmembership, or to membership in a new system. These costs, which vary greatly from case to case, can be considerable. Finally, participation in the system influences the domestic political economy of the member state in a way that makes its interests converge toward the interests of the core state. It must be stressed once again that the term "dependence," as employed here, refers to a political relationship: the exploitation of monetary dependence in order to coerce other states or alter their preferences. Economic flows are not unidirectional, nor are they the focus of attention here; actually, the "victims" in these cases will often be net economic winners.

---

[1] Some terminology: "core" refers to a currency at the center of an international monetary system. "System" refers to all of the formal and informal arrangements associated with a given core currency—it is the broadest term used here. An "area" is a currency system with a recognized core and established patterns and practices, with few or no legal barriers to trade and exchange between members and nonmembers. A "zone" is a restricted area with rules that give preferences to members over nonmembers. A "bloc" is a zone where the core currency is not freely convertible into other core currencies or recognized commodity bases. For example, in the sterling system, the pound was the core currency. The system was an area until 1931, when it became a zone, and then a bloc in 1939. In 1958, with the restoration of full convertibility, it was once again a zone.

[2] Albert O. Hirschman, *National Power and the Structure of Foreign Trade* (Berkeley: University of California Press, 1980).

The Theory of Monetary Dependence

The Forms of Monetary Dependence

There are four principal ways in which monetary dependence[3] is exploited: through enforcement, expulsion, extraction, and entrapment. *Enforcement* is the manipulation of the rules of the system in order to sanction (or support) member states. This can take place in two ways, reflecting the fact that dependence comes from two sources. First, it can involve the suspension of privileges within the framework of the system. Alternatively, enforcement can involve taking advantage of the fact that the target state's economy has been reshaped by its participation in a given international currency system. For example, if the target country depends on the core currency for transactions (and not simply reserves) the core country can move to interrupt the flow of such currency for a period of time.

Enforcement is a good starting point for the study of dependence because it is methodologically closest to the study of currency manipulation. Enforcement and manipulation are interesting, if ultimately distant, cousins. Manipulation attempts to coerce by altering the nature of the target's currency. Enforcement, on the other hand, is often an attempt to coerce by altering the nature and availability of the home currency, which is itself important to the target state.

Expulsion can be a conduit of power for the core state in two ways. First, it can be a simple punishment. Expelling a member of the system causes that party to lose the benefits of membership. Such a state will also incur the one-time cost of conversion from an economy based on participation in the system to one based on its own, or some other, currency. Secondly, and perhaps more usefully, expulsion provides power to the dominant state, as a coercive threat. That is, an awareness of the pain of expulsion by both core state and member state means that the former can coerce the latter simply by threatening to expel it. Assuming that the core state can make the threat credible, threats of expulsion are more useful than actual expulsion because they can change behavior, as opposed to punishing undesired acts, and they can be used over and over again. Beyond this, the implicit threat of expulsion can constrain the behavior of member states within tacitly understood boundaries.

Enforcement and expulsion are overt forms of the exploitation of monetary dependence. They take advantage of the explicit rules of the institutions, and the patterns of economic activity generated by membership in the system. These components should prove quite powerful under the right circumstances (more on this below) but there are important limitations on their use. These

---

[3] The phrase "monetary dependence" will often be used in place of the cumbersome "the exploitation of monetary dependence."

limits stem from feedback, which results from the power associated with the other two forms of monetary dependence, extraction and entrapment. The practice of enforcement and expulsion risks tempting states to abandon the system. This would cause the core state to lose the power it derives from the very existence of the system, or from the "structural" forms of dependence.

Extraction is the use of the rules and consequences of the system to extract wealth from the member states. (To the extent that this wealth is used for security-related goals, for example, to mobilize resources for war, it is of interest here.) Most significantly, nominally dormant mechanisms of extraction can provide mechanisms for mobilizing resources to meet emergencies. Extraction can take a number of other forms, such as tribute or paying dues in order to be a member of the system. However, tribute is more likely to take subtle forms, such as various economic concessions that member states are willing to make to the core state as the price for membership.[4] Extraction in general can also be more subtle, through a process by which the leader exploits its position as issuer of the core currency for the system. Such a currency is often de facto legal tender in the member states and of restricted transfer within and beyond the system. Under such circumstances, the dominant state can create forced loans or even gifts from member states, by transferring currency to the periphery and then inhibiting its movement. Thus extraction, or the potential for extraction in an emergency, can lead core states to limit the use of enforcement or expulsion, in order to ensure continued membership by all participants. One important result of the possibility of extraction is that dominant states do not just exercise power over their dependent partners, but can gain power from them.

Entrapment is the most fascinating form of the exploitation of monetary dependence. On one hand, it is a powerful instrument of coercion, like enforcement or expulsion. On the other hand, it derives its power from the structure of the system, as does extraction, and therefore it is also a net inhibitor of the use of the two overt components. This is important, because entrapment represents not simply a means of power, as do the other forms—it is the primary goal for core states. Although most states welcome the opportunity to wield the other forms of monetary dependence, their primary motivation for leading monetary systems, often at considerable cost, is to reap the benefits of entrapment. It should be noted that this creates a visibility problem for some aspects of the study of dependence.[5]

---

[4] Once again, *net* economic benefits for the member can be positive, if it values the rewards from participation in the system more than it does the price of the tribute.

[5] With regard to entrapment and threats of expulsion, successful implementation of techniques associated with these forms of monetary power may be hard to identify. This is because such successes preempt unwelcome behavior, as opposed to reversing it. Evidence can be marshaled to support the hypothesis of entrapment, such as a demonstration of the degree of dependence, or an observation of behavior that would be incongruous in the absence of such dependence. But ulti-

Entrapment is the transformation of interests that results from participation in a currency system. Entrapment takes place at two levels: at the level of the firm (or, more accurately, the sector) and the level of the government. Many of these issues have been explored in analyses of the effects of trade,[6] but they carry over to monetary relations, in some respects to an even greater extent. Firms and sectors engage in patterns of activity based on economic incentives. This constellation of incentives is transformed when a state accepts membership in a monetary system. Decisions based on these new incentives give firms a stake in their nations' continued participation in the system, and they will direct their political energies to that end. Further, the simple act of participation in the system strengthens those who benefit from the system relative to those who do not (by definition). This strength should translate into political power. Thus, participation in a currency system shifts the preferences of the nation as a whole, and strengthens those who most value continued membership in the system.

Although none addressed the monetary implications, studies of trade relations laid down the foundations and implications of these findings: (1) sectors will respond to external economic incentives, and (2) these groups will form political coalitions to advance their interests. Hirschman showed how this can affect international politics. He argued that "these regions or industries will exert a powerful influence in favor of a "friendly' attitude toward the state to the imports of which they owe their existence."[7]

Such considerations can also be forged by monetary dependence. (Actually, this was very much the case in the "trade" episode examined by Hirschman, as will be discussed below.) In fact, monetary considerations usually operate at an additional level. As with trade, monetary arrangements change interests

---

mately it is very difficult to measure the extent to which the relationships under consideration have caused desired, or altered undesired, preferences in the absence of overt coercion. Finally, even if the case has been established, and the outcome of inaction is logically attributable to dependence, determining the degree of the success (or relative importance or absolute strength of monetary power) is a subtle, and therefore even more challenging, undertaking.

This is compounded by a numbers problem. Because of the hierarchical nature of international currencies, there have not been a large number of distinct monetary systems—few states are capable of leading such organizations. (Thus, one would expect fewer episodes involving dependence and disruption than episodes involving manipulation.) Given the number of forms and conditions described above, it may be difficult to establish generalizable conclusions from the episodes considered. At the very least, a sensitivity to the restrictions imposed by the number of cases is important. The two primary goals, though, demonstration and enhanced understanding of the mechanics of dependence, should not be greatly affected by this problem.

[6] Hirschman, *National Power*; Charles P. Kindleberger, "Group Behavior and International Trade" (1951; reprinted in Kindleberger, *Economic Response* [Cambridge: Harvard University Press, 1986]); Peter Gourevitch, *Politics in Hard Times* (Ithaca, N.Y.: Cornell University Press, 1986).

[7] Hirschman, *National Power*, p. 29. On sectors, see Kindleberger, "Group Behavior"; on coalitions, see Gourevitch, "Hard Times."

OVERT   STRUCTURAL

Expulsion   Enforcement   Extraction   Entrapment

Low   Moderate   Moderate   High

RELATIVE UTILITY FOR CORE STATE

Figure 4.1 The Forms of Monetary Dependence

and strengthen "rightminded" (from the perspective of the core state) interest group coalitions that exercise political power in the member state. Further, as a result of this, member governments' preferences should shift as a result of both changing domestic political realities and an altered national interest, which is increasingly harmonious with that of the core state, other things being equal. Monetary power fosters even greater entrapment, moreover, because governments are an important, in fact, the dominant, monetary participant.

In contrast to most trade transactions, the member government is likely to have a stake in monetary affairs. It will also usually come to hold significant balances of the core currency. The government of the member state therefore has a direct interest in the fortunes of that currency. For example, in order to preserve the value of its assets, such as reserves, it does not want to see the value of that currency decline. This will also give member governments an interest in the more general political fortunes of the core state itself, which will, especially in the case of war, importantly affect the future value of the core currency. The power of entrapment is that it can alter the preferences of states without resort to threats or coercion.

In sum, leaders of monetary systems gain power over the dependent participants, and in some cases gain power from them as well. There are a number of conduits through which this power can be channeled. Some of these powers are limited, however, especially in their "traditional," or overt, implementation, to the extent that the potential gains from the structural components deter the use of overt ones. These forms of power are presented schematically in Figure 4.1.

The Conditions for Dependence

Two broad factors determine the prospects for the exploitation of dependence: the prevailing global economic conditions, and the degree of economic and political asymmetry between the core state and a given member or potential member of its system. The prevailing global economic conditions, broadly, the existence and degree of "prosperity" or "depression" in the international economy, determine the opportunity cost of nonmembership in a monetary system.[8] During general prosperity, the benefits from participation in a given system are at their relative nadir. Whatever the benefits of membership, the ability to replace them would tend to be greatest at this time. With global demand high, guaranteed markets are less important. If temporary balance-of-payments difficulties do arise, short-term financing should be available, because of the prospects for the potential debtor and the soundness of potential creditors. During depression, all of these conditions are reversed, and the benefits of membership are maximized. The ability to exploit monetary dependence directly depends on these opportunity costs. The higher the costs, the greater the power of overt threats, and the more punishment will be tolerated without unilateral withdrawal from the system.

Economic conditions are a vital, but not the only, determinant of the opportunity to exploit monetary dependence. A second fundamental consideration is the nature of each bilateral relationship between core and member. This relationship has an economic and a political component, and these components can in turn be further subdivided. The economic component has three important elements: the economic attractiveness of the core, the economic development of the member, and the extent and nature of their traditional economic relationship. The economic attractiveness of the core (specifically, to the member) affects the relationship through the same opportunity cost mechanism as do global economic conditions. The economic development of the member reflects its ability to adjust to new conditions, and thus is a measure of that state's ability to maneuver. For example, economies based on one commodity are less flexible and therefore more vulnerable than highly differentiated ones.

The extent and nature of the economic relationship between core and member also establishes opportunity costs. The former is the familiar Hirschmanesque mechanism. It is significant independent of prevailing economic conditions because involvement in a system with an important partner during prosperity provides insurance against eventual recession. The latter (the nature of the relationship) is more a monetary phenomena: regardless of size, states can be net sources or drains of foreign exchange. This can result from trade balances or financial flows, such as debt service. Dependent states that are net sources of foreign exchange will be better able to protect themselves than those that are net drains, because of feedback effects for the core state.

The political component of the relationship between core and member is simpler, involving the potential for political domination of the small state by the larger one. Even in the absence of economic incentives, militarily domi-

---

[8] "The opportunity costs of non-membership" is a bit cumbersome, but technically accurate. It is what one gives up by *not* being a member state, which, discounting transition costs, is equivalent to the cost of the loss of the benefits of membership to an exiting state. This cost is primarily relevant to member states, so the phrase "nonmembership" might be confusing. Therefore, the short phrase "opportunity cost" will be used. Higher opportunity costs reflect greater costs of exit.

Relative Bilateral Economic-Political

Position of the Core

		Strong	*Not Strong*
Global	*Prosperity*	Moderate	Low
Economic			
Conditions			
	Depression	Very High	Moderate

Figure 4.2 The Opportunity for Monetary Dependence

nant states may be able to bully weaker ones into economic relationships and agreements they might not otherwise initiate. This depends on the ability of the core state to bully each particular partner, and the ability of small states to find an external protector. For example, during the interwar period, because of its geographic position (and other factors), Belgium was less likely than Bulgaria to be forced into an unattractive exchange agreement with Germany.

These considerations can be summarized in a two-by-two matrix, which is presented in Figure 4.2. The vertical axis indicates general global economic conditions, represented by the ideal types of "prosperity" and "depression." The horizontal axis shows the relative position of the core to the member. (This is different for each pair of states.) This dimension is represented by the types "strong" and "not strong," and is an amalgamation of all of the bilateral economic and political elements discussed above.

Focal Case: The Mark Bloc and Entrapment

The German international monetary experience in the 1930s featured the most coordinated and aggressive exploitation of monetary dependence ever attempted. The German government completely subordinated its international monetary relations to overall political considerations. Germany was particularly well suited both to foster and to exploit monetary dependence in this era. Since Germany was a very powerful state in the midst of a major world depression, our theory would suggest that such opportunities would be very high. Furthermore, the illiberal economic ideology of the German government did not stand in the way of the overt politicization of monetary affairs. Ideological concerns, which might inhibit the exercise of monetary diplomacy by some states (Great Britain being the most obvious example), actually contributed to German efforts.

The primary targets of these efforts were the small states of southern and eastern Europe. It is generally accepted that German national strategy, at least after 1934, called for an economic mobilization for warfare, and the establishment of economic self-sufficiency within continental Europe. These objectives were pursued to facilitate the German national strategy directed at the domination of all Europe. In retrospective analyses, what stands out from this era most prominently, is a *trade* strategy, employed in the service of an overall national strategy. Often overlooked in this shuffle is the vital role of monetary politics.

The employment of currency power was embedded in a trading strategy, which was further embedded in national strategy. However, as we shall see below, the fostering and exploitation of monetary dependence was critical to the employment of such a strategy. Monetary power was introduced by the Germans for three primary purposes: to insulate the domestic economy, that is, to protect it from international market forces; to entrap Germany's small neighbors, which, as defined, would alter the preferences of those states in such a way as to harmonize them with German interests; and to extract from those countries the materials needed for war.

Germany's international monetary practices during this period were fantastically complex.[9] Its ability to exploit dependence was based on the introduction and manipulation of exchange control practices, especially bilateral exchange clearing.

Exchange Control and Exchange Clearing

Exchange control can be defined in a number of ways. Technically, it includes "every form of intervention on the part of the monetary authorities . . . aiming at interfering with the tendencies affecting exchange rates." These methods of interference can be direct methods, such as intervention in the market to support exchange and the introduction of exchange restrictions, or indirect methods, such as import restrictions. Under this broad definition, almost every international monetary regime involves some degree of exchange control.[10] The study of exchange control is usually limited, therefore,

---

[9] It is highly doubtful that there was any one individual in Germany (or elsewhere) who fully understood all of the subtleties of the German exchange system. The most successful attempt to disentangle the primary regulations that I have found is U.S. Tariff Commission (U.S.T.C.), *Foreign Trade and Exchange Controls in Germany*, Report, 2d ser., no. 150, (Washington, D.C.: U.S. Government Printing Office, 1942). Also recommended is Allen Thomas Bonnell, "German Control over International Economic Relations," *Illinois Studies in the Social Sciences* 13, no. 1, (1940).

[10] Paul Einzig, *Exchange Control* (London: Macmillan, 1934), pp. 9 (quote), 11, 12, 16. Exchange control can also vary dramatically in intensity. Mild forms include unofficial and official discouragement of capital export and speculation; further measures can involve legal prohibitions on the transfer of foreign capital, and the seizure of the foreign exchange of exporters; severe measures can ultimately include the complete suspension of foreign exchange dealing. Ibid., ch. 11.

to "abnormal" (at least in the view of the analyst) intervention or temporary, exceptional official measures.

Exchange control is introduced by governments for a number of reasons, but there are three principal motivations: to defend, stabilize, and exploit. Defensive exchange control usually involves restrictions designed to prevent capital flight or a forced devaluation of the home currency. Stabilization measures are typically those taken to smooth out fluctuations in foreign exchange receipts. Exploitative exchange control can aim to secure "unfair" trade advantages, or a variety of political objectives.[11]

Most nations resort, at the very least, to defensive exchange control from time to time. Economists consider any introduction of exchange control to be inefficient, causing disequilibria by distorting prices, but recognize that such practices may be required as temporary, emergency measures.[12] One such emergency occurred in 1931, with the failure of the Austrian Creditanstalt. In the four months that followed, Germany, Hungary, Greece, Yugoslavia, Czechoslovakia, Austria, Bulgaria, Denmark, Estonia, Latvia, and Lithuania suspended the convertibility of their currencies and instituted strict exchange control.[13] In this new international environment, a number of important questions surfaced. The most general one was how trade could continue without the transfer of foreign exchange. A second important issue was the ability of creditors to receive payments from countries that had blocked international transfers.

One answer to these problems was provided by the Swiss. Hungary, in an effort to prevent the collapse of the pengö, introduced vigorous exchange control restrictions on August 8, 1931, including a provision stipulating that Hungarians would pay for imports by depositing pengö into a blocked account held by Hungary in the name of the exporting country. Switzerland, faced with the alternative of suspending exports to Hungary or accepting blocked pengö balances as payment, came up with a third alternative. With Hungary's approval, the Swiss government created a parallel blocked account in Switzerland, where Hungarian imports were paid for in Swiss francs. Local exporters would be paid, in both countries, from the blocked balances in local currencies. With balanced trade, the two accounts would cancel each other out. Trade could take place in the absence of international payments and without resort to barter: bilateral exchange clearing had been invented.[14]

---

[11] Howard S. Ellis, *Exchange Control in Central Europe* (Cambridge: Harvard University Press, 1941), ch. 1 and p. 290.

[12] Representative of this view is Charles R. Whittlesey, "Exchange Control," *American Economic Review* 22, no. 4:585–604 (1932), esp. pp. 597, 601. For a strongly negative view of exchange control, see League of Nations, *Report on Exchange Control* (Geneva: League of Nations, 1938). The report argues that control "affords no remedy . . . but results in perpetuating those difficulties, and, in certain cases, in accentuating them."

[13] League of Nations, *Report*, p. 10.

[14] Einzig, *Exchange Control*, pp. 134–36.

Bilateral exchange clearing can be modeled in the following way[15]: Two countries participate: country X and country Y. Each country has importers, I(x) and I(y), and exporters, E(x) and E(y). Each country has a clearing authority, C, usually located at its central bank. The domestic currency of country X is dollars, and the domestic currency of country Y is francs.

The two countries establish an exchange rate between dollars and francs, and a period length for the effectiveness of the agreement. The exchange rate remains unchanged during this period. This period is usually short term (three months to a year), with the expectation that it will be extended, with revisions, at the end of the period. Assume an exchange rate of $2/Fr.

Given these parameters, trade, at the individual level, takes place in the following way: Importer $I^1(x)$ purchases steel worth Fr100 million from exporter $E^1(y)$. $I^1(x)$ pays $200 million into an account held at C(x) (its own country). This account, x[Y]x, is *owned* by C(y) (the exchange authority of the exporter's country), but it is *controlled* by C(x). C(x) must therefore authorize any payments out of account x[Y]x that Y wants to make. C(x) notifies C(y) that this payment has been made. After receiving notification, C(y) can release Fr100 million, from the account y[X]y held at C(y), to $E^1(y)$. The francs in account y[X]y were deposited there by importers in Y. For example, if Importer $I^2(y)$ purchased $200 million worth of grain from $E^2(x)$, $I^2(y)$ would deposit Fr100 million to y[X]y.

Under this model, trade must balance. (These requirements will be modified below.) If, at the end of the agreement, one account has a surplus of currency, it is expected that the new agreement will be refined to eliminate it. This can take place through a change in the exchange rate, or through changes in tariffs and quotas to eliminate the surplus and bring trade into balance. Direct transfers to balance accounts are considered to be against the spirit of exchange clearing. This simple model, for the aggregate economy, is presented in Figure 4.3.[16]

Although the simple model calls for bilateral trade to balance, in practice it often does not. This result can occur for two reasons. First, an imbalance of trade may be established by the agreement for the repayment of debts. If a debtor country (X) runs a trade surplus under exchange clearing with a credi-

---

[15] This description is a simplification. Exchange-clearing agreements are complex. They vary in detail from country to country, with substantial differences in the established exchange rate, items covered under the agreement, length of the agreement, establishment of trade ratios (Swedish clauses), and provisions for side payments. The best analysis of exchange clearing I have seen is P. Nyboe Andersen, *Bilateral Exchange Clearing Policy* (London: Oxford University Press, 1946). Other useful sources include Margaret S. Gordon, *Barriers to World Trade* (New York: Macmillan, 1941); and Paul Einzig, *The Exchange Clearing System* (London: Macmillan, 1935).

[16] Each analyst of exchange control offers slightly different interpretations of various aspects of the system. The simple model presented and diagramed in this chapter is my own interpretation, drawing on the work of Gordon, *Barriers*, esp. pp. 110, 136–37, 144; Einzig, *Exchange Control*, esp. chs. 12–14; Einzig, *Exchange Clearing*; Andersen, *Bilateral*; and League of Nations, *Enquiry into Clearing Agreements* (Geneva: League of Nations, 1935).

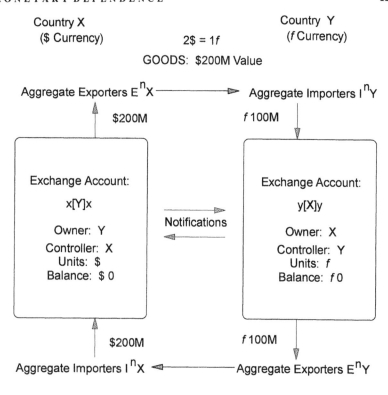

Figure 4.3 Simple Balanced Bilateral Clearing

tor country (Y), X will accumulate franc balances in y[X]y, because more importers in Y will be depositing than exporters will be withdrawing. If X and Y agree, those surplus francs can be used to pay X's debt to Y. The debt is thus paid without the international transfer of currency, but, in essence, is paid for with exports from debtor to creditor. For this reason, many Western European creditors imposed exchange clearing on their Eastern European debtors unilaterally.[17]

[17] Occasionally it was unilateral, but often it was by agreement. As is the tendency with clearing, each agreement was unique. For example, in the Swiss/Romanian agreement, it was recognized that Romania had an export surplus with Switzerland. Thus only 45 percent of the Swiss francs collected from Swiss importers of Romanian goods was used to pay Swiss exporters. Thirty-five percent was paid to Swiss exporters for exports delivered to Romania *before* the agreement (clearing blocked balances), 10 percent went to Swiss creditors against Romanian debts, and 10 percent was placed at the disposal of the Romanian government. Einzig, *Exchange Control*, p. 156. On the inclusion of payments arrangements in clearing agreements in general, see also Andersen, *Bilateral*, pp. 19, 21; Gordon, *Barriers*, pp. 121–22; League of Nations, *Enquiry*, pp. 1–3.

Trade also need not balance if one of the parties would prefer to accumulate blocked balances, rather than face a termination of the agreement. Accumulations of blocked balances will occur any time trade is imbalanced. The rate at which balances accumulate depends on the method by which the exchange authority in each country pays its exporters. Under the "waiting principle," exporters are only paid from the specific deposits of local importers. If imports are less than exports at any given time, exporters must wait for a new import, so that the importer can make a deposit into the clearing account. Under the waiting principle, exporters are paid off in the chronological order of their claims. Even if trade balances over the period of the agreement, there will naturally be times when exporters are waiting. This has a tendency to reduce liquidity and even to create negative multipliers on the economy. Therefore, although the original concept of exchange clearing envisioned the waiting principle, many participants turned to the "financing principle."

The financing principle is followed when the exchange authorities do not wait for domestic importers' payments, but pay domestic exporters with currency created (or "financed") against payments to the blocked accounts by foreigners.[18] Under the expectation of balanced trade, this is much more efficient. If trade does not balance, however, the financing principle can exacerbate the situation and result in an even greater imbalance than would have resulted under the waiting principle.[19] A diagram of unbalanced aggregate trade is presented in Figure 4.4.

Exchange agreements proliferated throughout Europe during this period, and were very important aspects of the trade of many of the states there. This was especially true in the case of Germany. Essentially, clearing is the ultimate form of exchange control, and the debate over the relative merits of such a system was similar to the debate over exchange control in general. Opponents stressed the distortions created, especially between "free" and "blocked" currencies, while proponents argued that clearing trade was superior to no trade at all.[20] Regardless, exchange control and bilateral clearing were the mechanisms through which German currency power operated.

---

[18] Andersen, *Bilateral*, pp. 37–39, 122, 150. On the economic implications of and distinctions between the two methods, see ibid., ch. 5.

[19] Under the waiting principle, if there is a "long line," or wait, exporters may be reluctant to sell. Additionally, foreign importers may have to offer higher prices to compensate for the longer wait. These two factors tend to be equilibrating with regard to the balance of trade between the two nations.

[20] At the start of 1935, there were 74 clearing agreements involving twenty-three countries. In 1936, the corresponding figures were 119 and thirty-five; in 1937, they were 151 and thirty-eight; and in 1939, they were 138 and thirty-seven. Andersen, *Bilateral*, p. 31. The League report, *Enquiry*, is critical of clearing, though members' responses to the League's survey characterized it as a "necessary evil" (p. 17). (Germany did not respond to the survey.) Einzig *Exchange Clearing* is a supporter of clearing, arguing that it (a) offers a compromise between orthodoxy and radicalism, (b) helps those states worst hit by the financial crisis, and (c) can be reformed and expanded to reduce problems associated with it (pp. viii, 8, 9, 99, 109).

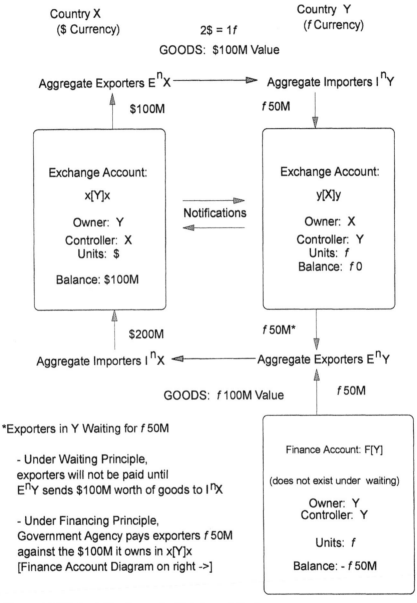

Figure 4.4 Bilateral Clearing under Unbalanced Trade

Germany and Exchange Control before the New Plan

Germany adopted exchange control measures on August 1, 1931, in the wake of the Creditanstalt collapse. Its motives were primarily defensive. Germany was in a precarious financial position, and its options were limited. Although not established for aggressive intentions, it was these mechanisms, created in the wake of this crisis and the years that followed, that were ultimately transformed into the tools of Nazi currency power.[21]

The alternative (to control) of devaluation was neither credible nor desired. It was not a credible response to the crisis, because it was common knowledge that in 1931 Germany had debts of RM26 billion, including RM15 billion in short-term liabilities, but only possessed gold and foreign exchange reserves worth RM3 billion. Instead of easing pressure on the mark, devaluation might have signaled weakness and finished it off. Devaluation was also not desired because it would have increased Germany's debt burden and heightened fears of inflation. Such fears were pervasive throughout southeastern Europe, but especially in Germany, where the mark had only been rescued from hyperinflation seven years earlier. In this region, stable money was viewed as a political necessity.[22] To prevent a flight of foreign capital, Germany introduced a series of control measures, which included provisions mandating that

1. all exchange transactions be cleared by the Reichsbank;
2. exchange take place only at the official gold parity;
3. all trade in futures be abolished;
4. the import and export of all currencies and monetary metals be prohibited; and
5. permits be required to purchase exchange.[23]

---

[21] Frank C. Child, *The Theory and Practice of Exchange Control in Germany* (The Hague: Martinus Nijhoff, 1958), p. 3; see also Ellis, *Exchange Control in Central Europe*, p. 166. Child's book is one of the more useful guides through the maze of German regulations. On the domestic financial side, see K. E. Poole, *German Financial Policies, 1932–1939* (Cambridge: Harvard University Press, 1939). On German economic thought, see Howard S. Ellis, *German Monetary Theory 1905–1933* (Cambridge: Harvard University Press, 1934), pt. 3.

[22] On the debt issue, Karl Ritter, "Germany's Experience with Clearing Agreements," *Foreign Affairs* 14, no. 3:466–75 (1936), p. 466. On inflation and political sensitivity, see Antonín Basch, *The Danube Basin and the German Economic Sphere* (New York: Columbia University Press, 1943), pp. 70–72. Basch argues, "Any change in the official parity would have increased nervousness and intensified capital flight." Ibid., p. 72. See also Child, *Exchange Control in Germany*, p. 13; Gordon, *Barriers*, p. 54. On the insufficiency of devaluation, see Paul Einzig, *Monetary Reform in Theory and Practice* (London: Kegan Paul, 1936), p. 50. Specifically on the option of adopting a floating exchange rate, see Knut Borchardt, "Could and Should Germany Have Followed Great Britain in Leaving the Gold Standard?," *Journal of European Economic History* 13, no. 3:471-97 (1984).

[23] Child, *Exchange Control in Germany*, pp. 15–16; Also U.S.T.C., *Trade and Exchange Controls*, pp. 55–57.

Despite these measures, new problems soon surfaced. The devaluation of the pound left the unchanged mark overvalued. Given Germany's unwillingness to devalue, the Brüning government attempted to solve this problem through the pursuit of a deflationary economic policy. When Brüning was overthrown, however, first Chancellor Franz von Pappen (in the second half of the year) and subsequently Hitler (after 1933) pursued inflationary policies.[24] Another problem involved the disposition of the mark balances of foreigners, which were now trapped within Germany under exchange control restrictions.[25]

The Germans now faced a multifaceted problem: how to protect the value of the mark, maintain exports given an overvalued mark, and solve the problem of the blocked balances. At this point, the Germans still considered it to be in their interest to gradually liquidate the blocked accounts in order to reestablish Germany's future creditworthiness. One integrated solution to this problem was to use blocked marks in partial payment for new transactions. Since these blocked balances were de facto devalued, Germany could implicitly manipulate the exchange rate when its officials saw fit by "watering down" international payments of transferable marks with blocked marks. And, of course, another response to these problems was an increase in bilateral agreements and clearing arrangements in order to "demonetize" trade transactions.[26]

[24] U.S.T.C., *Trade and Exchange Controls*, p. 70.

[25] At this point, there were only five types of blocked marks: (1) standstill credits, from agreements with short-term creditors; (2) blocked commercial accounts, which were proceeds from goods delivered before the controls of July 10, 1931; (3) old accounts, which were the other holdings of foreigners before that date; (4) blocked credit marks, comprising the proceeds from the sales of assets other than securities; (5) blocked security marks, which were the proceeds from the sale by foreigners of German securities in Germany. Child, *Exchange Control in Germany*, pp. 33–34. These blocked marks were frozen assets, and distinct from any accumulated marks in clearing accounts.

[26] On the blocked balances and trade, see H. K. Heuser, "The German Method of Combined Debt Liquidation and Export Stimulation," *Review of Economic Studies* 1, no. 3:210–17 (1934), pp. 210, 213. Heuser attempts to sort out the specific mechanics. Ibid., pp. 212–14. The varying rates of the balances allowed the Germans great price flexibility in trade without altering the legal value of the mark. Child reports the following values of some types of blocked marks as percentages of official gold parity:

Year	Registered	Travel	Credit	Security
1934	—	—	53.9	43.0
1935	56.3	65.6	37.3	28.2
1936	53.0	61.2	28.3	23.1
1937	51.2	61.2	22.4	21.6
1938	46.5	58.4	13.4	11.8

Child, *Exchange Control in Germany*, p. 123. For quarterly data for March 1935–December 1938, see League of Nations, *Money and Banking*, vol. 2, *Commercial and Central Banks*

During this first period of exchange control, German motives evolved. Initially, there was an attempt to defend the mark from the financial instability and crisis sweeping across the continent. Within one year, however, the goals of German policy expanded to include the maintenance of an overvalued mark, and the gradual insulation of the domestic economy from the demands and pressures of international market forces. By 1934, the aspirations of German monetary policy were again raised, and in this instance fundamentally transformed the basic purpose of German international monetary practices.

The New Plan

In the summer of 1934, the Germans encountered new exchange difficulties. In September, the New Plan was unveiled. Technically, the New Plan involved few new regulations, but rather involved a tightening of the interpretation and enforcement of old regulations, and a change in the purposes of German exchange control. Two important new features, developed during the year preceding the introduction of the New Plan, were formalized. One was a complete transfer moratorium, ending interest payments on German debts. The second was a change in the procedures for providing foreign exchange to importers. The existing quota system was replaced by a system whereby German officials would allot exchange for those exports deemed most important to the German economy.[27] The architect of the New Plan was Hjalmar Schacht. In his previous tenure in government, Schacht had been credited with ending the hyperinflation. Now, Schacht's system allowed Germany to vastly reduce the burden of its massive foreign debt, and facilitated the use of the monetary system as a political instrument.[28]

With regard to the direction of trade, the German government employed the

---

(Geneva: League of Nations, 1937 and 1939), pp. 72 and 85, respectively. On increasing bilateralism in German trade in this period, see U.S.T.C., *Trade and Exchange Controls*, chs. 4 and 5.

[27] Ellis, *Exchange Control in Central Europe*, p. 211; U.S.T.C., *Trade and Exchange Controls*, p. 113. For more on the measures leading up to the introduction of the New Plan, see Paul Einzig, *Germany's Default: The Economics of Hitlerism* (London: Macmillan , 1934), esp. 39–53, 78–86, 107–24.

[28] Karl R. Bopp, "Hjalmar Schacht: Central Banker," *University of Missouri Studies* 14, no. 1, (1939), offers a concise summary of Schacht's career. Mühlen Norbert, *Hitler's Magician: Schacht* (London: Routledge, 1938), presents a very negative portrait. Norbert argues that Schacht's "unlawful intervention against foreign creditors" won for Germany between RM17 billionand RM18.95 billion. This sum not only exceeded German reparations payments (which totaled RM10.096 billion from August 31, 1924, to June 30, 1931) but was seven times the French military budget of 1936 (pp. 212–14). Schacht's memoirs, promisingly titled *Confessions of the Old Wizard* (Boston: Houghton Mifflin, 1956), yield little insight into the intricacies of the New Plan. Exchange issues are discussed at a high level of abstraction, pp. 181–83, 189–91, 287–93, 302–5, 337. (As a point of interest, Schacht was acquitted at the Nuremburg trials.)

New Plan toward a number of specific ends. The Nazis aimed to reduce imports of finished and semifinished goods (especially from western Europe) and exports of raw materials; they also wanted to increase exports of finished goods and imports of raw materials, and to increase national self-sufficiency in general. Capital exports were also to be held to a minimum.[29]

The small nations of southeastern Europe were the logical focus of the new policy, given their geographical relationship to Germany. Much has been written about the German trade relationship with this region.[30] The focus here is on the importance of monetary power in establishing and enforcing these relationships. As one study noted,

> The German system of regulating foreign trade as developed by the National Socialist Government before the outbreak of the present war was based fundamentally upon the official control of foreign exchange transactions.[31]

Monetary influences were also important for a number of other reasons. Much of the New Plan was directed at "nullifying the importance of foreign exchange rates and foreign prices on the domestic economy." This was essential if rearmament was to take place without new inflation, which remained politically taboo in Germany.[32]

According to the theory of dependence, Germany should have been especially well placed to foster and exploit monetary dependence in this region. Germany was not only a very strong state, especially in relation to these neighbors (from both an economic and political perspective), but the prevailing economic conditions (international depression) were especially favorable for such activity. It should not be surprising, therefore, given German national strategy and economic ideology, that Germany used monetary power to achieve a number of political ends. Germany aimed to entrap those states, and to extract from them the necessary materials for its war machine. Entrapment was pursued through the practice of exchange clearing and other mechanisms that left Germany's trading partners holding large amounts of blocked marks. This created in those states a stake in both the viability of the mark and continued good relations with Germany. This entrapment is complementary to but distinct from the traditional discussions of trade dependence.

---

[29] Ellis, *Exchange Control in Central Europe*, p. 212; Child, *Exchange Control in Germany*, p. 133; Basch, *German Economic Sphere*, pp. 3, 171–72.

[30] See, for example, Hirschman, *National Power*; Basch, *German Economic Sphere*. See also Allan G. B. Fischer, "The German Trade Drive in South Eastern Europe," *International Affairs* 18, no. 2:143–70 (1939); and R. M. Spaulding, "The Political Economy of German Foreign Trade Policy in Central Europe, 1890–1960" (Ph.D. diss., Harvard University, 1989).

[31] U.S.T.C., *Trade and Exchange Controls*, p. 51.

[32] On insulation, Arthur Schweitzer, "The Role of Foreign Trade in the Nazi War Economy," *Journal of Political Economy* 57, no. 4:322–37 (1943) pp. 322–24; on continuing fears of inflation, Burton Klien, "Germany's Preparation for War: A Re-examination," *American Economic Review* 38, no. 1:56–77 (1948), pp. 51, 74.

The monetary system also facilitated extraction. The manipulation of currency arrangements served to channel certain trade flows toward Germany, but, as discussed in the theoretical section, this did not necessarily entail economic exploitation. The goal of entrapment, through which, in this case, extraction was facilitated, is not to exploit the target, but to cause its preferences to change in an appropriate direction. Such goals are often met through net economic transfers from the agent to the target, as opposed to the reverse.

To summarize, German strategy was to create a series of currency relationships that would facilitate and orient the flow of certain raw materials, to make it difficult for such flows to be altered, and to shape the preferences of its trading partners. The key instrument in this strategy was the use of bilateral clearing agreements, which were negotiated under the shadow of German power and the economic depression.

External Economic Relations under the New Plan

German economic relations with other states were dominated by three groups: southeastern Europe (henceforth referred to as eastern Europe), western Europe, and Latin America. Although Germany's general goals were those enumerated above, different patterns of relations with each group emerged. In eastern Europe, there was a successful strategy of entrapment and extraction. In western Europe, Germany aimed to retain traditional export surpluses, but at the price of gradually releasing blocked mark balances. In Latin America, German strategy was similar to the eastern strategy, but was less successful. The differences in the patterns of German relations with these three regions resulted from variations in the political and economic elements of the relationships between Germany and the states of each region.

Starting with the introduction of exchange control in 1931, and beyond the introduction of the New Plan, Germany reached exchange-clearing agreements will all of the nations of eastern Europe, with the exceptions of Poland, Albania, and Lithuania. These agreements, taken as a whole, made up the core of what could be considered the mark system. One important feature of these agreements was the establishment of the exchange rate, which was the official mark rate. Since this represented an overvaluation of the mark, trade did not balance, and most of Germany's trading partners accumulated new unused mark credits on their clearing accounts in Germany.[33] These balances were not blocked in the traditional sense, but restricted in their use. If at prevailing relative prices (and, importantly, given what the German authori-

---

[33] Child, *Exchange Control in Germany*, pp. 134, 150–54. See also U.S.T.C., *Trade and Exchange Controls*, pp. 95–97, which includes the terms of the first clearing agreement that Germany participated in, with Hungary, in April 1932.

ties would allow to be exported) Germany's partners exported more than they imported, those restricted balances represented claims against future German production.

The eastern Europeans were willing to accept this state of affairs for a number of reasons. One vital one was economic. These countries, with primarily agricultural economies, were devastated by the Depression, selling large production surpluses at "ruinously low prices." The Germans offered long-term contracts to purchase large amounts of goods from these countries at high prices, in some cases over 30 percent higher than the world price.[34]

The mark balances accumulated by these nations represented, in effect, a forced loan from those states to Germany. Why did these nations accept such a result? They accepted it because of entrapment, which was possible given the prevailing economic conditions, and facilitated by exchange clearing. Entrapment was taking place at two distinct levels in each of the small states of eastern Europe, at the level of the firm and the level of the state.

Under the financing principle, exporters are paid in local currency at a fixed rate regardless of the trade balance. Because of this there is a divergence in the value of trade for society as a whole on the one hand and individual exporters on the other. Given an exchange rate of Fr4/RM, an export for which a German importer offers to pay RM250 is worth Fr1,000 to the local exporter, even if control of a restricted RM250, which the local government would receive, is worth (in real terms) about Fr700. This would be pure economic exploitation if the free market value of the export were less than Fr700. In most cases, though, high German prices more than compensated for the overvaluation of the currency,[35] leaving the value of the export somewhere between Fr700 and Fr1,000. Regardless, the result of this arrangement was that exporters in the local country prefered to export to Germany, and the local government accumulated an increasing number of restricted marks.

This process would appear to drive a wedge between the preference of the exporters and that of the government. (This would be entrapment at the level of the firm.) However, in a depression, governments may embrace such arrangements as "the best means available of financing economic recovery." De facto government financing of exports to Germany was one way to create a domestic monetary expansion. Under the prevailing economic conditions, governments had reason to believe that such an expansion would be more likely to increase employment and output, rather than inflation.[36] Governments, then, the apparent victims of German policy, also had a stake in that policy and were thus entrapped as well. (This is beyond the entrapment asso-

---

[34] Fischer, "German Trade Drive," p. 143 (quote); Basch, *German Economic Sphere*, pp. 174–78.

[35] Basch, *German Economic Sphere*, p. 178.

[36] Larry Neal, "The Economics and Finance of Bilateral Clearing Agreements: Germany, 1934–8," *Economic History Review*, 2d ser., 32, no. 3:391–404 (1979), p. 393.

ciated with the mere accumulation of large mark balances by governments.)
In this case, they depended on German absorption of their products to provide
a monetary mechanism for domestic recovery.

It should be clear that this interpretation of events depends not only on the
existence of bilateral exchange clearing, but also on the conscious preference
on the part of Germany for employment of the finance principle. Under the
waiting principle, entrapment does occur to some extent. In a given period,
German imports could exceed German exports. This would give the local
government a stake in new restricted balances, but exporters, though satisfied
with the nominal price, would have to wait for payment. It would also limit
the magnitude of the accumulated balances, and therefore the degree of entrapment. Also, under waiting, the system could not be used by governments
to facilitate domestic recovery through monetary expansion. Therefore, if the
German policies described above were part of a purposeful strategy, one
would expect to find Germany a proponent of the use of the financing principle. In fact, Germany did favor the financing principle; moreover, so did the
foreign exporters that it successfully entrapped:

> The Struggle for the Financing Principle has primarily been fought by *Ger-*
> *many.* . . . Such German desires were supported by the influence of exporters on
> internal policies. In most states of South Eastern Europe, where a great proportion
> of the populations were dependent on German purchases, the Financing Principle
> was accordingly introduced.[37]

German trade policy, through the monetary mechanism, also encouraged its
small partners to further embrace the German economy. With mounting stacks
of restricted marks, those states moved to import as much as Germany was
willing to part with, even though these imports were often inappropriate and
of inferior craftsmanship.[38] But the balances continued to accumulate. In
1935, Greece held RM37 million, while Hungary held RM35 million, Romania held RM25 million; Turkey held RM60–80 million; and Yugoslavia
held RM23 million. In a powerful testament to the extent of their entrapment,
many of these states intervened in free markets to support the value of the
mark. Given their mark holdings, the value and stability of the German currency had become part of their national interest.[39]

Thus, through the use of exchange clearing to direct trade into fixed bilateral channels, and through the accumulation of mark balances, Germany tied
the economies of the eastern European states intimately with its own. These

---

[37] Andersen, *Bilateral*, p. 40 (emphasis in original).

[38] Fischer, "German Trade Drive," p. 157; Basch, *German Economic Sphere*, p. 154.

[39] Child, *Exchange Control in Germany*, pp. 153–54, 156. The degree of intervention varied.
Yugoslavia allowed clearing marks to fall to as low as 12.5 dinars, when the official rate was
17.5. Yugoslavia was the exception, however. Fischer, "German Trade Drive," p. 153. Greece,
more typically of the eastern European states, maintained the official rate by steady intervention.

small states were left with an increased stake in Germany's economic and political future. It should be stressed, however, that the measures discussed up to this point are best described not as economic exploitation, but rather as an aggressive attempt to reorient the economic priorities of Germany's small trading partners. However, these "economically neutral" actions do not tell the whole story. Although it could be argued that Germany's economic relations with the states of southeastern Europe were a *net* benefit for those states, there was a good share of tension and devious maneuvering. Germany was able to take advantage of its relationships with these states because of its relative economic and political power. The Berlin government was able to exploit these asymmetries, though its power was limited by changes in economic opportunities.

One activity in which the Germans engaged was to use the mark system to acquire "hard," or convertible, currencies. Germany did this by dumping some of the raw materials it acquired from the east in the western part of the continent. Germany technically lost "money" on these deals, but it paid for the imports with blocked marks (that is, essentially on credit), and was paid for the reexports with hard currency. Germany was able to do this because the huge, long-term contracts entered into in the east provided it with more of these materials than were required for domestic use. This was especially easy to arrange in depressed markets. The process not only raised hard currency but also further detached the German (and southeastern European) economies from the market price structure of the rest of the world. (Eastern primary producers were literally priced out of markets by reexports of their own goods, and made even more dependent on the German purchases.)[40]

As mentioned earlier, Germany's ability to foster and exploit monetary dependence was a function of its relative bargaining power. This power rested on German political power, which was high and stable during this period, but also on prevailing economic conditions. In the depths of the depression, Germany was the only viable export market for these countries, especially given the demonetization of their trade caused by the Depression but exploited by the Germans. But as economic conditions changed, so did Germany's bargaining power.[41] For example, because of German domination, Berlin was able to maintain the overvalued clearing-exchange rate between the mark and the pengö, against the wishes of Hungary. But as economic conditions improved, Hungary was able to revise aspects of the deal with Germany. This was the case in 1937, when the Hungarians threatened to sell all of their mark balances at any price necessary to clear the market.[42] Similarly, with the gen-

[40] Paul Einzig, *Hitler's New Order in Europe* (London: Macmillan 1941), p. 97; Fischer, "German Trade Drive," p. 160; Child, *Exchange Control in Germany*, p. 163.

[41] For more on the importance of power asymmetries in the negotiation of clearing agreements, see Andersen, *Bilateral*, pp. 113–14.

[42] Fischer, "German Trade Drive," p. 159; Ellis, *Exchange Control in Central Europe*, p. 87.

eral recovery of 1936–1937, and the opportunity this presented for many states to shift to new export markets, Germany had to increase prices, speed up delivery of its own exports, and relax some clearing regulations. With the new economic downturn at the end of 1937, though, Germany's bargaining power rebounded, as it was able to prove that the German market would remain stable through the ups and downs of business cycles.[43]

Regardless of these fluctuations, Germany's experience in southeastern Europe in the 1930s shows clearly its ability to exploit monetary dependence. By capitalizing on economic conditions and political position, Germany was able to use the mark system for both entrapment and extraction. Specifically, Germany was able to alter and harmonize the preferences of its neighbors, so that those states would view their fates as tied to Germany's. The Nazis were also able to use the system to facilitate their policy of regional autarky, insulating their national economy, separating the region from the world economy, and mobilizing, often on forced credit, the materials needed in the preparation for war.

The importance of relative German power, both political and economic, is fundamental in explaining its success in exploiting monetary dependence. This point is underscored by the German experience in Latin America and western Europe. In neither of these regions was Germany as successful as in southeastern Europe. In the western European case, comparing the small states there with the small states to the east leaves the political variables relatively constant, but changes the economic variables dramatically. With the large states of this region, both the political and economic variables are changed. In Latin America, many of the economic elements are similar to those in eastern Europe, but the political variable shifts. With two broad variables (political and economic relations), and approximately three and one-half cases (southeastern Europe, Latin America, western Europe [small states/ large states]), some conclusions can be reached about the relative importance of these variables, broadly defined.[44]

Germany's economic relations with the states of western Europe were quite different than its relations with the rest of the continent. Even relations with the small states, such as Belgium, which from a purely bilateral power perspective was similarly situated to the small eastern states, were different. These states had more multifaceted economies and, importantly, traditionally imported from Germany more than they exported. Because of these considerations and the realities of political geography, Germany was less well placed to dictate the terms of economic agreements to these countries, and furthermore wanted to preserve the earnings of hard currency that its export sur-

---

[43] Basch, *German Economic Sphere*, pp. 197, 201.

[44] Note that the other important variable for the study of dependence, prevailing economic conditions, is a constant across all three of the areas.

pluses to these states yielded. For this reason, even though Germany had bilateral clearing arrangements with most of the states of western Europe, those agreements usually included provisions for the payment of German debts and against the accumulation of new blocked balances. In exchange for these "concessions," the agreements specifically fixed trade ratios near the preclearing level, ensuring German export surpluses.[45]

The larger states of western Europe were in particularly strong positions. Britain, for example, never even had a clearing agreement with Germany, but rather reached a "payment agreement," which regulated trade between the two states and contained provisions for the repayment of German debts.[46] When the agreement with France resulted in the accumulation of mark balances by that country, supplementary agreements were established to reduce them. Western states were also more likely to employ the waiting principle. Even small states, such as Belgium, were able to reduce their German clearing debts—in that particular case a debt of RM30 million in 1935 was liquidated by the end of 1936. During these years, German clearing debts with western European states fell while in eastern Europe and Latin America they rose.[47]

The Latin American states were also uniquely situated. On the one hand, they shared some features with the eastern European states. They were primary product producers, suffering through the depression, carrying surplus production. On the other hand, they were well beyond Germany's political grasp. German goals with regard to Latin America were similar to those it had for its small neighbors to the east—to extract materials necessary for rearmament and industrial production, and to entrap in order to shift Latin American political preferences in Germany's favor. The principal difference between the two regions for Germany was the relative importance of the relationships. Latin America could never be as important to Germany as eastern Europe was, and Germany could never be as important to Latin America as it was to the eastern Europeans.

Germany's strategy with regard to Latin America was to control trade by inventing a mechanism, which, in essence, was a unilateral imposition of bilateral exchange clearing. This instrument, the aski mark (Ausländer Sonderkanten Für Inlandszahlung, or Foreigner's Special Accounts for Inland Payments) was actually the only completely new invention of the New Plan.

As with all aspects of German international monetary relations, the Aski system was both complex and confusing. Basically, the Aski system worked

[45] Child, *Exchange Control in Germany*, pp. 168–69; Gordon, *Barriers*, pp. 157–59.

[46] Payments agreements regulate trade but do not involve clearing accounts and provide for international transfers. See Gordon, *Barriers*, p. 189; and U.S.T.C., *Trade and Exchange Controls*, ch. 14.

[47] For a general discussion, see U.S.T.C., *Trade and Exchange Controls*, ch. 13; on France, see ibid., pp. 209–13. On the Belgian (and other) balances, see "Germany's Clearing Debts," *The Economist*, December, 1938, pp. 485–86.

in the following way: German importers of goods from states that had reached such agreements with Germany would pay for their imports, in marks, into Aski accounts. Those marks could then be used to purchase certain approved German exports. There are a number of interesting wrinkles with this system. First, each Aski transaction could carry a different exchange rate, although this usually meant different but consistent rates for specific types of imports. Thus "cotton askis" might be worth more than "copper askis." Second, there were different transfer restrictions on various askis. "Bank askis" (the vast majority) were transferable within countries, but "individual askis" were not, making the latter only one step above barter. Because it was transferable, the bank Aski rate could fluctuate within countries.[48]

The issues raised by the Aski procedure were similar to those raised in eastern Europe, but because the overall magnitudes were smaller and the distances greater, the resulting political implications were less significant. The Latin American countries were very similar to Germany's eastern neighbors, however, with regard to their vulnerable exchange position and resort to controls, which made them ripe for the German metier, fixed bilateral trade.[49]

Germany was able to dramatically increase its share of Latin American trade, providing about 14 percent of Latin American imports in 1939, up from 3.5 percent in 1932. Other features of Germany's eastern European system also surfaced, such as the depreciation of the Aski mark and the resale of Latin American goods by the Germans to raise hard currency. The fears of outside observers about German entrapment also rose as many Latin American states moved to support the value of the Aski in local markets.[50] The motivations of the Latin Americans were similar to those of the eastern Europeans. As one study noted,

> [O]n account of their need to maintain as large an export trade as possible, particularly in certain surplus commodities, they . . . were generally unable to limit their exports to Germany to the volume that was required to pay only for such imports from that country as would have been purchased under the normal foreign exchange procedure.[51]

[48] Child, *Exchange Control in Germany*, pp. 139–45. See also U.S.T.C., *Trade and Exchange Controls*, ch. 7; Ellis, *Exchange Control in Central Europe*, pp. 218–19; Gordon, *Barriers*, pp. 178–83.

[49] For more on the position of the Latin American states, see Herbert M. Bratter, "Foreign Exchange Control in Latin America," *Foreign Policy Reports* 14, no. 23:274–88 (1939).

[50] Trade figures are from "The Aski Mark," *The Economist*, August 12, 1939, p. 321. This essay also notes that each Latin importer became "a salesman of German exporters in his own market and a spokesman of German interests with his own government—an aspect not overlooked by Germany." (p. 322). For a specific review of the German trade drive in Latin America, see H. Gerald Smith, "German Trade Competition in Latin America," *Commercial Pan America* 53:1–12 (1936), esp. pp. 5–6. On the depreciation of the aski, Ellis, *Exchange Control in Central Europe*, p. 238. On Latin purchases and German dumping, Child, *Exchange Control in Germany*, pp. 145–46.

[51] U.S.T.C., *Trade and Exchange Controls*, p. 20.

The Aski system, while successful from the perspective of German trade objectives, failed to fully achieve the greater political objectives associated with the exploitation of monetary dependence (although Germany's political position was certainly enhanced in the region). Part of this is attributable to the fact that the Germans themselves successively moved to tighten the restrictions associated with the system, because it allowed for a greater flexibility on the part of foreigners than they originally envisioned or would tolerate.[52] Additionally, even though German trade in this region increased dramatically, Berlin was not able to capture market shares to the extent that it did with its eastern partners; and given the nature of trade route, it probably did not want to.

With the outbreak of World War II, the role of Latin America obviously dropped out of the mark system. Additionally, once open warfare is under way and member states are under direct military occupation, the concepts of entrapment and dependence become increasingly remote. Still, German efforts to finance its occupations by extracting wealth and resources from conquered territories represented a wartime tightening and transformation of its monetary bloc. Common techniques included the establishment of a new bank of issue, such as the one in Poland, which created new zloty notes to compensate peasants there for seized possessions. In Norway, this step was bypassed as the Germans simply seized the government's printing presses and ran off the currency they needed to meet expenses. Other monetary instruments were introduced more systematically throughout German-occupied Europe. The most significant of these was the Reichskreditkassenscheme, or the military currency paid to the German troops and circulated in those countries.[53]

Lessons from the German Experience

There are a number of significant findings from the German case. First and most important, the opportunity for and success of the implementation of monetary power in this case provides support for the hypotheses presented at the beginning of the chapter. Economic conditions were clearly important. It was the existence of the depression that led to the adoption of bilateral clearing by many states, and without clearing, many German techniques could not have been introduced. Further, and from a more general perspective, it was shown that German bargaining power was influenced by prevailing economic conditions. As expected, the greater the global economic distress, the greater

---

[52] U.S.T.C., *Trade and Exchange Controls*, pp. 141–43; Gordon, *Barriers*, pp. 182–83.

[53] On Poland and Norway, Paul Einzig, *Europe in Chains* (London: Penguin, 1940), pp. 65, 69. For specifics on the issue of the German military currency and the Kassen that issued them, see Bank for International Settlements, *Annual Report*, vol. 12 (Basle: BIS, 1942), pp. 28, 31, 180; vol. 13 (1943), p. 182; and esp. vol. 14 (1944), pp. 147–67.

the opportunity to exploit monetary dependence, because of the increased attractiveness of the central power.

The relative asymmetry of the economic and political relationship between central and satellite states was also demonstrated to be of significance. One finding in this regard is the importance of both economic and political elements. Judging from the German experience with the states of eastern Europe, western Europe, and Latin America, it would seem that both economic asymmetry and political asymmetry are necessary—neither is sufficient alone. Economic dominance is self-evidently important, but asymmetry with regard to the nature of the relationship and implicit political coercion was also vital in setting the terms of economic agreements. Unfortunately, the number of relationship types the Germans experienced does not allow for an exhaustive manipulation of all the variables. One particular question this analysis raises but leaves unanswered is the extent to which forms of dominance (in either the political or economic dimension) can substitute for the others in establishing and exploiting the dependent relationship.

Monetary power was of great, and perhaps indispensable, indirect importance to German national strategy. As discussed above, that strategy involved the complete reorientation of German trade, in order to mobilize and secure supplies of the primary products necessary for war. While this was a trade strategy embedded in an overall national strategy, its implementation was facilitated by monetary power, and it is hard to imagine that a similar degree of success could have been achieved without the skillful introduction of monetary diplomacy. The study of monetary dependence is plagued by the fact that it is hard to isolate the influence of underlying monetary arrangements. In this case, while monetary power was complementary to and overshadowed by a trade, and ultimately a military, strategy, its essential role should be clear.

One striking aspect of the German case is the complete politicization of German international monetary relations. This makes it easier to observe the indirect role of monetary power discussed above, and also provides a rare opportunity for the observation of the direct exploitation of monetary dependence. In this case, such exploitation allowed for the insulation of the German economy (and thus allowed for rearmament without inflation, which was of great significance), and the entrapment of neighboring states. The mark system of the 1930s also provides further demonstration of the conscious introduction of monetary power by states to achieve a variety of political ends.

Illustrative Cases

The Sterling System and Extraction

Because of the existence of the sterling area, Britain was able to increase the resources it mobilized to fight World War II and the speed of the mobilization. The mechanisms of the sterling bloc enabled Britain to borrow at will billions of pounds to fight the war, and to postpone ultimate repayment of these loans to ten years beyond the end of the fighting. This case also suggests the possibility for entrapment, especially after the war. The limited opportunities to exploit this entrapment, however, demonstrate the importance of the economic and political position of the core relative to the member states in determining capability. Because of its declining position, Britain acted to preserve the sterling area, and therefore the sterling balances, as they came to be known, were not a source of strength through entrapment, but a burden on the British economy.

Sterling emerged as the predominant international medium of exchange in the nineteenth century, displacing the Spanish silver dollar. Many states held their reserves in pounds, and almost all international transactions were denominated in the British currency. This was the result of British economic hegemony in the post-Napoleonic era, and its domination of international trade, which in turn contributed to primacy in international banking, shipping, and insurance. In this era, the sterling system could be visualized as a set of five concentric circles, with London as the focus. The innermost circles consisted of the colonies, which had no real monetary authority, followed by the new dominions, such as India and South Africa, which were closely linked to sterling but enjoyed some monetary discretion.[54] A third circle was composed of states, such as Japan and some nations in South America, which had close economic links with Britain and used sterling to back their own currencies. The two outer circles consisted of states that used sterling extensively, and were willing to absorb large amounts of the currency, though, in the case of the outermost circle, within certain limits.[55]

Only the inner two circles had explicit arrangements with London, and differentiated what, at this time, could be called members of the sterling zone from other participants in the sterling system. The relationship between Britain and the colonies was formalized in the early twentieth century with the creation of currency boards, which effectively maintained British control of the exchanges.[56]

The British dominions generally had a greater degree of monetary autonomy than did the colonies, but they played a more vital role in ensuring the smooth functioning of the sterling system. India, for one, served as an impor-

[54] Yusuf Bangura, *Britain and Commonwealth Africa* (Manchester: Manchester University Press, 1983), p. 25; A.C.L. Day, *The Future of Sterling* (Oxford: Clarendon Press, 1954), p. 24; H. A. Shannon, "The Evolution of the Colonial Sterling Exchange Standard," *IMF Staff Papers* 1, no. 3:334–54 (1951), pp. 334–37.

[55] Day, *Future of Sterling*, pp. 15, 25.

[56] W. T. Newlan and D. C. Rowan, *Money and Banking in British Colonial Africa* (Oxford: Clarendon Press, 1954), pp. 46, 57. See also Banguru, *Commonwealth Africa*, p. 38; and H. A. Shannon, "The Modern Colonial Exchange Standard," *IMF Staff Papers* 2, no. 2:318–62 (1952), p. 321. For a survey of colonial currencies before the currency boards, see Robert Chalmers, *History of Currency in the British Colonies* (London: H.M. Stationary Office, 1893); and G. L. M. Clausen, "The British Colonial Currency System," *Economic Journal* 54:1–25 (1944).

tant pivot in the British payments system. Britain had a trade deficit with the rest of the world, but enjoyed a trade surplus with India. This triangular balance (India was in surplus with the rest of the world) allowed Britain to recycle its investment income and provide liquidity for the international (sterling) system. Britain could also tap India's monetary reserves if they were required to supplement Britain's, ensuring its stability as the center of the financial system.[57] South Africa also played an important role in the maintenance of the system, as the key supplier of new gold.[58]

The sterling system changed dramatically in September 1931, when Britain went off the gold standard and effectively devalued the pound. While this did not reflect a sudden shift in the strength of the British currency, it did represent a basic transformation of the purpose of the sterling area. For the remainder of its existence, the sterling system would be a "defensive organization."[59] The "sterling area" was a currency zone formed by those currencies that followed sterling off gold, matched its depreciation, and pegged their values to the pound. There were three types of members. First were the colonial empire, Iraq, Egypt, and some new mandates, which continued to be administered by currency boards. Second were the semi-independent and closely associated economies, such as India, Australia and New Zealand, South Africa, and Portugal. These countries also participated in monetary cooperation and informal currency pooling. Finally, there were autonomous states, which participated primarily for stability, such as the Scandinavian countries and France after 1936.[60]

From 1931 to 1939 the sterling area was a zone, not a currency bloc: membership was somewhat flexible, and since the pound was convertible into other currencies and gold on the London market, Britain could not force sterling on

[57] Marcello de Cecco, *The International Gold Standard* (New York: St. Martin's Press, 1984), p. 62. The primary monetary controversy associated with India was the extent to which the silver standard imposed upon it by the East India Company in 1806 was used to extract gold from that country. The economic consequences of the silver standard in India became acute with the global fall in the price of silver in the 1870s. This issue is of only passing interest here because it represents an *economic*, as opposed to political, extraction. See DeCecco, *International Gold Standard*, p. 63; and also S. E. Harris, *Monetary Problems of the British Empire* (New York: Macmillan, 1931), book 8; Dwijendra Tripathi, "The Silver Question: India and America," *Journal of Indian History* 44, no. 3:789–98 (1966), esp. p. 793 (1966); and Dietmar Rothermund, "An Aspect of British Monetary Imperialism," *Indian Economic and Social History Review* 7, no. 1:91–107 (1970), esp. p. 93.

[58] See Bruce R. Dalgaard, *South Africa's Impact on Britain's Return to Gold, 1925* (New York: Arno Press, 1981), ch. 5.

[59] Day, *Future of Sterling*, p. 3 (quote).

[60] Ian M. Drummond, *The Floating Pound and the Sterling Area, 1931–1939* (Cambridge: Cambridge University Press, 1981), p. 5. Drummond offers the most comprehensive consideration of this period. Useful earlier analyses are offered by Robert B. Stewart, "Instruments of British Policy in the Sterling Area," *Political Science Quarterly* 52, no. 2:174–207 (1937); and A. S. J. Baster, "A Note on the Sterling Area," *Economic Journal* 47:568–74 (1937).

reluctant holders.[61] In fact, in order to mollify captive members of the system, Britain established the "Ottawa policy" of cheap credit, extensive exchange support, and the system of imperial preference within the commonwealth.[62] It was at this time that Britain began consciously to attempt to salvage the prestige of sterling through the existence of a thriving monetary area. Membership was, therefore, a natural policy for many countries. Holding reserves in London and pegging to the pound held no significant disadvantages. In fact, trade within the sterling area recovered from the depression at a faster rate than did total world trade.[63]

The sterling zone was transformed into the sterling bloc shortly after the start of World War II. With the war on, Britain moved to protect sterling from external forces while preserving liquidity within the sterling area. The system was restructured to act as a single unit with regard to exchange control purposes. Reserves were formally pooled, members' hard currency was sold to the Bank of England, and by 1940 members of what was by then the sterling bloc strictly regulated the flow of pounds between accounts of residents and nonresidents of the system. Under these circumstances, foreign members of the system dropped out.[64]

The changes in the sterling system were not superficially significant, but they fundamentally changed the relationship between the center, Britain, and the members. For example, reserves were pooled before 1939, but after that point drawings from the pool were restricted and became increasingly difficult. The transfer of sterling out of the bloc, or its conversion into dollars or other foreign currencies, was greatly reduced. This was achieved at first

[61] Drummond, *Floating Pound*, p. 257. In fact, the treasury had decided that it would not be British policy to ask states to join the sterling area, in order to avoid responsibility for supporting another currency in the future. Ibid., p. 72. South Africa did not immediately join the area: it floated on December 28, 1932, and did not peg to sterling until fifteen months after the September crisis, in February 1933. See Chapter 6. Canada never joined the sterling area. Drummond, *Floating Pound*, pp. 74–75.

[62] For a discussion of the Ottawa agreements of 1932, actually eleven bilateral agreements reached at the conference between different parts of the empire, see Stewart, "British Policy," pp. 176–81, 201–4; and Drummond, *Floating Pound*, p. 254. On British loans in the sterling area, see Stewart, "British Policy," pp. 184–91.

[63] On prestige, see Drummond, *Floating Pound*, p. 15. On "natural policy," see Philip W. Bell, *The Sterling Area in the Postwar World* (Oxford: Clarendon Press, 1956), p. 18. On trade recovery, see F. V. Meyer, *Britain, the Sterling Area, and Europe,* (Cambridge: Bowes and Bowes, 1952), p. 41.

[64] South Africa did not sell its hard currency reserves to the Bank of England. Economic Cooperation Administration, Special Mission to the United Kingdom, *The Sterling Area: An American Analysis* (Amsterdam: N. V. Arbenderspers, 1951), p. 26. See also A. R. Conan, *The Sterling Area* (London: Macmillan, 1952), p. 2; and Bell, *Sterling Area in Postwar World*, pp. 44–45. For more on South Africa and the sterling area, see N. N. Franklin, "South Africa's Balance of Payments and the Sterling area, 1939–1950," *Economic Journal* 61:290–309 (1951); and Chapter 6.

through tacit understandings, but increasingly through formal restrictions.[65]

World War II proved to be fantastically expensive for the United Kingdom. The war was financed in a number of ways, such as the running down of reserves, borrowing, and the sale of assets. Before the war, Britain's external assets exceeded its liabilities by over £4 billion. In 1948, the country was a net debtor. More dramatically, in 1938, British gold and dollar reserves stood at £864 million, while sterling liabilities, expressed in sterling balances held by outsiders, totaled £760 million. By 1948 these figures were £369 million and £2,700 million, respectively.[66] Britain was able to expand its sterling liabilities dramatically and in the face of declining reserves, largely because of the new mechanisms of the sterling bloc. Because sterling was de facto legal tender in the area, and given the restrictions on transfer and convertibility, Britain could spend pounds there without inhibition. Recipients of the British currency could purchase British goods and services (because of the war, this was a relatively limited option), they could hold the currency, or they could purchase sterling securities and hold them in accounts in London. These last two options were simply different forms of holding sterling, and represented future claims on British production, or future claims on British gold and foreign currency, when the pound was again convertible. These were, then, little more than imposed loans, facilitated by the existence of the sterling bloc.

In fact, the wartime current account deficit was financed through the transfer of inconvertible sterling, to the tune of £3 billion, of which £2.5 billion went to the sterling bloc. This creation of resources was of direct military consequence: about £1.5 billion of these balances went to meet military expenditures in Egypt and India.[67]

The implications of the wartime restrictions and the accumulation of ster-

[65] Bell, *Sterling Area in Postwar World*, p. 52. For a good review of Britain's formal exchange control regulations, see the report of the Economic Cooperation Administration, which summarizes the types of accounts associated with various countries. For example, sterling area countries held pounds in "resident accounts," and nonmembers held "nonresident accounts." Nonresident accounts could be "ordinary," "Central American," "bilateral," "transferable," or "American." Economic Cooperation Administration, *American Analysis*, p. 96. Different types of transfers were permitted between different accounts. For example, sterling in American accounts could be transfered to other types of accounts relatively freely, but bilateral and resident accounts were severely restricted. Ibid., p. 99.

[66] Economic Cooperation Administration, *American Analysis*, pp. 177–79. For a breakdown of the net disinvestment, see Bank for International Settlements (BIS), *Fourteenth Annual Report* (Basle: BIS, 1944), p. 135.

[67] A. R. Conan, *The Rationale of the Sterling Area* (London: Macmillan, 1961), p. 10; Economic Cooperation Administration, *American Analysis*, p. 28. H. A. Shannon, in "The Sterling Balances and the Sterling Area," *Economic Journal* 60:531–51 (1950), notes that since the Reserve Bank of India was obligated to buy sterling in unlimited quantities at a fixed exchange rate, India was "rapidly filled and flooded . . . with sterling" (p. 541). Similarly, "The Indian situation was reproduced in Egypt. The rise in holdings was largely due to British and American military expenditure, which, as elsewhere, was not offset by countervailing imports and services during the war" (p. 543).

TABLE 4.1
The Sterling Balances (millions of pounds)

	1945	1946	1948	1949	1950
All countries	3,688	3,721	3,424	3,425	3,757
"Blocked balance countries"	1,901	2,113	1,588	1,437	1,311
Southeast Asia	1,177	1,338	1,027	975	925
Middle East	587	575	427	395	353
South America	137	200	134	67	33
"Free balance countries"	1,787	1,608	1,836	1,988	2,446
Old Dominions	394	540	604	715	909
Dependencies	447	495	554	583	752
OEEC	421	424	371	441	398
Dollar area	36	35	24	36	85
Residual	489	114	283	213	302

Sources and notes: Economic Cooperation Administration, Special Mission to the United Kingdom, *The Sterling Area: An American Analysis* (Amsterdam: N. V. Arbenderspers, 1951), p. 195. "Blocked balance countries" and "free balance countries" are in quotes because the balances of the "free" areas were blocked by tacit agreements. In fact, as the table indicates, there was more pressure to release blocked balances than to release free ones. Areas are defined as follows: Southeast Asia includes India and Pakistan and Ceylon; Middle East includes Egypt, Palestine, and Iraq; South America includes Argentina, Brazil, and Uruguay; old Dominions include Australia, New Zealand, South Arica, and Ireland; dependencies include East Africa, West Africa, British Malaya and British Borneo, Hong Kong, and other colonies. For an analysis of the origins and distribution of these balances, see H. A. Shannon, "The Sterling Balances and the Sterling Area," *Economic Journal* 60:351–51 (1950).

ling balances (see Table 4.1) were not apparent until after the war, when it became clear that Britain would be unable to lift restrictions and return to the prewar sterling system. The wartime regulations were revised, though, and a more formal exchange control bureaucracy was established in 1947.[68] Sterling holders were not happy with this arrangement. The inability to draw on their own accounts caused some friction, and Egypt withdrew from the area over this issue in 1947. But for the most part, members felt the tug of entrapment: even if they were successful in accessing some of their balances quickly, if the result of such action was a fall in the value of sterling, then they could be net losers. This could result from the decrease in the value of their remaining balances, or the decrease in the value of their own currencies if those currencies were pegged to the pound.[69]

[68] On the postwar regulations, see H. A. Shannon, "The British Payments and Exchange Control System," *Quarterly Journal of Economics* 63, no. 2:212–37 (1949). See also Conan, *Sterling Area*, pp. 152–55; Economic Cooperation Administration, *American Analysis*, pp. 97–100; and R. F. Mikesell, *Foreign Exchange in the Post-war World* (New York: Twentieth Century Fund, 1954), chs. 10–11.

[69] On interdependence (entrapment), see Meyer, *Britain, Sterling Area, and Europe,*, pp. 24–25.

Britain, in a formal statement in 1949, recognized that "[i]n principle the whole of these balances represent[ed] a charge on the United Kingdom productions of goods and services."[70] But while the British government recognized this, London almost simultaneously demonstrated the privileged position of the state that occupies the center of any international monetary system. In the same month that British financial authorities made this statement, they demonstrated their ability to force a sharing of the burden of these debts. By devaluing the pound from $4.03 to $2.80, they were able to decrease the value of outstanding sterling balances by 30 percent. The reduction in the overall burden was even greater because the devaluation also increased the number of pounds needed by a given state to maintain the same amount of real reserves. It was expected that most states would continue to hold their reserves in sterling and such reserves would not be spent or encashed.[71] Britain did not intend to write off completely the sterling debts, however, since one of the central elements of its postwar foreign policy was to reestablish the pound as an international currency. Additionally, despite continued decline, Britain still had a number of things to offer, through the sterling area, to member states. Initially, British strength rested in the ability to release blocked balances, regulate and direct capital outflow, and manage and provide access to the gold and dollar pool.[72]

These considerations were able to keep the sterling bloc alive through the 1950s.[73] However, by 1958, conditions had changed. The blocked balances were all released,[74] the pound was fully convertible (ending the need for the pool), and the United States had replaced Britain as the principal source of credit. The sterling system became less significant, and was ultimately composed of Britain and its remaining colonies. The sterling system, which started with the colonies, ended with a sterling zone containing similarly situated members. Britain was able to ease the sting of releasing blocked balances

---

[70] Quoted in "The Sterling Balances," *The Economist*, May 13, 1950, p. 1075.

[71] Meyer, *Britain, Sterling Area, and Europe,*, p. 54. Obviously (and as would be seen) the policy of devaluation could only be used sparingly, or the currency would lose credibility as a reserve asset.

[72] On the importance of reestablishing sterling's international role to the British government, see Day, *Future of Sterling*, p. 115. On British bargaining power, see Bell, *Sterling Area in Postwar World*, p. 19.

[73] On the attraction of the pool, see Meyer, *Britain, Sterling Area, and Europe,*, pp. 92–93. On the mechanism of the gold pool, see Meyer pp. 74–75. Bell notes that Australia, which was a net dollar earner in 1950 and 1951, considered leaving the area, but thought better of it, aware that it was traditionally a dollar deficit country, both immediately before and after the war (pp. 62–63). For a summary of contributions and drawings from the pool by member countries during 1946–1952, see Bell, *Sterling Area in Postwar World*, pp. 56–57.

[74] As agreed to according to the Colombo plan of 1950. Economic Cooperation Administration, *American Analysis*, pp.181, 333–34; Bell, *Sterling Area in Postwar World*, pp. 22–24. Bell also summarizes the agreements regulating the blocked balances, pp. 39–42.

by increasing the balances of the colonies, postponing and stretching further into the future the ultimate repayment.[75]

With only the colonies remaining in the system, Britain sought to manage their decolonization in such a way as to preserve the sterling zone and thus the international status of the pound. Therefore, in their discussions with the colonies the British stressed the need to hold sterling and discriminate against the dollar. Initially, British attempts at monetary cooperation were successful. Even with the independence of most of these states in the late 1950s, and the full convertibility of the pound, the new states participated in the sterling area. This was a result of their concern for the viability of their new currencies, a desire to attract foreign investment, and the expectation of continued British economic assistance.[76] Ultimately, however, the continued weakness of the pound coupled with the former colonies' desire for complete independence served to doom the sterling zone. After the devaluation of 1967, most remaining members switched from the pound as a unit of account and withdrew substantial balances to defend their reserves against further devaluation. The sterling area limped along, but officially ended with the float of the pound on June 23, 1972.[77]

From its nucleus, the sterling zone established in 1825, the British pound rose to the status of international key currency for the nineteenth century. Almost the entire world participated in a sterling area. The twentieth century witnessed the contraction of this system, from area to bloc to zone, and finally, to ordinary currency. The specific example of power extraction considered here, the ability of Britain to mobilize large amounts of wealth for war, effectively demonstrates that monetary dependence can translate into real power. But there are a number of important limitations to this power. First of all, the British ability to exploit the sterling system depended on some degree

[75] On the colonial balances, see Sir Douglas Copland, *Problems of the Sterling Area*, Essays in International Finance, no. 17 (Princeton University, 1953), p. 12; Frederick Leith-Ross, "Sterling Convertibility," *South African Journal of Economics* 21, no. 1 (March 1953); Arthur Hazelwood, "Sterling Balances and the Colonial Currency System," *Economic Journal* 62:942–45 (1952); Ida Greaves, *The Colonial Sterling Balances*, Essays in International Finance, no. 20 (Princeton University, 1954); "Sterling Balances and the Colonial Currency System: A Comment," *Economic Journal* 63:921–23 (1953); and "The Sterling Balances of Colonial Territories," *Economic Journal* 61:433–39 (1951).

[76] Banguru, *Commonwealth Africa*, pp. 43, 72, 92. For a discussion of the postindependence sterling area members, see J. V. Mládek, "Evolution of African Currencies. Part II. The Sterling Area and Unattached Currencies," *Finance and Development* 1, no. 3:184–91 (1964); and Osman Hashim Abdel-Salam, "The Evolution of African Monetary Institutions," *Journal of Modern African Studies* 8, no. 3:339–62 (1970), esp. pp. 347–51.

[77] Banguru, *Commonwealth Africa*, pp. 79–80, 100, 113. On East Africa, see John M. Letiche, "Dependent Monetary Systems and Economic Development: The Case of Sterling East Africa," in Willy Sellekaerts, ed., *Economic Development and Planning* (essays in honor of Jan Tinbergen) (White Plains, N.Y.: International Arts and Sciences Press, 1974), esp. p. 212.

of cooperation from the member states. Membership did not force the hand of a participant, but it did allow for a number of important enhancements to British power, such as the actual mechanism of extraction. The ease, automaticity, and to some extent, invisibility of this mechanism made cooperation easier, and dissent more difficult.

A second point is the continued importance of both global economic conditions and specific asymmetries between the core state and individual members. The most important characteristic of the international economy during the period of extraction was not prosperity or depression, but war. The existence of major war can be considered a "poor" global economic environment, similar to depression, in that it provides opportunities to exploit dependence. Alternatively, major war could be seen as deemphasizing the importance of the global economic dimension, and magnifying the importance of bilateral asymmetries. Either way, political considerations, important at all times, were crucial during the war for explaining the comparative opportunity to exercise monetary power.

Just as in the German case, the firmer the British grasp became, the more states outside of the political influence of Britain began to slip beyond its economic reach. This is observable not only in the gradual contraction of the area, but in the nature of the contraction. Even with states closely associated with Britain, a politico-economic pecking order could be observed: Canada did not even join the sterling area in 1931, South Africa remained detached from the sterling bloc, and India maintained a greater degree of monetary autonomy than did the African colonies. When the war came, the greatest amount of extraction was from those states which were under the political domination of Britain.

Third, the British success at extraction suggests that there may be limits on this specific instrument in general. It is conceivable that extraction represents the expenditure of all of the goodwill accumulated during the previous life cycle of the system. To the extent that this is true, massive attempts at extraction may represent the nova of a given currency system.[78]

The Franc Zone and the Threat of Expulsion

Throughout the history of the modern international economy, France has been the most politically sensitive nation with regard to international monetary affairs. French sensitivity to currency affairs dates back to at least as early as

---

[78] On the other hand, a system might endure repeated minor episodes of extraction, if membership remains, on balance, attractive. Of course, a politically dominant state could conceivably use the monetary system to extract a constant flow of wealth from its subject members. This behavior, however, would represent the use of the monetary system to extract wealth for its own sake, and as such is outside the scope of this study.

Napoleon, who attempted to gauge the success of the "continental system" directed against Britain by carefully monitoring the fluctuations in the stability of the British exchange position.[79] France's first modern attempt to establish the franc as a core currency was in the 1860s, when, in the words of one scholar, "it was the Emperor's express desire to see all continental Europe united in a franc area which would exclude and isolate Germany."[80] This desire resulted in the Latin Monetary Union, which emerged from the Monetary Convention of 1865, where France, Italy, Switzerland, and Belgium agreed to closely coordinate their coinage and monetary policies. France was the driving force behind the union, through which Louis Napoleon hoped that the monetary standard of France would ultimately be imposed on states throughout Europe.[81]

Attempts were made to expand the union but ultimately France struggled simply to keep its original membership intact. Although disputes within the union continued, France held it together largely for political purposes, and in the 1930s made an effort to revive the Latin Monetary Union in the form of the gold bloc.[82] But limitations on its economic and political power ultimately prevented France from ever dominating the currency system of Europe. The story of the franc zone was destined to be limited to those countries outside of Europe, in areas where French predominance was unchallenged.

The French currency was used throughout French Africa. In 1901, the Banque de l'Afrique Occidentale Française (BAO), was founded and exclusively issued a franc-based paper currency throughout French West Africa.[83] As with the sterling area, the franc zone was tightened by both the Great Depression and World War II. The currency fluctuations of the interwar period increased transactions within fixed currency areas and dislocated trade between them. With the start of the war, increased regulation and exchange control reinforced this new pattern of trade and capital flows.[84] After the war, the system

[79] Eli Heckscher, *The Continental System: An Economic Interpretation* (Oxford: Clarendon Press, 1922), pp. 59–74, esp. pp. 65–66, 356–63, and passim.

[80] DeCecco, *International Gold Standard*, p. 44.

[81] Henry Parker Willis, *A History of the Latin Monetary Union* (Chicago: University of Chicago Press, 1901), pp. 46, 56.

[82] Willis, pp. 81–85, 108–11, 144. For more on the Latin Monetary Union, see H. B. Russel, *International Monetary Conferences* (New York: Harper, 1898), chs. 2 (esp. p. 34) and 3 (esp. p. 104). On the gold bloc, see Charles P. Kindleberger, *A Financial History of Western Europe* (London: George Allen and Unwin, 1984), pp. 395–96.

[83] Virginia Thompson and Richard Adloff, *French West Africa* (Stanford: Stanford University Press, 1957), pp. 278, 281.

[84] Thomas Balogh, *The Economic Impact of Monetary and Commercial Institutions of a European Origin in Africa* (Cairo: National Bank of Egypt, 1964), pp. 14, 16, 21. For an earlier treatment of similar material, see Balogh, "The Mechanism of Neo-Imperialism: The Economic Impact of Monetary and Commercial Institutions in Africa," *Oxford University Institute of Statistics Bulletin* 24, no. 3:331–216 (1962).

was restructured, with the creation of a separate colonial currency, the CFA (Colonies Françaises d'Afrique) franc.[85]

Although there was occasional dissent, the franc system continued without substantial change until the movement toward decolonization swept through Africa.[86] At this time, France restructured the franc zone and gave new states the choice of whether they wanted to participate. Three new regional central banks were established.[87] All of these three monetary systems shared certain vital features:

1. The central banks held the external reserves of their respective members. Reserves were held exclusively in the form of French francs, at the French treasury.

2. Payments and receipts in foreign currency were settled through an account in the French treasury, known as the Operations Account.[88] Through this account, France guaranteed the unlimited convertibility of CFA francs into French francs.

3. Management was shared by French and local authorities.[89]

France attempted to make membership in the franc zone as appealing as possible. It created a preference system for members' imports to France, waived import duties, and contributed to commodity stabilization funds. Members could also expect to receive more direct aid than did outsiders. As a result, French citizens paid high and stable prices for coffee, groundnuts, cocoa, bananas, cotton, and other products.[90]

---

[85] After independence, CFA stood for Communautés Financières Africaines. For more on wartime developments in the franc system, see Bank for International Settlements (BIS), *Fourteenth Annual Report (1 April 1943–1 March 1944)*, (Basle: BIS, 1944), pp. 265–71; see also Thompson and Adloff, *The Emerging States of French Equalatorial Africa* (Stanford: Stanford University Press, 1960).

[86] For a review of the franc zone, 1945–1964, see J. V. Mládek, "Evolution of African Currencies. Part I. The Franc Area," *Finance and Development* 1, no. 2:81–88 (1964); and Abdel Salam, "African Monetary Institutions," pp. 340–45.

[87] The Banque Central de Etats de l'Afrique de l'Ouest (BCEAO) was set up in West Africa, the Banque Central des Etats de l'Afrique Equatoriale et du Cameroon (BCEAEC) was set up in equatorial Africa, and a central bank was established for Madagascar and the Comoros.

[88] For more on the Operations Account, the cornerstone of the franc zone, see Holger L. Engberg, "The Operations Account System in French Speaking Africa," *Journal of Modern African Studies* 11, no. 4:537–45. (1973).

[89] International Monetary Fund, "The CFA Franc System," *IMF Staff Papers* 10, no. 3:345–96 (1963), pp. 346–47. Charter members of the BECOA were Dahomey, Ivory Coast, Mauritania, Niger, Senegal, Togo, and Upper Volta (but not Mali or Guinea, as discussed below). Charter members of the BCEAEC were the Central African Republic, Chad, Congo, and Gabon. Cameroon joined in November 1961. For more on the monetary, banking, and exchange system of the BECOA countries, see International Monetary Fund, *Surveys of African Economies*, vol. 3 (Washington, D.C.: IMF, 1970), pp. 71–91, 125–42. For the BCEAEC countries, see International Monetary Fund, *Surveys of African Economies*, vol. 1 (Washington D.C.: IMF, 1968), pp. 14–31, 43–53; and Peter Robeson, "Economic Integration in Equatorial Africa," in Arthur Hazelwood, ed., *African Integration and Disintegration* (London: Oxford University Press, 1967), esp. pp. 46–48.

[90] In 1961, the premium resulting from trade with France has been estimated at Fr343 million,

Even opponents of the system recognized its advantages. One critic counted monetary stability, a reduction in the risk of inflation and inflationary pressure, elimination of balance-of-payments difficulties, and the attraction of new capital and foreign investment among the benefits of membership. Because of these advantages, French colonial arrangements survived the transition to independence more fully than did their British counterparts. Another critic, commenting on the close relationship between France and its former African colonies, noted that "from the *economic* point of view, it is hard to argue that they were wrong."[91]

As the franc zone evolved into the 1970s and beyond, revisions to the system strengthened and broadened local monetary autonomy and promoted regional integration. But even with all of these developments, the franc zone remains in existence today, and France still guarantees the convertibility of the CFA franc. France also continues to provide relatively high amounts of aid to member countries, but most of the trade preferences were reduced or integrated into a larger arrangement with the European Common Market.[92] France's monetary relationships with its former colonies, however, were not always harmonious. Some members, such as Mali, had a stormy relationship with the franc system.[93]

Mali became independent on September 22, 1960, and continued its membership within the franc zone.[94] In 1962, Mali faced a debt crisis, and re-

from total exports of Fr3.2 billion, or 19 percent of total receipts. Direct aid in 1962 from France was Fr 1.4 billion. IMF, "CFA," pp. 357–60, 369, 376.

[91] On the advantages, see Aguibou Y. Yansane, "Some Problems of Monetary Dependency in French-Speaking West African States," *Journal of African Studies* 5, no. 4:444–70 (1978). On the survival of the franc zone, see Eghoisa Osagie, "Monetary Disintegration and Integration in West Africa," *Nigerian Journal of International Studies* 1, no. 1:453–63 (1975). (A slightly different version of this paper appears in *Economia Internazionale* 28, nos. 3–4:19–27 [1975].) On the "economic" logic, see Andrew M. Kamark, *The Economics of African Development* (New York: Preager, 1967), p. 225 (emphasis in original).

[92] For more on the revisions of 1974 and other new monetary developments, see Rattin J. Bhatia, "The West African Monetary Union," IMF Occasional Paper, no. 35 (May 1985), esp. p. 28. On integration, see Eghosa Osagie, "West African Clearing House, West African Unit of Account, and Pressures for Monetary Integration," *Journal of Common Market Studies* 17, no. 3:227–35, esp. pp. 227, 229, 231; E. C. Edozin and E. Osagie, eds., *The Economic Integration of West Africa* (Ibadan, Nigeria: Ibadan University Press, 1982; and John B. Mclenaghan et al., "Currency Convertibility in the Economic Community of West Africa," IMF Occasional Paper, no. 13 (August 1982).

[93] Although Mali left the franc zone voluntarily, the Malian experience with monetary independence, and the consequences of its withdrawal and return, demonstrate the real power of the threat of expulsion. The difference in the implications of exit, as opposed to expulsion, is considered in the conclusion of the franc zone discussion.

[94] Guinea, shortly after independence, created its own central bank and pursued a leftist agenda. The Guinean experience is therefore of interest for further study of the threat of expulsion. For more on the Guinean experience, see Yansane, "Monetary Dependency," p. 456; Kamark, *African Development,* p. 85; and Claude Riviere, *Guinea: The Mobilization of a People* (Ithaca, N.Y.: Cornell University Press, 1977), esp. pp. 7–8, 25, 103, 158, 194.

ceived $9 million from France to help see the country through its difficulties. Also during this year, negotiations were taking place with France to revise the monetary union and general bilateral cooperation. But even as these talks were in progress, on June 30, 1962, and against the advice of the government's chief economic advisor, Jean Bénard, Malian President Modibo Keita dramatically announced the introduction of a new, independent Mali franc, as troops surrounded the nation's banks.[95]

President Keita, in his announcement, stated

History teaches us that political power is always and necessarily accompanied by the royal prerogative of minting money, that monetary power is inseparable from national sovereignty, that it is the indispensable complement of it, its essential attribute.[96]

An expansion of the money supply initially relieved many of the constraints that had previously frustrated the government, but new difficulties followed. With no hard currency backing, foreign exchange holdings quickly fell. Since Mali traditionally imported most consumer goods, this combination led to an almost perpetual balance of payments crisis, and a shortage of consumer products. "Severe and unpredictable shortages" contributed to dislocation and smuggling, with further reduced government revenue and foreign exchange. The 1964 balance-of-payments crisis was alleviated by the diversion of Chinese and Russian investment credits to pay for current consumption. Subsequent crises were met with aid from the IMF and the International Development Association. Mali regularly violated the conditions of these loans, however, and by 1966 had run out of places to turn to.[97]

The Malian economy was in serious trouble without the support of the franc zone. Peanut exports declined from a peak of 98,000 tons in 1957–1958 to 22,000 tons in 1965–1966. Rice exports, at 34,500 tons in 1962, fell to 26,000 tons in 1967–1968. Inflation increased, as the government continued to borrow from the central bank. Consumer prices in unregulated markets rose 88 percent between 1962–1963 and 1967, and the value of the Mali franc declined steadily.[98] In this context, the government saw little choice but to

[95] William I. Jones, "Economics of the Coup," *Africa Report* 14:23–26, 51–53 (1969), p. 51. One interesting aspect of this episode is that the new Malian currency was printed in Czechoslovakia, technically an act of subversive disruption directed against the franc zone. Ibid. For general information on the mechanics and history of the Malian monetary system, see International Monetary Fund, *Surveys of African Economies*, vol. 7 (Washington, D.C.: IMF, 1977), esp. pp. 149–57.

[96] Quoted in Michael G. Schatzberg, "The Coup and After: Continuity or Change in Malian Politics?" African Studies Program, Occasional Paper no. 5, (University of Wisconsin, Madison, 1972), p. 2. For more on the political and economic thought of Keita, see John N. Hazard, "Marxian Socialism in Africa: The Case of Mali," *Comparative Politics* 1, no. 1:1–15 (1969).

[97] Jones, "Economics of the Coup," p. 51. See also "Mali—Six Years After," *West Africa*, January 21, 1967, pp. 79–81.

[98] Francis G. Snyder, "An Era Ends in Mali," *Africa Report* 14:16–22 (1969), p. 19. See also

enter into negotiations with France. These discussions led to an agreement signed in February 1967, under which Mali would be reintegrated into the franc zone. France would again have a role in dictating monetary and fiscal management to the Malian government. A new central bank was created, with France appointing half of the board members. President Keita was forced to "swallow his words," and in exchange for the ultimate French guarantee of convertibility, also agreed to devalue the Mali franc by 50 percent. The finance minister (and long-time Keita loyalist) Louis Nègre called the devaluation "an act of political realism."[99]

The move may have been realistic, but it presented Keita with a serious political problem. The true believers on the Malian left viewed the deal as a sellout, but at the same time the new deal promised no quick solution. French support could not undo the damage of five years of economic mismanagement. Mali's renewed participation in the franc zone expanded the resources available to the government, but at the same time imposed a new discipline. Consumer imports could only be increased gradually. The benefits of the deal with France and guaranteed convertibility were therefore not immediately apparent to the average citizen.[100]

President Keita reacted to this pressure by strengthening his power at home and attempting to reestablish his ideological credentials through rhetorical domestic initiatives. The national assembly was dissolved, and the political bureau of Keita's own monopoly political party was abolished. The president also sought to lead the nation through something of a "cultural revolution" based on the Chinese model.[101] Keita was apparently attempting to walk the tightrope of pursuing moderate economic policies under the cover of radical political rhetoric. This uneasy mix satisfied no one, and on November 19, 1968, Keita was overthrown in a military coup. The new government considered itself "socialist," but opposed the "excesses" of the previous government.

"Mali-Six Years After," *West Africa*, January 28, 1967 (continues article from January 21, concludes on February 11).

[99] On the new agreement, see IMF, *Surveys,* pp. 149, 150, 157; and Jones, "Economics of the Coup," p. 53. "Swallow . . .," is from Hazard, "Socialism in Africa," p. 3. The agreement was widely interpreted as a major failure for the government. See "Mali and the Franc," and "Franc devalued by ½," in *West Africa*, May 13, 1967, pp. 614, 639. Nègre is quoted in Snyder, "Era Ends in Mali," p. 19. For more on Nègre, reported to be one of only five men who knew in advance Mali was going to leave the franc zone, see "Portrait: Mali Technocrat," *West Africa*, June 3, 1967, p. 639.

[100] Jones, "Economics of the Coup," p. 19; Snyder, "Era Ends in Mali," p 23.

[101] On domestic rhetoric, Snyder, "Era Ends in Mali," p. 20. Mali's cultural revolution was also colorful, with the public denouncement of government employees, and radio exhortations, such as "What have you done for the revolution today?" On authoritarianism, Hazard, "Socialism in Africa," p. 3; and Schatzberg, "Coup and After," p. 4. For more on the consolidation of power, see "What's Happening in Mali," *West Africa*, September 2, 1967, p. 1135; and "Modibo and Mali," *West Africa*, September 9, 1967, p. 1161.

It moved to cut spending, encouraged the import of foreign capital, and sought closer ties with France.[102]

The efforts of France in general and Mali in particular offer a number of interesting lessons with regard to monetary dependence. First of all, in the French case we clearly see once again the core willing to make economic sacrifices to maintain the existence of a currency area, whether the Latin Monetary Union in the 1870s or the franc zone in the 1960s. Since France obviously valued the existence of such a zone, it had to be sensitive to the amount of political extraction that could be achieved without disrupting the area. This phenomenon applies to every leader of a currency area, but the extent to which it limits their ability to extract power depends on the values of the variables established in the introduction to this chapter. For France in the 1960s, the theory would suggest that its power for the overt exploitation of monetary dependence would be relatively low, given the general French position and the prevailing economic conditions. One important element in favor of the French was the distressed status of most of the members and potential members of the franc system, suggesting the possibility of high bilateral asymmetries.

France was willing to make sacrifices in order to lead a currency area, but what benefits did it expect? For the most part the French strategy seemed to have been one of entrapment: the belief that intimate and beneficial monetary association with France would facilitate close political and diplomatic ties. This especially seems to be the case with regard to France's European efforts. In its African endeavors, French policies were directed at rather specific goals. One was the use of the franc zone to expand French cultural and linguistic influence—or, more generally, prestige. Another was military—France hoped to mobilize African resources in order to compensate for increases in German economic and military might that could not be matched through domestic production. France retained these hopes into the 1960s, and attempted to integrate franc zone participants into its overall military strategy.[103]

The Malian experience raises two interesting issues for consideration. On the one hand, the utter collapse of the Malian economy cannot help but underscore the underlying power of the threat of expulsion, and the force of such an act as a specific sanction. Other similarly situated states could not help but observe the sequence of events: a defiant proclamation, followed by economic

[102] Snyder, "Era Ends in Mali," pp. 21–22. For more on the politics of the coup, see "A Coup to Stop a Coup," *West Africa*, December 28, 1968, p. 1553.

[103] On prestige, see Philip M. Allen, "Francophone Reconsidered," *Africa Report* 13, no. 6:6–11 (1968). On mobilizing African resources, Chester A. Crocker, "France's Changing Military Interests," *Africa Report* 13, no. 6:16–24, 41 (1968), pp. 16–17. In World War I, 225,000 Africans served in the French Army; 25,000 died. France planned to deploy over 500,000 African troops in World War II, but these plans were overtaken by the French defeat. Ibid., p. 17.

ruin, political instability, and ultimate surrender. French power, relative to the other members of the system, was enhanced by the episode.[104]

Why, given the obvious power of the sanction, do we not observe specific episodes of expulsion and threats of expulsion? Mali and Guinea, after all, were examples of exit, not expulsion. There are two reasons for this, beyond any consideration of feedback. Principally, by the mere act of its membership, each state is acceding to very specific demands, which strike at the heart of its political and economic sovereignty. In contrast to currency manipulation, where an influence attempt is accompanied by an overt action, with dependence, paradoxically, the influence is associated with the absence of overt activity. Members recognize, either implicitly or explicitly through the rules of the system, that their participation restricts the bounds of their behavior. Thus in order to engage in certain acts, they must leave. Whether this is because the rules simply prevent them from physically or legally performing certain actions, or because they are aware that such behavior would not be tolerated from the center, exit, for the purpose of pursuing a forbidden agenda, is not in practice distinct from expulsion. Specifically, Mali and other states, such as Guinea, simply could not have engaged in the economic and political acts they wished to pursue while remaining members of the franc zone.

This finding is generalizable to the question of expulsion in any currency area. The threat of expulsion will automatically limit behavior. Attempts to overcome those limits will result in an end to participation, and the distinction between exit and expulsion approaches mere semantics at the limit of the argument. This is the visibility problem (see note 5): each day that goes by during which friendly regimes remain in power, or behavior opposed by the core state is forsaken because of the benefits and constraints of membership, power is successfully exercised. The issue then is one of how significant monetary considerations are in achieving these ends. The Malian case is especially useful because it involves a state's explicitly accusing the franc zone of constraining policy, abandoning the zone, pursuing forbidden economic and political agendas, failing and being forced to accept a humiliating about-face, and ultimately losing power in favor of a government more friendly to the core currency country.

---

[104] Other episodes would confirm these beliefs. In 1962, a major capital flight from Senegal was touched off by rumors that the country intended to bolt from the franc zone. The Senegalese government was forced to "unambiguously declare that [it] would remain a member of the Franc Zone." Mauritania, in 1972, despite a "comfortable" reserve position, had to enact severe exchange control in the wake of its decision to withdraw from the West African Monetary Union. Engberg, "Operations Account," p. 541. For a discussion of some of the specific issues raised by "going it alone," see S. R. Dixon-Fyle, "Monetary Dependence in Africa: The Case of Sierra Leone," *Journal of Modern African Studies* 16, no. 2:273–94 (1978).

This is especially useful because the use of overt techniques in the French case, as with all such cases, will be limited by the usual conditions of dependence (economic conditions and bilateral asymmetries), and further restricted by feedback associated with the importance of structural goals (entrapment and the potential for extraction).

In the French case, though, there is also an additional reason why no overt attempts to exploit monetary dependence are observed: there was very little to exploit. Members of the franc zone in the 1960s included some of the world's poorest states. While this made them more inclined to participate in the franc zone, it also meant that they had little to offer France, beyond the fact that their membership allowed something called the "franc zone" to exist at all.

The Dollar and Enforcement

The United States during the postwar era was at the center of a dollar-based international economy. The nature and design of the system were not accidental, but were tailored to fit the economic and political goals of the United States in this era. After World War II, the United States was in a unique position to reshape the economic structure of the world. Its preference was for a system of payments that would be multilateral, nondiscriminatory, and based on the dollar. Under the Bretton Woods system, currencies would be fixed relative to the dollar and defended at those parities, primarily through the use of the dollar as a reserve currency. The dollar itself was fixed at $35 per ounce of gold. Parities could only be changed with permission from the International Monetary Fund, and then only to correct fundamental disequilibria. This system was designed to allow for some discretion without plunging into the monetary chaos and competitive devaluations of the 1930s.[105]

The United States wanted Britain and the rest of Western Europe to move to an open, multilateral payments system as quickly as possible. Its motives in this regard have been attributed to economic, ideological, and security considerations. From the economic perspective, the United States wanted to ensure access to important markets. This meant defeating any attempts at "national" capitalism that might arise in Europe, and dismantling systems of imperial preference, such as the British one. From both an economic and a security perspective, the United States, in a position of hegemony, stood to gain from an open international system.[106] More directly, entrapment of allies in a U.S.-

[105] For more on the early history and rules of the IMF, see J. Keith Horsefield, ed., *The International Monetary Fund 1945–1965: Twenty Years of International Monetary Cooperation* (Washington, D.C.: IMF, 1969); Richard N. Gardner, *Sterling-Dollar Diplomacy in Current Perspective* (New York: Columbia University Press, 1980); and Robert W. Oliver, *Early Plans for a World Bank*, Princeton Studies in International Finance, no. 29 (Princeton University 1971).

[106] Michael Hudson, in *Superimperialism: The Economic Strategy of the American Empire*

dominated monetary system was another important link in the emerging U.S.-led anti-Soviet alliance. Finally, and importantly, many officials in the United States believed that the breakdown of an open multilateral international economy had played a role in the causation of World War II.

For all of these reasons, the United States attached great value to the success of the dollar system, which was one of a number of economic and security arrangements founded by that state during this era. Therefore, even though the United States desired multilateralism and nondiscrimination, it embraced the comprehensive practice of permissive currency manipulation, tolerating temporary violations of both of these principles in order to allow states to recover from the war. Broad exceptions to the IMF rules were tolerated until 1958, when most Western European states finally restored full convertibility.

Because of the absolute size of the U.S. economy, and the system of payments and finance of which the United States was at the center, the world was on a de facto dollar standard. The theory of dependence would suggest that the United States would be well placed to exploit monetary dependence, especially during recessions. On the other hand, both theory and empirical findings, such as those from the British and French cases, would suggest that the United States would be reluctant to explicitly exploit this monetary dominance, because of the gains it accrued in terms of entrapment and prestige, and the implicit restraint on the behavior of others, resulting from the mere existence of the system. In the 1960s, however, the United States chose to extract wealth from the system and ultimately to free itself of the constraints that system imposed on its most privileged member.[107]

The end of the Bretton Woods system, however, did not end the opportunities of the United States to exploit monetary dominance. That dominance was based on three levels of relationships. First, and most broadly, was the dollar system, that is, the fact that the world used the dollar as its international currency. This relationship survived the collapse of Bretton Woods; in fact, in some ways the United States was less constrained and therefore more powerful at this level after the collapse than before it. However, in the absence of formal agreements and arrangements, this power was different—the oppor-

---

(New York: Holt, Rinehart and Winston, 1968), esp. pp. 59–70, argues that the United States used the monetary system to displace Britain and dominate Europe. Fred L. Block, in *The Origins of International Economic Disorder* (Berkeley: University of California Press, 1977), stresses the U.S. desire to defeat national capitalism, "which American policy-makers were more concerned about than a Russian invasion of Western Europe" (p. 10). On hegemony and openness, see Robert Gilpin, *War and Change in World Politics* (Cambridge: Cambridge University Press, 1981), esp. pp. 138–39. For an early statement on this issue, see John Gallagher and Ronald Robinson, "The Imperialism of Free Trade," *Economic History Review*, 2d ser., 6, no. 1:1–18 (1953).

[107] This period is examined more closely in Chapter 5.

tunity to foster and exploit monetary dependence at this level was rather small.

The second level was the Bretton Woods system, which could be called the outer dollar zone. Opportunities for the exploitation of dependence, however inhibited, did exist here. The end of Bretton Woods obviously had a major effect on this level, basically causing the collapse of the outer dollar zone. The members of this zone became members of the looser dollar system, and were less vulnerable to dependence.

The third level of monetary relationship consisted of a series of bilateral arrangements and even uncoordinated patterns of activity, which collectively could be considered the inner dollar zone. The inner dollar zone was not affected by the collapse of Bretton Woods, and the potential for the exploitation of dependence was similarly unchanged. This inner zone featured two distinct types of relationships, dollar backing and dollar substitution.

Dollar-backing relationships occur when the United States guarantees the convertibility of a foreign currency at a given rate, usually through the financing or operation of a local exchange equalization account. As mentioned in Chapter 1, the United States had such relationships with some friendly states in Southeast Asia during the Vietnam War. The issues associated with, and the implications of, these relationships, for both sides, are the same ones that surfaced in the consideration of the French and British systems in this chapter. Dollar substitution relationships, on the other hand, represent a type of relationship that has not been considered to this point. Dollar substitution occurs when the dollar is used as domestic currency outside of the United States. This substitution can be either partial or complete. Partial substitution is more common, with the dollar circulating side by side with a domestically issued currency.

Partial currency substitution, or, as it is called in this case, dollarization, exists to some extent throughout Latin America. With dollarization, citizens hold some of their wealth in dollars and use those dollars in domestic transactions. Additionally, citizens adjust their portfolios (the percentage of their wealth held in dollars) in response to economic and political variables. One important result of dollarization is that flexible exchange rates do not provide monetary independence. Policy actions taken by the government can be undermined by the demand-side portfolio shifts made by private individuals.[108]

---

[108] One critique of fixed exchange rates was that they did not allow for monetary independence, because increases in the domestic money supply would lead to automatic outflows of the domestic currency. Flexible exchange rates, it was argued, would insulate domestic monetary developments from international ones. But with currency substitution, "even perfectly flexible rates may not guarantee monetary independence." Marc A. Miles, "Currency Substitution, Flexible Exchange Rates, and Monetary Independence," *American Economic Review* 68, no. 3:428–36 (1978), pp. 428–29. See also Arturo Brillamburg and Susan M. Schadler, "A Model of Currency Substitution in Exchange Rate Determination," *IMF Staff Papers* 26, no. 3:513–42 (1979).

This leads to two important conclusions: first, that the availability of dollars will influence domestic economic policy, and second, that this influence will be greater the higher the degree of dollarization in the economy. Thus, under some circumstances, controlling the ability of foreign countries to gain access to dollars can be an instrument of monetary power.[109]

Most Latin American governments consider dollarization to be a problem and have moved to limit its degree in their domestic economies. Venezuela only allows its citizens to hold such balances in offshore accounts. Bolivia, Mexico, and the Dominican Republic are among the many states in the region that restrict dollar use. But dollarization remains significant, and is especially important for both political and economic independence in that currency substitution is highly responsive to changes in confidence in the local currency.[110]

Although most states fight dollarization in order to safeguard economic and ultimately political independence, on rare occasions, dollarization is embraced by a foreign government. Sometimes this results in complete dollarization —that is, there is no domestically produced currency; instead the dolllar circulates as legal tender. This is the case in Panama.[111] As discussed above, the degree of dollarization is highly correlated with the potential for the exploitation of monetary dependence. Complete substitution suggests high vulnerability, especially for a small country. This was the position of Panama, and the United States attempted to tap this resource when it came into conflict with Panama in the late 1980s.

The "Panama crisis" began as a domestic political conflict in that country in

---

[109] To "count" as monetary diplomacy, the sanction must be intended to influence monetary variables, as opposed to a seizure of wealth as a bargaining chip or for reparations. (Also, as long as this action takes the form of the manipulation of the value or availability of *dollars*, the effects are dependent on the importance of dollars to the target economy. Therefore this is the exploitation of dependence, and not an episode of "currency manipulation.") Given theses requirements, most cases where the United States has frozen the assets of a foreign power, such as Iran in 1979 and Iraq in 1990, do not qualify as episodes of the introduction of currency power.

[110] Jaime Marquez, "Money Demand in Open Economies: A Currency Substitution Model for Venezuela," *Journal of International Money and Finance* 6, no. 2:167–78 (1987), esp. pp. 167–68; Guillermo Ortiz, "Currency Substitution in Mexico: The Dollarization Problem," *Journal of Money, Credit and Banking* 5, no. 2:174–85 (1983), esp. p. 174; on Bolivia, Mexico, and public confidence, Michael Melvin, "The Dollarization of Latin America as a Market-Enforced Monetary Reform: Evidence and Implications," *Economic Development and Cultural Change* 36, no. 3:543–58 (1988), pp. 543, 551–52; Victor A. Canto, "Monetary Policy, Dollarization, and Parallel Market Exchange Rates: The Case of the Dominican Republic," *Journal of International Money and Finance* 4, no. 4:507–21 (1985). The Dominican case is particularly interesting because of the high degree of dollarization there and the conscious attempt of the government to integrate the demand for dollars into its monetary policy.

[111] On the costs and benefits of complete currency substitution, see Eugene A. Birnbaum, "The Cost of a Foreign Exchange Standard or the Use of a Foreign Currency as the Circulating Medium," *IMF Staff Papers* 5, no. 3:477–91 (1957); and Stanley Fischer, "Seigniorage and the Case for a National Money," *Journal of Political Economy* 90, no. 2:295–313 (1982).

June 1987.[112] At that time, Roberto Díaz-Herrera, former chief of staff of the Panamanian Defense Forces (PDF), publicly charged General Manuel Noriega, commander of the PDF, with corruption. These accusations led to protests and general political upheaval in Panama. In response, President Eric Delvalle declared a state of emergency.

The U.S. Senate, at the end of the month, passed a resolution calling for an investigation into Herrera's charges. This resolution stirred up anti-Americanism in Panama, which led to a riot outside the U.S. embassy. The Reagan administration accused General Noriega of instigating the protest, and suspended U.S. economic and military aid until Panama paid for the damage visited on the embassy. That aid was worth $14 million in fiscal 1987 and about $32 million the following year. The Panamanian government paid $106,000 for damages on July 29, but the United States opted not to resume aid. U.S.-Panamanian relations continued to sour throughout the year, and on December 22, President Reagan suspended Panama's sugar quota and moved to prevent Panama from gaining new loans from international organizations, such as the IMF. The situation escalated dramatically on February 4, 1988, when General Noriega was indicted by Florida federal grand juries on charges of drug smuggling, money laundering, and racketeering. The nature of these charges raised the stakes of the conflict, and politicized the crisis within the United States.

The situation further intensified in Panama three weeks later when President Eric Arturo Delvalle attempted to dismiss General Noriega. Instead, Noriega had Delvalle dismissed, during a five-minute midnight meeting of part of the military-dominated Panamanian National Assembly. Delvalle went into hiding in Panama, and Vice President Manuel Palma was appointed acting president. The United States continued to recognize Delvalle as the legitimate leader of Panama, and with his cooperation, it froze Panamanian assets in U.S. banks on March 2. The following week the United States moved to prevent all payments and other dollar transfers to Panama, with the creation of escrow accounts. These sanctions were formalized by an executive order, signed on April 8. U.S. sanctions had a major effect on the Panamanian economy, but did not force Noriega out of power. This stalemate continued into the

---

[112] The following summary is based primarily on three sources: (1) Gary Clyde Hufbauer, Jeffrey J. Schott, and Kimberly Ann Elliot, *Economic Sanctions Reconsidered*, 2d ed. (Washington, D.C.: Institute for International Economics, 1990), pp. 249–58; (2)Testimony and prepared statement of Frank C. Conhan, Assistant Comptroller General, U.S. General Accounting Office, reprinted in U.S. House of Representatives, Committee on Foreign Affairs, Subcommittee on Western Hemisphere Affairs and International Economic Policy and Trade, "U.S. Policy toward Panama in the Aftermath of the May, 1, 1989 Elections," 101st Congress, 1st session, July 25–27,1989, pp. 86–143; (3)Testimony and prepared statement of Michael Kozak, Deputy Assistant Secretary of State for Inter-American Affairs, reprinted in U.S. House of Representatives, Committee on Foreign Affairs, Subcommittee on Western Hemisphere Affairs, "The Political Situation in Panama and Options for U.S. Policy," 100th Congress, 2d session, April 20, May 4, and June 1,1988, pp. 120–40.

Bush administration, which continued the sanctions policy. The general remained in power until December 20, 1989, when the United States invaded Panama and installed a new government, led by Guillmero Endara, leader of the opposition party that had won the May 1989 elections, which had been subsequently nullified by General Noriega.

The United States failed to remove General Noriega from power through the use of sanctions. This was widely perceived to be another case in which sanctions "didn't work." Although such conclusions are usually reached without consideration of the costs of compliance to the target, this issue is not the primary concern here. Of greater interest is how powerful monetary power was in this instance, what factors could have increased or decreased its effectiveness, and what lessons can be learned from this episode about the exploitation of monetary dependence in general.

Panama was already in considerable economic trouble before the sanctions of March 1988 were imposed. As a global banking center that depended on international confidence in its stability, the Panamanian economy suffered from the turmoil associated with the crisis from its inception. In 1987, foreigners began to withdraw billions from the estimated $40 billion deposited at over one hundred foreign banks in Panama, with local Panamanians also withdrawing several hundred million dollars.[113]

The exercise of U.S. monetary power made a bad situation much worse, and, initially, demonetized the economy.[114] Sanctions were both swift and severe in their effect. The banking system was shut down, and within a week the government did not have enough cash to pay its employees, except for the armed forces. Barter increased, and grocers refused to accept checks or credit cards. The government attempted to meet its payroll ($62 million for 150,000 employees) by issuing checks in denominations of $20, $30, and $100, and persuading the recipients to treat them as cash. Between the sanctions and the recession that was already taking place, the Panamanian GDP fell by a whopping 17.8 percent in 1988.[115]

It was widely recognized that the monetary sanctions were devastating. The former U.S. ambassador to Panama stated that the U.S. government had done

[113] Economist Intelligence Unit, *Country Report: Nicaragua, Costa Rica, Panama*, no. 4 (1987), pp. 7, 20; "The Color of Money," *Newsweek*, August 4, 1987, p. 27.

[114] The legal actions taken by the United States to block Panamanian assets and prevent other dollar transfers or payments to the government of Panama were complicated. They involved the creation of a number of accounts at the Federal Reserve Bank of New York, one of which was put at the disposal of President Delvalle. For a discussion of these accounts and the magnitudes of the blocked Panamanian assets, see the statement of R. Richard Newcomb, Director, Office of Foreign Assets Control, Department of the Treasury, in U.S. Congress, "U.S. Policy toward Panama," (1989), pp. 241–67.

[115] Economist Intelligence Unit, *Country Report: Nicaragua, Costa Rica, Panama*, no. 2 (1988), pp. 18, 20, 21, and no. 4 (1990), p. 7; "The Big Squeeze" *Time*, March 21, 1988, pp. 34–36; "Short on Cash, Long on Coping," *Time*, May 23, 1988, p. 43.

the most damage "to the Panamanian economy since Henry Morgan, the pirate, sacked Panama city in 1671." Another expert commented that the sanctions "completely derailed the Panamanian economy." One Panamanian religious leader urged that the sanctions be lifted on humanitarian grounds, since the citizens of Panama were "living through one of the most difficult periods in [their] history."[116]

The impact of these sanctions came very close to toppling the Noriega regime. The Economist Intelligence Unit reported that "the resulting dollar shortages [had] led to a rapid acceleration in the domestic opposition to the Government, making general Noriega's position as effective ruler look increasingly untenable." Protests by the opposition reached a new level of intensity, and on March 16, there was an unsuccessful coup attempt against the general by a faction within the military. This action represented the first split in Panama's previously "monolithic" military forces.[117]

Despite this crisis, General Noriega was able to cling to power, even in the face of severe economic sanctions. By the first week in April, those sanctions included not only the asset seizure, but a suspension of payments to the government of Panama from the United States for the operation of the Panama Canal and the use of the trans-Isthmian oil pipeline, a suspension of trade preferences, and a suspension of tax and other payments from American businesses operating in Panama.[118]

Once Noriega had survived the initial crisis, he was slowly able to right the ship of state, which had come so close to capsizing. Although Panama could not find important new sources of dollars (no international institution would grant it credit, and rumors of Libyan support never materialized), several factors operated in the general's favor. First, given time, the economy could adapt to demonetization. Although the economy was operating at only 40 percent of capacity, debt payments had been suspended, and unemployment had increased to 25 percent (from 14 percent in 1987), the government was able to allow banks to reopen on May 9.[119] Second, the U.S. government, under pressure from domestic business interests, successively eased restrictions on private transfers to Panama on May 31, June 23, and August 24. These regulations had begun to make it virtually impossible for U.S. businesses to operate in Panama, and those interests were able to have the restrictions eased. This became a significant source of dollars for the Panamanian

---

[116] Testimony of Ambler H. Moss, Jr., Eva Loser, and Rev James H. Ottley (Episcopal Bishop of Panama), U.S. Congress, "The Political Situation in Panama," pp. 37, 77, 99–100.

[117] Economist Intelligence Unit, *Country Report*, no. 2 (1988), pp. 8, 18.

[118] Conahan, Testimony in U.S. Congress, "U.S. Policy toward Panama," pp. 116–17. Economist Intelligence Unit, *Country Report*, no. 2 (1988), p. 21.

[119] There were still severe restrictions on withdrawals, however. Economist Intelligence Unit, *Country Report*, no. 3 (1988), pp. 22–23.

government.[120] Finally, the severe impact of the sanctions themselves increased sympathy throughout Latin America for the Noriega regime.[121]

The crisis continued for another year and a half, with occasional variations in intensity. Although the Panamanian economy continued to suffer, in 1989 the economy stabilized, with GDP falling only slightly (beyond the depths of 1988).[122] Ultimately, the situation was militarized and resolved by U.S. intervention. Economic sanctions were widely held to have "failed" in this instance.[123] However, this Roman Coliseum–style thumb up/thumb down analysis is of limited value. What must be considered, along with degree of success in attaining specific objectives, is the cost of exercising various forms of power and the degree of difficulty associated with achieving success. By this yardstick, monetary power looks rather impressive, coming close to achieving extremely difficult goals at little or no cost. As one analyst noted,

> Well timed, sudden and concentrated financial pressure alone stood a reasonable chance of toppling Noriega in the short run in March 1988; in retrospect, it came very close to doing so. Had Noriega fallen, the objective would have been achieved with none of the costs associated with broader measures.[124]

As in the Suez crisis, monetary power was directed against policies that were highly valued by the target state. Although the Suez case was an episode of predatory currency manipulation, and the Panamanian episode featured an attempt at enforcement through the exploitation of monetary dependence, the strength of monetary power is evident in both cases. Both applied swift and severe pressure. Another aspect the two episodes have in common was the reason decisionmakers chose monetary power in those cases. Along with other considerations, sanctions were chosen that would inflict great pain on the leadership without permanently damaging the economy.

This was of great concern in the Panamanian case. Because of the importance of future U.S.-Panamanian relations, U.S.-Latin American relations,

---

[120] Hufbauer et al., *Economic Sanctions*, p. 254; Conahan, Testimony, p. 117. For a specific list of exceptions granted, ibid., p. 122. Most business groups argued that sanctions were counterproductive and hurt U.S. companies. See the prepared statement of the American Chamber of Commerce and Industry of Panama, U.S. Congress, "U.S. Policy toward Panama," pp. 202–8.

[121] Economist Intelligence Unit, *Country Report*, no. 3 (1988), p. 8. This result (the generation of international sympathy or domestic support) offers a practical demonstration of why private sanctions can be more effective than public ones.

[122] Economist Intelligence Unit, *Country Report: Nicaragua, Costa Rica, Panama* no. 4 (1990), p. 7.

[123] See quotes by Chairman Sam Gejdenson, Secretary of State for Inter-American Affairs Elliot Abrams, and Jeffrey Schott, in U.S. Congress, "U.S. Policy toward Panama," pp. 63–65, 175, 179–99.

[124] Joseph C. Lombard, "The Survival of Noriega: Lessons from the U.S. Sanctions against Panama," *Stanford Journal of International Law* 26, no. 1:269–323 (1989), pp. 271–72.

and U.S. business interests, the U.S. objectives were to rid Panama of Noriega without undermining the long-term health of the country as a whole. Monetary power is excellently suited for this type of mission. Attacking a country's liquidity is like turning off a faucet. Once the objectives are met, the faucet can be turned back on. Turning off the water and electricity can often cause a fugitive to surrender without setting fire to the building in which the fugitive has taken refuge.

In pursuit of this policy, the United States explicitly refrained from taking certain measures. Even though the United States purchased more than half of Panama's exports and was the leading source of its imports, a trade embargo was never imposed. Such action was avoided because it was viewed as being against the interests of the entire population of Panama, and not well focused on the interests of the government. Similarly, the United States considered but never banned Panamanian-flag ships from entering U.S. ports, which would have damaged a major Panamanian industry.[125]

Interestingly, it is possible that trade sanctions, which would have primarily hurt the citizens of Panama, would not have been decisive anyway. Because Panama's economy is dominated by services, it was not highly vulnerable to such sanctions. Additionally, the Nicaraguan embargo had proven rather easy to circumvent, and resulted in the displacement of U.S. businesses.[126] Some argued that U.S. policy failed because it held conflicting goals: ridding Panama of Noriega without seriously damaging the Panamanian economy or U.S. business interests.[127] This argument highlights the relaxation of the transfer restrictions, since introducing additional sanctions probably would not have affected the outcome. Even such a limited argument, however, does not seem persuasive for two reasons. First, these relaxations occurred after the sanctions had had their initial ferocious bite, when the chance of success was greatest. Second, these loopholes were created because of a lagged feedback effect. Initially, these sanctions could be introduced without cost to U.S. inter-

[125] For trade figures, Economist Intelligence Unit, *Country Profile: Nicaragua, Costa Rica, Panama, 1990–91*, p. 64. Pp. 44–68 provide a concise political and economic description of the country. On motives for limiting sanctions, see Economist Intelligence Unit, *Country Report*, no. 3 (1989), p. 8, and *Country Report*, no. 4 (1989), p. 18, which reports that a U.S. ban would "have harmed the country's ship registration industry irretrievably." The report added: "The USA is seeking to take measures which increase the pressure on General Noriega without doing long term damage to the country."

[126] Lombard, "Survival of Noriega," pp. 295–99. See also Schott, Testimony in U.S. Congress, "U.S. Policy toward Panama," p. 185.

[127] Congressman Gejdenson repeatedly argued this to be the case. U.S. Congress, "U.S. Policy toward Panama," pp. 63 ("we wanted to have our cake and eat it too"), 123–24, 138–39. Schott's testimony also cited "conflicting goals" as a source of failure, pp. 186–87. Conahan, in his written statements, asserts that the exceptions granted to protect the U.S. business community allowed almost half of the funds that could potentially have been denied the Noriega regime to get through, pp. 102–3. Lombard, "Survival of Noriega," on the other hand, minimizes the importance of the relaxations, pp. 301–2.

ests. Over time, however, the balance of pain shifted to include U.S. companies, which were able to mobilize to defend themselves. Thus, while the sanctions imposed on Panama were swift and powerful, they were simply not strong enough in this case to overcome the resistance of the target to compliance. This is not surprising, since the goal of the sanctions was so high: the overthrow of the target government.

From a broader perspective, the dollar system demonstrates once again the willingness of a core state to make economic sacrifices to establish and maintain a currency system, as the United States did during the first fifteen years of the postwar era. The United States was further motivated by a superpower competition and did not want to scare small states off, which explains why the United States would have been reluctant to engage in overt coercion, through the use of the monetary system, against small states. The United States preferred to promote entrapment and secure the potential for extraction. The circumstances surrounding the Panamanian case, however, provided an excellent opportunity to practice enforcement.

Because enforcement is a distant cousin of currency manipulation, it should not be surprising that it shares some of the features of that instrument. Enforcement was stunningly swift and severe in its implementation and effect. While the severity may vary from case to case, the swiftness of monetary power in general seems to be an enduring property, and one with great significance. Compared to other forms of economic coercion, such as trade sanctions, this episode confirms that monetary sanctions are generally more focused on the government, which is usually the target of sanctions. Additionally, the policymakers in the core state were aware of this fact.

However, one consequence of the swiftness of monetary sanctions is that if they do not work quickly, they may not work at all. Except to the extent that their effect is delayed by the running down of defenses, monetary sanctions, such as enforcement, may get successively weaker as time goes by. One possible explanation of this is that the sanction forces the target state to confront demonetization. If the government is willing to accept the consequences of demonetization, and proves able to survive the political climate created by the economic consequences of such a decision, it may have done all it needs to do to survive. Once complete demonetization is reached, the target country should slowly be able to adjust.

Another issue raised by this episode is the resurgence of private interests. It was asserted earlier that one of the advantages of monetary power is its relative freedom from domestic political pressures. This finding may have to be modified in some cases of enforcement. If the case is one of currency substitution (or dollarization), and the method of enforcement is to stop all payments to the target regime, private business interests must be reintegrated into the process, since they are important sources of payments through taxes and other fees to the target government. They will therefore be directly affected by the sanctions and possibly disposed to mobilize in order to oppose or weaken them. On the other hand, this problem is limited by the fact that if monetary sanctions are going to work, they will probably work quickly. Thus, if companies can mobilize to defeat sanctions, by the time they do so, if sanctions have not yet worked, it will not really matter. This would not be the case with other instruments of economic coercion, where private interests would be involved from the start, and when the instrument of coercion naturally takes longer to become effective.

The Theory and Practice of Monetary Dependence

Because of a number of methodological difficulties, generalizable conclusions about the exploitation of monetary dependence will be somewhat restricted. A recurrent theme is the measurability problem, a result of both the nature of the forms of dependence and the fact that those forms often conflict with, as opposed to complement, one another. However, one fundamental conclusion is clear: techniques that exploit monetary dependence exist, they have been introduced in a purposeful and systematic way by a variety of states throughout the twentieth century, and they have demonstrated considerable power to advance a number of security-related interests. The major influence attempts are summarized in Table 4.2.

To summarize this table, the analysis looked at four international monetary systems, led by Germany, Britain, France, and the United States. In the 1930s, Germany created the mark system, with three political objectives in mind: to isolate itself from the international economy, in order to facilitate

TABLE 4.2
The Practice of Monetary Dependence

Core/System	Target	Form/Objective	Evaluation
Germany/mark	Southeastern Europe	Isolation	Success
		Entrapment	Success
		Extraction	Success
Britain/pound	Sterling System	Entrapment	Unknown
		Extraction	Success
France/franc	Franc system	Entrapment	Unknown
	Mali/franc system	Expulsion/enforcement	Success
U.S./dollar	Outer dollar system	Entrapment	Success
	Panama (inner dollar system)	Enforcement	Failure

Note: All these episodes were major attempts.

autarky-based recovery and rearmament; to entrap its southeastern neighbors; and to extract from them the resources necessary for war. On all three counts, the policy was highly successful, as monetary diplomacy was integrated into the overall economic and national security strategy of Germany.

While the mark system lasted about a decade, the sterling system had the longest existence, close to 150 years, and furthered British interests through both entrapment and extraction. Extraction in this case was a significant, quantifiable emergency measure taken by Britain, and that particular episode offers a good example of how monetary systems can provide a reservoir of resources that the core can tap. The significance of entrapment, on the other hand, is more difficult to assess. While the characteristics of entrapment—patterns of economic interrelationships and political activity—can be observed, the weight and depth of those arrangements and the significance of their political consequences are virtually unmeasurable. This is not to say that they cannot be of tremendous importance, but rather that determining the true magnitude of that importance is difficult, making assessments of entrapment similarly problematic.

This pattern, the difficulty of measuring the outcome of structural as compared to overt forms of dependence, is repeated in the French case. Entrapment obviously occurred, and economic and political patterns were certainly affected by participation in the franc system, but what is difficult to measure is how tight those binding ties were. The French experience with the threat of expulsion, on the other hand, was highly and measurably successful, forcing Mali to return to the fold and clearly enforcing the policy preferences of France throughout the system. However, this success should be qualified by the observation that Guinea escaped such enforcement by paying the full price of exit.

The U.S. case is similar to the German case in that the success of entrapment is sufficiently apparent to code it "successful." The establishment of the outer dollar system was one of the pillars of the postwar international system established by the United States to further its interrelated economic and security-related goals. The U.S. attempt at enforcement (monetary sanctions against a deviant member of the inner dollar zone) was not successful, but did demonstrate the considerable weight of potential enforcement techniques available to system leaders.

There is a strong pattern of success suggested by the summary. Only the U.S. attempt to coerce Panama can be coded as a failure, and even that episode shows how vulnerable member states are to powerful sanctions imposed by core states. However, the "success" of monetary dependence is overstated, if the implicit conclusion is for states to run out and become core leaders. For the table does not include a number of failures, because in this case, most failures occur in what should be called the "presystem" stage. For example, as discussed above, France expended a great deal of energy in attempting to create franc systems in the nineteenth and early twentieth centuries, failing both times. These were both failed attempts to foster and exploit monetary dependence, but because they failed at the fostering stage, they could not be evaluated with regard to their success at exploitation. Basically, any functioning monetary system already represents some level of success. Another bias in the summary is that practice of many techniques of dependence carries with it greater risks than does the practice of manipulation. Attempts at expulsion, enforcement, and extraction are inhibited by fears of undermining entrapment. It is logical to assume, therefore, that the riskiest influence attempts (that is, those most likely to fail) will not be attempted by core states. Understanding the practice of dependence, then, requires a sensitivity to both when it will be introduced and its chances for nominal success.

Two broad considerations shape the opportunity to practice monetary dependence. The first of these is global economic conditions, which directly affect the relative benefits of membership and thus the leverage of the core state. The second is a more complicated amalgamation of bilateral economic and political relationships between core states and individual members. These establish the relative bargaining power between the core and member state, and it appears that both the economic and political variables are important. Similarly, the nature of both general economic conditions and specific bilateral relationships are important in explaining the opportunities for dependence. In wartime, though, the economic conditions aspect may be submerged. There is no reason why the prevalence of peace, on the other hand, should similarly cause the submersion of the bilateral relations dimension. Underlying power considerations will always be significant, and explain, for example, why France was unsuccessful in its repeated attempts to establish monetary dominance in Europe, the pattern of German relations, and the opportunities for British extraction.

One striking finding is that in all of the cases considered, core states actively wanted to be the leaders of monetary systems, and were willing to make repeated economic sacrifices in order to establish and maintain such positions.[128] This was not simply to enhance prestige, although this was often a motive, especially in declining states, such as Britain and France, in the postwar era. Rather, it was because those states recognized that thriving monetary systems provided them with three important enhancements of their power: first, insulation from the world economy, and thus increased autonomy; second, increased leverage over member states, due to asymmetric contribution-to-benefit ratios; and third, increased power from those states, through the potential for extraction, and especially from the transformation of the preferences of the members.

---

[128] This conforms with a general pattern whereby virtually every state that has had the opportunity to extend its monetary influence has done so.

No matter which of the other instruments they employed, all of the system leaders were very interested in entrapment, and although other concerns may have temporarily eclipsed that goal, over the long run it was dominant. After entrapment, leadership of currency systems is attractive because it provides the opportunity for extraction. For core states, sacrifices to maintain an area can be interpreted as a long-term investment. Extraction is probably not useful as a continuous flow of income, because this would undermine entrapment. However, as a mechanism that can facilitate the mobilization and coordinate the flow of needed resources under emergency circumstances, the potential of the instrument is great.

Because entrapment and the potential for extraction are coveted by states, the overt coercive instruments of dependence, enforcement, and expulsion, are somewhat inhibited by feedback. This is more important with regard to enforcement, because the tacit threat of expulsion will constrain the behavior of member states even in the absence of specific threats. However, given the right circumstances, enforcement will be practiced.[129]

The other side of this story is the process by which a peripheral state weighs the costs and benefits of membership. In choosing whether or not to participate in a monetary system, states must evaluate the international political consequences, as well as their own domestic political and economic circumstances. If they join, they will be vulnerable to the exploitation of their dependence. However, as members in a currency system, they may be better able to exercise monetary power of their own, through the practice of strategic disruption.

[129] Issues associated with when the "right circumstances" arise are considered in Part III.

5

Systemic Disruption

The Theory of Systemic Disruption

Systemic disruption is a distinct form of monetary power, although it is not unrelated to currency manipulation. Currency manipulation, it will be recalled, is any attempt to influence the value, stability, or other attributes of a specific currency. The use of this type of monetary power was defined by the ends—effect on the target currency—and not by the means, or method of manipulation. Systemic disruption is also defined by the ends: effect on a given international monetary regime, whether regional or global. However, although often complementary, the two instruments are distinct. Disruption aims at the system. The threat or sanction emanates from the dissolution of such a system. Two themes call attention to this distinction. First, as noted, the crucial difference is the source of the power of the sanction. Under currency manipulation, the sacrifices taken to defend the currency, the concessions made to stop the attack, and the political losses suffered as a result of the weakness of the currency, represent the sources of the power of the sanction. Under disruption, those sacrifices, concessions, and losses are associated with the attempt to maintain, and the cost of losing, the existence of a particular monetary system.

Secondly, and even more clearly, although techniques associated with currency manipulation may be introduced to further the goal of disruption, it is not necessary that such methods be introduced. That is, disruption can take place in the complete absence of currency manipulation–like techniques. Systemic disrupters can make threats or promises, unrelated to the monetary regime, designed to force the dissolution of a given system. Disrupters can also attempt to foment defection from the regime. In some cases, acting from within, such states might try to alter the existing rules in order to weaken the system or, alternatively, might simply withdraw from the organization and hope that others will follow.

All of these techniques challenge the system, but none of them involves affecting a target currency. The goals of such disruption remain numerous. One might want to weaken the leader of a monetary regime, which enjoys the prestige associated with, or any of the other benefits[1] resulting from, the existence of the system. Under such circumstances, the disruption aims to alter

---

[1] For the political benefits of leadership, see Chapter 4.

the balance of power between two states by undermining one source of the adversary's strength. On the other hand, the goal might be more indirect: a disrupter may wish to increase its own influence in the (would-be) former members of some other state's international monetary regime.

The Forms of Systemic Disruption

Systemic disruption comes in two varieties, strategic and subversive. Subversive disruption simply aims to destroy an existing international monetary regime, to weaken its leader or participating states, for any number of reasons. Strategic disruption, on the other hand, is a form of coercion: attempts to parlay the ability to undermine such a system into tangible gains without actually destroying the monetary regime. Subversive disruption is most naturally the province of states outside of the target monetary regime. This is because such states are less likely to suffer from the consequences of the system's collapse, and more likely to gain from the resulting weakness of the core state or states, and also have the ability to profit from sifting through the rubble of the devastated system. As outsiders, subversive disrupters have a limited number of options. Some of these have been mentioned above, such as overt threats or promises to the core or member states, directly intended to undermine the system. In such cases, it is logical to assume that the ability of the disrupter to offer some alternative monetary regime would enhance its position. However, the most compelling vision of subversive disruption is the doomsday scenario: the collapse of the core upon which a monetary regime is founded. Two of the most obvious techniques here are the massive counterfeiting of the core currency and the manipulation of the production or distribution of a commodity, such as gold, upon which a monetary system might be based.

Subversive disruption is a very blunt and therefore limited weapon. It is not a negotiated form of power but a one-time act of aggression. This may serve as an effective form of punishment, or as part of a broader and ongoing campaign to weaken an adversary in any way possible. As such an instrument, though, it is inhibited by the fact that it is a single-shot weapon, and once fired, its power is expended. The practice of strategic disruption is much more complicated. Strategic disruption is more naturally the province of insiders, that is, participants in the monetary system that is being threatened. Working from within better positions the state to interfere with the functioning of the system. However, it also means that the disrupting state usually wants the system to survive. States within a system are therefore endowed with a broader range of capabilities but are more inhibited from taking actions that might destroy the regime.

An analysis of strategic disruption also reveals additional differences between the practice of disruption and the practice of currency manipulation.

While manipulation almost always involves "aiming down," that is, supporting or attacking the currencies of weaker states, strategic disruption almost always involves "aiming up": challenging the interests of a stronger power. This form of currency power, therefore, runs a dual risk: one associated with the possibility that actions taken will inadvertently destroy the system, and another associated with the possibility of antagonizing a great power.

The theory of strategic disruption owes much to Schelling, and his development of the concept of "rocking the boat." The technique of boatrocking capitalizes not on the incredible threat that you will intentionally tip over the boat and drown both yourself and your opponent, but rather on the possibility that because of the rashness of your actions, the boat may accidentally overturn. The strategy is not to punish the adversary by destroying the system, but to extort side payments: that is, rewards for promising not to rock the boat any more.[2]

This nautical theme was applied to the international monetary system by Charles Kindleberger at a conference in 1965, when he noted:

> If a boat carries ten people six life preservers are more than enough in case anyone falls overboard. However if there is one neurotic aboard who won't sail unless he can keep a life preserver on there is danger of everyone else fighting for life preservers or even upsetting the boat.[3]

Most considerations of boatrocking focus on this possibility that the boat might be inadvertently overturned. But for a state practicing strategic disruption, this danger is only half the problem. To extend this analogy, the people in this case sailing in the monetary boat are not the same size: the disrupter is much lighter than the core country. To rock the boat, the smaller person may have to exert himself greatly, even to the extent of standing on the sides of the craft. In this case, he may simply fall overboard, without upsetting the boat.

To be more "money-specific," strategic disruption will usually involve a mid-sized power, since, to quote Kindleberger again, such states "have the power to hurt the system, generally insufficient power to steady it . . . but are tempted to pursue national goals which diverge from the interest of the system."[4] As a disrupter will usually be weaker, in an overall sense, than the state at the center of the system (the most likely target of such an influence attempt), boatrocking is even more hazardous than it would be were the risk limited to inadvertent capsizing. In these cases the challenger will also have to

---

[2] Thomas C. Schelling, *The Strategy of Conflict* (1960; reprint, Cambridge: Harvard University Press, 1980), ch. 8 and p. 196; see also Schelling, *Arms and Influence* (New Haven: Yale University Press, 1966), ch. 3.

[3] Quoted in the *Atlantic Community Quarterly* 3, no. 1 (1965), p. 101.

[4] Charles P. Kindleberger, "The International Monetary Politics of a Near Great Power: Two French Episodes, 1926–36 and 1960–70" (1972), reprinted in Kindleberger, *Keynesianism versus Monetarism* (London: George Allen and Unwin, 1985), p. 119.

be sensitive to its own weakness, and to the possibility that the strain of disruption might tax its own power too greatly, without affecting the system. More generally, even if the act of disruption itself were risk free (to the challenger's economy), such a state would still have to be sensitive to the fact that inclement weather in the form of unrelated events might toss it off the boat, leaving only the stronger state behind to save it from drowning.

The Monetary System and the Opportunity for Disruption

As with currency manipulation, the techniques of disruption are affected by the nature of the monetary system: specifically, the type of economic regime in effect. Systemic disruption depends on the ability to undermine specific promises or agreements. The nature of those agreements also defines the potential pressure points. (This is less important, but still the case, for subversive disruption.) As James Tobin noted, "Once a banker has solemnly assured the world and his depositors that he will never fail, he is at the mercy of those depositors capable of making him fail."[5] Once again, these promises can be categorized in terms of the oversimplified but sufficient dichotomy, fixed and floating exchange rate regimes.

FIXED EXCHANGE RATES

The ability to disrupt a fixed-rate system based on a specific commodity, such as gold or silver, depends on the ability to influence either the supply or the price of the key commodity.[6] Suppliers of the metal can obviously attempt to disrupt a system, for either strategic or subversive purposes, by increasing or decreasing production and distribution. Nonproducers can disrupt the system by changing the volume of their purchases of the commodity. For example, U.S. purchases of silver in the early 1930s raised the price of silver, and caused a great deflation in China, ultimately forcing that country off the silver standard. Had China been at the center of a silver-based regional international monetary arrangement, and had the United States wished to eliminate such a system in order to reduce Chinese influence in those countries, these actions would have represented a subversive disruption of the Chinese system.[7]

---

[5] James Tobin, "Europe and the Dollar," *Review of Economics and Statistics* 46, no. 2:123–26 (1964), p. 124.

[6] Technically, there is little difference between influencing "supply" and influencing "price." These signposts are used to represent the distinction between actions available to producers and those available to nonproducers.

[7] Actually, the U.S. action was taken with indifference to the Chinese situation, and there was no Chinese international monetary regime. For more on China, see Chapter 3.

The more complex the system design, the greater the opportunity for disruption. Thus, commodity-exchange standards are even easier to disrupt than pure commodity standard systems. This is because aside from preserving those elements of the latter system that are vulnerable to disruption, an exchange standard system adds additional rules, which can be exploited. States that engage in policies with the expectation that the rules will be followed may leave themselves vulnerable to actions taken by others that violate those norms. Even without this "expectations based policy shift," all systems with rules are vulnerable to disruption, and the degree to which they are vulnerable is determined by the importance of those rules to the survival of the system. Most important, in a gold-exchange standard system, surplus states (those with a positive balance of payments) must be willing to accept payment not in gold but in the form of recognized reserve currencies. Without such behavior, an exchange standard system cannot hope to survive.[8]

FLOATING EXCHANGE RATES

This regime appears to be the most difficult to disrupt, because the fewest explicit rules are associated with it. It is somewhat odd to consider the "disruption" of such a system. However, there are rules implicit in such a system, such as the commitment to maintain an open, market-dominated system of international monetary relations. The smooth operation of such a system could be disrupted by state intervention aimed at making foreign exchange markets unpredictable. Other states could violate the spirit of the system, maintaining inappropriate exchange rates and leaving target states uncomfortable with the system. Aside from the extraction of side payments, a disrupter could be motivated, for example, by a desire to compartmentalize the system in order to enhance its own power in a particular region. As always, the potential for subversion through the counterfeiting of one of the dominant currencies also exists.

Regimes featuring considerable inconvertibility also offer opportunities for disruption, as the "inconvertibility" is rarely universal, but usually takes place between established monetary blocs, with each bloc having its own rules. Here, subversion of these subsystems can take place both from within and from without. From outside the system, states can act to disrupt the enclosed regime, for example by encouraging or facilitating the exit of member states. As discussed in Chapter 4, Czechoslovakia disrupted the franc system in this way when it provided Mali with the ability to print its own currency. Disruption from within an externally inconvertible system is to some extent a microcosm of all of the techniques of disruption discussed above. However, since

---

[8] Alvin H. Hansen, *The Dollar and the International Monetary System* (New York: McGraw Hill, 1965), p. 57 (necessary behavior for the survival of a gold-exchange standard).

such regimes are usually based on the currency of the core state and not on a commodity, disruption is more likely to focus on the viability of the system's core currency. Additionally, states that are relatively important sources of reserves and foreign exchange can threaten to withdraw from the system, for either strategic or subversive reasons.

Under almost any international monetary regime, then, the opportunity for both strategic and subversive disruption exists in some form. In practice, as the following examples illustrate, the employment of these instruments has been more limited. There have not been any significant episodes of subversive disruption, and, not surprisingly, floating rate "systems" have not been disrupted.

Focal Case: France, Britain, and the Gold-Exchange Standard

The fifty-eight months from January 1927 to October 1931 featured the almost constant practice of monetary diplomacy. Most of these displays of currency power revolved around attempts at strategic disruption by France. This activity is reflected in the singular monetary trend of the era, the accumulation of gold by that country. In December 1926, France held 7.8 percent of the world's monetary gold reserves. Six years later, more than 27 percent of the world's gold reserves could be found in Paris. (At the end of 1914, the figure was 15.2 percent).[9]

France used its ability to accumulate gold to threaten the viability of the gold-exchange standard, or more specifically, the ability of Britain to manage and serve as the foundation of such a system, in the hope of extracting concessions on what were essentially political issues. These issues centered almost exclusively on some aspect of the German question. It merits repeating that a gold exchange standard cannot survive unless surplus countries are willing to take payment, and hold reserves, not simply in gold but also in designated key currencies. In this instance, France's position as such a surplus country put it in a position to challenge the convertibility of the pound, which was the linchpin of the monetary system.

The practice of currency power by France was a multilayered tapestry of disruption, aimed primarily at Britain, interwoven with additional specific currency manipulations, usually directed at Germany. These varied influence attempts were highly complementary, as pressure on Germany often resulted in indirect pressure on Britain, the system's banker. These interrelationships manifested themselves in an intriguing golden waltz, featuring the cunning French, the dutiful British, the enigmatic Germans, and the powerful American wallflowers.

[9] Gold holdings calculated from *Federal Reserve Bulletin* 19, no. 6 (1933), p. 368.

The Economic Backdrop

After World War I, it was the official expectation and preference of most states that the international gold standard would be restored in a timely fashion. However, because of the great inflations associated with that conflict, there was a relative shortage of gold. This led to the creation of a gold exchange standard system, in which key currencies (in this case, the pound and the dollar) would be used as international reserves to supplement gold holdings. For such purposes, (intervention to maintain par, settlement of international accounts, and as a store of reserve assets) dollars and pounds were to be as good as gold.

Such a system could only function if the key currencies were legally convertible into gold at a fixed rate. The last barrier to this was surmounted when Britain restored its prewar parity of $4.86/£, which became law on April 28, 1925. This restoration, especially in retrospect, appears to have been an overvaluation of the pound, and therefore had a negative effect on the British balance of payments. For this reason, and because the defense of such a par would require deflationary government policy (unless the Americans were willing to inflate) the restoration was criticized by some individuals at the time, most notably by John Maynard Keynes.[10] However, the politics of the restoration of the pound are not of concern here. What is important is that the effect of the restoration would be, among other things, a net drain on British gold reserves.

France, on the other hand, stabilized the franc at one-fifth of its prewar level, or Fr124/£. This was accomplished de facto in December 1926, though it would not become de jure until June 1928. This parity represented a relative undervaluation of the franc. The motives for stabilizing the franc at this level are unclear, though most recent analyses stress the dominance of domestic politics. It is notable that Emile Moreau, governor of the Bank of France and an uninhibited champion of French international monetary power, was the figure most dogmatically in favor of a low restoration (as compared to Prime Minister Raymond Poincaré, for example, who at one time considered allowing the franc to appreciate to Fr100/£).[11] Regardless, the undervaluation of the

---

[10] See John Maynard Keynes, *The Economic Consequences of Sterling Parity* (New York: Harcort Brace and Co., 1925); also D. E. Moggridge, *British Monetary Policy 1924–31* (Cambridge: Cambridge University Press, 1972).

[11] Gustav Cassel, in *The Crisis in the World's Monetary System* (Oxford: Clarendon Press, 1932), argued that "[t]he French learned from the British episode . . . [and] chose an external value distinctly below the internal purchasing power of the franc" (pp. 28–9). This is not incompatible with recent interpretations that stress domestic politics, such as Gregory C. Schmid, "The Politics of Currency Stabilization: The French Franc, 1926," *Journal of European Economic History* 3, no. 2:359–377 (1974), p. 377; and Pierre Sicsic, "Was the Franc Poincaré Deliberately Undervalued?" (unpublished photocopy, Department of Economics, Harvard University, November 1989), p. 2; ibid., pp. 18–20 (on Poincaré and Moreau).

franc would have a positive effect on the French balance of payments, which was to become one of the primary reasons why foreign exchange flowed to France in this period. Even before long-term payments patterns had this effect, the Bank of France, in order to keep the franc from appreciating, intervened in the market to support the stabilization. Since the goal was to keep the franc down, this meant selling francs and buying pounds. These operations were an important early source of the increase in the bank's holdings of foreign exchange[12], and as long as the franc was perceived to be undervalued, it would be a continuous phenomenon.

Thus there were natural economic forces at work to explain the flow of foreign exchange to France. These flows were the result of private international transactions and official intervention, and were usually denominated in pounds, which could be converted into gold on demand. However, the fact that this flow of foreign exchange was somehow "natural" did not detract from three important and troubling observations. First, France, unlike the United States (the other great gold absorber of the era), when forced to choose, "valued supremacy over international stability." Second, the new par value of the franc "inevitably constituted a weapon which France could use against Britain." Third, Moreau viewed British monetary policy as "a new kind of imperialism."[13]

The Consequences of the Restoration of the Franc

The accumulation of gold by France grew into one of the most widely discussed and hotly debated issues in international economics. This especially became the case as the world moved first into recession, and then into prolonged depression. There was little disagreement over the reasons for the flow of gold to France. Three causes in particular stood out. First was the undervaluation of the franc, which caused a flow of foreign exchange to France, as discussed above. Second was the movement of capital into France, in the form of both repatriation and flight from other sources, each attracted by the restoration of French financial stability. Third, at least until mid-1929, was the sterilization of gold imports and the direct liquidation of foreign exchange by the Bank of France.[14] There was great disagreement, though, regarding the motives behind the French gold absorption and the solution to the problem.

[12] Nearly £100 million was acquired by the Bank of France in this way before the end of May 1927. Andrew Boyle, *Montagu Norman: A Biography* (London: Cassell and Co., 1967), p. 227.

[13] On stability versus supremacy, Paul Einzig, *The Fight for Financial Supremacy* (London: Macmillan, 1931), p. 6. Einzig's argument echoes Kindleberger's discussion of the role of middle powers in a monetary system, discussed above. "Weapon" and "imperialism" are from Susan Strange, *Sterling and British Policy* (London: Oxford University Press, 1971), p. 52.

[14] Paul Einzig, *Behind the Scenes of International Finance* (London: Macmillan, 1932), p. 38;

There were three contending interpretations of French behavior. France could have been encouraging the inflow, in order to advance a political or financial strategy. France could have been passive in the face of the inflow, statutorily unable to act or otherwise disinclined to intervene. Finally, France could have been embarrassed by and opposed to the inflow, taking steps to counter it.[15] As for solutions, the debate inevitably reduced to whether it was the system or France that was the source of the problem, and accordingly to which of the two should bear the brunt of the adjustment necessary to resolve it.[16] The position sympathetic to France held that Britain must act to cut the flow of gold from Britain by restricting foreign lending and raising the interest rate. The opposing point of view held that halting the inflow of gold to France could easily have been accomplished, "had the French monetary authorities desired," and questioned whether French policy "ha[d] been influenced by purely economic considerations."[17] One critic argued, "I have not found a satisfactory explanation of what is going on, other than the will to acquire gold." Others countered that the movement and distribution of gold represented "a consequence, not a cause" of the world's problems.[18]

Regardless of the merits of this debate, as W. A. Brown has observed, "even by remaining passive in the foreign exchange markets . . . [France] was in a strategic position to get gold from abroad."[19] Additionally, the evidence supports the contention that the Bank of France both welcomed such an accumulation, because it complemented French financial and political strategies, and often enhanced it by active and purposeful intervention. Arguments challenging this interpretation rest on two erroneous assumptions regarding, first, the capabilities and, second, the relative significance of the Bank of France.

---

also John C. DeWilde, "French Financial Diplomacy," *Foreign Policy Reports* 8, no. 20:232–42 (1932), p. 237. Einzig, a British journalist, was one of the leading critics of French policy in this era.

[15] Einzig, *Financial Supremacy*, p. 104.

[16] Two principal fora in which this debate was carried out were the Royal Institute for International Affairs, which held a quasi-monthly seminar on the gold issue from December 1929 to February 1931, and the Gold Delegation of the Financial Committee of the League of Nations, which published numerous papers on the issue in the two years leading up to its final report in 1932. Royal Institute of International Affairs (RIIA), *The International Gold Problem* (London: Oxford University Press, 1932); League of Nations, *Report of the Gold Delegation of the Financial Committee* (Geneva: League of Nations, 1932) and two volumes of *Selected Documents* Submitted to the Gold Delegation of the Financial Committee (1930, 1931).

[17] For the French, Albert Aftalon, "The Causes and Effects of the Movement of Gold into France," pp. 9–10; for the British, T. E. Gregory, "The Causes of Gold Movements into and out of Great Britain, 1925–29," p. 25; both in League of Nations, *Selected Documents* (1931).

[18] "Will to acquire," C. H. Kisch, "Memorandum on Legal Provisions Concerning Reserves of Central Banks," RIIA, *International Gold Problem*, p. 149; Rist, "The International Consequences of the Present Distribution of Gold Holdings," RIIA, *International Gold Problem* p. 194.

[19] William A. Brown, Jr., *The International Gold Standard Reinterpreted 1914–34* (2 vols.) (New York: National Bureau of Economic Research, 1940), p. 766.

It has been argued that the Bank of France was legally powerless to stop the flow of gold. This position is based on the fact that unlike other central banks, the Bank of France could not engage in open market operations. While this is true, it is also the case that, as one observer noted, "it is contrary to reason" that France could not have limited gold imports. It was legal, for example, for the Bank of France to buy foreign currencies. France also could have increased its foreign loans and investments. Either of these two actions would have equilibrated the flow of gold into France, and they do not represent the universe of possible French steps in this regard.[20]

It has also been put forth that while the Bank of France did purchase gold during 1927–1929, perhaps even with malice aforethought, the bank was not the source of the gold drain to France in subsequent years. Instead, it was French commercial banks, motivated by domestic economic imperatives to increase reserves, and other French private interests, that imported the gold after 1929. To focus on the bank, this argument holds, is to ignore the more significant actors.[21]

It is certainly true that the Bank of France did not run down its remaining stock of foreign exchange in the later period, and that the gold that flowed into France was primarily the result of private transactions. In fact, however, there is no difference, in either the motive or the "blame," in the source of the gold flow between the two periods. This is because the reason why private actors were forced to encash their foreign exchange earnings (usually sterling) for gold is that the Bank of France announced that it would no longer accept any additional foreign exchange. Thus if private actors wished to convert their international earnings into francs (obviously the logical step for domestic firms and other French private citizens), they were forced first to convert them into gold, and then bring the gold to the Bank of France in exchange for francs, a transaction that the bank was legally bound to carry out.[22] There is

[20] "Contrary to reason," Kisch, "Memorandum," p. 149. On open market operations versus foreign currency purchases, R. G. Hawtrey at the RIIA, RIIA, *International Gold Problem* p. 157; see also Sicsic, "Franc Poincaré," p. 16. On lending, Brown, *Gold Standard, p.* 766; and Cassell, Crisis, p. 58. Thomas Balogh, in "The Import of Gold into France: An Analysis of the Technical Position," *Economic Journal* 40:442–60 (1930), p. 446, argued that lending would not solve the fundamental problem, the structure of the monetary system.

[21] M. Wolfe, *The French Franc between the Wars: 1919–1939* (New York: Columbia University Press, 1951), p. 98; Balogh, "Import," p. 445; "Review of the Month," *Federal Reserve Bulletin* 16, no. 1 (1930), p. 2; Even if this were the case, it would not have satisfied critics such as Einzig, who argued that it was "the duty of the authorities of any country to pursue a constructive policy and not merely abstain from the working of destructive factors." Paul Einzig, *The World Economic Crisis* (London: Macmillan, 1931), p. 40.

[22] "Review of the Month," *Federal Reserve Bulletin* 16, no. 11 (1930), noted that French "commercial banks . . . have drawn upon their foreign balances for the purpose of importing gold to be exchanged for notes at the Bank of France." Therefore, although "the Bank of France has not directly imported gold since the spring of 1929, about $550,000,000 of gold has been added to its reserves between that time and the autumn of 1930." Ibid. See also Walter R. Gardner,

no significant difference, then, between the Bank of France's refusing to accept additional foreign exchange from its citizens, forcing them to convert their holdings into gold, and its accepting the funds and exchanging them for gold itself.

France, then, was purposefully, if effortlessly, converting the large amounts of foreign exchange it acquired into gold, and could continue to do so indefinitely at any pace it saw fit. Governor Montagu Norman of the Bank of England realized this, stating that "the Bank of France has enough sterling to create a situation at any given moment which would endanger the maintenance of the pound on gold." Moreau was also well aware of the power his sterling holdings gave him over the Bank of England.[23] Thus the consequence of the stabilization of the franc and the pound at their respective levels (complemented by other elements present in the system) was that France had a remarkable instrument at its disposal with which to coerce Britain. France could step on one pedal, and increase the pressure on Britain; touch another, and the pressure was gone.

The Political Issues

France therefore had a method of coercing Britain, but to what ends would the bank employ its power? After all, it was the French view that France needed British political and military support. It would be illogical for France to attempt to undermine British power, since France hoped to tap that resource should another conflict with Germany erupt.[24] However, despite the underlying harmony of the two nations' long-term interests in containing German power, there was disagreement about how best to achieve this. This was a very emotional issue in France, and Paris and London repeatedly came into conflict over various aspects of the German question.

Still, the two nations were not "enemies." Nor does the following argument attempt to suggest that they were. The French actions were, however aggressive, strategic rather than subversive. This distinction must be kept in mind, in order to understand that French actions were aimed at modifying British behavior, while preserving the understanding that Britain would fight alongside France in any future war with Germany.

According to E. H. Carr, "The most important and persistent single factor

---

"Central Gold Reserves, 1926–31," *American Economic Review* 22, no. 1:56–65 (1932), pp. 60–61.

[23] Sir Henry Clay, *Lord Norman* (London: Macmillan, 1957), p. 231 (Norman quote); Kindleberger, "Two French Episodes," p. 121 (on Moreau).

[24] Arnold Wolfers, *Britain and France between Two World Wars* (New York: W. W. Norton, 1966), p. 77.

in European affairs following 1919 was the French demand for security."[25] France wanted to keep Germany as weak as possible, while Britain was more inclined to see German recovery as necessary for the smooth functioning of the overall European economy. Britain was also not opposed to a Germany just strong enough to balance French power on the continent.[26] These contrasting visions of Europe by the two states could not help but become more acute with the onset of the international depression in the middle of this period.

In one episode, the Ruhr occupation of 1923, France resorted to the use of force in the pursuit of its policy to guarantee the terms of the Versailles Treaty and keep Germany weak. This act reflected the titular theme of France's overall foreign policy: maintenance of the status quo (that is, preservation of the Versailles Treaty). The resort to arms was a failure, reflecting the postwar pacifism, and highlighting the weakness and instability of the franc at that time.[27] Among the lessons France extracted from the experience were the ineffectiveness of the use of preemptive force in containing Germany, and an acute awareness of currency power. Left these two ingredients, it is not surprising that France would, as soon as it was able, cook up a policy that attempted to use economic power to contain German strength.[28]

French policy conflicts with Britain over the German question fell into two broad categories: the extent to which Germany should be kept weakened, and the struggle for influence in those countries that were potential allies against Germany. This first category could be further subdivided into issues associated with Germany's internal strength on the one hand and its external relations on the other. These groups are represented by three specific issues: the size and disposition of German reparations, the proposal for a customs union between Germany and Austria, and the extension of loans by Britain to countries in eastern and central Europe.

France was prepared to use its monetary power to coerce Britain over each of these issues. The recourse to such action was made all the more likely by the constellation of participants at the heart of the drama: Norman, Moreau, Hjalmar Schacht, and Benjamin Strong, the central bankers of Britain, France, Germany, and the United States, respectively. Norman and Moreau simply did not get along. Norman, who was fluent in French, would speak only English in Moreau's presence, thus necessitating the presence of Charles Rist as a translator. Moreau, for his part, felt that Norman was an "imperialist," who

---

[25] Carr, *International Relations between the Two World Wars* (London: Macmillan, 1947), p. 25. Wolfers concurs, stating that France was "hypnotized by the 'German menace'" (*Britain and France*, p. 2).

[26] S.V.O. Clarke, *Central Bank Cooperation 1924–31* (New York: Federal Reserve Bank of New York, 1967), p. 21; Carr, *International Relations*, p. 50.

[27] This episode will be considered in Chapter 6.

[28] Einzig, *Financial Supremacy*, p. 5; id., *Behind the Scenes*, pp. ix, 8.

was "very close to Dr. Schacht," and that Norman and Schacht met frequently to "hatch up their secret plots." Strong was very close personally to Norman, but attempted to stay above the fray and play the role of peacemaker.[29]

Over all three of these issues, then, British and French policies clashed and the use of French currency power was, at the very least, threatened. For example, when both Britain and France were contemplating loans to Yugoslavia in 1927, Moreau noted in his diary: "If the Bank of England takes away from us these customers, whom we are anxious to hold for political reasons, I shall show my displeasure by buying gold in London."[30] In the clash over reparations, such threats were delivered more directly. According to Sir Frederick Leith-Ross, then deputy controller of finance at the British treasury, officials from the Bank of France, including its influential secretary, Pierre Quesnay, explicitly threatened the position of the pound over the reparations issue. Sir Frederick recalls that

> Quesnay . . . said that Mr. Snowden's attempt to alter the Young plan was inadmissible and that he must ask me to persuade him to abandon his objections and accept the Plan: otherwise the French Government would feel it necessary to convert all the sterling held in London by the Bank of France into gold and transfer it to Paris. I knew that at the time the French assets were estimated to amount to something like £240 million and . . . the French could easily demand gold to an extent which would force us off the gold standard: but I also felt sure that any threat of such action was in the nature of a political bluff as the Bank of France would certainly not want to see the collapse of sterling.[31]

Over the third issue area, conflict arose when Britain explicitly undermined a French attempt to employ currency power. On June, 18, 1931, the Austrian government resigned, rather than accept a French-backed loan to support the schilling, which was contingent upon an abandonment of the proposed customs union with Germany. The fate of both Austrian solvency and the customs union was at that moment undetermined. One day later, Britain stepped in with an unconditional loan (which was also substantially larger than the French offer). This strained Franco-British relations, as France saw the act as political interference, while the British, highly sensitive to the precarious state of the international monetary system at that particular moment, were outraged by the cavalier French power play.[32]

---

[29] Boyle, *Montague Norman*, p. 199 (animosity); pp. 198–99 (Moreau quotes). For more on Strong, see Lester V. Chandler, *Benjamin Strong, Central Banker* (Washington, D.C.: The Brookings Institution, 1958). For more on Schacht, see Chapter 4.

[30] Quoted in Clarke, *Central Bank Cooperation* p. 146.

[31] Sir Frederick Leith Ross, *Money Talks: Fifty Years of International Finance* (London: Hutchinson and Co., 1968), p. 124.

[32] Edward W. Bennett, *Germany and the Diplomacy of the Financial Crisis, 1931* (Cambridge: Harvard University Press, 1962), pp. 150–52; also Brown, *Gold Standard*, p. 1041; Clarke, *Central Bank Cooperation*, pp. 186, 189.

The Techniques of Disruption

Thus, France had an instrument with which to coerce Britain, and indicated, both privately and publicly, an awareness of its existence and the intention to use it. What remains to be considered is whether any such steps were actually taken, under what circumstances, and with what degree of success. According to Paul Einzig, it was his suspicion that "whenever relations between France and Britain became strained, the franc moved invariably against sterling and large amounts of gold were shipped . . . to Paris."[33] Through an investigation of this claim, the employment of French disruption will be evaluated.

The data in Figures 5.1, 5.2, and 5.3 shed some light on the reserve positions of the principal European states during this period. Figure 5.1 is the most comprehensive, showing gold reserve movements, monthly, from July 1928 to December 1931. Figure 5.2, which show net gold imports to England, is an attempt to understand what was happening in the previous year and a half, January 1927 to June 1928, a period for which I could not uncover data for monthly gold reserves. Since Figures 5.1 and 5.2 show movements, not levels, Figure 5.3 is presented to give a sense of absolute trends over a longer period of time.[34]

The first conflict that engaged the two powers was over attempts to gain influence in eastern Europe. France was determined to enhance its position in this region, as part of its strategy to attract allies against Germany. France was particularly interested in courting the favor of Poland, Yugoslavia, Romania, and Czechoslovakia. In May 1927 this conflict boiled over when Moreau ordered a withdrawal of gold from London to express his displeasure over the fact that the stabilization of the Polish currency would take place through the League of Nations, which the Frenchman viewed as an English-dominated organization.[35] This abrupt withdrawal of gold from London is reflected in Figure 5.2.

It was the apparent strategy of France that gold withdrawals in this case would not simply register French disapproval through disruption, but rather would also directly influence the situation. Not for the last time, French policy was aimed at forcing Britain to counter the gold outflow stimulated in Paris by raising the discount rate, which would, incidentally, inhibit the British ability

[33] Paul Einzig, *International Gold Movements*, 2d ed. (London: Macmillan , 1931), p. 33.

[34] Figure 5.1 is calculated from *Federal Reserve Bulletin* 19, no. 6 (1933), p. 368; the year-end statistics in Figure 5.3 are from this source as well. The statistics in Figure 5.2 are from *Federal Reserve Bulletin* 15, no. 1 (1929), p. 33. It should be remembered that since Figure 5.1 shows movement, not level, a flat line represents a constant rate of loss (or gain) from month to month, not a constant level of reserves. A constant level of reserves would be a flat line superimposed on the x-axis.

[35] On France's aims in eastern Europe, see Carr, *International Relations*, p. 43; see also Wolfers, *Britain and France*, ch. 8. On the Moreau order of withdrawal, see Boyle, *Montague Norman*, pp. 225–26.

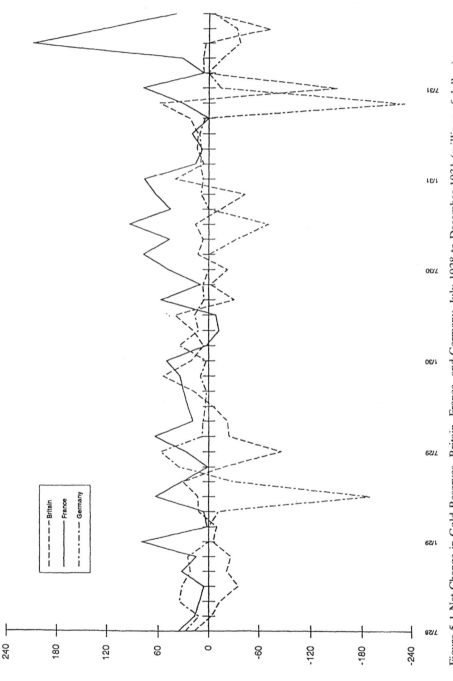

Figure 5.1 Net Change in Gold Reserves, Britain, France, and Germany, July 1928 to December 1931 (millions of dollars)
Source: *Federal Reserve Bulletin*, June 1933, p. 368.

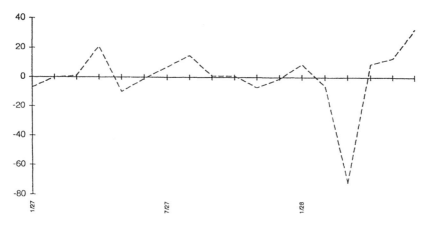

Figure 5.2 Net Gold Imports into Britain, Monthly, January 1927 to June 1928 (millions of dollars)
Source: Federal Reserve Bulletin, January 1929, p. 33.

to make foreign loans. Norman responded that he could not do this because it would cause domestic political upheaval.[36]

In this particular instance the conflict seems to have been resolved at a meeting in July, attended by Norman, Schacht, Strong, and Rist in Long Island, New York. No records were kept of the discussions or any agreements reached, but the pound did not come under any pressure for the rest of the year, though Figure 5.2 reveals a small net export of gold in November, which does not appear to have been the result of political influences. In fact, net British gold exports to France for all of 1927, including the May losses, amounted to only about $4 million.[37]

It soon became clear, however, that Moreau's fuse with regard to Britain had only been lengthened, not extinguished. On February 6, 1928, he recorded in his diary:

I had an important conversation with Mr. Poincaré over the issue of the Bank of England's Imperialism . . . [it has built] the foundation for a veritable financial domination of Europe. The Financial Committee in Geneva has been an instrument of this policy. . . . England has thus managed to install itself completely in Austria, Hungary, Belgium, Norway and Italy. It will implant itself next in Greece and Portu-

[36] Brown, *Gold Standard,* pp. 453, 456; See also Clarke, *Central Bank Cooperation* p. 30.
[37] Clarke, *Central Bank Cooperation* p. 123; Einzig, *Gold Movements* (1st ed., 1929), p. 26. Net exports to France are calculated from *Federal Reserve Bulletin* 15, no. 1 (1929), p. 33. It is possible that Strong offered to lower U.S. interest rates, and supply gold to France at the same price that it would cost France to purchase it from England, as part of a package deal. (Boyle, *Montague Norman,* p. 231.)

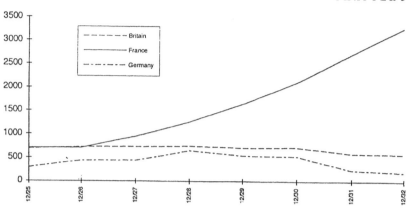

Figure 5.3 General Trend in Gold Reserves, Britain, France, and Germany, Year's End, 1925–1932 (millions of dollars)
Source: Federal Reserve Bulletin, June 1933, p. 368.

gal. It is attempting to get a foothold in Yugoslavia and it is fighting us on the sly in Rumania. Should it be allowed to go forward? . . . our political influence in places where our vital interests are at stake will be compromised seriously.

We now possess powerful means of exerting pressure on the bank of England. Would it not be in order to have a serious talk with Mr. Norman and attempt to divide Europe into two spheres of financial influence assigned respectively to France and England?

Mr. Poincaré seemed very much interested . . . [and] told me that it was absolutely necessary that I have a conversation with Mr. Norman in three weeks at the latest, since the political situation in Yugoslavia is disquieting and the situation in Rumania does not inspire any confidence in him either. He is concerned that Mr. Titulesco may distance Rumania from us and bring it closer to England and Italy.[38]

Moreau left for London on February 21, 1928, so that he might, in his own phrase, "offer Norman war or peace." A face-to-face meeting with Norman did not take place, though, as the latter suddenly took ill. Norman's subordinates were left to deal with Moreau, and reached an agreement that included a British promise to recognize "complete equality" between the two banks, and assurances that the Bank of England would not intervene in the negotiations over the Romanian stabilization. These agreements, however, were re-

---

[38] Emile Moreau, *The Golden Franc: Memoirs of a Governor of the Bank of France: The Stabilization of the Franc (1926–1928),* translated by Stephen D. Stoller and Trevor C. Roberts (Boulder, Colo.: Westview Press, 1991), pp. 430–31. See also ibid., ch. 15.

nounced by Norman upon his (swift) recovery, and this fact was communicated to the Bank of France. The French were predictably furious, and the
incident led to a tremendous row between Strong and Norman, only months
before the former's death.[39]

As the data in Figure 5.2 clearly illustrate, the French attempted to force
Britain to comply with the agreement reached in London, or at least to demonstrate the seriousness and depth of their anger, with massive purchases of gold
immediately following the Norman renunciation. For all of 1928, Britain
would end up exporting $96 million worth of gold directly to France.[40] How-
ever, the remarkable display of French monetary power does not appear to
have altered British behavior, although it did serve as a signal that could not
be misunderstood.

The next movement of reserves that bears consideration occurred from
April to July, 1929.[41] This incident reflected a conflict of the second type,
over German reparations. These transfers were being renegotiated, and obviously France was interested in bleeding Germany white to keep its nemesis as
weak as possible. In this episode, France leveled its monetary power directly
at Germany. One interesting aspect of this effort to coerce Germany is the
revelation that French influence attempts directed elsewhere could put pressure
on Britain through the indirect disruption of the system. During a meeting
of the experts' committee in Paris, in April 1929, there was a dramatic running down of the German reserves. The Germans were convinced that these
movements were encouraged by the French, both directly and through the
spread of rumors placed in the press, in order to improve their bargaining
position. Germany was vulnerable to such pressure, since the stability of the
mark depended on a large and steady flow of short-term international credits.[42]

The data in Figure 5.1 support this version of events, revealing a tremendous drop in German reserves and a significant peak in those of the French.
Even more fascinating is the international pattern that followed. As the Germans recovered their reserves, there was a corresponding drop in British gold
holdings. This is because the Germans purchased their replenishing gold in
London[43], which was the typical procedure for any European state. Thus significant French pressure on Germany (or, for that matter, any European currency) would indirectly pressure Britain.

This pattern can be observed once again in the following summer. Also at

[39] Boyle, *Montague Norman*, pp. 232–44; Chandler, *Benjamin Strong*, pp. 407, 409, 417.

[40] *Federal Reserve Bulletin* 16, no. 1 (1930), p. 22.

[41] The French peak in January 1929 resulted from purchases in the American market, and
hence is not of direct interest here.

[42] Hjalmar Schacht, *The End of Reparations* (New York: Jonathan Cape, 1931), pp. 87, 89;
German Reichsbank, *Annual Report*, excerpted in *Federal Reserve Bulletin* 16, no. 5 (1930),
pp. 298–99 (on German accusations); Bennett, *Financial Crisis*, p. 7 (foreign credits).

[43] Brown, *Gold Standard*, p. 767.

that time, France was attempting to influence the outcome of the Young negotiations through the manipulation of the German currency. Significant French
accumulations coincided with German losses. After a lag, German reserves
rebounded, and British holdings dropped. There were some differences from
the previous pattern: in this case, the movements were less severe, the lag
time was shorter, and more of the British losses appeared to have gone directly
to France, but the underlying pattern and causes were the same.

It is hard to measure the "success" of the French manipulations and disruption over this issue. The Young plan included a reparations scheme that many
considered impractical, suggesting France had been somewhat successful during the negotiations.[44] However, since these reparations were not ultimately
paid, the "success" of French policy, and any contribution made to it by the
practice of monetary diplomacy, must be highly qualified.

Finally, the monetary gyrations of the spring and summer of 1931 must be
considered. These months would witness the fleeting triumph and ultimate
failure of the French policy of strategic disruption of the gold-exchange standard. The specific issue at this stage of the ongoing influence attempt was the
proposal for an Austro-German customs union. In this instance, France came
into direct monetary conflict with both Germany and Britain. France remained
primarily motivated by political concerns at this time, and would continue to
be so at least until August. France was strongly opposed to the union, or for
that matter any agreement that would in essence result in a larger Germany.
Britain, on the other hand, was motivated by economic considerations, sensitive to the links that might spread a financial crisis from Austria to Germany
and then to Britain itself.

Austria was strongly in favor of a customs union with Germany, as many
both there and abroad doubted the economic viability of an independent Austria. This problem became acute when, on May 11, it was announced that the
Creditanstalt, the most important bank in Austria, was in serious trouble. This
was especially significant because of the close relationship between this bank
and German financial circles, which meant that Germany would be "at once
exposed to the danger of panic withdrawal of capital." As the data in Figure
5.1 indicate, this clearly occurred.[45]

The international financial crisis moved on to Germany, and, as discussed
above, it was in this context that Britain and France clashed over loans to
support the Austrian schilling. In July, France registered its displeasure with
British policy through a renewed attack on sterling, and although this was
complemented by a panic-driven international movement in the same direction, at this point France was still of a political mindset. France did participate
in an international credit to assist Germany on June 25, splitting a $100 mil-

---

[44] See, for example, Wolfers, *Britain and France*, p. 63–64.

[45] Bennett, *Financial Crisis*, pp. 40, 100 (on Austria); League of Nations, *World Economic Survey 1931–2* (Geneva: League of Nations, 1932), p. 72 (Germany).

lion loan with the Bank of England, the Bank for International Settlements, and the U.S. Federal Reserve banks.[46]

However, this was as far as France was willing to go. When Germany required additional funds, France attempted to attach conditions to any new loan, including stipulations concerning reparations, the customs union, and the rate of German military spending. Rather than agree to these terms, the Germans withdrew from international finance into a protective shell of exchange control.[47] With the German avenue effectively dammed, the crisis floodwaters were diverted to Britain.

With Britain experiencing financial crisis, France finally achieved some of the goals at which its four-year policy of strategic disruption had been directed. In order to stay on the gold standard, Britain was forced to accept loans from France, at both the beginning and the end of August. In this condition, not only was Britain dependent on French policy, but France was finally in a position to dictate the financial politics on the continent. France extended loans to Yugoslavia and Poland, and in August a loan to Hungary was provided, contingent on the removal of a revisionist (that is, anti–Versailles Treaty) minister. In September, the Austrian situation worsened, and French financial pressure could no longer be resisted. The customs union was abandoned in exchange for a £7.1 million loan, provided on September 17.[48]

However, at the very moment the French achieved financial supremacy, the rug was pulled out from under them. Despite French assistance, which had been substantially if belatedly extended to Britain in August, when the reality of the financial crisis finally began to dawn on France, Britain was forced off the gold standard on September 20. This was not what France wanted. Britain was now beyond the reach of French disruption, as the mechanism of French influence, the Anglocentric gold-exchange standard, no longer existed.

The French attempt at strategic disruption failed. Simply put, France could not create the circumstances under which its will would be heeded until the boatrocking became so daring and vigorous that it was inevitable that the craft would soon be upset. France attempted to shift its influence attempt toward the United States (reflected in the huge mid-1931 peak shown in Figure 5.1),[49] but the United States was both too remote and too secure for this to have any significant effect.

The failure of French policy was evident from every quarter. The policy of

[46] Bennett, *Financial Crisis*, p. 248 (French attack); *Federal Reserve Bulletin*, November 1930, p. 383 (loan to Germany).

[47] Clarke, *Central Bank Cooperation* pp. 195–96. For more on German exchange control, see Chapter 4.

[48] John W. Wheeler-Bennett, *The Wreck of Reparations* (New York: Howard Fertig, 1932), p. 112 (Austria); DeWilde, "French Financial Diplomacy," pp. 236–38 (Hungary and others). Brown, Gold Standard, p. 949, calls these loans both "critical" and "a form of political conflict."

[49] DeWilde, "French Financial Diplomacy," p. 233; Paul Einzig, *Finance and Politics* (London: Macmillan, 1932), pp. 54–55.

gold absorption had contributed to the depression. The attempts to coerce Germany contributed to the economic difficulties there, which led to exchange control (and the end of any French monetary leverage in that direction) and the radicalization of politics in Germany. The collapse of the international monetary system also isolated eastern Europe from French influence, and eliminated the ability to pressure Britain over the position of sterling.[50] If nothing else, the episode reveals the dangers inherent in boatrocking.

Was This Strategic Disruption?

French policy cannot be considered a failure, however, unless its goals were disruptive and not subversive. Obviously, if the French goal had been to destroy the system, the policy would have been successful. However, the evidence overwhelmingly supports the argument that the policy was one of disruption. The problem, as one observer noted, was that "France . . . never for one moment dreamed that Great Britain would take the final step of going off the gold standard." Even during the first crisis of May 1927, "Mr. Moreau felt more strongly inclined not to throw the pound sterling to earth." France wanted to reveal and exploit British weakness, not cause the collapse of the pound.[51]

France had good reasons for wanting to keep the gold-exchange standard alive, beyond the awful consequences of its collapse recounted above. A break with gold would surely mean British devaluation, which would undermine France's trading position. This was especially unwelcome during the depression. Secondly, it would reduce the role of gold in the world economy, and France had obviously put most of its eggs in that basket. Finally, France stood to take a loss in the event of any British devaluation from the reduction in the value of its substantial remaining sterling balances.

France, accordingly, acted to support sterling, once it realized that the gold link was truly vulnerable. It began to buy pounds hastily in August, and on August 1, it participated in a £50 million Franco-American credit to bolster the British position. A second such credit of £80 million was advanced on August 25. The French were willing to go ahead with still another credit, but decided it would not be wise when the Americans declined to participate. As a

---

[50] Others have been more critical of the French failure. Einzig (*Behind the Scenes*, p. 145), stated: "A collapse of the Reichmark is certain to bring about a complete political upheaval in Germany. It is highly probable that the extreme nationalists or the communists will then acquire power." R. G. Hawtrey, in *The Art of Central Banking* (1932; reprint, London: Frank Cass and Co., 1962), offered the not uncommon opinion that "French absorption of Gold from January 1929 to May 1931 was one of the most powerful causes of the world depression" (p. 38).

[51] Wheeler-Bennett, *Wreck*, p. 105 ("never dreamed"); Brown, *Gold Standard*, p. 458 (strongly inclined); see also Einzig, *Behind the Scenes*, p. 99.

result of the subsequent devaluation, France lost some Fr2,432 million on its sterling assets.[52]

In fact, the two nations had rarely seen more eye to eye on the explanation of a monetary phenomenon than they did over the September crisis. Rist wrote in *The Economist* that the pound fell "like a good soldier, fighting for the stability of the currencies of Europe." And when Clément Moret (Moreau's successor) traveled to England in October, he was awarded an honorary KBE as a token of gratitude for France's support.[53]

To summarize, France's logical interests, its actions, and the perception of both participants and observers all support the interpretation that France's policy was strategic, and explicitly undermine the argument that it was subversive.

Lessons from the Interwar Disruption

The French experience suggests a number of generalizable findings with regard to the practice of strategic disruption. Two stand out in particular. The first is the large number of paths to influence afforded to the potential disrupter. To this point, only direct attempts at monetary power in general, and systemic disruption in particular, have been considered. This episode revealed that disrupters can challenge system leaders through monetary diplomacy introduced in almost any direction, since that action will have systemwide repercussions. Most often, this results from the leader's role as reserve custodian and lender of last resort of the member states. Member states are likely to call on these functions when their positions become threatened. In a more general sense, monetary difficulties anywhere in the system can unleash private market forces that pressure the reserve currency. Both of these phenomena resulted from French currency manipulation directed at Germany, which led to considerable pressure on the pound.

The second prominent generalizable finding is the considerable difference between the power to disrupt the system and the capability to extract concessions on the basis of this strength. France clearly had the former, as its power was both recognized by participants on each side and reflected in the gold movements associated with specific influence attempts. Possessing the latter was a much more difficult task, and was only attained for a brief moment at great cost.

[52] Wheeler-Bennett, *Wreck*, p. 113 (credits); DeWilde, "French Financial Diplomacy," p. 238 (losses). One economist, challenging arguments that France forced Britain off gold, emphasized the role of small countries and private actors, each protecting its own interests, as the proximate cause of the collapse. Willard Hurst, "Holland, Switzerland, and Belgium in the English Gold Crisis of 1931," *Journal of Political Economy* 40, no. 5:638–60 (1932), esp. pp. 655, 657.

[53] Hurst, "English Gold Crisis," p. 655 (Rist quote); Leith Ross, *Money Talks*, p. 139 (Moret).

This difference between power and influence stems from the fact that Britain recognized France's actions as being disruptive as opposed to subversive. Convinced that France would not push too hard, Britain could maintain a stiff upper lip in the face of French pressure, aware of the seriousness of the situation but convinced that France would not push too hard. This conviction was expressed explicitly by Leith-Ross, as discussed above, and enabled Britain to dismiss one particularly clumsy effort.

France, though, reacted to the British silent treatment with increasingly aggressive attempts to demonstrate its seriousness. This policy was finally successful, but the threat that left something to chance came back to haunt France, as it unleashed, or at the very least contributed significantly to, forces that were beyond its ability to contain. Thus the system was overturned, and the ability to extract concessions was no longer inhibited by a lack of credibility, as it was initially, but rather by the flip side of that coin, the all too real fulfillment of France's threats, which drowned French interests, along with those of the other passengers.

Illustrative Cases

France and the Dollar System

During much of the 1960s, the U.S.-led international monetary system came under the attack of the golden sword of France. The monetary regime was a gold exchange standard system established by the United States through negotiations with Great Britain at Bretton Woods, New Hampshire, at the close of World War II. France, a surplus country, in this era as in the 1920s, chose to use the flow of foreign exchange resulting from its position to attempt to coerce the leader of the system. Although cloaked in economic arguments, the French challenge to the U.S.-led monetary system was politically motivated. Specifically, during this era the French were interested in limiting U.S. influence in Europe, and were prepared to employ any lever at their disposal to pursue this end. By this reasoning, French monetary diplomacy was not primarily motivated by desire to reform the monetary system, but rather was opportunistically employed to further France's broader international strategy.

From all outward appearances, 1958 should have represented the fruition of U.S. efforts to construct a stable, self-sustaining U.S.-led international monetary system. After ten years of U.S. support and acquiescence in unilateral monetary discrimination, the major European currencies had finally achieved complete external convertibility. The primary monetary challenge of the 1950s, the "dollar shortage," had been overcome, and the International Monetary Fund was ready and able to oversee the system of fixed exchange rates.

In reality, 1958 was the apogee of the dollar system. As the previous fifteen years told the story of its construction, so the next fifteen would tell of its decline. Starting in that pivotal year, U.S. payments (though not yet U.S. trade) went into stubborn and persistent deficit. The problem of the dollar shortage would soon be displaced by the problem of the dollar surplus, or "overhang." Robert Triffin had exposed this paradox for key currency countries in an exchange standard system.[54] In this context, the abundance of dollars in the international economy would be a constant source of pressure on the monetary system.

These problems were not unnoticed by governments or individuals. It was also noted that U.S. short-term liabilities to foreigners at this time exceeded $21 billion, while the U.S. gold stock stood at $17.5 billion. In November 1960, the spot price of gold reached $40 an ounce on the London market, and sent the monetary circus of the 1960s on the road.[55]

After the November gold price shock, the United States moved to gain control of the gold market and protect the dollar and other vulnerable currencies (usually the pound). In 1961, the gold pool was formed, and the first Basle agreement was reached. The gold pool was made up of contributions by

[54] Robert Triffin, *Gold and the Dollar Crisis* (New Haven: Yale University Press, 1960).

[55] The response of the academic community to the "dollar problem" was striking. It is perhaps here that the profession earned its reputation for having more opinions than economists. Peter Kenen's was an early voice that agreed with Triffin's diagnosis that it was time to seek substitutes for both gold and the dollar as international reserves. Kenen, "International Liquidity and the Balance of Payments in a Reserve Currency Country," *Quarterly Journal of Economics*, November 1960. The first published "symposium" on this issue was edited by Seymour E. Harris (*The Dollar in Crisis* [New York: Harcourt, Brace and World, 1961]) and included contributions by leading economists, such as Harrod, Harbeler, Galbraith, and Triffin. This was followed by a flood of analyses, including the following: Francis Cassell, *Gold or Credit? The Economics and Politics of International Money* (New York: Praeger, 1965); Sidney E. Rolfe, *Gold and World Power* (New York: Harper and Row, 1966); Robert Z. Aliber, *The Future of the Dollar as an International Currency* (New York: Praeger, 1966); John Parke Young, *United States Gold Policy: The Case for Change*, Essays in International Finance, no. 56 (Princeton University, 1966); Miroslav Kriz, *Gold: Barbarous Relic or Useful Instrument?* Essays in International Finance, no. 60 (Princeton University, 1967); Richard N. Cooper, *The Economics of Interdependence: Economic Policy in the Atlantic Community* (New York: McGraw Hill, 1968); Gordon L. Weil and Ian Davidson, *The Gold War* (London: Selker and Warburg, 1970); Sidney E. Rolfe and James Burtle, *The Great Wheel: The World Monetary System* (New York: Quadrangle, 1973). Marxist perspectives include Ernest Mandel, *Decline of the Dollar: A Marxist View of the Monetary Crisis* (New York: Monad Press, 1972); and A. Stadniochenko, *Monetary Crisis of Capitalism* (Moscow: Progress Publishers, 1975), which is a retrospective view. Non-Marxist postmortems on the system include Anthony Lanyi, "Political Aspects of Exchange-Rate Systems," in Richard L. Merritt, ed., *Communication in International Politics* (Urbana: University of Illinois Press, 1972), which adopts a game-theoretic approach; Robert W. Russell, "Transgovernmental Interaction in the International Monetary System 1960–72," *International Organization* 27, no. 4:431–64 (1973); and "The International Monetary System; A Symposium," *Journal of International Economics* 2, no. 4:315–453 (1972), which includes contributions by Jagdish Bhagwati, Cooper, J. M. Fleming, Triffin, Harry Johnson, Charles P. Kindleberger, and Paul Samuelson.

member states (almost all the industrial countries, including France). Sales from the pool would relieve upward pressure on the gold price. The Basle agreement was an understanding that central banks would be willing to hold foreign exchange for extended periods of time (three to six months), with a guarantee that when the notes were converted, they would be redeemable at the original rates of exchange. This would help ameliorate short-term foreign exchange crises. These agreements operated successfully throughout the first half of the decade. However, as Susan Strange pointed out, the need for international cooperation in these endeavors represented the end of dollar hegemony, and the start of Anglo-American dependence on Europe to ensure the stability of the monetary system.[56] For the rest of the decade, the reform of the system would not be dictated by the United States to grateful dependents, but negotiated with increasingly assertive allies.

As the Kennedy administration came to power, it was aware that there was a potentially serious dollar problem. At his successor's first White House briefing, President Eisenhower "pummeled" President-elect Kennedy for two hours about the dollar. This treatment was obviously effective, because according to Arthur Schlesinger, Jr., Kennedy, "used to tell his advisors that the two things which scared him most were nuclear war and the payments deficit."[57] It was not Kennedy, however, but rather his successor, Lyndon Johnson, who would have to deal with the French challenge to the dollar. This was because during the early 1960s, the French nation was still preoccupied with the issues that had swept General de Gaulle suddenly back to power in 1958: the Algerian War, and the creation of the new constitution of the Fifth Republic. Even as he first came to power, though, the significance of monetary power was not far from the thoughts of de Gaulle. On December 28, 1958, he devalued the franc by over 15 percent, on the heels of a 20 percent devaluation in 1957.[58]

This devaluation is significant for three reasons. First, it provides a lesson in the politics of devaluation: de Gaulle was able to escape any possible criticism for the act because of its context (during a crisis not of his making) and its timing (shortly after he took office). Second, he revealed how deeply ingrained the concept of monetary prestige was in his psyche. Concurrent with

[56] Susan Strange, *International Monetary Relations*, vol. 2. of Andrew Shonfield, ed., *International Economic Relations of the Western World 1959–71* (London: Oxford University Press, 1976), ch. 3 (on the gold pool and the Basle agreement), p. 87 (dependence). Strange's book offers an excellent monetary history of the period. Also useful are Stephen D. Cohen, *International Monetary Reform 1964–69: The Political Dimension* (New York: Praeger, 1970); and John S. Odell, *U.S. International Monetary Policy* (Princeton: Princeton University Press, 1982).

[57] Martin Mayer, *The Fate of the Dollar* (New York: Times Books, 1980), p. 83 ("pummeled"); Arthur M. Schlesinger, Jr., *A Thousand Days* (Boston, Houghton Mifflin Co., 1965), p. 654 ("nuclear war").

[58] Edward L. Morse, *Foreign Policy and Interdependence in Gaullist France* (Princeton: Princeton University Press, 1973), p. 216; also Weil and Davidson, *Gold War*, p. 77.

the devaluation, he also ordered a one-hundred to one conversion of franc notes, because he wanted, in his words, "the franc . . . to have a substance commensurate with the respect that it is due."[59] By this act the franc would trade at 4.92 to the dollar, as opposed to 492. Finally, after the devaluation the franc would be relatively undervalued. Thus, as in the late 1920s, France could expect a flow of foreign exchange into the nation. Should it be desired, the dollars coming into France could be exchanged for gold.

It was indeed likely that the French would pursue such a course. The French had been consistent critics of Anglo-American–dominated monetary systems in general and gold exchange standard systems in particular, as evidenced in the 1920s episode discussed above. These criticisms became more aggressive as the French nation emerged from the shadow of its domestic problems, but they were not new. When Jacques Rueff called for a doubling of the gold price, his arguments were almost precisely those previously put forth by Charles Rist, who had preceded him as the most prominent economist in France.[60] As shall become clear, however, de Gaulle was less wedded to any one economic philosophy than his advisors. His success lay in tapping into the politics of gold, which festered in France, and not in a desire to improve the functioning of the monetary system.

Still, the French attempt to disrupt the dollar system was cloaked in the legitimacy of economic righteousness. France argued that the United States unfairly gained from its position as the key currency of the system. De Gaulle called it an "extraordinary advantage." Rueff spoke of deficit without tears, noting that the United States, as the reserve currency country, could run balance-of-payments deficits indefinitely with "no pain." It could indefinitely postpone the adjustment that would of necessity be swift and harsh for other countries.[61]

The economic costs and benefits of the U.S. position in the payments system were widely debated. In retrospect the net economic magnitudes were marginal.[62] But the issue had an emotional resonance. A book entitled *Le Défi*

[59] General Charles de Gaulle, *Major Addresses, Statements, and Press Conferences, 5/19/58–1/31/64* (New York: Press and Information Division, French Embassy, 1964), p. 32.

[60] Jacques Rueff, *The Monetary Sin of the West* (New York: Macmillan, 1972), is a summary of Rueff's diagnosis of and prescription for the problems of the 1960s; see ibid., pp. 141 ff., on the need to double the gold price. Rueff's *Balance of Payments* (New York: Macmillan, 1967) is a collection of essays tracing the history of his thought on similar issues. On Rist, see Rist, *History of Monetary and Credit Theory*, translated by Jane de Gras (1940; reprint, New York: Augustus M. Kelley, 1966) and Rist, *The Triumph of Gold*, translated by Philip Courtney (New York: Greenwood Press, 1961).

[61] General Charles de Gaulle, *Major Addresses, Statements, and Press Conferences, 3/17/64–1/16/67* (New York: Press and Information Division, French Embassy, 1967), p. 80 (de Gaulle quote); Rueff, *Monetary Sin,* p. 78 (Rueff quote). See also William M. Clarke, "What the General Meant about Gold," *Westminster Bank Review*, May 1965, pp. 5–6.

[62] For this debate, see Cassell, *Gold or Credit?*, p. 38 (net benefit unclear); Robert Z. Aliber,

Américan, which focused on this issue of U.S. investment in Europe, enjoyed a stay on the bestseller list in France.[63] At the official level, France expended a great deal of effort in its critique of the gold exchange standard regime. It did so even though this greatly antagonized the United States, and ran the risk of destroying, rather than reforming, the entire international monetary system. Given the small magnitude of the potential economic gains to the United States from the system (and thus the relative economic losses to France), it seems unlikely that the strategy was motivated simply by a concern for marginal wealth or global economic efficiency.

De Gaulle's monetary diplomacy was a tool he employed to further his overall foreign policy. This is because, in the words of one observer:

> The one weakness in the American armor, trivial though it is when considered in the perspective of real American economic strength, is the U.S. payments deficit. Manifestly this can be exploited in a number of ways to irritate the U.S. administration and to embarrass the conduct of American foreign policies.[64]

Monetary relations between the United States and France were a "microcosm" of the relations between the two powers. The same basic approach and purpose was evident in France's withdrawal from NATO's integrated military command, and its pursuit of an independent nuclear force. Because of the

---

"The Costs and Benefits of the U.S. Role as a Reserve Currency Country," *Quarterly Journal of Economics* 78, no. 3:442–56 (1964), p. 454 (net benefit); William A. Salant, "The Reserve Currency Role of the Dollar: Blessing or Burden to the United States?" *Review of Economics and Statistics* 46, no. 2:165–72 (1964), p. 167 (1950–1956, net benefit; 1958–1963, net cost); Herbert G. Grubel, "The Benefits and Costs of Being the World's Banker," *National Banking Review* 2, no. 2:189–212 (1964), p. 205 (net cost); Robert Z. Aliber, "The Costs and Benefits of Being the World's Banker: A Comment," and Henry N. Goldstein, "Does It Necessarily Cost Anything to Be the World's Banker?" both in *National Banking Review* 3, no. 2:409–15 (1965) (critiques of Grubel; for Grubel's reply, see ibid., pp. 416–17; John R. Karlik, "The Costs and Benefits of Being a Reserve Currency Country," in Peter Kenen and Roger Lawrence, eds., *The Open Economy: Essays on International Trade and Finance* (New York: Columbia University Press, 1968), p. 338 (net benefit). For an interesting analysis of the potential for seigniorage, see Benjamin J. Cohen, "The Seigniorage Gain of an International Currency: An Empirical Test," *Quarterly Journal of Economics* 85 (1971). For a European perspective, see E. J. Kirschen, "The American External Seigniorage: Origin, Cost to Europe, and Possible Defenses," *European Economic Review* 5, no. 4:355–78 (1974).

[63] J. J. Servan-Schreiber, *The American Challenge* (New York: Atheneum, 1968). For more on this issue, see Robert Gilpin, *France in the Age of the Scientific State* (Princeton: Princeton University Press, 1968), ch. 3; and Allan W. Johnstone, *United States Direct Investment in France: An Investigation of the French Charges* (Cambridge: MIT Press, 1965). Later in the decade, the focus of the criticism shifted. It was then charged that the United States was exploiting the dollar system to finance the Vietnam War. See, for example, Henry Magdoff, *The Age of Imperialism: The Economics of U.S. Foreign Policy* (New York: Monthly Review Press, 1969), pp. 80–88.

[64] Peter Jay, "Why France Balks," *Interplay*, December 1967, p. 40.

structure of the international system, though, monetary diplomacy afforded the French greater leverage than did those issues related to defense.[65]

What were the French goals, and how were they advanced by conflict with the Americans? According to Stanley Hoffmann, de Gaulle desired a Europe under French leadership that would be "apart from and above" the cold war conflict. He traces the French desire to be a "principal player" on the world stage to the humiliation of defeat and occupation in World War II. Others point to the lesson of Suez: that France must have the ability to go it alone. Most explanations of French policy also stress the feeling that France was constantly chafing under the dominance of an Anglo-American international order.[66]

In his own speeches, de Gaulle stressed the theme of French independence: "Above all it is a question of keeping ourselves free of vassalage."[67] Conflict with the United States, therefore, to quote Hoffmann, served de Gaulle "as an elevator."[68] By attempting to restrict the game to the playing field most tilted in France's favor, General de Gaulle could appear as an equal to the United States. He could also use the opportunity to question the viability of U.S. leadership, and promote the concept of France as the alternative.

Evidence for the interpretation that de Gaulle's monetary diplomacy was a means to other goals, as opposed to an end in itself, is provided by his own monetary philosophy, and the style in which he pursued "reform." The most striking aspect of de Gaulle's critique of the gold-exchange standard was that he never offered a specific alternative. His ministers sometimes did, but they often found the rug pulled out from under them. When Finance Minister Valéry Giscard d'Estaing's idea for a Composite Reserve Unit (CRU), which would undermine the reserve role of the dollar, was opposed by the Americans, de Gaulle appeared to support it. However, as the idea began to gain popularity, he backed off from the proposal and ultimately sacked Giscard in favor of Michel Debré.[69] Additionally, if it was reform of the monetary system

---

[65] Morse, *Gaullist France*, p. 204 ("microcosm"); Harold van B. Cleveland, *The Atlantic Idea and Its European Rivals* (New York: McGraw Hill, 1966), pp. 75, 83.

[66] Stanley Hoffmann, "De Gaulle, Europe, and the Atlantic Alliance," *International Organization* 18, no. 1:1–28 (1964), pp. 1, 2, 17, 19 (1964). John Newhouse, in *DeGaulle and the Anglo-Saxons* (New York: Viking Press, 1970), emphasizes Suez and the desire to "rid France of Anglo-Saxon influence" (pp. 8, 31–2). Restoration of France's "position of greatness" is also stressed by Cecil V. Crabb, Jr., "The Gaullist Revolt against the Anglo-Saxons," *Atlantic Community Quarterly* 2, no. 1: 35 (1964); and Weil and Davidson, *Gold War*, p. 74.

[67] "Vassalage," is from a radio address, December 31, 1964; on independence, see also de Gaulle's twelfth press conference, September 9, 1965. Both reprinted in de Gaulle, *Major Addresses*, pp. 75, 98.

[68] Hoffmann, "Atlantic Alliance," p. 20. Stephen Cohen agrees, noting that in the pursuit of great power status, "anti-U.S. thrusts" were not ends, but a "means to attain French goals" (*International Monetary Reform*, p. 50).

[69] Peter B. Kenen, "The International Position of the Dollar," in Benjamin J. Cohen, ed.,

that he had in mind, de Gaulle was not going about it in the most efficient way. Raymond Aron, for example, agreed that the United States was abusing the system, taking an unjust profit by borrowing official dollar balances at 4 percent or less, and then turning around and investing in European industry at rates of 5 percent or more. However, Aron argued that "the technico-psychological guerrilla warfare" being waged against the dollar accomplished nothing and was a poor substitute for constructive solutions to real problems.[70] Monetary diplomacy reflected, but did not represent, French aims. In the words of James Tobin, "General de Gaulle's monetary restlessness . . . [was] of a piece with his general restlessness."[71]

Clearly, it was French policy to challenge the leadership role of the United States in the Western world, and the most efficient path to this end was through the monetary system. The French thrusts fell into three general categories: the highly public encashment of dollars for gold, overt rhetorical challenges to the system, and the subversion of international monetary conferences. Each of these instruments was a significant source of disruption, and all were consciously and repeatedly employed.

Although it was not the first example of French disruption, comments made by General de Gaulle at his eleventh press conference, on February 4, 1965, stand out as the high-water mark of this episode. In response to a question on monetary reform, de Gaulle gave a sweeping historical evaluation of the situation, criticizing the "gold exchange standard" (always referring to it in English, as if it could not be translated into French[72]). His answer included the following comments:

The conditions which formerly were able to give rise to the "gold exchange standard" have changed. . . . The custom of ascribing a superior value to the dollar as an international currency no longer rests on its initial foundation.

Circumstances are such today that it is possible to wonder how far the difficulties would go if the States which hold dollars sooner or later reached the point where they wanted to convert them into gold.

France recommends that the system be changed.

American Foreign Economic Policy: Essays and Comments (New York: Harper and Row, 1968), p. 68; also Jay, "Why France Balks" (on CRU), p. 40; Strange, *International Monetary Relations*, pp. 219, 225 (also CRU).

[70] Quoted in Strange, *International Monetary Relations*, p. 244.

[71] James Tobin, "The Future of the Dollar as International Money," in Cohen, *American*, p. 176; see also Cassell, *Gold or Credit?*, pp. 11, 177.

[72] As Rueff followed Rist, so did de Gaulle follow in the tradition of French disruption. On December 16, 1931, the French finance minister stated: "The Gold-Exchange Standard is an Anglo-Saxon phrase which cannot be translated into French," quoted in Margaret G. Myers, *Paris as a Financial Center* (New York: Garland Publishing, 1936), p. 31.

Doubtless, no one would think of dictating to any country how to manage its domestic affairs. But the supreme law, the golden rule—and indeed it is pertinent to say it—that must be enforced and honored again in international economic relations, is the duty to balance, from one monetary area to another, by effective inflows and outflows of gold, the balance of payments resulting from their exchanges.[73]

The importance of rhetoric as an instrument of monetary power should not be underestimated. This is especially true if the technique is introduced against a currency or system that is already recognized as potentially vulnerable. Just as a run on deposits can ruin a sound bank, a run on the "American bank" (exchanging what were technically short-term liabilities, dollars, for assets, gold) could undermine the dollar system. De Gaulle was not quite yelling "fire" in a crowded theater, but he did loudly announce that the place was a firetrap and it was his intention to leave as quickly as possible.

These monetary shots were heard around the world. De Gaulle's "attack . . . gave rise to a world-wide echo." The president of France had openly "declared war" on the dollar system.[74] This rhetorical campaign complemented other French monetary maneuvers, such as the "well publicized" action on the part of France to "accelerate the conversion into gold of their substantial dollar balances." Such encashment was the second instrument of French disruption, a policy that was followed in the early 1960s and peaked in 1965. Nor was it sufficient simply to transfer ownership of the gold, as was standard practice. Rather, de Gaulle had the gold transported back to Paris from New York.[75] The magnitudes of the gold-purchasing policy are presented in Figure 5.4.[76]

Aside from publicly challenging the viability of the dollar and exchanging its dollars for gold, France also took a contrary and obstructionist position at the many international monetary conferences held during the decade. As early as the 1961 Vienna meeting, the French, along with the Dutch, attempted to exploit their increasingly strong position. This posture continued through the March 1968 Stockholm conference, which is considered the last hurrah of French monetary diplomacy in this era. As one observer noted, "Far from seeking to contribute to these talks, President de Gaulle may have intended to bring them down to a level at which French tactical strength could exert its greatest influence."[77]

[73] de Gaulle, *Major Addresses,* pp. 79–81.

[74] F. E. Aschlinger, "The Gold Standard—The French Proposal and the American Answer," pts. 1 and 2, *Swiss Review of World Affairs,* March 1965 ("echo") and May 1965, p. 3; and id., "The French Monetary Campaign," ibid., July 1965, p. 13 ("war"). Kindleberger, "Two French Episodes," concurs that at the press conference, de Gaulle "declared war on the dollar standard" (p. 124).

[75] "Gaullefinger," *Atlantic Community Quarterly* 3, no. 1:98–101 (1965), p. 98 (gold purchases); Weil and Davidson, Gold War, p. 89 (gold repatriation).

[76] Figures are from Strange, *International Monetary Relations,* p. 296.

[77] On the Vienna meeting, Strange, *International Monetary Relations,* p. 110; "Far from seek-

Gold Holdings, 1,000 - 6,000

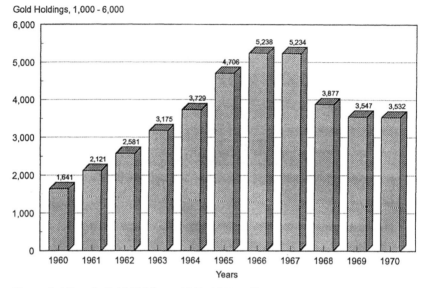

Figure 5.4 French Gold Holdings, 1960–1970 (millions of dollars)

Despite these numerous and varied efforts, the French attempt at strategic disruption, in the end, failed. In the 1920s, failure resulted when French boat-rocking finally contributed to the destruction of the system. This time, although the American system was ultimately doomed, it was French internal weakness that caused the collapse of its monetary strategy. In May 1968, only two months after the Stockholm meeting, France was rocked by an internal political crisis. Capital fled the nation, which lost over $2.8 billion of its $7 billion reserves of gold and foreign exchange. The United States came to France's assistance, supplying dollars to support the franc by buying back gold from France, and arranging a $1.3 billion dollar standby credit for the beleaguered nation. The franc was "enfeebled" by this crisis and would not soon recover. Figuratively speaking, France's monetary surrender was officially delivered with the announcement by the Bank of France in March 1969 that it no longer was in favor of an increase in the gold price.[78]

ing," Clarke, "What the General Meant," p. 2. For more on the Stockholm conference, see Robert Triffin, "DeGaulle at Stockholm: Villain, Hero, or Sphinx?" *Interplay*, May 1968, pp. 15–17. On the French personalities associated with these conferences, see Paul Fabra, "The Moneymen of France," *Interplay*, January 1968, pp. 37–40. For a discussion of the French negotiating positions at these conferences, with an emphasis on France's European relations, see Jacques Wolff, "La Diplomatie du franc," *Revue de Science Financière* 60, no. 4:782–829 (1968), 61, no. 1:5–76 (1969), 61, no. 2:206–70 (1969).

[78] Meyer, *Fate of the Dollar,* pp. 152, 160; Morse, *Gaullist France,* p. 246; Newhouse, *De-Gaulle,* p. 320 ("enfeebled"); Lyndon Johnson, *The Vantage Point* (New York: Holt, Rinehart and Wilson, 1971), p. 319 (credit); Strange, *International Monetary Relations,* p. 302 (Bank of France).

Given the zest with which France pursued its assault on the dollar, it is reasonable to ask whether French intentions were strategic or in fact subversive. The evidence supports the view that they were strategic. First and most obviously, as in the 1920s case, as a gold-hoarding country, France could only be hurt by a complete collapse of the system, which would certainly include the United States's abandoning the gold-dollar link, thus reducing the role of gold, and hurting France's competitive position. Actually, the only truly subversive diplomacy, in the form of a threat to break with gold, was a weapon in the U.S. arsenal, not the French one.[79]

Secondly, France was apparently sensitive to the underlying power of the United States to fundamentally subvert the system. Anti-French sentiment in the United States grew throughout the mid-sixties, and by 1967 there were calls from a number of influential circles for the United States to break with gold. That year was a very shaky one for the international monetary system (culminating in the British devaluation). Yet when the system was relatively weak, the United States was (unofficially) threatening to subvert the system itself, while French monetary diplomacy became less assertive, (though it did rebound somewhat in the wake of the British devaluation and through the Stockholm conference). This is reflected in Figure 5.4, with 1967 representing an abrupt break from the French gold accumulation policy. This suggests that the French were interested in manipulating, but not destroying, the international monetary system.[80]

Third, previous observers, though they did not use the term, maintained that the French policy was strategic, not subversive. French policy was seen as an attempt to embarrass the United States (and Britain) without "pushing them over the brink of devaluation . . . to weaken without pushing too far."

[79] H. G. Aubrey, in *Behind the Veil of International Money*, Essays in International Finance, no. 71 (Princeton University, 1969), argued that the U.S. ability to threaten to break with gold was its "financial deterrence." Aubrey also stresses political variables in "The Political Economy of International Monetary Reform," *Social Research* 33, no. 2:218–54 (1966).

[80] James Tobin was an early critic of France, arguing that the United States, having helped out the rest of the world during the dollar shortage, was now getting the "short end of the stick." Tobin, "Europe and the Dollar," p. 124. Many joined in Tobin's criticism. Though Rueff claimed that a doubling of the gold price would benefit the United States, after subsequent encashments, the net effect would be to double European gold holdings. Strange, *International Monetary Relations*, p. 239. In 1967, Kindleberger and other economists called for the United States to break with gold. The heads of the two largest banks, the Chase Manhattan Bank and the Bank of America, publicly called for such a policy in April. Anti-French sentiment also increased in Congress. "The French, chastened by these developments, took the point" (Strange, *International Monetary Relations,*, p. 245). Peter Kenen was a more technical critic of de Gaulle's monetary policy, in his "The General's Monetary Absurdity," *New Leader*, December 16, 1968, pp. 6–8. Not all Americans were critical of the French position, however. See John L. Hess, *The Case for DeGaulle: An American Viewpoint* (New York: William Morrow and Co., 1968). Hess, sympathetic to the French position, noted that unwarranted anti-French hysteria had reached a point where "A Boston landlord threatened publicly to make the French counsel pay his rent in gold" (p. 29).

France was thus described as "playing an opposition role in the Atlantic community, not a subversive or revolutionary one."[81]

Finally, the French monetary diplomacy was seen at the time as strategic, at least by American officials. They preferred to deal with de Gaulle, and viewed these issues as "family fights." Johnson reported that he was occasionally "tempted to abandon my policy of polite restraint toward de Gaulle, but I forced myself to be patient." He was also quick to come to France's assistance in the 1968 crisis, arguing that "[t]he international monetary system is not a field for pettiness or retribution."[82]

Given these considerations, it is difficult to argue that the French monetary diplomacy in the 1960s was anything but strategic. What is more puzzling is why the policy failed to produce any concrete gains. One of the striking aspects of this episode is the fact that France was so unsuccessful. On the one hand, the long-term failure of the French policy is not surprising. Strategic disruption is a tricky business, and sooner or later France was bound to be tripped up by its own relative weaknesses, or by the collapse of the system itself. It is only by chance that internal weakness was decisive in this case, predating the collapse of the doomed system by three years.[83] Additionally, as the monetary regime weakened in 1967, France's ability to extract concessions was inhibited by its own stake in the survival of the system.

However, there were still at least three years during which France could have strongly exerted its influence, 1964–1966. The elements were certainly in place. The system did have underlying flaws, and France was experiencing a sustained balance-of-payments surplus. This provided the opportunity to pull all three of the levers mentioned above: rhetoric, negotiation, and gold purchases. Yet despite an active introduction of all of these weapons, the results were minimal.

[81] Jay, "Why France Balks," p. 40 (1st quote); Strange, *International Monetary Relations*, p. 301 (2d quote). Kindleberger (1972) agrees with Strange and Jay that French policy was strategic, stating: "The U.S. must have known that the French dollar conversions of 1965 were undertaken only because France believed that the U.S. could resist them. The episode was maneuvering, not warfare" (p. 126). However, Kindleberger also emphasizes the reassertion of French policy toward the end of 1967, and his analysis provides support for the argument that balance-of-payments difficulties in France in late 1966 contributed to the abatement of the the French strategic disruption in 1967 (p. 125).

[82] Newhouse, DeGaulle, p. 319 ("family fights"); Johnson, *Vantage Point*, pp. 315–16. This did not mean, however, that Johnson did not take the threat of monetary diplomacy directed at U.S. interests seriously. On June 16, 1965, Johnson wote a memorandum to the secretary of the Treasury on the subject of "Forward Planning in International Finance." In that memo, Johnson ordered the creation of a "small high level study group" to consider a number of questions, first among which was, "What are the possible means of reducing the United States' vulnerability to political and economic pressure through the threatened conversion into gold of any overhang of official dollar balances?" Memorandum, reprinted in Johnson, *Vantage Point*, pp. 597–98.

[83] On the end of Bretton Woods, see Odell, U.S. *International Monetary Policy*, chs. 4–5; and Joanne Gowa, *Closing the Gold Window* (Cornell: Cornell University Press, 1983).

This was due to the nature of French goals. Instead of a specific objective, France was pursuing a "milieu goal": enhancement of French power and prestige, in order to displace the United States as the leader of Western Europe. This approach was flawed for two reasons. First, France's reach exceeded its grasp. France sought to displace the United States, but could not afford to destroy the dollar system and replace it with a monetary regime financed and managed by Paris. This recognition of weakness was one reason that the French pursued strategic, as opposed to subversive, disruption. Thus the goal itself had inherent contradictions.

Secondly, and of more general relevance for the study of strategic disruption, France was not pursuing a tangible goal. While foreign policies can certainly be introduced to achieve intangible goals, strategic disruption may not be a good instrument for such pursuits. As discussed in the theory section, disrupters walk a tightrope between their own weakness and the survival of the system. It is therefore logical that the shorter the trip, the greater the chance of success (if one holds constant the degree of difficulty). Instead of attempting to walk from point A to point B (attempting to extract a specific concession), France set out on a path of indefinite length. Such a course invites catastrophe. Specific goals or side payments may not have been the French objective, but they could have left France with something at the end of the struggle.

Zambia and the Sterling System

On November 11, 1965, Rhodesia, a self-governing colony of the United Kingdom, proclaimed a Unilateral Declaration of Independence (UDI). This action was taken to preserve the system of white minority rule, which would have been incompatible with the British policy of establishing majority rule upon decolonization. At the time the UDI was announced, Rhodesia's 210,000 whites ruled over 4.2 million blacks.[84]

The question of how to deal with Ian Smith's rebel regime became one of great controversy. At the center of this dispute stood Britain on one side and Zambia on the other. The specific dispute between these two states was the unwillingness of Britain to use force to end the rebellion. A swift and decisive suppression of the uprising was demanded by all of the newly independent African states through the Organization of African Unity (OAU), and, indeed, by the whole world at the United Nations. While Rhodesia was an issue of great importance to all black African states, Zambia was the only such state on the "front line."

[84] Robert C. Good, *UDI: The International Politics of the Rhodesian Rebellion* (Princeton: Princeton University Press, 1973), p. 15. The author was the U.S. ambassador to Zambia from March 1965 to December 1968.

After an initial period of patience, Zambia, led by President Kenneth Ka-unda, attempted to force Britain to intervene militarily to end the rebellion. The three instruments at his disposal were the threat to leave the British Com-monwealth, the threat to cut off copper exports to Britain, and the threat to sell Zambia's sterling holdings and possibly destroy what remained of the sterling area. The last two of these threats were taken seriously by the British govern-ment, although the copper cutoff was not a credible option, given the impor-tance of copper to the Zambian economy. Sales of sterling, however, being virtually costless, represented a credible threat.[85] Interestingly, it was Britain, more than Zambia, that was walking a monetary tightrope in this case. For while too little action might end the sterling area, too much action could also threaten to destroy the system.

During the first decade after World War II, independent members of the sterling area reduced their large sterling balances while those of the colonial members increased.[86] During the next ten years, these newly independent countries would run down their balances as well. This was a natural result of the establishment of independent monetary institutions in those countries, and was accelerated by a downward trend in commodity prices and a shortage of external capital. In all, African sterling balances declined from their record high of £755 million in 1954 to £254 million in 1966. The traditionally large reserves of Ghana and Nigeria dwindled especially quickly, leaving Zambia, with reserves of £80 million, as the largest holder in Commonwealth Africa.[87]

At the center of the system, Britain continued to suffer from the monotonic decline of the pound as an international currency. Sterling was under almost constant pressure. The weakness of the pound dominated both the domestic and the foreign policy agenda in Britain. Austerity measures to prop up the currency contributed not only to domestic belt-tightening, but to pressure to reduce overseas commitments as well. Sterling was under severe pressure in December 1964, and was rescued by $3 billion in short-term credits provided by a consortium of central banks at the last minute. Other crises that required international support erupted in the summers of 1965 and 1966. The 1967 crisis led to the devaluation of the pound on November 18, and was accom-panied by an additional $3 billion of international credits.[88]

The particular position of sterling in this era meant that Britain could be

---

[85] This once again demonstrates the relative freedom from "feedback" effects (discussed in Chapter 2) that monetary sanctions enjoy compared to trade sanctions.

[86] See Chapter 4.

[87] Yusuf Bangura, *Britain and Commonwealth Africa* (Manchester: Manchester University Press, 1983), p. 97. While a substantial amount, Zambia's £80 million did not qualify that state as one of "five heavyweights," each of which held at least £200 million: Australia, Malaysia, Kuwait, Hong Kong, and Ireland. Strange, *Sterling*, p. 89.

[88] Strange, *International Monetary Relations*, pp. 135–40; See also S. Brittan, *Steering the Economy* (New York: Library Press, 1971); and H. Brandon, *In The Red: The Struggle for Ster-ling 1964–1966* (London: Andre Deutch Ltd., 1966).

squeezed from two sides. On the one hand, the country clearly could not afford to get involved in a costly and protracted war.[89] At the same time, sterling appeared to be vulnerable to external pressure, from sources that were agitating for military action.

If Britain was squeezed in the 1960s, the Rhodesian declaration of independence left Zambia in a stranglehold. Geographically landlocked, Zambia, formerly "Northern Rhodesia," was also politically landlocked, surrounded in southern Africa by white-dominated Rhodesia, South Africa, South West Africa, Mozambique, and Angola (the latter two still Portuguese colonies) and a handful of similarly situated, weak states, such as Malawi. As the Zambian government itself noted: "Zambia and Southern Rhodesia's economies have for the past seventy years been inextricably joined like siamese twins."[90]

Zambia was completely dependent on Rhodesia, a state of affairs primarily due to the importance of the copper industry to the Zambian economy. Zambia produced 12 percent of the world's output of the metal, and copper production accounted for 96 percent of its exports, 60 percent of the government's revenue, and 44 percent of the country's GNP. The industry depended on Rhodesian-controlled railways to transport the metal to the sea, Rhodesian-controlled power plants, and imports of coal and petroleum. Zambia could perhaps redirect its imports of consumer goods away from Rhodesia, but the dependence of the copper industry and thus the entire Zambian economy could not easily be undone.[91] As one observer noted, "Hit Rhodesia with sanctions, and Zambia must flinch."[92] This ceased to be a hypothetical issue with the declaration of Rhodesian independence.

[89] Neera Chandhoke, *The Politics of U.N. Sanctions*, (New Delhi: Gitanjali Publishing House, 1986), p. 47.

[90] F. Taylor Ostrander, "Zambia in the Aftermath of the Rhodesian UDI: Logistical and Economic Problems," *African Forum* 2, no. 3:50–65 (1967), pp. 51–52.

[91] For the percentages, Richard Sklar, "Zambia's Response to the Rhodesian Unilateral Declaration of Independence," in William Tardoff, ed., *Politics in Zambia* (Berkeley: University of California Press, 1974), pp. 320–21; For more on dependence, see Jan Pettman, *Zambia: Security and Conflict* (London: Julian Friedman Publishers , 1974), ch. 4. J.D.B. Miller, in *Survey of Commonwealth Affairs* (London: Oxford University Press, 1974), states that "South Africa, Rhodesia, and Zambia form a single economy, linked by rail" (p. 221). On the railway linkages, and the dependence of the copper industry on this network, see Richard Hall, "Zambia and Rhodesia: Links and Fetters," *Africa Report* 11, no. 1:8–12 (1966), pp. 8–10.

[92] "Hit Rhodesia . . .," Good, *UDI*, p. 86. "Highest price," Richard Hall, *The High Price of Principles: Kaunda and the White South* (London: Hodder and Stroughton, 1969), p. 5.

It was not inevitable that Zambia would come into conflict with Rhodesia, though. Malawi, a similarly situated state, followed the strategy of accommodation, a form of bandwagoning that would be predicted by international relations theory. Zambia defied this logic and pursued a strategy of confrontation, a course of action that has been attributed to the "burning idealism" of President Kaunda. (Miller, *Survey*, p. 200). For more on Kaunda's ideology, see Hall, *High Price*, p. 39, passim. On balancing and bandwagoning, see Stephen M. Walt, *The Origins of Alliances* (Ithaca, N.Y.: Cornell University Press, 1987).

The Rhodesian UDI was not a bolt from the blue, but an anticipated tactic, which was of great concern to both Britain and the black African states. Britain had warned Rhodesia that grave consequences would result from such an action. In the wake of the declaration, Britain suspended all privileges that Rhodesia had enjoyed as a member of the Commonwealth and imposed economic sanctions. Rhodesian sugar and tobacco exports were boycotted. There was optimism that these sanctions would be effective, since exports accounted for 40 percent of Rhodesian GNP, and the tobacco and sugar exports alone accounted for £22 million of Rhodesia's exports of £31 million to Britain in 1964. Within two months of the UDI, *The Economist* proclaimed that "everything now points to the ultimate defeat of the Rhodesian rebellion."[93]

However, the economic sanctions did not bring down the rebel regime, and would not, at least in the near term. The sanctions came to be criticized as limited, gradual, and unfocused.[94] In fact, the rebel regime's sterling balances in London were not immediately frozen.[95] But the greatest international criticism of the British government was Prime Minister Harold Wilson's explicit and repeated renunciation of the use of force, predating the UDI. President Kwame Nkrumah of Ghana angrily argued that the renunciation of force was "a direct invitation to the rebellion."[96]

The black African states pressed hard for British military intervention, in international organizations such as the UN, the OAU, and the Commonwealth. One month before the UDI, the UN General Assembly voted 107–2 to call on Britain to use force to prevent any such rebellion. At the OAU, in the wake of the UDI, members voted to break off diplomatic relations with Britain if it failed to bring an end to the rebellion by December 15. In this atmosphere, the meetings of the Commonwealth in 1965 and 1966 "took the air of trials."[97]

[93] Good, *UDI,* pp. 69–71.

[94] R. B. Suttcliffe, "The Political Economy of Rhodesian Sanctions," *Journal of Commonwealth Political Studies* 7, no. 2:113–25 (1969), pp. 114, 117; see also Good, *UDI,* p. 82.

[95] For more specific details of the sanctions, see Chandhoke, *Politics of U.N. Sanctions,* passim. Elaine Windrich, in *Britain and the Politics of Rhodesian Independence* (London: Croom Helm, 1978), argues that more swift and comprehensive payment prohibitions could have caused a severe economic crisis (p. 64). Thomas M. Frank, in "Must We Lose Zimbabwe?" *African Forum* 2, no. 3 (1967), is also highly critical of Wilson's handling of the crisis.

It is interesting to note that in its initial reluctance to freeze Rhodesian sterling balances in London, the British government was again walking the monetary tightrope. The initial hesitation was criticized by President Julius Nyerere of Tanzania as an act of complicity, but in fact the British government did not want to do anything to undermine the reputation of sterling as an international reserve asset. (Bangura, *Commonwealth Africa,* pp. 108–9).

[96] Olajide Aluko, *Ghana and Nigeria, 1957–1970* (London: Rex Collings, 1976), p. 179.

[97] On the UN, Donald Rothchild, "Rhodesian Rebellion and African Response," *Africa Quarterly* 6, no. 3:184–96 (1966), p. 186; on the OAU, Good, *UDI,* p. 103; on the Commonwealth, James Barber, "The Impact of the Rhodesian Crisis on the Commonwealth," *Journal of Commonwealth Political Studies* 7, no. 2:83–95 (1969), p. 85. For more on the commonwealth, especially

The emerging African states were furious over Britain's refusal to contemplate the use of force in this instance, noting that the imperial power had not hesitated to crush colonial rebellions in the past. Many argued that this was racism. Indeed, given the number of references to Rhodesian "kith and kin" (that is, whites) to be heard in Britain during the crisis, it is hard to ignore this as a factor. However, there were a number of other reasons why Britain did not intervene, the most important of which was domestic politics. Most British citizens did not care about Rhodesia and, given the prevailing atmosphere of austerity, would be unlikely to support any costly overseas adventures. Additionally, while Britain could afford a "swift and decisive" military victory, there was the real possibility that such a conflict would become difficult and expensive, and neither the British economy in general nor the pound in particular had the stamina for such an undertaking.[98]

With the passing of the December 15 deadline, only a handful of African states broke off relations with Britain. If the UDI revealed British weakness, it demonstrated even more clearly the weaknesses of the newly independent states of Africa.[99] The two states that vied for pan-African leadership, Ghana and Nigeria, were in precarious positions. Both states, once important earners of foreign exchange for the sterling system, had almost completely run down their reserves. In 1965, Ghana's finances were "in chaos." Thus President Nkrumah's attempt at subversive disruption of the sterling area—a call for the pooling of African reserves and the creation of an African currency area— amounted to mere rhetoric. Also, both states were preoccupied by domestic affairs: each suffered a coup in early 1966, and the Nigerian civil war erupted in 1967.[100]

Even if their own actions were ineffective, the new African states were

---

the September 1966 meeting, Brain Lapping, "The Commonwealth and Rhodesia," *African Report*, November 1966, pp. 10–14, esp. pp. 12–13.

[98] On African anger, R. C. Pratt, "African Responses to the Rhodesian Crisis," *International Journal* 21, no. 2:186–98 (1966), p. 192. On domestic perceptions of the crisis, R. B. Suttcliffe, "Zambia and the Strains of the UDI," *World Today* 23, no. 12:506–11 (1967), pp. 507–9. On domestic politics, see Paul Foot, *The Politics of Harold Wilson* (Middlesex: Penguin Books, 1968); see also Lapping, "Commonwealth and Rhodesia," p. 11.

[99] On the break in relations, Good, *UDI*, p. 103; Rothchild suggests that this allowed for a "dual approach" strategy of pressure from within and without ("Rhodesian Rebellion," p. 193). Anirudha Gupta, in "The Rhodesian Crisis and the Organization of African Unity," *International Studies* 9, no. 1:55–64 (1967), pp. 61, 63, argues that the black African states not only were weak, but allowed criticism of Britain to substitute for a comprehensive strategy.

[100] On African leadership, Aluko, *Ghana and Nigeria*, pp. 73–76. On foreign exchange earnings, Miller, *Survey*, p. 279. "Chaos," Aluko, *Ghana and Nigeria*, p. 176. President Nkrumah called for the pooling of African reserves in the speech to the National Assembly on December 16, 1965, announcing the break of relations with Britain. Kwame Nkrumah, *Rhodesia File* (London: Panat Books, 1976), p. 125. On domestic distractions, Aluko, *Ghana and Nigeria*, pp. 21, 25, 28. For more on Nigeria, see Ojalide Aluko, *Essays on Nigerian Foreign Policy* (London: George Allen and Unwin, 1981); see also Chapter 3.

correct in their perception that sanctions alone were not going to work. There were two principal reasons for this. First was the ability of the rebel regime to adapt to the sanctions, especially with regard to the maintenance of white living standards. Second was the support given to Rhodesia by the adjacent white-ruled African states, South Africa and Mozambique.[101] This allowed Rhodesia to secure vital imports and provided an outlet for its exports. This was especially true for the essential import of oil, which flowed to Rhodesia by rail from South Africa and also off-loaded at Mozambican ports. Because of these actions, there was no serious or protracted shortage of oil in Rhodesia, even after the United States and Britain agreed to a specific embargo on that commodity.[102]

In another of the subepisodes of monetary diplomacy during this crisis, South Africa also supported Rhodesia through the practice of protective currency manipulation. When the crisis initially broke, South Africa did not publicly embrace Rhodesia (for example, diplomatic recognition was not extended), and it was not clear that local earners of Rhodesian pounds would be assured that their profits could be converted into South African currency. However, the reserve bank in Pretoria did continue to accept the Rhodesian currency at par and act as that country's international clearing house. The South African Central Bank also provided seasonal support for the Rhodesian foreign exchange position.[103] Both of these actions were significant and benevolent acts of support (for the rebel regime). The Rhodesian pound was clearly a less attractive international currency after the UDI than it was before, without even considering the stark fact that the reserves traditionally used to defend the value of the currency lay frozen in London, and that the country had taken that opportunity to default on its international obligations.

Because of the aid and comfort offered to the Ian Smith regime, most of the hawkish states made the logical demand that the sanctions be extended to include "violators," which meant Portugal and South Africa. However, once again, monetary considerations dominated British thinking. Rhodesia was expendable, but good relations with South Africa were essential: without South African gold and trade, the sterling area would not survive. That nation owned 20 percent of the gold held by the Bank of England, and the British government did not need to be reminded of its precarious financial posi-

---

[101] On white living standards, Suttcliffe, "Rhodesian Sanctions," p. 117. T.R.C. Curtin, in "Total Sanctions and Economic Development in Rhodesia," *Journal of Commonwealth Political Studies* 7, no. 2:126–31 (1969), p. 130, argued that even if South Africa cooperated in a policy of total sanctions against Rhodesia, if Rhodesia followed the correct policies, economic collapse would not be ensured.

[102] Good, *UDI*, pp. 131, 134, 145; also Chandhoke, *Politics of U.N. Sanctions*, p. 85.

[103] On convertibility, Good, *UDI*, pp. 129, 258; on seasonal support, Suttcliffe, "Rhodesian Sanctions," p. 124.

tion.[104] Thus the monetary tightrope Britain was traversing became even thinner. Not only could Britain ill afford to risk a protracted war (had it the inclination to use force), it was equally important that relations with South Africa not be ruptured.

Given the fact that economic sanctions were not likely to succeed against Rhodesia (at least in the foreseeable future), and Britain was apparently extremely reluctant to use force, Zambia was left in an extraordinarily difficult position. Zambia was in a much stronger position to coerce Britain than any of the other African states that actively opposed the UDI. Zambia's copper industry gave it two potential levers: the copper itself, upon which Britain depended, and the large Zambian sterling balances, which had been accumulated as a result of previous copper sales. However, although in firm disagreement with Britain over the handling of the crisis, President Kaunda initially attempted to cooperate with the Wilson government.[105]

Given Zambia's dependence on Rhodesia and Kaunda's principled unwillingness to strike a deal with the rebel regime, it was essential from the Zambian perspective that the crisis be resolved as quickly as possible. In the first two months following the UDI, Zambia got a taste of what life would be like in confrontation with its southern neighbor. Almost every lever at Rhodesian disposal was employed against Zambia. On December 17, 1965, Britain and the United States agreed to introduce oil sanctions against Rhodesia. One day later, oil stopped flowing from Rhodesia to Zambia, and a dramatic multinational oil airlift was arranged in order to keep the Zambian economy afloat. The Smith regime also manipulated taxes and procedures associated with coal exports and rail transport, steps that further threatened the viability of the Zambian economy.[106]

Despite the hardship suffered in Zambia (and because of the limited options available), Kaunda was willing to give the sanctions policy an opportunity to show that it could get the job done. One reason for this was that Wilson had indicated to Kaunda that he, Wilson, would be in a better position to deal with the rebellion after the British elections in April. In January 1966, Kaunda told his cabinet: "I am sure that Harold will do the right thing at the right time."[107]

The April elections were a stunning victory for Labour, bringing the party a huge majority in Parliament. In the intervening period, sanctions had not

[104] P. Chandrasekhara Rao, "The Rhodesian Crisis and the Use of Force," *Africa Quarterly* 6, no. 4:285–96 (1967), p. 292; also Chandhoke, *Politics of U.N. Sanctions*, p. 51; Foot, *Harold Wilson*, p. 270; and Lapping, "Commonwealth and Rhodesia," p. 14.

[105] Banguru, *Commonwealth Africa*, pp. 109–10

[106] Good, *UDI*, pp. 95–99; 107–12.

[107] Hall, *High Price*, p. 137 (quote); Douglas D. Anglin and Timothy M. Shaw, *Zambia's Foreign Policy: Studies in Diplomacy and Dependence* (Boulder, Colo.: Westview Press, 1979), p. 122 (elections).

changed the situation in Rhodesia. Wilson then announced his next move, negotiations (or "talks about talks") with the rebel regime. President Kaunda was not notified of this move in advance, and reportedly heard of it by chance when monitoring the news via shortwave radio.[108] This double-cross was the single defining moment in relations between Great Britain and independent Zambia. Kaunda responded with an anti-British fury, which was reflected most obviously in his speeches. Indicative of the new state of relations, Kaunda refused to attend the Commonwealth conference in September, sending Foreign Minister Kapwapase and Finance Minister Wina instead. Kapwapase took the opportunity to call Wilson a racialist and walk out of the conference, leaving Wina behind to apologize.[109]

After the announcement of the negotiations policy, Zambian tactics shifted from attempting to nudge Britain in the right direction to confrontation. If Zambia could not convince Britain to use force, perhaps Britain could be compelled to intervene militarily. At the very least, Britain should provide compensation to Zambia for the continued suffering that persisted only because of British inaction.

The only real lever that Zambia had at its disposal was a threat to undermine the sterling system, that is, strategic disruption. Zambia could conceivably threaten to cut off Britain's vital copper supplies (it was often muttered in Zambia, "If Britain wants its copper, let it solve the whole issue"[110]), but given Zambia's dependence on copper exports, this was hardly a credible threat.

Zambia could challenge the sterling system in two ways. First, it could insist on dollar payments for copper exports. This was a much more credible use of the copper weapon, as it would be costless to Zambia but perhaps decisive with regard to the fate of the pound. Such threats were raised in July 1966. Second, Zambia could sell off its substantial sterling holdings. According to a report in the *Times of Zambia*, also in late July, a sudden withdrawal of Zambian reserves from London "would almost certainly have forced a devaluation of the pound." On July 21, Finance Minister Wina demonstrated his skill at passive aggression, announcing that it was "not his government's policy to increase sterling's international problems."[111]

The Zambian strategic disruption did not compel Britain to use force. There

[108] Good, *UDI*, pp. 150–55. Notably, the decision to enter into negotiations was popular in Britain (ibid., p. 150).

[109] Hall, *High Price*, pp. 149–52.

[110] Good, *UDI*, p. 163. Although hardly credible, the threat to cut off copper did raise eyebrows in Britain. Prime Minister Wilson noted in his memoirs that "Britain was utterly dependent on [Zambia's] copper supplies." Harold Wilson, *A Personal Record: The Labour Government 1964–1970* (Boston: Little, Brown , 1971), p. 182.

[111] Banguru, *Commonwealth Africa*, p. 110 (copper, Wina quote); Anglin and Shaw, *Zambia's Foreign Policy*, p. 122 (*Times* quote).

were a number of reasons for this. First, as in all cases of strategic disruption, Zambia was on its own tightrope. It would not profit from destroying the sterling system, but would instead be in the same situation with regard to Rhodesia, and have no chance to receive British aid. Strategic disruption, by its very nature, is almost always more effective as a threat than as a sanction. In this particular case, such disruption was even less likely to compel action, because Britain had reason to believe that complying with the demands of the disrupters would not save the sterling system, as the weight of war itself might bring the system down.

However, the Zambian tactics were successful in extracting side payments, in the form of increased aid. The July saber rattling over sterling occurred at the same time that the two nations were discussing a compensatory aid package for Zambia, given that copper production in that nation was down by one-third, and GNP off by a striking 25 percent. Britain first offered £7 million, and when this was rejected as insufficient and followed by renewed threats against sterling, ultimately doubled the offer. This may not appear to be a great amount, but it must be considered in context. In that same July, Prime Minister Wilson announced new austerity budget cuts of £100 million annually. As one observer noted, the Zambian aid package was a "generous proposal presented at a time when Britain was retrenching its commitments throughout the world." Notably, in the "memorandum of understanding" ultimately signed in February 1967, British aid was explicitly linked to continued Zambian participation in the Commonwealth and the sterling area, underscoring the linkage between the aid and the pound.[112]

The Zambian episode offers a number of interesting lessons. Up to this point, the consideration of strategic disruption has focused on the fact that given its position, the initiator of the action must walk a tightrope: it may exhaust itself in the influence attempt, or may destroy the system, failing to achieve its objectives and losing whatever benefits the system provided. In this episode, the target state was found to be walking a tightrope as well, and a highly paradoxical one. Giving in to demands will save a monetary system from disruption only if the actions demanded do not in themselves do the job. The paradox is that those states that are most vulnerable to strategic disruption, that is, those leader states in monetary difficulty, may have the least ability to deliver.

One consequence of this is that the goals of disruption must be specific and nonperverse. Highly successful disrupters, if this logic is correct, would engage in short-term disruption in the pursuit of specific goals, goals that would not excessively tax the foreign exchange position of the target state. Less successful disrupters, on the other hand, are likely to be those that pursue

---

[112] Good, *UDI,* pp. 105, 167, 168 (quote); Bangura, *Commonwealth Africa,* pp. 110 (renewed threats), 111 (membership links).

long-term goals that may in and of themselves destroy the system. Zambia's disruption, which was concentrated in July, when the aid package was being negotiated, did not succeed in compelling Britain to use force, but it was influential in determining the outcome of a nonmonetary issue.

This episode also contains an interesting counterfactual. One of the factors that motivated Britain during this crisis was the need to maintain good relations with South Africa. Had South Africa been ruled by the black majority instead of the white minority, Britain's need to remain friendly with that state would have led to a different set of circumstances. Given the passions associated with the issue, such a South African state would surely have engaged in strategic disruption against the sterling system to compel the British to intervene with force. Given the position of South Africa, the threat would be credible—it could have easily tipped over the boat of British finance, especially given the state of the pound at that time. It is not clear that Britain would have opted to crush the rebellion, since this might have destroyed sterling anyway (though perhaps not with the cooperation of South Africa). It is clear, however, that under those circumstances, Britain would have had to choose between monetarily hazardous intervention in Rhodesia and the demise of the sterling system.

The Theory and Practice of Systemic Disruption

The three cases examined, considered in conjunction with the theoretical sections, afford the opportunity to draw some general conclusions about systemic disruption. To frame the analysis, these cases are summarized in Table 5.1. Taken together, the cases confirm a number of the hypotheses generated in the introduction to the chapter, but also hold a number of surprises.

To expand on this shorthand, in the first episode, France engaged in strategic disruption of the gold exchange standard system during 1927–1931 in order to alter British behavior over issues associated with the German question. While France was able to disrupt the system, it was unable to extract specific concessions from Britain, and the influence attempt ended in failure when the monetary system collapsed in 1931. In the second episode, France again attempted strategic disruption of a gold exchange standard system during 1964–1968, this time in a struggle with the United States over leadership in Europe. This attempt ended in failure when the franc weakened in 1968 and was supported by the United States Finally, in 1966, Zambia engaged in strategic disruption of the sterling system in order to force Britain to intervene militarily to crush the Rhodesian rebellion. Zambia failed to achieve its nominal goal, but did extract significant side payments, and so this episode's result is evaluated as mixed, having elements of both success and failure.

Two notable findings stand out immediately. The first is the failure to dem-

TABLE 5.1
The Practice of Systemic Disruption

Agent/Year	Target	Issue	Resolution	Evaluation
France, 1927–1931	Britain	German question	Systemic collapse	Failure
France, 1964–1968	United States	Leadership in Europe	Fall of the franc	Failure
Zambia, 1966	Britain	Rhodesia	More aid	Mixed

Note: All these episodes were major attempts.

onstrate the practice of subversive disruption. This was attributed to the relatively small number of candidate targets, a similarly small number of possible agents, and a natural bias of candidate agents in favor of strategic disruption. Clearly, it has been demonstrated that strategic disruption has been consciously employed by states, but the inability to demonstrate subversion represents the first theoretically generated form of monetary power that has failed to pass the test of existence. This question is revisited in Part III.

The finding that leaps from the table is the difficulty of disruption: the "scorecard" shows two failures and one mixed outcome, with no examples of clear success. This is especially surprising because all three of the systems disrupted appear to have been vulnerable: none of the three survived seven years after the initial disruption. This suggests either that disruption is very hard to execute successfully, or that vulnerable systems are not the best ones to disrupt.

Both of these factors seem to be true. Disruption is very difficult, for a number of reasons. As discussed in the introduction, and confirmed by the cases, this form of monetary power is unique in that the agents are "aiming up": they are weaker than the target states. This leaves such disrupters vulnerable to being trumped by the target on an unrelated issue. This underscores yet again the significance of the tightrope analogy, in which disrupters are vulnerable because of both their own weakness and the possibility that their actions will inadvertently destroy the system. A target state, aware of the preference of a strategic disrupter not to destroy the system, and also cognizant of the relative overall weakness of its adversary, may adopt a passive strategy, attempting to wait the agent out. This strategy was successfully employed by the United States in the 1960s, and was also attempted with less overall success by Britain in the 1920s.

With respect to the second possibility, it may be difficult to engage in the successful strategic disruption of a weak system. While it may be possible to disrupt the system, parlaying that capability to extract concessions from the leader of a declining system may not be possible, due to the fact that the concessions themselves might undermine the regime. In that case, the system leader has no incentive to give in to the disrupter's demands, which would not solve the problem raised by the influence attempt, that is, preserving the monetary regime. This suggests that in some cases the opportunity for successful strategic disruption rests at an unstable equilibrium between the relative strengths of the two participants. When the system is very vulnerable to disruption, it is likely that the concessions that can be extracted will also be limited. On the other hand, when the system is strong, the ability to disrupt will be reduced. This yields the paradox that the greater the ability to disrupt, the smaller the ability to extract. However, this paradox is overstated, and such an interpretation does not eliminate the possibility of successful strategic disruption; it simply limits the range of the types of payments that can be extracted. A number of concessions can occur at no risk to the monetary system. Thus the lesson is one of tactics, not strategy. The French tactics seemed to be especially sound in this regard (though they were ultimately unsuccessful)[113] in the 1927 attempt to force Britain to raise interest rates. In that action, the French policy goal was to force Britain to take steps that would be necessary to protect the system from further disruption, the exact opposite of steps that would undermine the system.

A number of other tactical lessons emerge from the case studies. Since disruption is so difficult, experience suggests that specific, short-term goals are more likely to be achieved than more general, long-term ones. Rhetoric also appears to be an important instrument. On this point, strategic disruption provides another example of monetary sanctions which attempt to call forth market bandwagoning, as opposed to pressing against "natural economic forces." Calling attention to the weakness of a given regime may unleash atomistic and complementary speculative forces.[114] Unexpected tactical strengths of disruption include its ability to function effectively in both direct and indirect capacities. As demonstrated in the French attempts to coerce Germany, disruption is a flexible instrument in that the successful practice of monetary power anywhere within a system will have effects that will work their way back to the center. Therefore, even if the core appears impregnable, it may still be sensitive to more circuitous coercion. Additionally, in all three

[113] As discussed above, this attempt, tactically sound with regard to the monetary system, would have forced Britain to take actions that were incompatible with more dominant domestic political considerations.

[114] Chapter 2 discussed when market forces would be likely to complement or inhibit the practice of monetary power. Market forces are likely to complement attempts at disruption directed at monetary systems based on rules, since the respect of those rules represents implicit deviations from market outcomes. Deviations from the rules can allow market forces an avenue of expression, which would logically be destabilizing. This also explains why, as expected, disruption took place under fixed exchange rate regimes.

cases considered, strategic disruption had a direct and successful effect: it functioned as a signal. In every case, the practice of disruption, even when ultimately unsuccessful, imposed real economic costs on the target and accurately communicated a policy preference and depth of commitment on specific issues to the target country.

Part III

THE POTENTIAL OF MONETARY POWER

6

The Opportunity for Monetary Power

Introduction

Part I considered the theory of monetary power, generating hypotheses about what forms such power could take and establishing the viability of those forms. Part II examined the practice and mechanics of monetary power, satisfying the question of existence by demonstrating that states had practiced monetary diplomacy throughout the twentieth century. Part II also examined how that power worked, explored the attributes of its various instruments, and considered the question of when attempts at monetary coercion will be successful. This part looks at the potential of monetary power. This chapter attempts to evaluate that potential by looking at a number of apparent "missed opportunities" to practice monetary diplomacy. Chapter 7 summarizes the findings of the book, considers more closely the issue of the sources of success and failure, and explores those issues in contemporary international politics, which can better be understood with a sensitivity to the concept of monetary power.

This chapter examines a number of cases when the exercise of monetary power by a given state seemed to be a logical option, yet was not exercised. By comparing these episodes with the episodes from Part II, the analysis considers why and when states choose to engage in (or refrain from) the practice of monetary diplomacy.[1]

Currency Manipulation

In theory, there should be a large number of opportunities to practice currency manipulation, and therefore this form of monetary power should also be likely to have the greatest number of "missing cases." There are three levels of decisionmaking at which the chance to introduce techniques of monetary power in general and currency manipulation in particular can be missed: the level of the influence attempt, that of economic diplomacy, and that of monetary power. At the first level, states may fail to attempt monetary diplomacy

---

[1] Of course, just as in Part II, the episodes here do not represent the complete universe of possible cases. The "missed opportunities" chosen represent distinct examples, illustrate unique aspects of the question, and showcase a variety of monetary regimes.

because they have made the political decision not to attempt to influence the outcome of a given situation. Alternately, intervention with other components of power may eliminate the need to consider monetary tactics.

At the second level, monetary power may also be ruled out because of limitations on the practice of economic diplomacy in general. Although it has been argued that monetary power is less vulnerable to such problems than other instruments of economic power, this does not mean that it will never be undermined by such pitfalls as feedback or domestic politics. Finally, states may fail to introduce manipulative techniques for reasons particular to monetary power. Decisionmakers may be unaware of the opportunity, either because they are not sensitive to the economics of the issue, or because the vulnerability of the target was not known to the home state at the time. On the other hand, a home state may be aware of the target's vulnerability, but because of its own currency position find itself unable to practice monetary diplomacy at that time.

France and the Occupation of the Ruhr

As discussed in Chapter 5, France's policy during the interwar period was dominated by its desire to keep Germany as weak as possible. In the early post–World War I period, this meant ensuring a large and steady stream of reparations from Germany. In 1923, because of their dissatisfaction with the flow of reparations from Germany, France and Belgium occupied the Ruhr in order to take the matter into their own hands and focus attention on the issue. The occupation was neither short nor successful, and economic conditions in both France and Germany deteriorated as a result. Finally, in October 1924, the Dawes plan fixed a new reparations schedule, facilitated by the "Dawes loan" to Germany, and the occupation ended in August 1925.[2]

The occupation of the Ruhr contributed to the subsequent hyperinflation of the German mark, and greatly weakened the French franc. In fact, the "shadow of the Ruhr Conflict lay over the exchange markets of the world."[3] What is surprising in this case is that neither Britain nor the United States attempted to manipulate the French currency in support of its own foreign policy goals during the crisis, despite the fact that those states opposed the

---

[2] General Charles Dawes would later become vice president of the United States. Perhaps of even greater significance, he also wrote the song "It's All in the Game," which was covered by Van Morrison in his landmark 1979 album, *Into the Music*.

[3] William Adams Brown, Jr., *The International Gold Standard Reinterpreted, 1914–34* (New York: National Bureau of Economic Research, 1940), p. 307 (quote). For more on the currency situation in this period, see D. T. Jack, *The Restoration of European Currencies* (London: P. S. King and Son , 1927).

occupation, could have engaged in decisive manipulation, and were aware of the monetary power at their disposal.

France's foray into the Ruhr was initially part of a risky bargaining strategy adopted by Prime Minister Poincaré. He was dissatisfied with the difficulty his country was experiencing in extracting reparations from Germany, adamant that any German economic recovery take place within a framework that guaranteed France's economic and military security, and dismayed by the apparent emergence of an Anglo-German entente. The first two problems could be eased by either a forgiveness of the Allies' debts to one another or new loans to Germany. France unsuccessfully pressed for both of these in international negotiations, and in order to shock the rest of the world into action, moved into the Ruhr with Belgium on January 11, 1923.[4]

Thus the occupation, nominally to extract reparations, was actually a "political maneuver," designed to "raise the necessary fears" in Washington, London, and Berlin. The move was legally justified when the reparation commission ruled on December 26, 1922, and January 9, 1923, that Germany was in "voluntary default" of timber and coal deliveries, respectively. Both Britain and the United States were opposed to the move, but it was popular in France, where Poincaré received a vote of confidence, 452–72.[5]

The Germans met the occupation with a strategy of passive resistance, and a suspension of reparation payments. France responded by imposing a total economic blockade and seizing assets in the region. Each side adopted a strategy based on waiting the other out. The French hoped to create conditions that would alarm the German government, and more specifically, powerful German industrialists. Germany hoped to increase the costs of the occupation until they reached unsustainable levels. Unfortunately, both sides were successful in fomenting discomfort but not retreat. Costs to France increased and reached an unexpected Fr50 million per month, but this was met in France by a corresponding increase in the goals of the operation. In August 1923, economic pressure on Germany resulted in the resignation of the Cuno government and the final fall of the mark into hyperinflation, but it did not bring about surrender.[6]

The value of the mark had been eroding steadily as a result of domestic

---

[4] Walter A. McDougal, *France's Rhineland Diplomacy, 1914–24: The Last Bid for a Balance of Power in Europe* (Princeton: Princeton University Press, 1978), pp. 215, 240, 243, 250.

[5] "Political maneuver," McDougal, *Rhineland Diplomacy*, p. 215; confidence vote, ibid., p. 251. For the legal justification and opposition, Hermann J. Rupieper, *The Cuno Government and Reparations, 1922–23: Politics and Economics* (The Hague: Martinus Nijhoff, 1979), p. 78; also Marc Tractenberg, *Reparation in World Politics: France and European Economic Diplomacy, 1916–23* (New York: Columbia University Press, 1980), p. 288.

[6] McDougal, *Rhineland Diplomacy*, pp. 258, 262, 278, 290; Tractenberg, *Reparation*, pp. 295–96; Rupieper, *Cuno Government*, p. 81.

inflation, and the process greatly accelerated with the onset of the Ruhr crisis. The mark fell from 27,000/U.S.$1 on January 28, 1923, to 47,000/U.S.$ three days later. The Bank of England advanced credits to the Reichsbank at this time, in the hope of stabilizing the mark.[7] In a brief episode of successful self-protective currency manipulation, the Reichsbank intervened on the foreign exchange markets, in February 1923, and the mark doubled its value in two weeks. However, the mark subsequently resumed its fall, and was soon considered a lost cause by the British. It fell from 1.3 million/$ to 5 million/$ in August, and bottomed out at 4.2 trillion/$ in November.[8]

As the hyperinflation made it almost impossible to extract resources from Germany, France reacted with a further expansion of its tactics and a dramatic increase in its objectives. France supported a separatist movement in the occupied territory, which favored the creation of an independent Rhenish state. Further, the Poincaré government contemplated the introduction of a new Rhenish currency. Aside from being an essential aspect of sovereignty, such a move could drive the mark out of the region and make it difficult to finance the resistance there.[9]

However, although it supported the separatist movement, as well as the declaration of the Rhenish republic on October 21, 1923, France did not introduce this dramatic attempt at currency manipulation, an effort that would have predated the comparable Japanese efforts in China by more than a decade. The scheme was initially grounded by the objections of Finance Minister Charles Lasteyrie, who did not think the franc could bear the burden of underwriting such a currency. In the wake of the November declaration, this issue resurfaced, but was dismissed, again because of the weakness of the franc, but also because of the stabilization of the mark, which by January of 1924 appeared to be successful and would make the new currency less attractive.[10]

The stabilization of the mark was masterminded by Hjalmar Schacht, with the introduction of the rentenmark in November 1923.[11] It was this shift in fortunes—the stabilization of the mark and the continued deterioration of the

[7] Rupieper, *Cuno Government*, pp. 107–9. Britain also cooperated with Germany over the final restoration of the mark in November 1923. British aid to Germany obviously contributed to the French suspicion of British monetary motives (discussed in Chapter 5). However in both that period and during the Ruhr crisis (Rupieper, *Cuno Government*, p. 79), Britain and France were pursuing differently ordered preferences: British priorities rested with the overall economic stability of Europe.

[8] McDougal, *Rhineland Diplomacy*, p. 272 (February intervention) and p. 316 (4.2 trillion); Rupieper, *Cuno Government*, p. 108 (January fall) and p. 187 (lost cause).

[9] On the Rhenish separatism and currency issue, McDougal, *Rhineland Diplomacy*, pp. 262–63, 304–5, 326–29; Tractenberg, *Reparation*, pp. 299–301, 306–9, 322.

[10] McDougal, *Rhineland Diplomacy*, pp. 263, 316 (Lasteyrie opposition initially and again in October), also p. 304; Tractenberg, *Reparation*, p. 324.

[11] For more on this, see Hjalmar Schacht, *The Stabilization of the Mark* (New York: Adelphi Co., 1927). On issues related to the Ruhr crisis, see esp. ibid., pp. 53, 62, 134, 136, 189.

franc, as well as the increasing international unpopularity of the French position—that eventually led France to agree to the negotiations that resulted in the Dawes loan.[12] While the loan did represent the fulfillment of one of France's initial goals, neither side was satisfied with the outcome and both were the worse for wear.[13]

The single most important element determining the course and the outcome of the Ruhr crisis was the state of the French franc. As long as it occupied the Ruhr, France held all the cards. But France's ability to sustain such an occupation was suspect from the very beginning. At the cabinet meeting of November 27, 1922, the only opposition to the proposed strategy came from Finance Minister Lasteyrie, who feared that the operation might cause the collapse of the franc.[14]

The franc did come under repeated pressure. The costs of the occupation, which were exacerbated by persistent government budget deficits and an unwillingness to raise taxes, led to the expectation that the franc would depreciate. These underlying economic conditions, combined with political instability in France, invited the speculative attacks that rocked the franc repeatedly during this period. More than any other approach, speculation was "the determining factor" of the value of the franc, which was floating during this period.[15]

The franc came under extraordinary pressure during the first quarter of 1924. In January, the franc began a precipitous fall. Finance Minister Lasteyrie claimed that the drop was a result of German dumping of francs for dollars, motivated by a desire to "bring pressure to bear on the foreign policy of France and to induce M. Poincaré's government to renounce its action in the Ruhr." Lasteyrie made specific reference to a meeting of November 6,

[12] France's relations with the United States and Britain were already strained; those with its key ally, Belgium, also deteriorated as the crisis wore on. The Belgian currency came under pressure, and France engaged in protective manipulation. However, Belgium became increasingly dissatisfied with the extent of French support and nervous about British displeasure with Belgium's participation. McDougal, *Rhineland Diplomacy*, pp. 288–89, 327; Rupieper, *Cuno Government*, p. 126, 221.

[13] McDougal, *Rhineland Diplomacy*, p. 356; Rupieper, *Cuno Government*, p. 253.

[14] McDougal, *Rhineland Diplomacy*, pp. 227, 345. The Belgian foreign minister, Henri Jasper, also recognized the risk, but defended the policy, stating: "The occupation of the Ruhr was a considered gamble. It exposed the French and Belgian currencies to considerable risk. Not to do so might have exposed them to greater risks." (p. 240).

[15] McDougal, *Rhineland Diplomacy*, pp. 350–51 (economic conditions in France); "determining factor" is from Eleanor Lansing Dulles, *The French Franc 1914–1928* (New York: Macmillan, 1929), p. 37.

During this era, speculation was not only the key factor in explaining the value of the franc (as opposed to, for example, purchasing power parity or the balance of payments); it also pushed the franc *away* from its "market" equilibrium. See Robert Z. Aliber, "Speculation in the Foreign Exchanges: The European Experience, 1919–26," *Yale Economic Essays* 2, no. 1:171–245 (1961), esp. pp. 199–219.

1923, at which bankers from the occupied regions of Germany, under the guidance of the Reichsbank, decided to sell off the francs at their disposal for dollars.[16]

While the Germans did sell francs during this period, it is difficult to determine whether this was currency manipulation (that is, politically motivated). Many francs spent in the Rhineland filtered back into Germany, and there were good economic reasons for Germany to sell this accumulated currency, including recent devaluations in other European currencies, which left the franc even more apparently overvalued than before. Regardless, the franc was rocked by much more powerful speculative forces, which included a "coordinated" effort by the "gnomes of Zurich" (in this case, operating out of New York and Amsterdam) to induce panic selling of the franc in order to enhance the profitability of their own short positions.[17]

The political implications of the fall of the franc were considerable. Alexandre Millerand, president of France from 1920 to 1924 and an early promoter of plans to occupy the Ruhr, observed: "My country . . . can stand anything except a financial crisis." But a financial crisis is exactly what confronted France. The franc, which had traded at Fr13/£ before the crisis, reached Fr96.11/£ in January, bottoming out at Fr117.54/£ on March 8. France was forced to seek international support to protect the franc.[18]

The United States and Britain were the two states in a position to save the franc. But they also had a major political dispute with France: they both opposed the Rhineland occupation and wanted the situation resolved as quickly as possible. With the franc under pressure, these states had the opportunity to practice monetary power. There were three such possible responses to France's request for assistance. The Anglo-Americans could ignore such requests and engage in their own predatory acts against the franc; they could ignore the requests and hope that France would be forced to abandon the occupation; or they could tie assistance to specific political conditions (that is, withdrawal).

In fact, the United States and Britain pursued a fourth course. Instead of capitalizing on France's weakness, those nations chose to offer support for the franc with no political conditions. The U.S. government allowed the J. P. Morgan Company to lend France $100 million (such a transaction required government approval), and loans of pounds were also forthcoming from Brit-

---

[16] Stephen Schuker, *The End of French Predominance in Europe* (Chapel Hill: University of North Carolina Press, 1976), p. 56.

[17] M. Wolfe, *The French Franc between the Wars 1919–1939* (New York: Columbia University Press, 1951), finds "good evidence that [the speculation] was not political" (p. 33). See also Schuker, *End of French Predominance,* pp. 91 (economic reasons), 94 ("coordinated"); McDougal, *Rhineland Diplomacy,* p. 351.

[18] Schuker, *End of French Predominance,* p. 106 (quote); McDougal, *Rhineland Diplomacy,* pp. 351, 356 (Fr/£).

ain. The French government was able to enter the foreign exchange market and ruthlessly squeeze the bears, whose losses led to a wave of bankruptcies and suicides. The franc rebounded quickly to Fr92.25/£ and reached Fr62.15/£ by mid-April.[19]

It would appear that the United States and Britain missed an obvious opportunity to practice currency manipulation. As noted above, one possible reason states miss opportunities to introduce monetary power is that they are unaware of them. In this episode, however, all of the participants were acutely aware of the importance of the currency issue, and discussed amongst themselves the possibility of exploiting France's vulnerability.

The Berlin government explored the possibility of a predatory attack on the franc as early as March 1923, when it became worried about Germany's ability to sustain passive resistance. The U.S. ambassador to that country, Alanson B. Houghton, took up the local cause and advised Secretary of State Charles Evans Hughes that France should be stopped, and that the franc "was the obvious point of weakness." All the United States and Britain really needed to do was "overcome the artificial support now given to the franc," in order to affect domestic politics in France sufficiently to bring about withdrawal.[20]

However, Washington was not inclined to engage in such aggressive acts against France. The United States preferred not to get involved, and when the crisis initially broke, removed its remaining forces from Europe. The issue resurfaced in the summer, when German officials made plans to sustain any run on the franc: that is, they decided to opportunistically bandwagon with any market forces that would move the franc in a desired direction. (Germany also attempted a rhetorical offensive against the franc in central Europe and Holland.) By this time, however, the weakness of the mark made any consequential manipulation coming from Berlin highly unlikely. This did not prevent the German government from seeking outside support. In July Secretary Hughes was approached, through informal contacts, about "cooperation by America in case of economic pressure by England on France . . . for example, if England were to withdraw her support of the French franc and French securities." Hughes declined to offer U.S. cooperation, claiming that U.S. banks were outside the control of the government.[21]

---

[19] Carl L. Holtfrerich, "Domestic and Foreign Expectations and the Demand for Money during the German Inflation 1920–23," in Charles P. Kindleberger and Jean-Pierre Laffargue, eds., *Financial Crises: Theory, History, and Policy* (Cambridge: Cambridge University Press, 1982), p. 135 (Morgan loan); Dulles, *The French Franc*, p. 175; Wolfe, *French Franc*, p. 35 (suicides); Schuker, *End of French Predominance,* pp. 109, 112 (State Department approval), 125; McDougal, *Rhineland Diplomacy*, p. 356 (Fr/£).

[20] Schuker, *End of French Predominance*, p. 96.

[21] Rupieper, *Cuno Government*, p. 118 (U.S. withdrawal) and ch. 5 (German attempts to elicit support from Washington and London); Schuker, *End of French Predominance*, p. 96 (propaganda attempts), p. 97 (bandwagoning, weakness, quote).

The British were also aware of both France's vulnerability and their own ability to exploit that weakness. Responding to a request from the Foreign Office to study possible British methods of influencing French policy, Controller of Finance Sir Otto E. Niemeyer reported at the close of 1923: "The only thing likely to move the present French government towards a more reasonable reparations policy . . . is a fall in the French franc sufficiently serious to shake the confidence of the French peasant in his national securities." Additionally, the Niemeyer study stated that it was well within British capabilities to bring about such a fall in the franc through a number of measures, for example, the seizure of French gold in London to pay interest on France's debts to Britain. Other techniques, such as selling French securities on the open market, would be more discreet. "A likely fear of this result," the report continued, "would make the French government very susceptible to pressure."[22]

Officials in Britain discussed introducing this "weapon of overwhelming power," but repeatedly hesitated at the moment of truth. At one time it was decided to wait at least until the outcome of upcoming elections in France. When France's policy did not change, they considered threatening France in an informal letter. As this was about to occur, however, the British Labour party suddenly came to power, and Prime Minister Ramsay McDonald was inclined to wait a while longer, expecting the known opposition of the Labour party to the occupation and the newly started Dawes negotiations to generate a momentum of their own. Those negotiations eventually led to the settlement described above, and the need to contemplate monetary diplomacy passed.[23]

The Ruhr episode offers an almost ideal example of a missed opportunity to practice currency manipulation. There was a political disagreement, a target with vulnerability to monetary sanctions, bandwagoning market conditions, agents with the capability to introduce techniques of manipulation, every expectation that such sanctions would be highly successful, and an awareness of all of these conditions by both the potential agents and the potential target. Yet in the final analysis, the most obvious opportunity to enact the predatory acts resulted instead in the provision of unconditional support for the target by the agents.

It is very difficult to explain why something did *not* occur. However, a number of considerations may make this episode somewhat less puzzling. German behavior, for example, requires no explanation. Germany's failure to engage in significant manipulation was a consequence of its own weakness. Explaining the behavior of the United States is somewhat more complicated,

---

[22] Schuker, *End of French Predominance*, p. 99 (also 1st quote); Rupieper, *Cuno Government*, p. 247 (also quotes in text).

[23] Rupieper, *Cuno Government*, pp. 247, 249–50; Schuker, *End of French Predominance*, p. 101.

but a reasonable model can be constructed. If U.S. interests are divided into the political and the economic, a consistency emerges. Politically, the United States was opposed to the occupation, but this was a relatively low-priority item, and the United States responded with a policy of isolation. Although the Americans disagreed with a particular French policy, in general economic considerations dominated political ones. With regard to Europe in this period, a view of the United States as economically sensitive and politically agnostic is consistent with a U.S. policy that opposed the Ruhr occupation but allowed private actors within its society to help prevent the collapse of the franc.

The behavior of the British is the most difficult to explain. Unlike the United States, Britain was strongly opposed to the Ruhr occupation, and took the initiative in investigating its own potential to practice currency manipulation. The shift from the precipice of predatory action to unconditional support seems highly inconsistent.

There are two types of possible explanations for the British reversal. First, Britain may have been inhibited by feedback. As discussed above, the stability of the European economy was always a high-priority item for the British government. In fact, it was the sanctity of this priority that brought British and French interests into conflict so often in the interwar period. Threatening to undermine the franc was one thing—its actual collapse would have been another. In the face of the actual crisis, the issue of European economic stability may have trumped the British government's desire to end the occupation.[24]

The second set of explanations complements the first. The January crisis may have represented a currency manipulation that was much stronger than the British had in mind. Britain made preparations to *threaten* France with currency manipulation, but at no time did it commit to actual engagement, and perhaps hoped that threats would be sufficient. Also, any manipulation that would have been employed could have been carefully modulated, and even initially introduced solely for signaling purposes.

It is also possible that the British officials considered themselves to be practicing a tactic of "implicit currency manipulation," a technique that would be undermined by a collapse of the franc. Under the implicit manipulation interpretation, France, aware of its own weakness and vulnerability to potential British pressure, alters policies of its own that reflect these realities. As these weaknesses and vulnerabilities become greater, the target policies retreat further and further. A sudden collapse, however, might unpredictably alter the final outcome.

[24] Once again, monetary power was free from standard bilateral feedback, which is the source of the central feedback paradox that undermines the utility of the other instruments of economic power. However, if the British were inhibited by feedback in this case, it would be a demonstration of environmental feedback, in which the manipulation threatens to undermine a broader monetary system. An example of this was discussed in Chapter 3—the Nazi pound-counterfeiting scheme in Europe.

It was the case that as the franc got weaker and weaker, France's demands diminished, and this process did lead to the final settlement.[25] It is therefore possible that the January crisis was in some ways "too good" an opportunity for currency manipulation, and given Britain's overall goals in Europe, a more patient policy of waiting out the more gradual decline of the franc was preferred.[26]

The League of Nations versus Italy

On October 3, 1935, Italy attacked Ethiopia in order to conquer that state and make it part of the Italian empire. This act was a clear violation of the Covenant of the League of Nations, of which both states were members. The League imposed economic sanctions on Italy, which did not influence the outcome of the conflict. The "failure" of economic sanctions in this case became the scarlet letter borne forever by both the League and the concept of economic sanctions.

In fact, the Ethiopian crisis is a better indictment of the League than of sanctions. As many have observed, sanctions were only half-heartedly applied. What is less well known, though, is that the Italian lira was very vulnerable to manipulation during this crisis, and that monetary sanctions could have had a decisive influence on the outcome of the crisis. However, no state moved to take advantage of this opportunity.

The invasion of Ethiopia was a direct challenge to the principles of the League of Nations. Small members in particular viewed the League's ability to deal with this issue as a "test case" of the viability of the organization as a legitimate actor in the international system.[27] On October 11, the League announced an arms embargo against Italy. Eight days later, a number of more substantial sanctions followed. All loans to Italy were prohibited, no imports from Italy were to be permitted to any member state, and certain exports to Italy were also prohibited, including rubber, tin, and transport animals.[28]

---

[25] McDougal, *Rhineland Diplomacy*, pp. 353–34.

[26] This argument would be strongly supported by evidence showing that the British attempted to gently nudge the franc downward whenever it stabilized during its general decline. It is highly unlikely, however, that such evidence exists.

[27] George W. Baer, *Test Case: Italy, Ethiopia, and the League of Nations* (Stanford: Hoover Institution Press, 1976), p. 23. For a pro-Italian view of the episode, see Luigi Villari, *Italian Foreign Policy under Mussolini* (New York: Devin Adair Co., 1956); one interesting claim in this polemic is that during the war, Italy was able to acquire one hundred Rolls Royce engines for warplanes (p. 151). For a perspective on the crisis in the context of overall Italian foreign policy, see Esmonde M. Robertson, *Mussolini as Empire Builder: Europe and Africa, 1932–36* (London: Macmillan, 1977).

[28] Gary Clyde Hufbauer, Jeffrey J. Schott, and Kimberly Ann Elliot, *Economic Sanctions*

These sanctions were expected to have considerable impact on the Italian economy, causing by some estimates a 50 percent reduction in Italy's exports, and thus its international purchasing power. However, the sanctions were also carefully limited. No decision was made on the export of coal, oil, iron, and steel to Italy, all of which, but especially oil, were vital to the war effort. Military and diplomatic sanctions, well within the legal responses available to the League, were not even discussed.[29]

Given the prevailing expectations and preferences of the dominant actors, this hesitation was not illogical. It was assumed, even by Italian military experts, that it would take at least two years to conquer Ethiopia. Therefore, more aggressive sanctions could be held in reserve while negotiations occurred to see if Mussolini could be satisfied with something short of total conquest. (Fear of further sanctions did bring the Italians as far as the bargaining table on October 16.) Both Britain and France, by far the most powerful states in the League, preferred to resolve the issue without rupturing their relations with Italy. Those states viewed Germany as their principal enemy, and Italy as an important member of a European coalition that would keep Germany in check.[30]

In accordance with this strategy, on November 2, Britain and France had the League postpone a consideration of oil (and other additional) sanctions. In December, the British foreign secretary, Samuel Hoare, met secretly in Paris with the French prime minister, Pierre Laval, in order to coordinate their proposal that part of Abyssinia be ceded to Italy as part of a negotiated settlement. However, these proposals were leaked, causing an uproar in Great Britain, which led to the resignation of Hoare on December 18.[31]

Oil was the crucial issue. Italy was vulnerable to oil sanctions, with no domestic production and most of its wartime advantage over Ethiopia based on the exploitation of petroleum products. If such sanctions were to be effective, however, they would have to be introduced relatively quickly, since there would be a lag of several months while Italy relied on its reserves. But when the League Council met again on January 23, a decision on oil sanctions was postponed once again.[32] Although Britain was moving in the direction of supporting oil sanctions, and indicated this to the League in March 1936,

---

Reconsidered: Supplemental Case Histories, 2d ed. (Washington, D.C.: Institute for International Economics, 1990), p. 33; Baer, *Test Case*, p. 23.

[29] Baer, *Test Case*, p. 24. In fact, the sanctions imposed were less than those called for automatically by the League covenant: a complete commercial and financial break with violators (p. 7).

[30] Ibid., pp. 9–10, 40.

[31] Hufbauer et al., *Economic Sanctions*, p. 34.

[32] Royal Institute of International Affairs (RIIA), *International Sanctions* (London: Oxford University Press, 1938), p. 67; Hufbauer (et al.), *Economic Sanctions*, p. 34.

France's position did not change, and oil sanctions were never introduced. At that point, such sanctions would have been too late, anyway. Overwhelming firepower, combined with the decisive introduction of poison gas into the conflict turned the tide for Italy, and by April, the war was essentially lost. League sanctions were formally lifted on July 15.[33]

Britain and especially France could not bring themselves to pull the trigger on the oil weapon when they had the chance. Such a move, they (reasonably) assumed, would rupture their relations with Italy, and possibly even bring them into direct confrontation with Mussolini's military. Given the prevailing European security environment, this risk was unacceptable. However, these states also had a weapon at their disposal that could have discreetly caused the Italian operation to fail: predatory currency manipulation of the lira. In this case, the practice of monetary power could have been done secretly. Thus the preferred outcome (end of the invasion) could have been achieved without the unacceptable risk (open conflict with Italy). If a financial crisis caused Italy to withdraw, Britain and France would not get the blame.

Italy in general and the Mussolini regime in particular were highly vulnerable to currency manipulation, especially with the added strain of the war. Mussolini had tied the fate of his regime closely to the prestige of the lira. On August 8, 1926, in a speech in Pesaro, he announced: "I want to tell you . . . from this square to all the world I say that I will defend the lira to the last breath, to the last drop of blood." In pursuit of this policy, the Italian Institute of Exchange intervened in the market to drive up the value of the lira, and on December 21, 1927, its value was officially fixed at L19/$ (L92/£). In order to be able to defend the lira at this rate, Italy arranged to borrow $75 million from the Bank of England and French sources, as well as an additional $50 million from an American banking syndicate. The rate left the lira somewhat overvalued, increasing unemployment and reducing exports (though inflation fell and Italy's terms of trade improved); but the purposeful overvaluation and its successful defense did serve its purpose: to enhance Mussolini's reputation as a leader.[34]

Mussolini recognized the link between his fate and that of the lira. Over two months before he ordered that the Pesaro declaration be carved in stone, he wrote to his finance minister, Giuseppe Volpi, that "the fate of the regime was tied to the lira." This explains why Mussolini refused to devalue the lira even when it made good economic sense to do so. Because of the overvalued lira, Italy entered the depression in 1926, as opposed to 1930. As one ob-

---

[33] Baer, *Test Case*, pp. 213–14, 219–20, 239, 243, 282.

[34] Joel S. Cohen, "The 1927 Revaluation of the Lira: A Study in Political Economy," *Economic History Review*, 2d ser., 25, no. 4:642–54 (1972), pp. 649, 654; also Brown, *Gold Standard*, p. 950.

server noted, the "Pesaro declaration . . . formed the basis of his whole monetary policy and to a very large extent his whole economic policy."[35]

The sacrifices associated with the maintenance of the overvalued lira continued to increase. In 1934, some domestic programs had to be scaled back to defend the currency, but Mussolini remained stubbornly opposed to any devaluation of the lira. Paul Einzig, a British financial journalist known at the time to be sympathetic to aspects of Italian fascism as an economic experiment, visited Mussolini in November of that year and urged him to devalue. Einzig reported: "I was told that when shortly before my arrival a leading Italian industrialist suggested to Mussolini that the lira should be devalued he flew into a fit of rage and banged his desk with such force that its glass top broke."[36]

Mussolini was well aware of the increasing costs of maintaining the overvalued lira, but he was so adamant about the necessity for maintaining it at its current level, he would not even consider a number of graceful ways to devalue. Einzig pointed out, for example, that because of domestic deflation and the devaluation of other currencies, the lira was actually even higher (in relation to other currencies) than ever, and therefore a change in parity would not truly "devalue" the lira, but simply restore its earlier value.[37] But Mussolini's commitment to the value of the lira was symbolic and political, not reasoned and economic: therefore economic arguments would not have been sufficient to force a change in policy.

Consequentially, Italy approached the Ethiopian war with a vulnerable currency, whose stability was intimately related to the survival of the Mussolini government. As noted above, foreign devaluations left the lira even more overvalued than before. In 1927, the dollar bought 19 lire; the pound fetched 92. By 1935, those figures stood at 12 and 58. The Italian economy was in depression, its trade was imbalanced, and pressure on the lira intensified in 1934. In May, the Instituto Nazional Cambi was created to enforce new exchange control restrictions. But for the year, reserves fell from L7.397 billion to L5.883 billion. By the end of 1934 those reserves were just slightly above the legal minimum reserve ratio of 40 percent. Following a pattern described in Chapter 2, simply approaching such a level stimulated market bandwagoning and further withdrawal of funds from Italy. This required the enforcement of restrictions on the movement of gold and capital, and a discount of 5–10

---

[35] Rowland Sarti, "Mussolini and the Italian Industrial leadership in the Battle of the Lira 1925–27," *Past and Present*, no. 47:97–112 (1970), p. 98 (Volpi letter); Paul Einzig, *Bankers, Statesmen, and Economists* (London: Macmillan, 1935), p. 100 (quote, economic conditions and policy).

[36] Paul Einzig, *In the Center of Things* (London: Hutchinson and Co., 1960), pp. 149, 150 (quote), 153.

[37] Einzig, *Bankers, Statesmen*, pp. 110, 114.

percent on the lira in relation to other gold-backed currencies emerged in free markets; this was the first tangible sign that the lira might be forced completely off gold.[38]

Pressure on the Italian currency continued into 1935, even before the invasion. The government was forced to take increasingly dramatic steps in order to acquire the foreign exchange necessary to defend the lira. In December 1934, all citizens were required to register their holdings of exchange and other foreign assets, and on May 21, 1935, Italians were given twenty days to turn these over to the government. On that day silver coins were also recalled, one week after a prohibition was placed on the export of that metal. As the summer arrived and war appeared likely, the pressure on the exchanges intensified yet again. On July 2, the 1927 statute stipulating that the gold reserve of the Bank of Italy be no less than 40 percent of the note issue was suspended. Within weeks, the lira was quoted at a discount of over 30 percent in the forward market. In the last ten days of the month the Bank of Italy lost L267 million worth of gold, a rate that would exhaust existing gold reserves in twenty weeks. The Italian government responded with a host of new restrictions, and the Bank of Italy raised its discount rate from 3.5 percent to 4.5 percent. However, the gold drain continued, and the bank lost over L723 million worth during the remainder of the summer, with gold reserves falling to L4.334 billion on September 20.[39]

Of course, both the war and the sanctions added nothing but additional pressure on the lira. In terms of gold and foreign exchange (holdings of which were relatively modest), Italy suffered both demand- and supply-side pressures. The cost of war preparations and the war itself increased the government's demand for foreign exchange greatly, but sanctions limited the supply. The preparations for war cost almost L1 billion three months before the invasion, and less than two months later, additional expenditures of L2.5 billion were announced. Trade sanctions, of course, drastically reduced Italy's ability to earn foreign exchange, and its biggest foreign exchange earner, tourism, also suffered greatly.[40]

On November 27, the Bank of Italy was forced to raise its buying price for gold from Italian citizens to L15.50 per gram, up from the statutory rate of 12.63. This was an implicit devaluation of over 20 percent on domestic trans-

---

[38] H. V. Hudson, "The Economic Aspects of the Italo-Abyssinian Conflict," in Arnold J. Toynbee, *Survey of International Affairs 1935*, vol. 2, *Abyssinia and Italy* (London: Oxford University Press, 1936), pp. 419–20. On lira exchange rates and the Instituto Nazional, Baer, *Test Case*, p. 166.

[39] Hudson, "Economic Aspects," pp. 420, 436; RIIA, *International Sanctions*, pp. 78–79.

[40] Hudson, "Economic Aspects," pp. 436–37. On Italy's trade before and during the conflict, M. Bonn, "How Sanctions Failed," *Foreign Affairs* 15, no. 2:350–61 (1937), pp. 351–53, 355–57. On Italy's tactical economic responses to the sanctions, see William G. Welk, "Sanctions and Trade Restrictions in Italy," *American Economic Review* 27, no. 1:96–107 (1937).

actions, but it did not stop the hemorrhaging of the gold reserves. On October 20, the last day the government published such statistics, the gold reserves stood at L3.936 billion, and it was subsequently revealed that by New Year's Eve they had fallen to L3.027 billion.[41]

The Mussolini government continued to search for creative ways to replenish the reserves. On December 18, it declared a "wedding ring day" of allegiance. Women were called upon to surrender their gold wedding rings. In Rome, 250,000 rings were turned in, and 180,000 were surrendered in Milan. This operation along with other donations raised almost four tons of gold (worth about $4.5 million, or L54 million at official rates) and over five tons of silver. However, Italy exported L1.926 billion worth of gold in the first quarter of 1936, meaning that existing reserves must have fallen by about one-third over this period.[42]

To summarize the monetary situation, the government's reserves were falling at a dramatic rate. Extraordinary measures taken to supplement the reserves may have enhanced them by as much as L2 billion, but this one-time boost did not change the fundamentals of the situation. Even with the new reserves, Italy lost between one-third and one-half of its reserves during the first six months of the invasion—and at the start of the war, those reserves already stood below the statutory minimum for the first time since its establishment over eight years previously.[43]

Such a reserve loss reflected a severe currency crisis, and one that took place in the absence of currency manipulation. The introduction of currency manipulation could have made the situation even worse, especially with the logical expectation of market bandwagoning in this case. Crucially, since Italy was experiencing a crisis in the absence of manipulation, predatory acts taken secretly to exacerbate the situation would not have necessarily cast suspicion on the agents of influence. If it was the intention of Britain and France to stop the invasion without appearing to have forced such an outcome, then currency manipulation would have been the appropriate instrument to bring this about.

There was good reason to believe that such manipulation would have been successful. The severity of the currency crisis even in the absence of manipulation is one indication of this. Another is the importance of the reputation of the lira to the Mussolini regime. Such a combination (a serious currency crisis coupled with a high degree of monetary politization) would be sufficient to

---

[41] Hudson, "Economic Aspects," p. 438.

[42] Baer, *Test Case*, pp. 159–60 (wedding rings); Hudson, "Economic Aspects," p. 438 (reserves).

[43] Hudson, "Economic Aspects," pp. 438–39. Hudson estimated a maximum of L750 million from private gold and assets, L750 million from foreign securities, and L500 million in retired silver coins. He further estimated that the L2.6 billion reserve loss from October 1935 to March 1936 represented one-third of Italy's exchange assets; Baer, *Test Case* (p. 245) puts those losses at one-half of exchange assets by March 23.

bring down most governments. Even if Mussolini had been able to survive a total collapse of the lira, however, monetary sanctions might have still stopped the invasion. Italy was highly dependent on trade for essential imports. As one analysis noted, an "exhaustion of the gold supply and the foreign exchange . . . might have brought about real scarcity." Thus, if the Western powers were unwilling to impose an oil embargo, their monetary sanctions might have eliminated Italy's ability to purchase that vital commodity. Such a result would have been even more effective than a legislated embargo, which could have been violated by nonparticipants.[44]

It would appear, then, that France and Britain missed an excellent opportunity to practice monetary diplomacy. It this case, because of its private nature, monetary sanctions were in fact one of the few potent instruments available to those powers, given their preferences. It is possible that they were not aware of the opportunity. However, in all likelihood, the issue of awareness was irrelevant. Had Britain and France been approached by the Ethiopian government with a plan to introduce monetary sanctions, they probably would not have implemented it.

Monetary sanctions were not implemented in this case (assuming the potential agents were aware of their availability) because Britain and France did not want the invasion to fail. It is not that they were in favor of the conquest, but that they were so Eurocentric in their thinking they did not want to undermine the Mussolini regime in Italy, even if they would not get the "blame." No one's candidate for Man of the Year, Mussolini did represent stability in Italy, and the Western powers believed that he would participate in a coalition designed to contain Germany.

There is very strong evidence to support this interpretation of the crisis. The British secretary for foreign affairs, Sir John Simon, told a colleague in January 1935 (nine months before the invasion), "The Italians intend to take Abyssinia." He also informed King George VI that he would handle the situation "in a way which will not affect adversely Anglo-Italian relations." Britain was prepared to look the other way, and would have done so quietly had its domestic population not been so outraged by the invasion.[45]

France was even less interested in the fate of Ethiopia than was Britain (which apparently became increasingly disenchanted with Italy over the course of the crisis). According to E. H. Carr, both France and Britain "became apprehensive that an Italian failure in Abyssinia might react on the situa-

---

[44] RIIA, *International Sanctions,* p. 78 (essential imports); Bonn, "How Sanctions Failed," p. 360 (quote).

[45] Dina Mazengia, "British Foreign Policy in the Italo-Ethiopian Conflict, December 1934–July 1936: A Study in Appeasement" (Ph.D. diss., Department of History, SUNY–Albany, 1979), pp. 29, 30, 171. On anti-Italian sentiment in the United Kingdom, see R.A.C. Parker, "Great Britain, France, and the Ethiopian Crisis 1935–36," *English Historical Review* 89:293–332 (1974), p. 298.

tion in central Europe." France, however, had the most to lose. In January 1935, Laval met with Mussolini in Rome, and signed eight agreements, four of which were secret. The secret agreements involved an understanding that Italy would have a free hand in Ethiopia, but would cooperate in the containment of any revisionist German ambitions in Europe.[46]

Therefore, sanctions against Italy were carefully modulated. Britain and France actively blocked the imposition of oil sanctions (and, of course, refrained from any monetary sanctions that would have eliminated Italy's ability to purchase oil, which would have stopped the invasion in its tracks and possibly finished Mussolini. There was no doubt that oil was critical. Mussolini himself told Hitler: "If the League of Nations had followed Eden's advice in the Abyssinian dispute and had extended economic sanctions to include oil, I would have had to withdraw from Abyssinia within a week. This would have been an incalculable disaster for me."[47]Italy threatened to refuse any new military agreements with France and to pull out of the League of Nations, the Locarno pact, and, of course, the entire Laval-Mussolini understanding if oil sanctions were imposed, and this was sufficient to keep the French in line. France's refusal to anger Italy also kept the British from acting on their nobler instincts toward the end of the conflict. However, France and especially Britain wanted to hold the League together, and went through the motions of opposing the invasion.[48]

Thus, the decision of Britain and France not to attempt currency manipulation in this case occurred at the first level of decisionmaking considered in the introduction. Those two nations did not wish to force the collapse of the Mussolini regime, and therefore did not truly attempt to stop the invasion from succeeding. While the opportunity for manipulation existed, with a good chance of "succeeding," the potential agents of influence were not actually interested in bringing about the results that monetary sanctions could deliver.

The United States and the Stabilization of the Lira

After World War II, the United States and the Soviet Union found themselves in confrontation over the future of Europe. The emerging conflict was played

[46] E. H. Carr, *International Relations between the Two World Wars (1919–1939)* (London: Macmillan, 1947), p. 227. Parker stresses Eurocentrism ("Ethiopian Crisis," pp. 293–96). On the Franco-Italian understanding, see D. C. Watt, "Document: the Secret Laval-Mussolini Agreement of 1935 on Ethiopia," *Middle East Journal* 15, no. 1:69–78 (1961), pp. 69, 71, 74–78 (text of agreements).

[47] Quoted in Mazengia, *British Foreign Policy,* p. 166.

[48] On Italian threats, Baer, *Test Case,* p. 221; also Mazengia, *British Foreign Policy,* p. 179. On saving face, Stephen V. Chukumba, *The Big Powers against Ethiopia: Anglo-Franco-American Diplomatic Maneuvers during the Italo-Ethiopian Dispute, 1934–8* (Washington, D.C.: University Press of America, 1979), pp. 234, 271, 378.

out in a number of theaters, most notably Germany. The less conspicuous struggle over the fate of Italy, however, also had the potential to alter the course of the conflict. As one observer stated at the time, the election in Italy of April 1948 was "one of the five or six main events in the international cold war."[49]

The United States intervened vigorously in that election, in support of the Christian Democrats against the Communists. What is puzzling in this case is that while the United States considered and deployed almost every instrument of persuasion at its disposal, it did not engage in protective currency manipulation of the lira. This is especially surprising given the fact that such protection could have eased pressure on the ruling Christian Democratic party, whose policies to defend the lira had a deflationary effect on the nation's economy on the eve of the election. The Christian Democrats did win the election, but the outcome was seriously in doubt: three months before the election, Western analysts thought the Communists had an "even chance" at victory.[50] Had the outcome been different, the failure of the United States to practice monetary diplomacy could have been one of the most serious blunders of the cold war.

The events in Italy were important in and of themselves, but were also considered influential in determining the extent to which communism would spread in Western Europe. George F. Kennan, then director of the State Department policy planning staff, told Secretary of State George Marshall in a top-secret memo: "As far as Europe is concerned, Italy is obviously key point. If communists were to win election there our whole position in Mediterranean, and possibly in western Europe as well, would probably be undermined."[51] This was an ominous statement, as the situation was thought to be a highly dangerous one by American analysts. There was a thriving communist movement in Italy, and coupled with a fragile economy, conditions were ripe for a communist takeover. Officials noted at the time that "there is no choice between becoming a communist on 1500 calories [a day] and a believer in democracy on 1000."[52]

Italy, like most of Europe, was devastated by the war. Aside from physical damage and dislocation, by 1943 the country had exhausted its foreign exchange reserves, and the Allied occupation forces and administration contributed to a great increase in inflation, which continued into 1944. United Nations (UNNRA) aid kept the economy afloat for the first year and a half after the war, with essential shipments of food, medicine, and coal. However,

---

[49] Howard K. Smith, *The State of Europe* (New York: Alfred A. Knopf, 1949), p. 202.

[50] Ibid.

[51] U.S. Department of State, *Foreign Relations of the United States [FRUS]*, 1948, vol. 3 (Washington, D.C.: U.S. Government Printing Office, 1974), p. 849.

[52] Quoted in James Edward Miller, *The United States and Italy, 1940–50: The Politics of Diplomacy and Stabilization* (Chapel Hill: University of North Carolina Press, 1986), p. 183.

this assistance was scheduled to be terminated in June 1947, and Italy would subsequently be hard pressed to come up with the foreign exchange necessary to pay for essential imports.[53]

The situation became particularly critical at the end of 1946. The United States had always been concerned about the viability of the Italian economy, fearing that economic chaos there would lead to a Marxist takeover. However, although the United States bankrolled UN relief efforts, its bilateral aid to Italy was minimal, such as a $25 million export-import loan. In 1946, the United States did practice permissive currency manipulation, accepting lire as payments for the surplus goods it sold to Italy. However, these modest efforts were not enough to keep the economy on its feet, and Prime Minister Alcide De Gasperi traveled to Washington in January 1947 to explain directly the gravity of the situation.[54]

The United States took the communist threat in Italy very seriously,[55] and as a result of the January meeting, decided to commit to the De Gasperi regime, with the view that his Christian Democratic party offered the best chance to defeat communism there. The United States extended a new $100 million export-import loan. Even more important, from this point on (and especially in the wake of the Truman Doctrine, announced two months later), the United States became an active participant in the domestic politics of Italy, aiming to keep the Christian Democrats in power and the leftists out.[56]

With promises of additional U.S. aid in hand, De Gasperi moved sharply to the right, although there is no evidence that this was an explicit quid pro quo. On May 12, De Gasperi resigned, and formed a new government, which had no leftist ministers. Less than a month later, the Marshall Plan was announced.[57] However, that aid would not reach Italy until June 1948. As UN relief was to end in June 1947, this left a one-year gap to bridge, which included the period leading up to the Italian national elections of April 1948.

---

[53] Muriel Grinrod, *The Rebuilding of Italy: Politics and Economics 1945–55* (London: Royal Institute for International Affairs, 1955), p. 47; also Miller, *United States and Italy*, pp. 151–52 (wartime).

[54] Miller, *United States and Italy*, pp. 181, 188; also Miller, "The Search for Stability: An Interpretation of American Policy in Italy: 1943–46," *Italian Historical Journal* 1, no. 2:264–86 (1978), p. 279.

[55] The United States planned a number of possible responses to a communist ascension in Italy, either through elections or extralegal techniques. See *FRUS*, 1947, vol. 3 (Washington, D.C.: U.S. Government Printing Office, 1972), pp. 976–83; also *FRUS*, 1948, vol. 3, pp. 816–70.

[56] Grinrod, *Rebuilding*, p. 47; James Edward Miller, "Taking Off the Gloves: The U.S. and the Italian Elections of 1948," *Diplomatic History* 7, no. 1:35–55 (1983), p. 36 ; Alan A. Platt and Robert Leonardi, "American Foreign Policy and the Post-war Italian Left," *Political Science Quarterly* 93, no. 2:197–215 (1978), pp. 197, 199–200 ; Miller, *United States and Italy*, p. 223, 228.

[57] Grinrod, *Rebuilding*, p. 55; Miller, *United States and Italy*, pp. 219–20, 228, 230; also Joyce and Gabriel Kolko, *The Limits of Power: The World and U.S. Foreign Policy* (New York: Harper and Row, 1972), pp. 147, 371.

Obviously from the perspective of the ruling party, this was a rather unfortunate time to be without external support. Not surprisingly, the economic situation in Italy deteriorated in the spring and summer of 1947. In May, the U.S. undersecretary of state for economic affairs warned that the European economies were "careening toward disaster," with Italy "leading the race towards bankruptcy." Without increases in aid, he added, Italy would be out of foreign exchange by the end of the year, with highly destabilizing consequences. The United States responded with a number of improvised aid programs that helped keep the economy afloat.[58]

The United States intervened more systematically in the Italian political system, obsessed with the possible outcome of the 1948 elections. The Americans gave a number of high-profile gifts to Italy, engaged in a public relations campaign touting the benefits of the Marshall Plan (and threatened to withdraw such aid if the Communists won the election), and encouraged American celebrities of Italian descent to involve themselves in the campaign. The United States also engaged in its "first significant" peacetime covert operations, which included funneling millions of dollars to individual political parties, and even drew up military contingency plans in the event of a Communist victory. A related plan to secretly reinforce Italy's police and military forces was called off by De Gasperi at the last minute.[59]

The elections were a success for the Christian Democrats, who received 48.5 percent of the vote and an absolute majority in Parliament. The "most important reason" for this victory was the intervention of the United States in the campaign, but there were additional factors that contributed to the sizable victory. The Czech coup, which had occurred less than two months before the vote, had increased anticommunism in Italy and spurred the United States to increase its efforts. Also, the Church had finally entered the fray in favor of the Christian Democrats.[60]

One remarkable omission from the list of factors that influenced the 1948 election was the practice of protective currency manipulation by the United States. The introduction of such techniques could have eased the economic hardships with which Italy was confronted during the months leading up to the election. The restoration of the lira was neither simple nor painless, and the Italian currency problems represented a double-edged sword: instability in the currency could undermine confidence in the economy and the government, but the steps taken to ensure stability would be deflationary, causing economic hardship.

[58] Miller, *United States and Italy,* pp. 210, 230 (quote).

[59] Smith, *State of Europe,* p. 205; Miller, "Taking Off the Gloves," pp. 35 (quote), 36–37; Miller, *United States and Italy,* pp. 245–49.

[60] Miller, *United States and Italy,* pp. 247, 249; Miller, "Taking Off the Gloves," p. 36; Smith, *State of Europe,* pp. 203, 205 ("most important reason").

Immediately after the war, all international transactions were tightly controlled by the Italian government, through the use of techniques such as clearing. In early 1946, however, improvements in the financial picture led private interests to press for the introduction of measures to stimulate trade. The official exchange rate of L100/$ represented a severe overvaluation of the lira, whose real value had been undercut by domestic inflation, and this made exports unprofitable. On January 18, it was decided to create a "commercial" rate of exchange of L225/$ (L907.3/£) to help exporters. Further liberalizations were introduced on March 23, when half of the foreign exchange earned through exports to nonclearing countries (that is, the United States and most of the sterling area) was put at the disposal of the exporters. Those recipients were restricted in what they could do with the exchange, but the new privileges included the right to sell it freely to importers.[61]

These changes established a free exchange market in Italy, although a limited and imperfect one. For example, in this multiple exchange rate system, significant discrepancies emerged in cross-rates between clearing and nonclearing currencies, between the dollar and the pound, and across commodities. Still, the experiment was initially successful, and it was not until the end of the year that the financial picture again turned sour. Some analysts have argued that the 50 percent rule was too much too soon, and set off a spiral that weakened the lira and stimulated inflation (further weakening the lira).[62] The value of the lira on the new free market in Milan (see Figure 6.1) offered a good barometer of the financial picture in Italy.[63]

The lira stabilized toward the end of the year, but in 1947 came under increasing pressure. In the spring and summer, this blossomed into a full-blown crisis of confidence in the currency. In May, Luigi Einaudi, who had been the governor of the Bank of Italy, became deputy prime minister and minister of the budget. Einaudi strongly believed that "should the currency collapse in Italy, everything would collapse on the social-political level." He initiated strong measures on the monetary side of the economy to bolster the value of the lira, introducing a host of new banking regulations, streamlining the 50 percent rule, devaluing the "official rate" of the lira to 350/$, and, importantly, imposing "vigorous and ruthless" credit control.[64]

The measures were successful in stabilizing the lira, and in November, the

---

[61] Bruno Foa, *Monetary Reconstruction in Italy* (New York: King's Crown Press, 1949), pp. 48–49; Karel Holbik, *Italy in International Cooperation* (Padova: Casa Editrice Dott. Antonio Milan, 1959), pp. 31–33.

[62] Foa, *Monetary Reconstruction,* pp. 50, 53, 55, 56 ("premature"); also Holbik, *Italy,* p. 35.

[63] Foa, *Monetary Reconstruction,* p. 54. For more detailed figures, including the black market rates for dollars and pounds (monthly, May 1946–October 1949), see Friedrich Lutz and Vera C. Lutz, *Monetary and Foreign Exchange Policy in Italy,* Princeton Studies in International Finance, no. 1 (Princeton University, 1950), table 11.

[64] Holbik, *Italy,* p. 27 (and quote); Foa, *Monetary Reconstruction,* pp. 103–4.

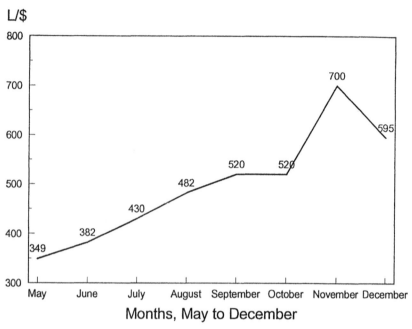

Figure 6.1 The Market Value of the Lira in Milan, 1946 (L/$)

government felt secure enough in the stability of the currency to implicitly devalue it to the free market rate, by floating the official value of the currency. A stabilization fund was established to keep the currency within preferred parameters.[65] Changes in the free market value of the lira in Milan (see Figure 6.2) trace the course of this monetary crisis and recovery.[66]

The "successful" stabilization of the lira presented in Figure 6.2, however, does not tell the entire story. The measures introduced under Einaudi's plan had a strong deflationary impact on the Italian economy. In fact, from the third quarter of 1947 through the first quarter of 1948, which was the heart of the crucial campaign season, Italian industrial production fell by 12 percent. This was a direct result of the deflationary policies designed to bolster the lira. The contraction was so severe that the emergency aid offered by the United States in December 1947 was undercut by the fact that the Italian economy could not absorb the fuel and industrial products that were provided.[67]

Obviously, the deflationary policy imposed to protect the lira deflated the economy at the worst possible time for U.S. interests. However, a failure to

[65] Foa, *Monetary Reconstruction*, pp. 111–12; Holbik, *Italy*, p. 38.
[66] Foa, *Monetary Reconstruction*, p. 104.
[67] Kolko and Kolko, *Limits of Power*, p. 371.

L/$

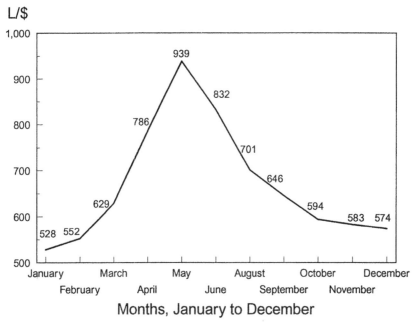

Months, January to December

Figure 6.2 The Market Value of the Lira in Milan, 1947 (L/$)

stabilize the lira could also have undermined those interests. The practice of protective currency manipulation at either of two stages could have eased the undesired pressures.

During the inflationary stage, particularly from September 1946 to May 1947, the United States could have intervened in the exchange markets, mopping up the excess lire and stabilizing the lira's value. This would have allowed the Italian economy to continue to expand without suffering any destabilizing inflationary pressures. During the deflationary stage, U.S. intervention could have mitigated the severity of the required deflationary measures. This is particularly apparent with regard to the second half of this stage, December 1937 to April 1948. At that time, the Italian government had two levers at its disposal to protect the value of the lira: monetary policy and its stabilization fund. The stronger one lever was, the less need there was for the other. Therefore, while monetary policy had to be sufficiently strict to allow the lira to be managed without exhausting the stabilization fund, the larger the pool of reserves was, the less tight monetary policy needed to be. Thus, once the Italian stabilization fund had been established, instead of buying lire, the United States could have contributed directly to the fund, or sold the fund dollars and precious metals in exchange for lira.

The United States did not take any of these steps, and allowed the Italian economy to deflate on the eve of an election in which the United States was doing everything in its power to support the ruling party. There are a number of possible explanations for this apparent blunder. The United States may not have been aware of the opportunity to exercise monetary power. Alternatively, the United States might have preferred not to use that particular instrument of economic power.

It is almost impossible to tell how cognizant U.S. policymakers were of their monetary powers.[68] However, the United States had been reluctant to engage in currency stabilization schemes previously, suspicious that its support would be exploited for personal gain by unscrupulous insiders.[69] In this case, such a tendency might have been complemented by an emphasis on the real side of the economy, which was for good reason the focus of concern in the immediate postwar era. Additionally, when the Americans did contemplate the monetary side of the equation, it was to encourage multilateralism and free convertibility under the auspices of the IMF. The United States showed an insensitivity to monetary pressures when it forced Britain to reestablish convertibility in 1947; it may have been reluctant in the Italian case to encourage any bilateral arrangements that would undermine the development of the IMF system.

Given traditional U.S. preferences, and perhaps even more appropriately in this case, the United States might have taken the attitude, You take care of the monetary side of the economy, we'll supply the goods. This was certainly one of the outcomes of the Marshall Plan.[70] But if this was the case, then the United States made a serious blunder in underestimating the consequences of failing to sufficiently fill the gap between the UN and Marshall Plan relief efforts, a gap that imposed hardship on the Italian economy during the elec-

---

[68] Some aspects of the U.S. position are clear, however. The United States was very sensitive to the precarious economic position of Italy during this period, and was aware of the additional strain imposed by Einaudi's deflationary tactics. See *FRUS*, 1946, vol. 5 (Washington, D.C.: U.S. Government Printing Office, 1969), pp. 890–46, esp pp. 907, 915, 931, and 934–35; and *FRUS*, 1947, vol. 3, pp. 942–51, 958–67, and 971–77. Further, U.S. Ambassador Dunn sent two top-secret cables from Italy to Marshall, one on September 17, 1947, and one marked "urgent" five days later. In the first cable, Dunn stated: "It can be frankly said, therefore, that Italy is on the verge of a dollar crisis, which if allowed to break, will inevitably so restrict production, transportation and employment as to cause an inflation, with attendant political upheaval, so far unmatched in Italy. If it does not break in a few weeks, it cannot be held off for long. While the Marshall plan is still a light of hope on the dismal road Italy walks, it is a dim and distant one for the weary traveler." Dunn went on to recommend that the United States advance to Italy dollars, a stabilization loan, and additional export-import credits, and possibly arrange for IMF support. *FRUS*, 1947, vol. 3, pp. 974–75. Similar measures were also urged by the ambassador in the second cable (p. 976). However, these do not appear to have generated any further discussions on this issue in Washington.

[69] See the discussion of the China case in Chapter 3.

[70] Foa, *Monetary Reconstruction*, p. 140.

tion season. Monetary diplomacy could have been an important element of the U.S. strategy to influence the outcome of the crucial 1948 elections in Italy.

The Opportunity for Currency Manipulation

The decision to engage in currency manipulation can be derailed at three distinct levels: by inhibitions on influence attempts in general, at the level of economic diplomacy, and with regard specifically to monetary power. During the Ruhr occupation, the behavior of the United States is easily explained away at the first level (that is, it was not inclined to force a resolution of the conflict), but the British behavior is more puzzling. Britain may have blundered (at the first level), been inhibited by "environmental feedback" (at the third), or perceived itself to be following a consistent policy of monetary diplomacy: "implicit currency manipulation" (also a third-level decision). Perhaps it was some combination of the three; there is no simple answer. A less perplexing case of a missed opportunity for manipulation during this crisis was the French decision not to support an independent Rhenish currency. In this episode, the decision was made at the third, or explicitly monetary, level of decisionmaking: France did not have the monetary capability to bring off such an attempt. German manipulation (against France) was similarly inhibited by a deficiency of its own monetary power.

The failure of Britain and France to engage in monetary warfare against Italy over the Ethiopian war is best understood in the context of decisions made at the first level. However, had preferences been slightly different, the ability to undermine the lira without getting the "blame" for it would have meant that monetary power in this case could have been an extraordinarily powerful tool. If growing British disenchantment with Italy had led to the decision that Mussolini was expendable, currency manipulation would have been the best instrument at Britain's disposal to bring about his downfall. It is not clear, however, that the British were aware of Italy's vulnerability.

In the postwar Italian episode, the failure of the United States to protect the Italian currency could have had disastrous consequences. In this case, the oversight by the United States may have been the result of an understandable focus on the real side of the economy, a reluctance to engage in currency stabilization schemes, and possibly environmental feedback associated with the evolution of the IMF system. Still, given the importance the United States attached to the outcome of the election, the failure to engage in protective manipulation in this case appears to be a serious error.

These episodes reveal that inhibitions to the practice of currency manipulation can be traced to a variety of sources. At the same time, they also reinforce some of the general arguments raised previously regarding monetary power.

Once again, monetary stability is shown repeatedly to be highly valued by political leaders and consequential for core security interests, across different settings and monetary regimes.

Dependence and Disruption

Missed opportunities of monetary dependence and systemic disruption are more difficult to evaluate than those involving currency manipulation. This is because, as discussed in Chapters 4 and 5, there are fewer total opportunities to practice these forms of monetary power. Also, the definition of "opportunity" is less straightforward in these cases. Further, with regard to disruption, there are fewer total cases (and fewer "missed opportunities") because this type of monetary power is so difficult to practice.

The Issue of Dependence

The study of dependence is particularly challenging, for two reasons. As discussed previously, some of these forms are exerted invisibly, which makes it difficult to tell if there is an influence attempt in effect. It is consequentially difficult to determine, therefore, if an opportunity is being missed. Other techniques of dependence are inhibited by a fear that overt influence attempts at expulsion and enforcement will undermine structural attempts at extraction and entrapment. Again, aside from a general sensitivity to this issue, it is hard to be certain when this factor is at work.

The second challenge is that states, even mid-sized ones, have consistently attempted to extend their monetary influence as far as possible. Therefore, there are very few missed opportunities with regard to dependence: almost every state given the opportunity to create a subordinate currency system has done so.[71] There do appear to be at least two states that did not extend their monetary influence under circumstances where it might be expected that they would. The United States in the first third of the twentieth century and France in the years immediately following World War I each had apparent opportunities to create currency areas but did not.

From 1900–1933, the United States overtly asserted its dominance in the Caribbean Basin. Following the "Roosevelt corollary" to the Monroe Doc-

---

[71] Of course, possible examples of missed opportunities to exploit dependence are embedded within those attempts at monetary dependence that did occur, such as the mark, pound, franc, and dollar systems examined in Chapter 4. While core states did act on their opportunities to create currency systems in these cases, they may have passed up opportunities to introduce specific forms and techniques of dependence that surfaced from time to time.

trine, the United States actively intervened in the region not simply to prevent European intervention, but to prevent the rise of conditions that might provoke such intervention. The United States established a military presence in a number of countries, often taking over control of customs administration in order to ensure the repayment of international debts. Despite the fact that the United States dominated the region with its "big stick" diplomacy, and even though it also became actively involved in the finances of a number of states there, it never attempted to create a "dollar system" in the region. This is more surprising given the fact that there was little uniformity amongst the various currency systems of the region.[72]

With the study of dependence, it is difficult to point to specific moments or episodes (as in the study of manipulation) to consider "missed opportunities." However, a number of complementary explanations help explain the U.S. attitude during this period in a general sense. Specifically, there are three types of likely reasons why this period did not witness the birth of the "dollar system." Each of these hypotheses also reveals something about when states will seize the opportunity to practice monetary power in general.

One reason the United States did not foster and exploit (or "practice") dependence in this period may have been that its policy goals were met with other components of state power. Through the overt use of force and the implicit threat of its introduction, the United States was able to impose on the Caribbean nations the behavior that it desired without having to resort to the practice of monetary diplomacy. For example, although the weakness in the Nicaraguan currency was a principal contributing factor to the revolutions there from 1907 to 1910, the United States intervened directly and decisively to ensure its preferred result, eliminating any need to take advantage of the weakness of the peso.[73] In general, then, states may "miss opportunities" to practice dependence (or monetary diplomacy in general) simply because the desires that would have motivated such attempts were satisfied by resort to other methods.

The United States may also have been motivated by ideological concerns in this period. The creation of a formal currency area would have been an explicitly imperial act, since typically each European power was the leader of its own currency area, with its colonies as members, down to Belgium, Spain, and Portugal. Although the United States was wrestling with the concept of its own emerging imperialism, it in no way viewed itself as an imperial power in the European sense, and the creation of a currency area may have seemed

[72] On these currency systems, see John Parke Young, *Central American Currency and Finance* (Princeton: Princeton University Press, 1925). For a broad overview, see Charles A. McQueen, "Foreign Exchange in Latin America," U.S. Department of Commerce Trade Information Bulletin no. 316 (Washington, D.C.: U.S. Government Printing Office, 1925).

[73] See Young, *Central American Currency,* esp. pp. 126, 132, 133, 135, 137.

dangerously close to an acceptance of that status. In general, ideology—specifically the state's interpretation of the proper relationship between economics and politics—will be an important determinant of how a leader exploits dependence.

Finally, the United States may have failed to exercise dependence in this era because it was unable to do so. That is, at this stage of its own development, the United States may have been technically ill equipped to manage such a system. It must be remembered that the U.S. government and financial institutions were not well developed at this time. The Federal Reserve System itself was only established in 1913. The creation of a dollar system, with reserves, exchange rates, and capital flows, all financed and regulated from Washington, was probably beyond the capability (and inclination) of the U.S. political system at that time. This finding also has an associated general corollary: states may be unable to exploit an opportunity for dependence because of their own limitations. This may have been the case in the French episode.

As discussed above, France's foreign policy after World War I revolved around attempts to limit German power. France hoped to build up alliances with the small and newly independent states that bordered Germany. What is surprising is that France, a power that was historically sensitive to monetary politics and would remain so in the future, did not become more actively involved in the creation of and stabilization of the new currencies that emerged in those states.

France instead relied on two other economic instruments of state power: aid and finance, in its attempt to court these countries. No attempt was made to integrate these states into a greater franc system. French assistance to states such as Poland, Czechoslovakia, Yugoslavia, and Romania took the form of military assistance and assurances of access to loans. This aid was consequential, and often linked to the establishment of formal military alliances.[74]

While they were perhaps necessary, however, aid and financial diplomacy were not sufficient to meet France's policy goals. The currency question was a crucial one in all of these countries, especially Czechoslovakia, newly independent from Austria-Hungary and a vital eastern ally against Germany. France did not involve itself in the dramatic stabilization of the Czech crown. This is surprising, since, in the words of one Czech government official, "The first, greatest, and most anxious question claiming attention after the revolution was the regulation of the currency and the monetary standard."[75]

Not only did France fail to become involved in the stabilization (fostering dependence, for example, by financing an exchange equalization fund), but it

---

[74] Carr, *International Relations*, p. 61; Piotr S. Wandycz, *France and Her Eastern Allies 1919–25* (Minneapolis: University of Minnesota Press, 1962), pp. 221, 291.

[75] Alois Rasin, *Financial Policy of Czechoslovakia during the First Year of Its History* (Oxford: Clarendon Press, 1923), p. 7.

allowed the currency to become increasingly dependent on the German mark. Germany was interested in establishing close ties between the two currencies. The Czech crown was initially able to resist falling into the mark's orbit, remaining unexpectedly strong through 1923, but weakened in the following few years and became increasingly close to the German currency.[76]

France's failure to establish a franc bloc not only is surprising, given that country's historical tendencies, but may have been a significant error, especially with regard to Czechoslovakia. France showed a preference to court relations with these states through the use of aid and finance, both of which yielded a number of successes, but neither of which established the more enduring pattern of intimacy that monetary dependence might have been able to foster.

One possible explanation for the French inaction was an inability to aggressively pursue monetary diplomacy in this period. As discussed earlier in this chapter, the franc was under substantial pressure throughout this period, especially during the Ruhr occupation. It should be recalled that Finance Minister Lasteyrie twice shot down plans to introduce an independent Rhenish currency, because such a currency would have to be supported by the franc. The creation of a franc system in eastern Europe would have been at least as ambitious, and therefore probably beyond France's capabilities at that time.

Additionally, the overt extension of France's monetary influence into eastern Europe might have greatly angered the British. The two nations' interests often conflicted in this period, but France did not wish to antagonize Britain unnecessarily. As discussed in Chapter 5, these states clashed in the second half of the 1920s over the share of their respective influence in eastern Europe. These disputes were primarily over finance, but represented the more general attempt to establish economic dominance in the region. Any attempt by France to establish an explicit currency area in the region would have been a dramatic escalation in that competition, probably with unwelcome consequences.

The Opportunity to Foster and Exploit Monetary Dependence

The cases above, along with the experiences of other system leaders, contribute to the general theory of dependence. Germany's mark system represented the most explicit attempt to exploit monetary dependence. Since the influence attempts were continuous throughout the life of the system, there are no missed opportunities to speak of. Germany was quick to take advantage of its opportunities for two reasons. First, it had specific goals: isolation, entrap-

---

[76] Rasin, *Financial Policy of Czechoslovakia*, p. 73; Brendan Brown, *Monetary Chaos in Europe* (London: Croom Helm, 1988), pp. 110, 115, 123.

ment, and extraction, which it pursued aggressively. Second, the German economic ideology explicitly subordinated economic concerns to political ones. This was just the opposite of the British ideology, which at the very least explicitly separated the two.

Few real opportunities existed for Britain to exploit dependence. As discussed in Chapter 4, for the last forty years of its existence, the sterling area was primarily a "defensive organization"[77] (and in the last twenty, particularly so), and thus Britain would have been unlikely to take any steps to undermine the system. The form that was introduced during this period, extraction, was an emergency wartime measure. Some opportunities may have arisen before 1931, but these, too, would have been inhibited for good reasons. In most of the areas under formal British control, more direct methods of influence were available. Vis-à-vis the more independent participants in the sterling system, attempts to exploit dependence would surely have threatened the benefits that accrued to Britain as a result of entrapment, and would therefore have inhibited such attempts, even if a British government had ever been inclined to contemplate such measures.

The French were not restricted by a laissez-faire economic philosophy, but still engaged in few overt attempts to exploit dependence. This is because there was little that France could extract from the relatively weak members of its system. Instead, an ongoing attempt at entrapment was in place, with overt instruments inhibited not simply by a fear of undermining structural goals but also by a lack of good targets. The enforcement that did occur reinforces this interpretation, as it was an attempt to maintain the general conformity of the policies of the members.

The United States certainly passed up opportunities to overtly exploit monetary dependence in the outer dollar system. Once again, however, the system leader's goals focused on entrapment. The goal of entrapment in this case was rather specific (compared to the more heuristic goals of most states that attempt to encourage dependence), and highly valued: the integration of an international economic policy into a broader national security strategy. In this case, threats to successful entrapment stemming from the introduction of overt techniques of dependence emanated from two sources. On the one hand, states observing enforcement or expulsion could withdraw from the system, threatening the open multilateral international economy that the United States had so painstakingly constructed. On the other hand, the use of a Western economic organization to coerce small states would be a public relations coup for the Soviet Union, and might possibly affect the loyalties of developing states during the cold war. This possibility would have been taken very seriously in the 1950s and 1960s, when the Soviet economic philosophy still actively competed with that of the West.

---

[77] A.C.L. Day, *The Future of Sterling* (Oxford: Clarendon Press, 1954), p. 3.

The sum of these experiences suggest that there are two types of missed opportunities to practice dependence, the failure to extend monetary influence and the failure to take advantage of opportunities that present themselves within established systems. Reasons for the failure to create monetary systems can also be explained at the three levels of decisionmaking used to evaluate the practice of currency manipulation. The French case had two possible causes at the third (or explicitly monetary) level, the absence of monetary capability and feedback.[78] The U.S. case could be explained at the first level (resort to other instruments) or the third level (inability). This case also featured an explanation that technically fits at either the second or the third level, economic ideology. This influence is highly significant for the study of monetary dependence, though it is much less important for the evaluation of manipulation or disruption.

For established systems, four factors appear to dictate whether states will embrace specific opportunities to exploit monetary dependence. Three of these were observed with regard to the nonsystems: First, other instruments may be preferred, because for a particular confrontation, they are especially efficient. Second, states must have the capacity to capitalize on the situation. It is difficult (though certainly possible) to measure this capability, which will fluctuate over time given prevailing economic conditions in the home state. Third, states have differed markedly in their willingness to explicitly politicize international monetary relations. This preference can make the difference between action and inaction in a number of potential cases, and will be crucial in understanding the "shape" of the system. Finally, and peculiar to the practice of monetary power within established currency systems, leader states are always inhibited in their use of overt forms of dependence by the fear of undermining their structural goals, which over the long run are always held more dearly.

South Africa and the Opportunity for Strategic Disruption

South Africa was an essential player in the sterling system led by Great Britain. As the principal source of the system's essential gold reserves, the Union of South Africa would appear to have been well positioned to practice strategic disruption. In the thirty-year period from 1920 to 1950, there also would seem to have been a number of specific opportunities to introduce this form of monetary power. However, South Africa never attempted to take advantage of

---

[78] The feedback in this case was not a special monetary type, and could therefore arguably be considered a second-level consideration. But the other instruments of economic power (aid, finance) were not inhibited by this feedback, and therefore in this case normal bilateral feedback was special to monetary power, which makes it a third-level inhibitor.

TABLE 6.1
Britain, South Africa, and Gold, 1920–1925

Year	S.A. Gold Exports (thousands of pounds)	% of S.A. Gold Production	% of U.K. Gold Imports
1920	25,757	57.1	77.7
1921	29,018	67.4	78.5
1922	29,649	91.7	96.6
1923	37,424	90.0	96.9
1924	27,739	62.0	95.6
1925	23,665	58.1	82.3

Source: Bruce R. Dalgaard, *South Africa's Impact on Britain's Return to Gold, 1925* (New York: Arno Press, 1981), pp. 134–35.

the potential power at its disposal in order to extract political concessions from Britain or other member states. It is surprising that this powerful instrument was not employed to advance such goals as increased autonomy from the center.

The first opportunities South Africa had to coerce Britain were during the period leading up to, and the decision over, the restoration of the gold standard in 1925. For several years, neither party had been on the gold standard, for reasons dating back to World War I. During that war, the South African pound was pegged to the British pound, which was technically still on the gold standard. After the war, the British pound floated and depreciated, but South African pounds were still convertible into gold and British pounds at parity. This led to an outflow of gold coins from South Africa, which was severe enough to force a suspension of the gold standard there.[79]

The first five years of the 1920s found South Africa well placed to practice disruption, and aware that the threat of a financial break with London could be an effective lever with which to force greater independence. Britain was highly dependent on South African gold at this time (as shown in Table 6.1):[80] it was through the outflow of gold that Britain was able to finance its trade deficit with the rest of the world. The British government also hoped to restore the gold standard, in which case it would require access to South African gold to cushion its reserves.[81]

South Africa never attempted to exploit British dependence in this period (basically because of its own dependence on Britain), but such considerations did influence South Africa's decision to unilaterally restore the gold standard.

[79] Edwin Cannan, "South African Currency" [review of "Report of the Select Committee on the Embargo on Export of Specie"], *Economic Journal* 30:519–30 (1920), pp. 519–20, 522.

[80] Bruce R. Dalgaard, *South Africa's Impact on Britain's Return to Gold, 1925* (New York: Arno Press, 1981), pp. 134–35.

[81] Ibid., pp. 13, 19, 136, 138, 143, 145.

Separatists thought that the move would humiliate Britain, while others simply hoped that the move would prod Britain into taking a similar step.[82] As early as March 1920, the South African government appointed a committee to report on the consequences of inconvertibility and "the desirability and practicability of removing the embargo." The committee decided that such a move would be premature, citing possible capital flight from the country and general economic instability.[83]

Inconvertibility was set to expire in 1923, but was extended until July 1, 1925. In 1925, another committee, this one composed of two famous economists from abroad, was formed to decide whether the embargo should be extended yet again. The Kemmerer-Vissering committee was warned of the same risks that its 1920 predecessor had been warned of: a devaluation of sterling would make it impossible to maintain the South African currency's exchange rate and cause an efflux of capital; there would be greater fluctuation in exchange rates; and the domestic economy would no longer be linked with its most important trading partner. However, these men were not as easily intimidated as their less eminent predecessors, and agreed with the majority of the witnesses called that the gold standard should be unilaterally reestablished. The controversy over whether South Africa could support a gold standard independent of Britain became an academic one when Britain restored the system just before South Africa did.[84]

The South African decision to return to the gold standard was partially motivated by politics, but there is no evidence that it was explicitly employed as an instrument of influence against Britain. Montagu Norman, the governor of the Bank of England, wanted Britain to return to the gold standard ahead of the dominions. South Africa could have used promises to postpone its own restoration until Britain was ready as a bargaining chip. However, officials there seemed satisfied with the possibility that their actions would prod Britain into an early restoration, which they seemed to do.[85]

One factor inhibiting South Africa at this juncture was that, as a major gold producer, it wanted as many nations as possible to embrace the gold standard.[86] Thus, to the extent that its policy moved Britain and the rest of the

---

[82] Dalgaard, *South Africa's Impact*, pp. 18, 103, 157. For more on this issue and the members of the sterling system in general, see L. S. Pressnell, "1925: The Burden of Sterling," *Economic History Review*, 2d ser., 31, no. 1:67–88 (1978).

[83] Cannan, "South African Currency," pp. 523, 525.

[84] C. S. Richards, "The Kemmerer-Vissering Report and the Position of the Reserve Bank of the Union of South Africa," *Economic Journal* 35:588–67 (1925), pp. 558–59, 561; Brian Kantor, "The Evolution of Monetary Policy in South Africa," *South African Journal of Economics* 39, no. 1:42–72 (1971), pp. 54–56; Cannan, "South African Currency," p. 524.

[85] Dalgaard, *South Africa's Impact*, pp. 150, 154.

[86] This is not a surprising posture for producers of base commodities to adopt. During the American Civil War, for example, California and Oregon retained the gold standard because "[t]he people of the West Coast were sellers of gold and they were reluctant to set a bad example

sterling area toward convertibility, that policy was highly successful. However, this concern would inhibit South Africa's ability to practice disruption at certain times. For example, the period of instability leading up to September 1931 was an excellent opportunity for a country such as France to practice disruption. This was not the case for South Africa. Great Britain's suspension of the gold standard came as a shock to the South Africans, whose monetary authorities did not expect the break. In fact, they had been assured by "quarters of the highest responsibility" that "sterling would not be forced off gold."[87] Any opportunity to practice disruption over this issue was completely undercut by South Africa's strong preference for Britain to remain on the gold standard. Because of this, South Africa was unlike some potential disrupters (but perhaps more like many others) in that its preferences were so strongly held and widely known that its opportunity to practice disruption would be at it lowest when the target (Britain) was most vulnerable, as it was in 1931. Under such circumstances, if anything, South Africa would be expected to offer any assistance necessary to help maintain the system's link to gold.

Once Britain had gone off gold, South Africa was confronted with the question of whether to follow suit. It was decided that South Africa would independently maintain the gold standard. This decision, and the consequences of it, were among the most important formative experiences of the state's currency history.

The policy of staying with gold was initially popular, but the opposition party soon favored a break with gold and a link with sterling at its new level. A major controversy over this issue developed as the orthodox policies adopted seemed to be making the ongoing depression in South Africa even worse. Within months, the agricultural sector was in serious trouble and export industries were decimated, although the gold-mining industry was relatively well off, as the price for its product remained stable within the country while other prices fell. The economy was also rocked by a speculative flight of capital, reacting to the uncertainty of the monetary situation there and the possibility of a matching devaluation. The balance-of-payments position was "worsening daily," and South Africa found itself in the midst of "a somewhat desperate situation."[88]

---

by using paper money and reducing their own monetary demand for gold." Richard A. Lester, *Monetary Experiments: Early American and Recent Scandinavian* (1939; reprint, New York: Augustus M. Kelley, 1970), p. 170.

[87] Gerhard De Kock, *A History of the South African Reserve Bank (1920–52)* (Pretoria: J. L. Van Schaik, 1954), p. 139.

[88] W. J. Busschau, "Changing Ideas on Gold since 1933," *South African Journal of Economics* 22, no. 1:32–39 (1954), pp. 32 ("worsening") and 34 ("desperate") ; De Kock, *South African Reserve Bank*, pp. 140, 142, 145–47. High speculative demand for sterling caused a "severe" exchange loss in South Africa. The reserve bank required, for the first time, assistance from local commercial banks, and was forced to raise interest rates to defend the currency. De Kock, *South African Reserve Bank*, pp. 171, 173, 177.

Once again, the country was in the midst of a debate over its ability to unilaterally adhere to the gold standard, as it was in 1920 and 1925. Those in favor of the gold standard argued that a break with gold would be inflationary, immoral, and a benefit to the gold industry that would not extend to the rest of the economy. Opponents argued that a devaluation would correct imbalances in export prices; end the credit crunch, which resulted from capital flight; link the economy with its most important trading partner; and given prevailing economic conditions, not be inflationary.[89]

In retrospect, the antigold arguments were correct.[90] However, the proximate cause of South Africa's eventual split with gold was a political, not an economic, crisis. When a key political figure suddenly announced his opposition to the maintenance of the gold standard, a flurry of resignations followed, and speculation against the South African pound took off. Within three days, almost SA£3 million was withdrawn from banks for encashment into gold. The reserve bank felt that it could defend the exchange position of the currency from normal economic forces, but not from hoarding demand, and was forced off gold on December 28, 1932. The currency floated until February, when it was pegged to sterling.[91]

The period during which South Africa was unilaterally on the gold standard was in fact a "test of [its] ability to go it alone."[92] South Africa passed this test in one sense, in that it was able to maintain convertibility (at least until the political crisis). However given the economic consequences, especially when compared with the improvements that occurred after its reintegration into the sterling area, South Africa must have found the waters of unilateralism to be uncomfortably chilly.

[89] De Kock, *South African Reserve Bank*, pp. 150–57 (arguments for gold standard), 158–61 (arguments against); also Ian M. Drummond, *The Floating Pound and the Sterling Area, 1931–1939* (Cambridge; Cambridge University Press, 1981), p. 92.

[90] "The decision of December 1932 has proved to be the right policy." A. J. Limebeer, "The Gold Mining Industry and the Gold Standard," *South African Journal of Economics* 3, no. 2:145–57 (1953), p. 149. Given the prevailing economic conditions, the move did not rekindle inflation (prices actually fell in 1933 and 1934), and expansion in the mining sector did stimulate other sectors of the economy (pp. 148–50). De Kock concurs, stating that "South Africa erred in trying to maintain the gold standard independently" (*South African Reserve Bank*, p. 138), and noting that policies were "contractive when they should have been expansionist" (p. 188).

[91] De Kock, *South African Reserve Bank*, 161–63; Drummond, *Floating Pound*, p. 97. That South Africa was forced off gold, despite the fact that "clearly, the *basic and purely economic conditions* prevailing during 1931 and 1932 did not affect the Union's balance of Payments in such a way as to *necessitate* the depreciation of the currency" (De Kock, *South African Reserve Bank*, p. 163, emphasis in original), offers yet another example of the fragility of "technically" sound currencies and their vulnerability to sudden noneconomic shocks, as discussed in Chapter 2. This case also offers another example of domestic hoarding demand representing a major source of the reserve losses that force states to abandon commodity standards.

[92] Limebeer, "Gold Mining Industry," p. 146. Given the depression, this was not an easy test, but it was the correct test: as discussed in Chapter 4, one of the factors that attracts members to monetary systems is protection during downturns in the international economy.

The decision was made to match the devaluation of the British pound, and to intervene in the markets to defend this new parity. It became increasingly clear that "the abandonment of the gold standard and the depreciation of the South African pound to the level of sterling were decidedly beneficial to the Union." The break signaled the triumph of the "pragmatic school" over the "conservative, fundamentalist view," and the authorities were able to ease monetary policies that improved domestic liquidity. With the link to sterling, South Africa became a member of the then-formalized sterling area, with its privileged access to trade and capital markets. These effects multiplied throughout the economy and "effected a remarkable improvement in the more basic economic conditions in the country." From 1933 to 1939, South Africa had a surplus on current account.[93] Given these conditions, disruption during this period seems extremely unlikely, and there is no evidence to suggest that it occurred.

As discussed in Chapter 4, the outbreak of World War II led to the imposition of exchange control and transformed the nature of the sterling system. South Africa imposed exchange control and discriminated in favor of the area, but did not embrace all of the new regulations, such as the pooling of member reserves in London. Sizable amounts of South African gold were transferred to Britain through the repayment of South Africa's debts, which was a successful method of contributing gold to the war effort without stirring domestic opposition to the cost.[94]

Britain and South Africa also reached agreement on large sales of gold, which the British would pick up directly from South African ports. Both sides benefited from this arrangement: Britain got the gold it needed, and South Africa had guaranteed sales in large quantities, without having to worry about the hazards of shipping the metal during wartime.[95] The war was good for the South African economy, which enjoyed a favorable balance of payments. The Reserve Bank there was able to dramatically increase its holdings of gold and foreign exchange, from £46 million in August 1939 to £267 million in December 1945.[96]

South Africa emerged from the war, therefore, in sound economic shape

[93] De Kock, *South African Reserve Bank*, pp. 212 (1st quote), 214, 221–22 (2d quote); D. G. Franzen, "Monetary Policy in South Africa 1932–82," *South African Journal of Economics* 51, no. 1:88–133 (1983), pp. 95 ("pragmatists vs. fundamentalists"), 99 (liquidity, sterling area, current account).

[94] By 1945, South Africa's external debt had been reduced from £81.57 million to £18.2 million. Kantor, "Evolution," p. 59.

[95] Those sales of gold to Britain were as follows: £90.4 million in 1940, £118.9 million in 1941, £54.9 million in 1942, £90.0 million in 1943, £78.2 million in 1944, and £79.6 million in 1945. N. N. Franklin, "South Africa's Balance of Payments and the Sterling Area," *Economic Journal* 61:290–309 (1951), p. 291 (figures); De Kock, *South African Reserve Bank*, pp. 237–8, 243–44, 251.

[96] Franklin, "South Africa's Balance of Payments," p. 291.

and with very high reserves. Although under less pressure to restrict imports than were other members, South Africa decided to stay in the sterling area. The access to the London capital market and the British economy in general were strong incentives to retain membership. But South Africa was not a full member of the area. Instead, it was able to establish a special relationship through a series of bilateral agreements with Britain. Initially, South Africa promised to sell Britain £70 million worth of gold each year, while the British agreed to supply South Africa with any foreign exchange it required. South Africa was also to sell gold directly in the New York market in order to limit the amount of foreign exchange it would depend on the sterling system for, but South Africa's drawings of dollars from the London pool still exceeded expectations (and were larger than the gold contributions), and the agreement had to be revised. The new deal ended South Africa's ability to draw from the London dollar pool, and involved a gold "loan" to Britain (repayable in sterling) of at least £80 million a year. South Africa retained the other privileges of membership (outside of the right to draw from the dollar pool), and under this particular agreement, Britain agreed to buy £12 worth of South African fruit, wine, brandy, and other products. This bargain satisfied both sides, and was extended through 1949.[97]

Although the South African economy emerged from the war in good shape, shortly thereafter the country began to experience balance-of-payments difficulties, resulting from huge increases in imports, adverse movement in the terms of trade, and a decline in gold production. The problems started in 1946 and worsened in the following year. In 1946 the deficit was met by running down foreign exchange reserves, and in 1947, by selling more gold. By 1948, these measures were supplemented by import restrictions. If not for capital imports from the sterling area, the problem would have been much worse. Still, the payments situation continued to deteriorate. The Reserve Bank's holdings of gold and foreign exchange fell from £247,809,000 at the end of 1947 to £80,663,000 at the end of the following year. Further import restrictions did not stop the net balance-of-payments deficit for the first nine months of 1949 from ballooning to £109 million, which was only £26 million less than the net deficits of 1946, 1947, and 1948 combined. South Africa once again drew on its gold and foreign exchange reserves, and called in the £80 million in sterling it was entitled to against the gold it had loaned to Britain.[98]

Faced with pressures on its own currency during this period, Britain deval-

[97] Ibid., p. 306–7; De Kock, *South African Reserve Bank*, pp. 287, 289–95; also Economic Cooperation Administration, *The Sterling Area: An American Analysis* (Amsterdam: N. V. Arbeiderspers, 1951), p. 253; A. R. Conan, *The Sterling Area* (London: Macmillan, 1952), p. 77.

[98] Franklin, "South Africa's Balance of Payments," pp. 294–96; De Kock, *South African Reserve Bank*, pp. 299–300, 302–9; Kantor, "Evolution," pp. 60–62; Franzen, "Monetary Policy," pp. 101–4.

ued in September 1949.[99] South Africa was then left with the same decision that had confronted it in 1931. This time, with the benefit of experience, the government chose to match the devaluation. Officials did not think that the South African currency would withstand the capital flight in this case, and hoped that the devaluation would ease balance-of-payments pressures. These hopes were realized, and a £4 million surplus on current account combined with a £36 million surplus on capital account meant that the balance of payments for the following year was £40 million in surplus.[100]

South Africa signed a new agreement with Britain in 1950, trading increased gold sales for continued access to the London capital market. This deal was extended in 1951 and again in 1952. South Africa, which had been drifting away from the sterling area from 1946 to 1949, actually became more closely associated with the system in the early 1950s. If anything, the new agreement was more favorable to the sterling area (as opposed to South Africa) than the previous ones. One reason for this was the devaluation, which changed the relative price of dollar and pound goods. As one observer noted, "The advantages of membership of the sterling area continued to exceed the disadvantages."[101]

The British system was vulnerable to disruption a number of times during the thirty-year period from 1920 to 1950. However, at each moment, important considerations inhibited South Africa from playing the role of disrupter. Three reasons for this stand out, and they underscore the difficulty any state has in practicing disruption. First, South Africa was highly dependent on the British economy. Second, it had a vital stake in the promotion of gold standard systems, and was therefore reluctant to take steps that would undermine the ability of such systems to flourish and expand. Third, South Africa did reach a number of important economic agreements with the sterling system, which were based on the importance of its gold holdings.[102]

At least one and often all three of these factors inhibited the South Africans at various points in time. During the first half of the 1920s, Great Britain was certainly dependent on South African gold, but that dependence was not unidirectional. In 1920, Britain took over 70 percent of South Africa's total exports, and only 17 percent of those exports were destined for ports outside of the sterling system. By 1925, these figures still stood at 51.7 percent and 22.8

[99] For more on the British devaluation, see Chapter 4.

[100] De Kock, *South African Reserve Bank*, pp. 312–17. Interestingly, Mr. N. C. Havenga was the South African minister of finance in both 1931 and 1949.

[101] A.C.L. Day, "The South African Reserve Bank," in R. S. Sayers, ed., *Banking in the British Commonwealth* (Oxford: Clarendon Press, 1952), pp. 381–85; Franklin, "South Africa's Balance of Payments," p. 309 (relative advantages); De Kock, *South African Reserve Bank*, pp. 319–22, 323 (quote).

[102] These agreements do not appear to represent the exercise of monetary power and would not "count" here anyway because they fall into the category of wealth effects.

percent, respectively. If anything, South Africa was even more dependent financially. The Reserve Bank had only been chartered in 1920, and there was "an absence in the 1920s of broad, active and well organized money and capital markets" in the country.[103]

There was little to be taken advantage of during the crisis that culminated in 1931 for a state such as South Africa, dedicated as it was to the preservation of the gold standard. More important, it was to find, in the following fifteen months, that the single life was not as fulfilling as it had first appeared to be. That experience would naturally inhibit further flirtation with monetary unilateralism, which the practice of strategic disruption would certainly entail. During and immediately after World War II, South Africa was able to strike a number of good economic bargains. These deals secured necessities for the country, especially with regard to access to the London capital market. Domestic capital markets were still not sufficiently developed to satisfy the country's requirements. Were South Africa to split with the area, or attempt to disrupt it, Britain might "be inclined to shut off capital imports."[104]

British weakness in the late 1940s, for example in 1947 or 1949, was also an unlikely target for South African aggression, not simply because of the dependence just mentioned, but also because of the deteriorating financial picture in South Africa. The country's monetary troubles meant that unilateralism would be just as dangerous as it had been in 1932. There also remained the possibility of renewed international recession. Given these considerations, in 1949 South Africa immediately matched the British devaluation, and in 1950 signed an agreement reflecting a balance of power that was tipping in the direction of the sterling area and away from South Africa.

It has previously been argued that strategic disruption would be (a) rarely within the capacity of states, and (b) difficult to successfully introduce even for states with the technical ability to practice it. The South African case provides further support for these arguments. With disruption, the decision-making is almost exclusively at the monetary level: the home state must consider the risks of bilateral monetary feedback (that its actions might undermine its own currency), and whether it has the capability to competently disrupt. This case also supports the contention that those factors that make the exploitation of dependence easier make the practice of disruption harder. In the current case, these factors included the nature of the bilateral relationship between Britain and South Africa, and the changing economic environments that make participation in a currency system attractive.

---

[103] Dalgaard, *South Africa's Impact*, p. 30 (trade figures); De Kock, *South African Reserve Bank*, p. 123 (quote).

[104] R. F. Mikesell, *Foreign Exchange in the Post-war World* (New York: Twentieth Century Fund, 1954), p. 256.

The Absence of Subversive Disruption

It is logical to assume that the greater a state's ability to disrupt a monetary system, the more likely it would be inclined to practice strategic, as opposed to subversive, disruption.[105] The South African case lends strength to this explanation for the absence of subversive disruption. South Africa was one of the few states in the international system capable of practicing subversion, yet its interdependence with the systems it could have potentially undermined was so great that it was inhibited from practicing even strategic disruption.

However, this hypothesis does not explain the absence of every possible opportunity for the practice of subversive disruption. This is the only form of monetary power that has apparently never been employed.[106] As the form of currency power that aims to fundamentally challenge the currency position of the strongest targets, its relative scarcity should not be a surprise. But there appear to be two types of "missed opportunities" with regard to subversive disruption not covered by the hypothesis above: (1) an attack on the Western monetary system by the Soviet Union during the cold war, and (2) interbloc warfare, that is, attempts by one bloc leader to destroy another system, perhaps in order to expand its own monetary influence into those areas.

The most puzzling is the apparent Soviet abstinence from the practice of monetary diplomacy. Lenin himself noted that "in order to destroy bourgeois society you must debauch its money."[107] Given what was revealed by the study of the South African experience, it is understandable that the Soviets did

---

[105] This is because producers of reserve commodities or holders of substantial balances of key currencies are likely to have a stake in the survival of the system.

[106] Technically, the Czechoslovakian printing of Malian currency was an attempt at the subversive disruption of the franc zone, but that act does not appear to have been part of a larger strategy. Nkrumah's rhetoric against the sterling system (discussed in Chapter 5) was also subversive, if insignificant. Fictional attempts are somewhat more interesting, but have unfortunately focused exclusively on wealth effects. Guy Hamilton's film *Goldfinger* (1964) involves an attempt to radiate all the gold at Fort Knox, causing a tenfold increase in the value of the world's unaffected gold, which the movie's villain has hoarded. In Arthur Hiller's *The In-Laws* (1979), a Central American dictator plans to flood the world economy with Western currencies, in order to escape a crushing debt burden.

[107] Quoted in Joseph A. Schumpeter, *Capitalism, Socialism, and Democracy* (1942; reprint, New York: Harper and Row, 1976), p. 227.

There is some controversy over whether Lenin actually said this. Schumpeter uses quotation marks, but provides no source. Schumpeter may have been thinking of Keynes, who wrote, "Lenin is said to have declared that the best way to destroy the capitalist system was to debauch the currency." Keynes went on to add, "Lenin was certainly right. There is no subtler, no surer means of overturning the existing basis of society than to debauch the currency. The process engages all of the hidden forces of economic law on one side of destruction, and does it in a manner which not one man in a million is able to diagnose." John Maynard Keynes, *The Economic Consequences of the Peace* (1920; reprint, New York: Penguin Books, 1988), pp. 235 (1st quote), 236 (2d quote).

not attempt to employ their gold reserves for subversion; those resources were too intrinsically important to be fooled around with. But the lack of the introduction of other techniques directed at this end (as far as we know) is surprising. The possibility that such attempts might occur was openly discussed in the West during the early years of the cold war.[108]

It is possible that the Soviets never mastered the technology necessary to attempt a counterfeiting scheme, the most likely technique they would have employed. In fact, outside of this, there may have been little disruption within the Soviets' power. Even if gold had been involved, a suspension of sales, already considered unlikely, would not necessarily (or even probably) have been successful. Sales of gold could have been used to accumulate dollars, which could then have been dumped at the right moment; but that would have involved a great sacrifice in consumption, required a great deal of expertise in order to be done correctly, and have been undercut by the increased gold reserves provided by the first phase of the operation.

Thus the Soviets were limited to counterfeiting or some other type of sabotage operation, such as terrorist attacks against financial centers or Western gold reserves. If they had had the capability to practice such techniques, however, they still might not have introduced them. At certain times, the Soviets may have expected communism to defeat capitalism naturally. At other times, they may have been dependent on the West for vital imports, and therefore would not have wanted to destroy the capitalist international economy. Since one of these forces would tend to be stronger as the other receded, there would always have been at least one good reason not to contemplate subversive disruption.

There is also no clear case of subversive disruption directed at one system from another. Given the nature of international relations, it is surprising that this form of monetary warfare has not been observed. Possibly this is because during those periods when multiple systems existed, the lines of demarcation were clearly drawn. Most of these areas evolved from colonial arrangements, and were complemented by trade, financial, military, and cultural ties. Thus, members from one area would not have automatically joined up with other systems if their own collapsed.[109] Additionally, as a result of the discriminatory rules and arrangements, it may have been difficult to penetrate other systems with attempts at disruption. Finally, taking on an entire system means that the target is of considerable size and power, so doing so may simply have been outside of the capability of most potential home states, of which there

[108] This was one reason why some of those involved in Operation Bernhard came forward. "It *could* happen again," George J. McNally, "The Great Nazi Counterfeit Plot," *Reader's Digest*, July 1952, p. 31 (emphasis in original).

[109] Courting defectors, of course, is not the only motive for interbloc disruption. The home state may wish simply to weaken the target by depriving it of the benefits it accrues from the existence of its system.

were quite a few to begin with. For all these reasons, attacking another system may have been a high risk maneuver (that is, one that invited retaliation) with a rather low probability of success.

The Option of Monetary Power

The goal of this chapter has been to uncover some general lessons about when states choose to embrace opportunities to practice monetary diplomacy. These findings also offer insights into the nature of monetary power in general. As discussed in the introduction, in order to exercise monetary power, decision-makers must clear three sets of hurdles along the way. First, a decision must be made to initiate an influence attempt. Monetary opportunities at this stage can be passed up either because no action will be taken at all or because another method of coercion quickly and successfully resolved the problem.[110] Second, monetary power must not be inhibited by factors related to the practice of economic diplomacy, such as standard feedback or domestic political objections. Third, monetary power may be overlooked or ruled out because of the nature of this instrument of coercion: it can be overlooked because a state is ignorant of either its own power or the vulnerability of the target, or it can be ruled out because the home state is unable to practice monetary diplomacy as a result of its own currency position or its sensitivity to specific kinds of monetary feedback. The three types of monetary power are affected in different ways by these hurdles.

Opportunities to practice currency manipulation are passed over for a broad spectrum of reasons. The episodes examined in this chapter (summarized in Table 6.2) do not suggest any generalizable pattern. However, when considered together with the examples from Part II, some tendencies do emerge. One is the importance of awareness. Political leaders who are sensitive to the political aspects of currency relations are more likely to engage in currency manipulation than those who are not. Treasury Secretary Morgenthau is a good example of this: U.S. monetary diplomacy was particularly active during his tenure. This tendency can also be extended to national ideology: certain states, such as France and Germany, were more likely to embrace opportunities that might have been disdained by states (such as Britain) professing a more liberal economic philosophy.

With monetary dependence and systemic disruption, because there are fewer missed opportunities, here, too, it is difficult to observe patterns. However, in these cases, certain themes stand out so clearly that general conclusions can be drawn. With regard to dependence, ideology is an important

---

[110] If the other method was clearly inferior to monetary power, then the source of the missed opportunity is considered to dwell in the second or third level of considerations.

TABLE 6.2
Missed Opportunities

Agent	Target	Opportunity	Possible Causes of Inaction
Manipulation			
Britain	France	Predatory/passive	Environmenal feedback
			Implicit manipulation
United States	France	Predatory/passive	Relative indifference
			Environmental feedback
France	Germany	Predatory	Bilateral monetary feedback
Germany	France	Predatory	Insufficient resources
United Kindom/	Italy	Predatory	Policy preference
France			
United States	Italy	Protective	Error of omission
Dependence			
United States	Caribbean	Entrapment	Other methods preferred
		Enforcement	Insufficient infrastructure
France	East Europe	Entrapment	Insufficient resources
		Extraction	
Various	Various	Overt techniques	Feedback (fear of undermining
			entrapment)
Disruption			
South Africa	United Kingdom	Strategic	Bilateral monetary feedback
USSR	United States/West	Subversive	Policy preference
			Environmental feedback

variable in explaining the way in which system leaders will attempt to influence member states. Still, the primary reason that states will fail to introduce overt methods of dependence remains how those actions will affect underlying structural goals.

Disruption has always appeared quite difficult. Apparently, only two states have even tried to practice strategic disruption, and none have attempted subversion. It is interesting to consider why South Africa did not attempt what Zambia and France did. Zambia engaged in disruption because it felt very passionately about a particular disagreement with Britain. Because of its high degree of difficulty, disruption may require a very special occasion for states to contemplate it, which South Africa never encountered. On the other hand, South Africa received a number of important benefits from the sterling system, which France did not. France did enjoy the ability to participate in a smoothly running international monetary economy, but it received no specific side payments, such as those enjoyed by South Africa. This suggests that while strategic disrupters are likely to be participants in the system, they are unlikely to be members of the "inner circle" (reducing even further the number of likely disrupters). In general, few practitioners of disruption would be sufficiently insulated from the economic chaos that might result from the actual destruction of the target system.

Two additional issues also appear significant with regard to the practice of monetary power. First of all, the analysis called attention to what is possibly a new form of currency manipulation, "implicit currency manipulation." This form rests somewhere between the passive and permissive forms. Technically, it would be a stretch to consider this a full-fledged form of manipulation. It is more of a condition, one that occurs when a currency is known by all concerned to be particularly weak. In some cases there may be a tacit understanding that in choosing its policies, the state with weak currency must keep its ambitions in close relation to the degree of its monetary vulnerability. This phenomenon may explain aspects of the behavior of both potential manipulators and their likely targets in a variety of cases.

Secondly, "missed opportunities" to practice monetary diplomacy were often attributable to some form of feedback. Thus, while it has been argued that monetary power is relatively free from feedback, as compared to other instruments of economic statecraft, feedback remains an important force in shaping the prospects for monetary power. Three distinct forms of feedback can be observed: standard bilateral feedback ("feedback"), in which the introduction of power undermines other goals, bilateral monetary feedback, in which the monetary diplomacy hurts the currency of the home state, and environmental feedback, in which the practice of monetary power upsets other valued monetary arrangements. While monetary power is remarkably free from standard feedback (although such feedback was important in the U.S.-Mexico case), the other forms of feedback can be more routinely consequential. Attempts at strategic disruption will often be vulnerable to bilateral monetary feedback. Additionally, the Nazi counterfeiting scheme, the Ruhr occupation, and the exploitation of dependence in general all suggest that environmental feedback will also at times be of considerable significance. A greater sensitivity to this phenomenon may contribute to the understanding not only of when states will practice monetary power, but also of when those forms introduced will be likely to succeed.

7

Monetary Power and International Relations

Introduction

In the United States, the same agency charged with protecting the president's life is also responsible for safeguarding the integrity of the dollar. The sanctity of the domestic currency is one theme that is common to states and leaders across place and time, and history supports the view that this concern is well founded. It does, however, create new opportunities for states to influence the course of international relations. This book has examined how states can use and have used international monetary relations and arrangements as an instrument of power. It has established a generalized framework of "monetary power," exploring its theory, practice, and potential. In order to isolate the causal relationships under consideration, the analysis was limited to the use of monetary power by states to advance security-related or other noneconomic goals. This restriction also serves to call further attention to the intimate relationship between issues of "political economy" and "national security."

The Practice of Monetary Power

Part I addressed a number of theoretical challenges to the viability of monetary power. Part II, which, among other things, demonstrated that monetary power had been purposefully introduced by states, in so doing surmounted another challenge to the concept of monetary power, that of its existence in practice. Those cases also revealed a number of lessons with regard to this instrument of economic power, many of which provided support for a number of the hypotheses generated in Part I. Some of those hypotheses focused on the difference between monetary diplomacy and the other economic instruments of state power.

It was hypothesized that fewer states would be disposed to be the agents of monetary power (as compared to aid, trade, and finance), because currency relations are typically more hierarchical than the other economic interactions. As expected, a relatively small number of regionally or globally dominant states had a hand in almost every case. These states, along with a number of strategically positioned smaller states, composed most of the set of the agents of monetary influence. However, the analysis did suggest that mid-sized states could play a significant role in specific regional cases, especially with regard to the practice of positive sanctions.

It was also hypothesized that the opportunity for monetary power would depend on the existence of a relatively well integrated world economy. This limitation turned out to be an overstatement. Some degree of modernity does seem to be essential for the systematic practice of monetary diplomacy, but in contrast to trade, it cannot be said that the extent of the openness of the economy determines states' vulnerability to sanctions.[1] There are a number of reasons for this, including the fact that opportunities exist to practice techniques of dependence within relatively closed subsystems, the ability to engage in manipulation in third markets, and the vulnerability of states to currency pressure from mobilized domestic pressures, such as local hoarding demand; these factors are often overlooked.

Monetary power was also found to be less "limited" than aid, trade, or finance. Limits were defined to include feedback, circumvention, and defense. As argued in Chapter 2, with monetary sanctions, defense would be expensive and "self-inflammatory." Thus, for example, Germany did not devalue in 1931, opting for exchange control instead, because officials there felt (among other considerations) that devaluation would set off further speculation against the mark. Also as anticipated, opportunities to circumvent monetary sanctions were severely limited. The most promising technique, finding a protector, is not a true solution, as it involves trading vulnerability for dependence.

Monetary diplomacy is less affected by feedback than the other instruments of economic coercion, but the cases suggested a potential for more feedback in some forms than initially predicted. This is not typically because of standard feedback (in which the sanction undermines other goals), but rather due to bilateral monetary feedback (particularly in strategic disruption), as well as general environmental feedback. The possibility that monetary sanctions may indirectly undermine a larger set of currency arrangements is one of the most important reasons why states refrain from engaging in techniques that might otherwise appear fruitful. This concern stopped the Nazis from introducing their forged pounds in occupied Europe, which may have undermined a potentially important currency manipulation.

On the other hand, the "efficiency" of monetary power, in both an absolute and a relative sense, exceeded expectations. As defined in Chapter 2, efficiency includes the independence of the central government with regard to currency relations, the ability to execute monetary sanctions privately or even secretly, and the extent to which the sanction is focused on the target government. It was hypothesized that monetary diplomacy would be highly efficient, and all of the attributes of such efficiency were featured in a variety of the cases considered.

[1] However, openness does increase vulnerability, other things being equal.

Many of the hypotheses generated in Part I, such as those relating to limits and efficiency, had to do with the practice of monetary power in general. The case studies in Part II also revealed a number of lessons and patterns with regard to each particular type of monetary power.

Currency Manipulation

Chapter 3 considered four forms of currency manipulation: protective, permissive, passive, and predatory. In all cases of manipulation, and in general with regard to monetary diplomacy, all of the definitions of these forms were ends oriented: that is, they included any action taken whose goal was to influence the value of the target currency. Also, these definitions did not say anything about the direction in which the manipulation moved the currency. However, in most of the cases (but not all of them; the Tripartite Monetary Agreement, for example, was an exception), positive manipulation supported the value of the currency, and negative sanctions sought to force it downward. This tendency was probably the result of two factors: first, that driving a currency upwards against a target's will is more difficult than attempting to force it in the opposite direction because defense is much more feasible for the target in the former case, and second, because conflicts that would lead to those types of actions are more likely to be economic than security related, and would therefore not "count" in the context of the current analysis.

There were also some variations on these forms. "Self-protection," that is, a state's taking actions to defend its own currency, was discovered to be a significant feature of monetary diplomacy, especially during wartime. This is because in wartime, expectations with regard to the course and outcome of the war are the best determinants of exchange rates on unregulated markets. States will often attempt to influence expectations by intervening in these markets, and in more authoritarian societies, draconian tactics will frequently be introduced to limit information and influence the domestic population's perception of the stability of the home currency.

"Implicit monetary power" and "implicit currency manipulation," introduced in Chapter 6, were not anticipated in the theoretical section. It is important not to overstate the importance of this pseudo-form of monetary diplomacy. However, with regard to currency manipulation, an awareness of one's own weak position, coupled with an awareness of potential agent states able either to support or to undermine that currency position, can cause a state to alter its policies so that they fall within a range acceptable to those potential manipulators. Thus the expectation that there is a threshold of dissatisfaction at which an adversary will successfully direct monetary sanctions may alter target behavior without the presence of any actual or threatened influence attempt.

Currency manipulation takes place within the context of a variety of different international monetary regimes and subsystems. This study has emphasized the distinction between fixed and flexible exchange rate regimes. Different regimes change the *techniques* of manipulation, but they do not appear to be among the most important variables in explaining whether opportunities for monetary diplomacy will arise or the chances that such attempts will be successful. For example, as discussed in Part I, under a fixed regime employing a gold standard, protective manipulation would involve selling gold to the target in exchange for the target's currency, while with floating exchange rates, protection would reverse this transaction: the home state would buy the target's gold in exchange for home currency. This may influence a state's ability to protect, given its endowments and domestic political constraints; however, as will be discussed below, other considerations will be more likely to influence the opportunities for manipulation.[2]

There are a large number of additional findings with regard to the practice of currency manipulation, beyond those already discussed. Five of the most salient of these are summarized below.

Currency manipulation is inexpensive. While it may require considerable resources to introduce them, techniques of currency manipulation are generally not very costly. This low cost is even more striking when compared with many of the outcomes associated with the practice of monetary power. In fact, many techniques of manipulation are profitable to the home state. Passive manipulation never involves an economic sacrifice on the part of the home state and is often profitable. Protective and predatory measures can involve a net economic loss or gain for the home state, but on average the actions examined here were profitable, and in none of the cases were any incurred costs consequential. Permissive power is the only form that always involves a sacrifice for the home state, and those costs are likely to be relatively minor and diffuse.

Currency manipulation is multifaceted. This is a consequence of the ends-oriented definition of monetary power. Because of this, a large number of different techniques can be employed in the service of currency manipulation. Rhetoric (or rumormongering) is often an effective form of manipulation. Additionally, a wide variety of apparently noneconomic techniques can be directed at the target currency. This allows a home state to attack (or support) a currency from its own position of strength and direct that pressure at the most obvious point of its adversary's vulnerability.

Currency manipulation is flexible. It is flexible in both intensity and implementation. With regard to intensity, the continuous nature of the value of the target currency and many of the techniques of manipulation (that is, market operations) mean that the extent of the pressure imposed by the manipulation

---

[2] The theoretical analysis in Part II also argued that the regime type could affect the distribution of capabilities and vulnerabilities with regard to monetary power. For example, a floating-rate system may further skew the differences between large and small states along these dimensions.

can be controlled by the home state. As observed in Part II, states can use this form of power simply to signal preferences to other states, or in an attempt to totally annihilate the target currency. The flexibility of monetary power also pertains to the independence of the central government with regard to its practice. Because of this autonomy, monetary power can be used in violation of the spirit of neutrality laws (as in the U.S. support for China) or in opposition to organized domestic interests (as in the U.S.-Mexico conflict). The ability of the home state to choose whether to introduce manipulation privately or publicly is another attribute of monetary power that enhances its flexibility.

Currency manipulation interacts with the target economy. In those cases where it is most successful, manipulation will set off complementary forces in the target economy. This can be seen in cases that involve a commodity standard, such as the Indian case, where domestic hoarding demand was the most important source of pressure on the currency. With floating rates, this same mechanism is manifested through increased currency substitution on the part of local actors. The domestic ramifications of manipulation also motivate actors within the target society. Especially important is the relationship of the banking community to the central government (as seen in the Agadir crisis), and particularly the relative political power of these two sectors.

Currency manipulation can be highly consequential. Currency manipulation not only has been shown to impose real economic costs on target economies, but also proved able to affect the outcome of shooting wars, which is usually considered to be beyond the capabilities of economic instruments of power. In Nigeria, Suez, and Japan's war in China, currency manipulation was decisive in determining the course and outcome of wars. Monetary considerations were also important in World War I. In all of these cases, given the importance of the goals to the target states, the power and significance of monetary diplomacy exceeded the expectations raised for it in Part I.

Monetary Dependence

As with currency manipulation, there are four forms of the exploitation of monetary dependence, which were introduced in Chapter 4: expulsion, enforcement, extraction, and entrapment. However, unlike currency manipulation, some of these forms are both instruments and policy goals for the agent of power, and therefore a preference ordering can be assigned to these forms for the home state. The opportunity for structural benefits, extraction and especially entrapment, is what motivates states to create monetary systems. Because of this, system leaders are less likely to practice the more overt forms of dependence, expulsion, and enforcement, because the more those techniques are employed, the more likely they are to encourage other states to exit from the system.

The overt practice of monetary dependence is also reduced by the presence of implicit monetary power, which, because of the particular circumstances associated with dependence, is a more significant and recognizable factor for this type of power than for either manipulation or disruption. This can be seen through a comparison of dependence and manipulation.

There are some similarities between currency manipulation and the overt forms of monetary dependence. Expulsion is similar to an extreme form of passive manipulation, as in a case where an extraordinarily high degree of protection practiced for a long period of time is suddenly abandoned and replaced by indifference. Enforcement is similar to predatory manipulation, although in practice the techniques and mechanisms are markedly dissimilar, as discussed in Chapter 4 with regard to the Panama episode. Implicit monetary power is more prevalent with dependence, then (and limits the need to use the overt instruments of expulsion and enforcement), because the sets of unacceptable behaviors associated with implicit monetary power are usually clearly defined, and the explicit nature of the relationship between the core state and each member heightens both sides' awareness of these limits and the likely consequences of such "unacceptable" behavior.

As discussed in Part I and Chapter 4, it is important to recall that monetary dependence involves *political* as opposed to *economic* exploitation. In fact, the source of the power of dependence comes from the fact that member states benefit asymmetrically from participation in the system, enjoying increased stability, privileges, and protection. The Malian case offered an excellent example of what happens when states lose the benefits of membership.

Both the high value attached to entrapment by system leaders and the prevalence of implicit forces in dependence relations create a measurability problem for the study of this type of monetary power. However, a number of findings can be identified even within this fog. It has already been noted, for example, that states are quick to take advantage of opportunities to create their own international currency systems. Some additional lessons are summarized below.

Monetary systems automatically foster entrapment. Without any overt effort, the most coveted aspect of dependence, entrapment, is cultivated by the simple act of participation in a monetary system. This occurs for a number of reasons. Participation will have a diversionary effect on trade, directing it toward other system members and thus making membership more important than it was initially. It will strengthen elements in society that benefit from membership relative to those who do not, shifting the balance of power within the member state toward those domestic actors that are favorably disposed toward retaining membership in the system. Also, the pattern of financial, trade, and currency relations that result from participation will give member states a stake in the value and stability of the core currency.

Monetary systems insulate the core state. Just as participation protects each member state from dangers in the international economy, such as global recession, the system as a whole insulates core states from the international economy. As seen most clearly in the German case, system leaders can protect themselves from monetary pressures in the international economy by discriminating against the outside world and relying on their own systems. This also evolved into the dominant function of the sterling system.

Monetary systems represent a reservoir of power. As demonstrated most clearly in the British case, the existence of a monetary system can be considered an investment by the core state. The rules of the system and the dependence of its members on the core currency provide mechanisms through which leaders can mobilize large amounts of resources in a short period of time. Thus monetary systems add to the underlying power of the core state. This does not imply, however, that the existence of systems are necessarily a net benefit to the core state. Such a determination also depends on the amount of resources that must be expended in order to maintain the regime.

Systemic Disruption

Chapter 5 considered systemic disruption, which has only two forms, strategic disruption and subversive disruption. As with dependence, some of the techniques of disruption are similar to those associated with some form of currency manipulation. Again, however, there are important differences. Because of the ends-oriented definition of both forms of power, similar means, or techniques, may be observed across different types of monetary diplomacy. Disruption may involve what looks like the manipulation of a target currency, but the target of disruption is the system, not the currency, and the sanction is associated with the threatened loss of the system, not the inherent costs of instability or a loss in the value of the target currency. Additionally, many techniques of disruption (for example, fomenting defection) could not be considered techniques of manipulation.

As expected, relatively few attempts at disruption were identified. This result was not surprising, given that few states were well positioned to practice disruption, and that doing so would have involved challenging targets that were stronger, in a general sense, than the home states. It was argued that this combination would make the introduction of this type of monetary power too risky for most states. If anything, the examination of the practice of disruption found it to be even more difficult an instrument to employ successfully than was initially expected.

No cases of subversive disruption were observed, because of the reasons just mentioned, but also because it was found that those states most likely to be in a position to practice subversion would probably be better served by attempting strategic disruption. Additionally, subversive disruption, as an act of brute force involving an all-or-nothing attack, is a less flexible tool of influence. It may therefore be that there are fewer occasions when such tactics will be among the most efficient ones at the disposal of a given state. Even strategic disruption, however, has been rarely practiced, and then with very limited success.

Strategic disruption is difficult because it is an attempt at boatrocking in which the agent state is weaker than the target. The agent's boatrocking can cause it to fall into the water without even upsetting the boat. A state in this situation may also be vulnerable to unrelated stormy waters, which may again send it overboard without affecting the stronger occupant in the boat. To extend this analogy, all attempts at disruption can also be undermined by the system leader itself overturning the boat in anger (for example, by devaluing[3]), which may in fact cause greater problems for the nominal agent of monetary power, as the target may well be a better swimmer.

Still, attempts at disruption can be highly consequential. As discussed in Chapter 2, the existence of rules in a given system creates viable opportunities to practice disruption, as does the international equivalent of the paradox that motivated actors can occasionally inspire a fatal run on an otherwise solvent bank. Thus, even though disruption is quite difficult and rarely successful, it remains a viable instrument of monetary power. There are a number of general lessons associated with this form of power, some of which are considered below.

Disruption can fulfill intermediate goals. Even if the overall goal of disruption is not met, the actions can fulfill other goals. Vulnerabilities to disruption, for example, provide excellent signaling opportunities for states wishing to get the attention of the core state. A more public attempt at disruption, on the other hand, can be used to enhance the status of the agent by engaging it in a conflict with a much stronger target on a battlefield that minimizes the difference between their respective power.

Disruption attracts a certain type of agent. As discussed in Chapter 5, midsized states (from the perspective of the system involved) are the most likely to practice strategic disruption. Chapter 6 revealed that the likely agents of disruption come from an even smaller pool. Because of the risks and the particular vulnerability to feedback of this form of monetary power, states that practice strategic disruption are likely either to have very strongly held views on a given conflict (making the risks worthwhile) or to be only partially integrated into the system (reducing feedback). These considerations help explain the pattern of French, Zambian, and South African attempts at disruption.

Disruption can have crucial economic consequences. Even in failure, disruption is similar to the other types of monetary power in that it has a signifi-

---

[3] This technique can only be used sparingly by the core state that wishes to preserve its system. As the British case illustrates, while devaluation can be a successful tactic, each additional devaluation stimulates further flight from the home currency as a reserve asset.

cant economic impact on the target. This is of particular importance with regard to disruption, because the ultimate target often encompasses a sizable portion of the international economy. This necessitates a sensitivity to the nature of strategic disruption on the part of core states (and interested observers), since disruption may be attempted (as it has been in the past) even though it typically has not been "successful" in achieving agents' goals. French disruption of the interwar monetary system, for example, contributed substantially to that system's collapse, and is the most important factor in explaining international gold movements from 1927 to 1931.

The Potential of Monetary Power

The Sources of Success and Failure

Any analysis that attempts to consider the "success" of economic instruments of state power must be initiated with a sensitivity to related theoretical issues. As Baldwin has pointed out, binary evaluations that simply focus on "success" and "failure" are deceptive and provide limited information. For a proper evaluation, one must consider the cost of economic sanctions compared to other forms of influence, the value the target attaches to defiance, and the secondary and tertiary effects on states' reputations and the behavior of third parties. Therefore this discussion will focus on identifying the factors that make a given attempt to employ monetary power more likely to be effective, other things being equal.[4]

With currency manipulation, two dominant factors explain whether the attempt is likely to be successful or not: the reaction of free market forces to the manipulation attempt, and the extent of the politicization of the currency question in the target country. These two factors have a number of subcomponents.

Currency politicization. States differ with regard to the extent to which the external stability and value of their own currencies are of domestic political importance. A number of factors determine the extent of currency politicization. Specific political leaders and parties can, purposefully or not, find their fates intimately intertwined with the destiny of their currencies. Mussolini

---

[4] This also entails distinguishing between those elements that make *any* attempt to practice economic diplomacy more likely to be successful and those that are specific to monetary power. It is the latter that are of interest here. For example, as mentioned above, with all economic sanctions the probability of success in altering the behavior of the target will be positively correlated with the ratio of the pain inflicted by the sanction to the value the target attaches to noncompliance with the demand. Similarly, the success ratio will be positively correlated with the ratio of the power of the home state to the power of the target within the given issue area. These general findings, which hold true for monetary power, fall into the former category (that is, they hold true for all economic diplomacy).

overtly politicized the lira in order to demonstrate his leadership. Politicization brings with it, however, the likelihood of being more vulnerable to currency manipulation. The British Labour party, blamed for the devaluations of 1931 and (especially) 1949, returned to power in 1964 determined not to devalue, and went to great lengths to avoid that measure. Currency manipulation should be more successful in these cases because rulers would be more likely to prefer to give in on unrelated issues rather than to risk devaluation, given the choice. Thus, if the Mexican government, in its dispute with the United States, felt that it could not devalue the peso and remain in power, U.S. currency manipulation might have been more successful in the late 1930s.

Beyond differences across possible leaders in a given target society, currency politicization can also exist at the national level. For example, countries that have experienced severe inflationary episodes within the collective memory of the population will be more vulnerable to currency manipulation. This is because the inflation that would follow forced devaluation, or perhaps even the devaluation itself, would threaten the position of the government. As discussed in Chapter 4, many states chose to adopt strict exchange control during the interwar period rather than allow either devaluation or inflation, both of which were still politically taboo in those nations that had had serious bouts with inflation after World War I. Once again, capitulation on an unrelated issue may be preferable to the risk of devaluation for leaders in such societies.

Finally, politicization is also determined by the type of political system in the target country. It may be the case that dictators are less sensitive to monetary pressure than democratically elected leaders. However, what is more important with regard to the type of regime for the success of currency manipulation is the extent to which the head of state, in either a democracy or a dictatorship, serves at the pleasure of interests that are affected by instability of the currency. Thus, a dictatorship that serves at the pleasure of oligarchic interests that dominate the production of the state's few export commodities will be more sensitive to monetary pressure than a more insulated self-sustaining military government. Although the Panamanian case was not technically one of currency manipulation, this factor contributed to the ability of the Noriega regime to resist the U.S. attempt at enforcement. A different type of regime would probably have been unable to resist the pressure imposed by the sanctions in that case.

Market reaction. Along with the extent of politicization, which influences success by affecting how vulnerable particular governments are to changes in currency value, market reaction is the most important determinant of the success of currency manipulation. This factor affects the outcome by determining how much pressure the manipulation will bring to bear on the target currency. There are three principal determinants of the market reaction, which is essentially the question of whether and to what extent the market will bandwagon with or balance against the manipulation. These factors are market size, economic conditions, and currency reputation.

The extent to which either balancing or bandwagoning occurs is determined by the size of the market in the target currency. It has already been assumed (see note 4) that the general influence of relative strength upon the outcome of attempts at economic diplomacy holds for monetary power. In monetary affairs, though, there is an extension of this phenomenon, having to do with the extent to which market forces are available to either balance or bandwagon. Each currency in the free market has a different typical volume of transactions. The smaller the average volume of transactions, the less significant is market reaction, in either direction. Thus it is not simply small states but states whose currencies are not widely traded that are relatively more vulnerable to manipulation.[5]

In many cases, usually those involving states with less widely traded currencies, balancing and bandwagoning will not be significant in determining the outcome. However, in other cases, whether the market balances or bandwagons will be the most important reason why a given attempt at monetary diplomacy succeeds or fails. Two vital considerations determining this are the perception of economic conditions in the target country and the reputation of the target currency.

Economic conditions in the target country determine whether there is an expectation that the country (a) is willing to devalue and (b) has the ability to prevent an unwanted depreciation. Thus those conditions that make a country devalue under "normal" circumstances, such as persistent inflation or balance-of-payments deficits, also make the target more susceptible to currency manipulation. With regard to ability, states may not have the resources to support their currencies. Further, as discussed in Chapter 2, an awareness that defenses are low not only makes a nation vulnerable, but also increases expectations of depreciation, placing additional pressure on the currency. Defensive capability may also be limited by the perception of political restrictions on action. Measures traditionally taken to protect the currency (that is, deflationary policies) may not be politically acceptable in the target country at certain times.

---

[5] It might be argued that a small market would not influence the opportunity for success in either direction, since both balancing and bandwagoning are less significant under such circumstances. However, this is not the case. Since it will constitute a larger percentage of total transactions, manipulation under these conditions will force the target currency down (or up) faster. Additionally, the manipulation would represent a particularly overwhelming share of the information available to those holders of the target currency that did exist, making then more likely to bandwagon than to balance. It should also be noted that there is a bias toward bandwagoning from domestic sources, since domestic hoarding demand is likely to cause an additional flight from the currency. There is no compensating domestic force that balances as naturally as these forces bandwagon.

Currency reputation is probably the single most important factor in determining the reaction of market forces to the observation of pressure on a given currency. The market will tend to balance with currencies that have good reputations and bandwagon against those with poor reputations. Reputation matters in currency affairs. A "good" reputation comes from a number of sources, such as the historical willingness to do what is necessary to defend the currency. Central bank independence may be another source of reputation. Reputations can change over time, suggesting that they are affected by both the underlying economic strength of the target (as opposed to the more temporary conditions discussed above), and the "monetary reputation" of the ruling party. Thus, leftist parties may be more vulnerable to currency manipulation than rightist governments.[6]

Factors that influence the chances of the success of currency manipulation carry over to the practice of monetary dependence and systemic disruption, especially with regard to those forms of dependence and disruption that share some of the attributes of manipulation. Certain other factors, however, are particularly important with regard to explaining the success of these other two forms of monetary power.

Obviously, the exploitation of dependence must never impose costs greater than the costs associated with exit. It adds little to note that influence attempts that involve costs to the target lower than the opportunity cost of nonmembership, as long as they do not generate the expectation that additional demands will follow shortly and exceed that level, should be successful.[7] An exploration of the factors that influence those relative costs, on the other hand, will be highly useful in the effort to understand success and failure. As discussed in Chapter 4, two factors determine this cost: general economic conditions and the bilateral economic relationship between each member state and the core.

The bilateral relationship includes two particularly important elements.

---

[6] It is interesting to contemplate why reputation is more important with regard to currency affairs than with other state attributes. There are a number of possible explanations. Currencies have long trading histories, which involve repeated trials over time on essentially the same issue, which is rarely the case in political confrontations. Currencies are also constantly being probed in contemporary international markets, so the current extent of government support is also continuously tested. Therefore, unlike most deterrence situations, the system engages in repeated and specific tests of a well-defined reputation attribute.

Commitment strategy is also different in currency markets. Greater central bank independence may represent a credible form of commitment. Finally, it is more difficult to "bluff," since there is less divergence between signals and policy. For example, a state that has no intention of using force may threaten to do so, or even put its troops on alert. These actions signal a willingness to use force, but are not a commitment to that policy. Actions taken to defend currencies, however, such as raising the domestic interest rate, not only signal a willingness to defend the value of the currency, but are in fact also actions that actually defend the currency.

[7] This is not necessarily the case, as domestic political opposition to compliance may make the government unable to pursue such a course.

One is the share of its total trade that the target conducts with system members. The higher this percentage, the greater the dislocation effects would be as a result of exit, and thus the higher the opportunity cost. The second element is whether the target tends to contribute to or draw from the system's reserve and financial capacity. Net contributors have less reason to fear going it alone than do those members that traditionally draw on the resources of the system.

It has become increasingly clear in the course of this analysis that in many ways, disruption is inversely related to dependence. Nowhere is this more apparent than with regard to the factors that determine whether specific influence attempts will be successful. In general, those factors that make states more vulnerable to dependence make them less likely to engage in disruption. Beyond this, the episodes considered in Chapter 5 also suggested specific lessons with regard to the prospects for the successful practice of this form of monetary power. Since disruption is difficult, the chances of success are better for specific short-term goals than for less well defined long-term ones. Also, because of the fact that weakened system leaders will be more vulnerable to disruption, demands have a greater chance of being accepted if their adoption would not in and of iself force the collapse of the system. For example, measures that force the target to raise interest rates are more likely to be successful than those that require the major outflow of reserve assets.

The Sources of Opportunity

Chapter 6 looked at the reasons why states do or do not take advantage of opportunities that arise to practice monetary power. But when are those opportunities likely to occur? Of course, opportunities will tend to arise when the conditions for success are greatest. But there are other factors at work as well. Most important are global economic conditions. A poor international environment, such as global recession, dramatically increases the benefits of membership in a currency system, and therefore increases the opportunity to practice techniques of dependence (and reduces the opportunity for disruption). The sensitivity to change of opportunities to exploit dependence, even during a recession, was observed in the German interwar case. A good (that is, prosperous) international environment, on the other hand, minimizes the risks associated with strategic disruption (and reduces the ability to exploit dependence). However, as the South African case showed, even the fear of renewed economic difficulties can inhibit the urge to disrupt. Additionally, states that specialize in the production of a small number of goods will be more sensitive to environmental concerns in general, and will therefore be more vulnerable to dependence and less likely to practice disruption.

The state of the international economy also influences opportunities to practice currency manipulation. Because targets will typically be weaker, and other states and institutions (such as private banks) will also be less able to help defend any target state, more opportunities for manipulation should arise during international recessions than in periods of prosperity. Beyond this, a variety of other influences shape the opportunity for currency manipulation in particular and monetary power in general.

Timing is crucial. Opportunities for the practice of monetary diplomacy arise at certain identifiable moments. Target state elections always allow a relatively heightened opportunity to practice either protective or predatory manipulation, as do moments of domestic political turmoil. Other cycles can also be identified: some states, such as those with economies based on agricultural exports, will have seasonal fluctuations in their earnings and reserve holdings. Opportunities are obviously highest when defenses are relatively low. Similarly, changes in market conditions can also be exploited. Thus the world silver shortage during World War I put pressure on the Indian rupee, leaving it more vulnerable to pressure. The rise in the price of silver left the Chinese currency very vulnerable to pressure in the early 1930s, although no actor appeared to take advantage of this particular opportunity.

Timing simply means taking advantage of those moments when the potential target is most vulnerable. These periods may arise for the reasons mentioned above or, in the context of an international conflict, may be the result of poor planning. A state preparing for war, or for an aggressive influence attempt, will be more vulnerable to monetary diplomacy if it has not anticipated the possibility that such power could be directed against it. As seen in the Italian war with Ethiopia, the apparent movement toward international conflict puts pressure on a state's exchange position from two directions. On one side, the government is drawing on its resources to prepare for war; on the other, its financial position is challenged by speculation, which tends to shift capital from belligerent to neutral currencies in times of conflict. Monetary power may be able to influence the target in any event, but opportunities should be greatest when targets have not sufficiently anticipated the consequences of monetary diplomacy directed against them.

Opportunities for dependence inhibit manipulation. Interrelationships among the types of monetary power are not limited to dependence and disruption. Just as the preference for entrapment can inhibit the practice of overt forms of monetary dependence, with larger systems, the opportunity for entrapment inhibits the practice of negative currency manipulation in general. This explains why the post–World War II era witnessed fewer episodes of predatory manipulation than did the previous era.[8] As discussed in Chapters 4

---

[8] There were, however, more episodes than were presented in Part II. Two of the predatory cases examined did come from the postwar era (as did three of the four cases of dependence and two of the three episodes of disruption), but there were also others. Some of these were mentioned

and 6, the U.S. attempt to construct and maintain the outer dollar zone could have been undermined by aggressive attempts at manipulation or the overt exploitation of dependence. Therefore, negative manipulation in this era was less common than it might otherwise have been. This suggests that periods in which established systems are disintegrating should feature an increase in the opportunity to practice manipulation.

Opportunities for disruption do exist. Despite the now-familiar difficulties regarding disruption, chances to practice this type of monetary power do exist. As discussed in Chapter 5, these opportunities increase the more rules there are associated with the target system, because the rules separate the system from market forces, which can then bandwagon with the disruptive actions, increasing the effective power of the agent relative to the target. Additional opportunities for disruption arise from indirect techniques, through pressure at the weakest link in a system (as seen in the interwar period) or through multiple diffuse pressures that overwhelm the ability of the system to respond.

Monetary power may be effective against friends. Monetary power may provide a relatively greater number of opportunities to coerce states with which the home state is traditionally friendly than do other forms of influence. This is because unlike many other instruments of economic power, monetary sanctions can be introduced to great effect without causing permanent damage to the target economy. This was a very important consideration for the United States with regard to its influence attempts directed at Britain and Panama. States positioned to exploit dependence and disruption are also usually friendly with the states they are trying to influence. Further, the private nature of monetary sanctions means that pressure can be introduced without long-term effects on relations because the parties involved need never appear to be in direct confrontation.

Finally, it should be kept in mind that the best "opportunities" to practice monetary power may be illusory. This is because they can in fact be "too successful." Therefore, some obvious instances may not represent "true" opportunities to influence targets because of the home state's fear that such overt efforts will persuade targets to remove themselves from further pressure. Vigorous and repeated attempts at manipulation can contribute to rigorous exchange control, and to an unwelcome retreat of the target to beyond the grasp of the home state. Strategic disruption can cause the unwanted collapse of an international monetary system. Thus, because of the remarkable force of cur-

---

in various parts of the book. These were not presented because the demonstrations from the earlier periods were more than sufficient for the purposes of the analysis, and because monetary power tends to be practiced discreetly, with the result that the data were usually much better for the earlier cases. Additionally, for reasons discussed below, monetary diplomacy in the cold war era was more likely to feature *economic* issues, outside the scope of this study.

rency power, true opportunities to practice monetary diplomacy entail both a vulnerability and the ability to use techniques which skillfully exploit it.

Monetary Power and Contemporary International Politics

It is highly likely that monetary diplomacy will become a more significant feature of the international system in the coming years. Three fundamental changes in the international system all create increased opportunity for the practice of monetary power: the end of the cold war, the dispersion of monetary power, and the growth of financial markets.

The End of the Cold War

For a number of reasons, the cold war tended to inhibit the practice of monetary power. The ideological aspects of the struggle contributed to this. Given the competition between the superpowers to demonstrate the superiority of their systems, the United States was reluctant to use the mechanisms of international capitalism to destabilize developing regimes. In fact, much of U.S. policy in this era was designed to get states to participate in an explicit international monetary institution, the IMF. Also, the nonmarket nature of the Soviet Union and its allies left little room for most forms of monetary diplomacy.[9] Finally, the cold war in general drove the capitalist economies together, harmonizing their basic security vision, thus reducing both the necessity and the inclination for coercive measures to shape security behavior between those states.

With the end of the cold war, all of these inhibitors have been eliminated. The practice of overt monetary power does not drive small states into the arms of Soviet-style command economies. New market economies provide targets where there were none before. The collapse of the common security threat uncovers dormant conflicts between the advanced capitalist states and reduces incentives to avoid conflict. Additionally, those conflicts that do boil over are more likely to be fought with economic, as opposed to military, measures.

Monetary power will be of increasing consequence in three post–cold war arenas. First is the evolution of monetary arrangements among the states of the former Soviet Union. These agreements will help define the balance of economic power between the Russian center and the other states, the relative insulation of the unit as a whole, and opportunities for entrapment and disruption. It must be recognized, then, that the choice of a system will have specific

---

[9] However, black market exchanges of local for hard currencies might have provided some opportunities.

political consequences.[10] Second is the monetary destiny of the states of Eastern Europe. Sandwiched between the mark system and a possible ruble system, saddled with internal instability, and confronted with regional conflicts, the states in this region are likely candidates to experience conflicting pressures of manipulation and dependence. Third, and related to this, is the general trend toward disintegration. As more and more states declare their independence, there will be an increasing number of small states with relatively weak currencies in the world. Such states will be particularly vulnerable to manipulation and excellent candidates for dependence.

The Dispersion of Monetary Power

The main trend in the international monetary system in the near future will be the continued dispersion of monetary power. Relative monetary power will shift away from the United States and toward Germany and Japan. Once again, this development will increase the salience of monetary power in the international system. With the continued decline of the outer dollar area, the United States is likely to become less inhibited with regard to the practice of currency manipulation. Additionally, the emergence of new monetary powers means that more states will have the capability to practice manipulation. As noted above, this increase in the number of those capable of practicing manipulation is taking place at the same time that the number of states vulnerable to manipulation is approaching a new high.

The rise of new currencies carries with it the expectation that these new core states will attempt to expand their monetary influence. One consequence of the dispersion of monetary power, then, will be the rise of new monetary systems, centered around the dollar, yen, and mark. The formation of these systems will feature monetary politics, and the structure of the systems will shape the opportunities of these states to exploit dependence. Coupled with the end of the cold war, these factors will make monetary conflict and competition between these areas likely. Given the emerging environment, small states may be forced to seek membership in monetary systems in order to avoid being frozen out of the benefits of these systems, which are likely to include trade and financial preferences, and to provide protection from the potential manipulation of others.

It should be noted that the formation of three distinct currency centers, one located in Europe, one in East Asia, and one in the western hemisphere, will have political consequences. While the specific rules will shape these influences, these currency systems will have diversionary effects with regard to all

[10] On the economics of a number of possible systems, see John Williamson, *Trade and Payments after Soviet Disintegration* (Washington, D.C.: Institute for International Economics, 1992).

other economic transactions. This should bring the members of each system closer together, insulate the systems, and increase the political power of the leaders vis-à-vis the members. Consequently, the currency associations of the states of Eastern Europe, including those of the former Soviet Union, will take on added significance. The prospects for the development of an independent and thriving ruble system will greatly influence the balance of monetary power.

The Growth of Financial Markets

The growth of financial markets represents the third fundamental change in the international system with implications for monetary power. This growth has been manifested in both size and permeability. The power of the market has grown fantastically in the last twenty-five years, and technological developments have integrated those markets to a greater extent than ever before. Both of these developments increase the opportunities for the practice of monetary power, and thus suggest that it will become an increasingly common feature of international politics.

The increased size of the market means that states will have less control over their monetary destinies. This will be particularly true in the near future, given the number of minor, weak currencies emerging in the system. It also means that the issues of market balancing and bandwagoning will be of increasing importance: it will become more and more difficult to overcome balancing, while bandwagoning might ensure the success of coercion. Since the market constantly hunts for new equilibria, is often self-inflammatory, and often acts on noneconomic data, the success of currency manipulation will increasingly be dependent on the ability of actors to skillfully manipulate market forces. Specific tactics, such as the mixture of public and private measures, and the timing of various acts will become decisive.

The absolute size of the market also means that disruption, which typically counts on inspiring market bandwagoning, will become an increasingly viable, if still challenging, form of coercion. The influence of these developments on dependence, however, is less clear. On one hand, the increasingly dangerous international environment makes membership more attractive. On the other, technological changes that foster permeability may undermine the ability of currency systems to insulate members from the international economy. Thus, changes in the financial system threaten the ability of leaders to gain the benefits of dependence. In the context of increasing regionalization, much depends on whether states will challenge market evolution and construct stricter rules to protect currency blocs, or whether they will embrace the market and allow monetary blocs to be functionally marginalized. Either way, these financial developments will increase the significance of monetary power. In the case of increased insulation, the practice of dependence will become increasingly overt and powerful. In the case of increased permeability, the exposure to market forces will leave all states more vulnerable to currency manipulation.

Regardless, new developments in the international system all create increased opportunities for the practice of monetary power, suggesting that this form of state power will become a more salient feature of international politics in the coming years.

Index

Abyssinia. *See* Ethiopia
Agadir crisis, 12, 82, 83–85, 113, 267
aid, 4, 21, 22, 24, 160, 246; attributes of,
  25–26, 26n.10, 27, 28–29; compared with
  monetary power, 31, 112, 263, 264; franc
  zone and, 150–52
Albania, 132
Algeria, 68, 194
appreciation, 9n.14, 177
Aristophanes, 48n.5
Aron, Raymond, 198
aski-mark, 137–39
Australia, 67, 142, 146n.73, 204n.87
Austria, 123, 181, 182, 185, 188
Austria-Hungary, 88, 246
Awolowo, Obafemi, 103

balance of payments, 176, 177, 202, 254,
  255, 256; concerns regarding, 3, 120,
  151, 152; crises in, 8, 10, 14, 40 deficits
  in, 18, 195
Balancing, 37–38, 273, 273n5, 274, 280.
  See also bandwagoning
Baldwin, David, 7, 21n.2, 271
Bandwagoning, 37–38, 39, 40, 214, 226,
  231, 233, 272–73, 273n.5, 274, 277,
  280. *See also* balancing
Bank for International Settlements, 189
Bank of England, 143, 180, 182, 185, 186,
  208, 222, 230, 251
Bank of Italy, 232, 239
Bank of Mexico, 98
Bank of France, 12, 176, 177, 178, 179,
  180, 182, 187, 200
barter, 18, 19, 138, 161
Basle agreement, 193, 194
Belgium, 92, 121, 136, 137, 149, 185, 220,
  221, 223n.12
Ben Gurion, David, 68
Bénard, Jean, 152
Bergsten, C. Fred, 10
Biafra, 102–6
bilateral exchange clearing, 123–27, 133,
  134, 135, 137; financing principle under
  126–27, 133, 134; waiting principle under

126–27, 134, 137. *See also* exchange
  control
bimetallism, 48
black markets, 23n.6, 25, 49, 103, 112,
  278n.9
boatrocking, 27, 172, 190, 200, 270
Bolivia, 159
Boyle, Edward, 74
Brazil, 97
Bretton Woods, 156, 157, 158, 192
British Commonwealth, 63, 64, 204, 206,
  210, 211; conference in 1952 of, 64;
  Ottawa policy of, 143
Brown, W. A., 178
Bulganin, Nikolai, 72, 73
Bulgaria, 121, 123
Bush Administration, 161
Butler, R. A., 69, 70n.68, 72, 74, 75

Canada, 143n.61, 148
Cardenas, Lazaro, 97
Carr, E.H., 180–81, 234–35
Cassel, Gustav, 34, 176n.11
Chen, K. P., 53n.15, 56
China, 3, 22, 152, 153, 173, 222, 276;
  Great Britain and currency stabilization
  boards for, 56–58; Japan and predatory
  manipulation against, 58–61; lessons from
  monetary warfare in, 61–63; monetary
  warfare over, 51–62, 107, 111, 112, 114,
  267; U.S. purchases of silver from, 52–56
Churchill, Winston, 10, 74
cold war, 101n.161, 236, 248, 258–59,
  278–79
composite reserve unit, 197
continental system, 149
counterfeiting, 3, 4n.4, 100–102, 110, 111,
  112, 171, 259, 262, 264
Cuno, Wilhelm, 221
currency manipulation, 8–12, 13, 41, 281;
  costs to sender, 62, 81, 91, 107, 111–12,
  266; costs to target, 10–11, 107, 267;
  defense against, 10, 110–11; forms of,
  46–7; lessons regarding, 265–67;
  opportunities to practice, 273–74, 260,

currency manipulation (*cont.*)
276–77; secrecy of, 36, 81, 111, 112,
226, 230, 233, 264, 277; theory of 46–
51, 110–14, 219–20, 243–44; theoretical
viability of, 31–38. *See also* implicit
currency manipulation; passive currency
manipulation; permissive currency manipulation; predatory currency manipulation;
protective currency manipulation
currency politization, 231, 233, 271–72
currency reputation, 16, 38, 39, 42, 273,
274, 274n.6; relationship between prestige
and, 11, 12, 14, 38, 194, 230
currency substitution, 106, 158, 158n.108,
165, 267
Czechoslovakia, 64, 123, 152n.95, 174,
183, 238, 246–47, 258n.106

Daniels, Josephus, 96, 97
Dayan, Moshe, 68
Dawes plan, 220, 220n2, 223, 226
Debré, Michel, 197
deflation, 92, 93, 110, 129, 176, 231, 236,
238, 240, 241, 242, 273
De Gasperi, Alcide, 237, 238
de Gaulle, Charles, 194, 195, 196, 197,
198, 199, 202
Delvalle, Eric, 160, 161n.114
Denmark, 123
depreciation, 9, 38n.50 39, 48, 138, 223,
273. *See also* devaluation
devaluation, 12, 16, 17, 38n.50, 39, 40, 47,
92, 93, 123, 156, 254, 272, 273; of
British pound 15, 63, 142, 146, 147,
255–56; of French franc, 194–95; and
Germany, 128, 129; and Italy 231, 233; of
Mexican peso, 97, 98; of U.S. dollar,
32n.28, 33. *See also* depreciation
Diaz-Herrera, Roberto, 160
dollar (U.S.), 11, 18, 30, 32, 33, 36, 59,
86, 101, 146, 176, 239, 263. *See also*
dollar system
dollar system, 13, 156–66, 167, 248, 277,
279; absence of in early twentieth century,
244–46; challenged by France, 192–203.
See also dollar (U.S.)
Dominican Republic, 159, 159n.110
Dulles, John Foster, 65, 65n.51, 67, 72
Dunn, James Clement, 242n.68
Dylan, Bob, 3

Eden, Anthony, 63, 65, 65n.52, 68, 70, 71,
72, 74, 75, 79
Egypt, 6, 64, 65, 66, 67, 68, 142, 144,
144n.67, 145
Einaudi, Luigi, 239, 240
Einzig, Paul, 179n.21, 183, 190n.50, 231,
Eisenhower, Dwight D., 66, 67, 72, 79, 194
Endara, Guillmero, 161
enforcement, 116, 163, 167, 168, 169, 248,
267, 268. *See also* Panama
entrapment, 40n.56, 117–19, 167, 168, 169,
248–49, 267, 268; Britain and, 141, 145,
157, 248; France and, 154, 157, 248;
Germany and, 122, 131–32, 136, 138,
247–48; U.S. and, 157, 165, 248 267,
268
Estonia, 123
Ethiopia, 93, 228, 229, 231, 234, 235, 243,
276
European Common Market, 151
exchange control, 54, 60, 85, 122–23, 239,
254, 277; German 128–32, 254; Italian,
231, 232, 239; wartime 85, 144–45, 254.
See also bilateral exchange clearing
exchange equalization account, 16, 92, 158
exchange rates; equilibria in, 32, 33, 34, 35,
36, 36nn. 40, 41, 280; theories of
determination of 34, 35; fixed and
flexible, 8, 9n14, 32, 36, 36n.43, 38n.50,
45, 48–50, 82, 82n.99, 113–14, 173–75,
266, 266n.2, 267
expulsion, 13, 14, 40, 116, 117, 154–55,
167, 168, 169, 248, 267, 268. *See also*
Mali
extraction, 117, 165, 167, 168, 169, 267;
British, 147–48, 165, 167, 168, 248, 269;
German, 122, 132, 136, 140, 248

Federal Reserve (U.S.), 11, 30, 68, 69,
161n.114, 189, 246
feedback, 25, 164, 169, 220, 227, 227n.24,
249, 249n.78, 262; bilateral monetary,
257, 262, 264; central paradox of, 27,
110; monetary diplomacy and, 99, 107,
117, 120, 169, 270; economic diplomacy
and, 25, 26, 27, 110, 264; environmental,
101, 110, 227n.24, 243, 262, 264
financial diplomacy 4, 7, 21, 22, 24–25,
246; attributes of, 26, 27, 29, 31;
compared with monetary power, 31, 263,

264; during the inter-war period, 182, 186, 189

financial markets, 280–81

franc (french), 85, 86, 88, 194, 223, 225, 226, 227; post world war I restoration of, 11–12, 176–80; weakness in, 200, 220, 222, 224. See also franc zone

franc zone, 13, 16n.36, 148–56, 166, 167, 168, 248, 249; failure to create in inter-war period, 244, 246–47; operations account of, 150. See also franc (french)

France, 12, 18, 137, 142, 157, 158, 177, 180, 190–92, 260, 261, 270; and Agadir crisis, 83–85; and crusade against dollar, 192–203; and inter-war disruption, 183–92, 271; and Italian invasion of Ethiopia, 229–30, 233–35, 243; and occupation of the Ruhr, 220–28, 243; and Suez Crisis, 64, 66, 67, 68, 70, 76–78, 80; and tripartite monetary agreement, 92–95. See also franc (french); franc zone

George VI, 234

German question, 175, 180–82

Germany, 6, 23, 89, 92–93, 149, 154, 175, 182, 229, 234–35, 246, 247, 260, 269, 279; and Agadir crisis 83–85; counterfeiting by, 83, 100–102, 110, 111, 227n24, 259n.108, 262; and currency manipulation during WWI by, 87–89; exchange control of, 123, 128–30, 189, 264; French manipulation against, 187, 191; and French occupation of Ruhr, 220–24, 243; "new plan" of, 130–32; relations of under new plan, 132–38. See also mark (German); mark bloc

Ghana, 204, 206, 207

Giscard d'Estaing, Valéry, 197

gold, 3, 48, 112, 146, 171, 190, 226, 259, 266, 272; inter-war flows of, 175, 182, 183, 184–86, 187; Italian losses of, 231–32, 233, 234; post-war flows of, 199–200, 201; price of, 32, 33, 195; as reserves, 41, 49, 144; South African, 208, 249, 250, 254, 255. See also gold exchange standard; gold standard; reserves

gold bloc, 92, 149

gold-exchange standard, 6, 174, 198n.72; inter-war, 175, 188, 189, 190; post-war, 195, 196, 198. See also gold

gold pool, 193–94

gold standard, 12, 50, 84, 85, 176, 189, 190, 251n.86; South Africa and, 250, 251, 252, 253, 254. See also gold

Goldfinger, 258n.196

good neighbor policy, 96, 99

Gowa, Joanne, 29n.20

Gowon, Yakubu, 102, 103, 105

Great Britain, 11, 12, 15, 23, 90, 121, 137, 156, 157, 158, 177, 190–92, 213, 260, 269; and Agadir crisis, 83, 85; and China, 51, 56–58, 60; and french occupation of Ruhr, 224–28, 243; and Italian invasion of Ethiopia, 229–30, 233–35, 243; and South Africa, 249–57; and Rhodesia, 203, 206–8; and Suez crisis, 3, 64–82, 277; and tripartite monetary agreement 92–95; and World War I, 86–7, 89. See also pound (british); sterling area

Greece, 101, 101n.159, 123, 134, 134n.39, 185

Gresham's Law, 48, 48n.5

Guinea, 16n.36, 150n.89, 151n.94, 155, 167

Heydrich, Richard, 100

Himmler, Heinrich, 100

Hirschman, Albert O., 12, 13, 14, 15, 115, 118, 120

Hitler, Adolph, 94, 129, 235

Hoare, Samuel, 229

Hoffmann, Stanley, 197

Houghton, Alanson B., 225

Hufbauer, Gary Clyde, 7, 21, 28

Hughes, Charles Evans, 225

Hull, Cordell, 56, 57, 96, 97, 98, 99

Humphrey, George, 68–9

Hungary, 123, 134, 135, 185, 189

ideology; role of in monetary diplomacy, 121, 131, 156, 248, 249, 260–61

implicit currency manipulation, 227, 243, 262, 265

inconvertibility, 27, 49–50, 90, 174, 251

India, 6, 89–91, 111, 113, 141, 142, 142n.57, 144, 144n.67, 148, 267. See also rupee

Inflation, 19, 90, 131, 140, 151, 152, 176, 253, 253n90, 272; and hyperinflation 128, 221–22; in Italy, 230, 239, 241, 242n.68; and monetary diplomacy 7, 9, 23, 272

In-Laws, The, 258n.106
Institute of Exchange (Italy), 230
Instituto Nazional Cambi, 231
International Development Association, 152
International Monetary Fund, 17, 69, 73, 77, 81, 152, 156, 157, 160, 242, 243, 278
International Monetary Relations, 5–6
Iran, 64, 159n.109
Iraq, 64, 65, 142, 159n.109
Israel, 24n.9, 66, 68, 71
Italy, 101, 149, 185, 186; and invasion of Ethiopia, 228–35, 276; missed opportunity to support, 235–43. *See also* lira (Italian)

Japan, 51, 53, 141, 222, 279; and China, 58–61, 83, 107, 112, 267. *See also* yen
Jasper, Henri, 223n.14
Johnson, Lyndon B., 12, 12n.30, 194, 202, 202n.82
Jordan, 65

Kaunda, Kenneth, 204, 205n.92, 209, 210
Keita, Modibo, 152, 153,
Kemmerer, Edwin W., 251
Kenen, Peter B., 40, 193n.55
Kennan, George F., 236
Kennedy, John F., 3, 194
key currency, 6, 18, 19, 23, 41, 42, 48, 147, 175, 176; benefits to issuer of, 195, 195n.62
Keynes, John Maynard, 87, 176, 258n.107
Kindleberger, Charles P., 11, 23, 172, 199n.74, 201n.80, 202n.81
Knorr, Klaus, 7, 26n.10
Krugman, Paul, 33n.32
Kung, H. H., 52, 61
Kunz, Diane, 69n.67, 77n.90

Laos, 15
Lasteyrie, Charles, 222, 223, 247
Latin America, 96, 97, 132, 136, 137, 139, 140, 163; fear of axis penetration in, 98, 138, 138n.50; dollarization in, 158, 159
Latin Monetary Union, 149, 154
Latvia, 123
Laval, Pierre, 229, 235
League of Nations, 183, 228, 229, 230, 235
Lenin, Vladamir, 258, 258n.107
Libya, 24n.9, 65, 162
lira (Italian), 12, 30n.22, 85, 230–34; post-war stabilization of 235–43

Leith-Ross, Frederick, 182, 192
Liska, George, 26n10, 28
Lithuania, 123, 132
LLoyd, Selwin, 68, 69, 70, 71, 74, 75, 78
locarno, treaty of, 92, 235

McDonald, Ramsay, 226
Macmillan, Harold, 63, 66, 67, 71, 72, 74, 75, 75n.76, 98
Madiebo, Alexander, 105
Malawi, 205, 205n.92
Mali, 150n.89, 151–55, 174, 258n.106, 268
mark (german), 37, 87, 221, 222, 222n.7. *See also* mark bloc
mark bloc, 13, 132–41, 166, 167, 247–48, 275, 279. *See also* mark (german)
Marshall, George, 236, 242n.68
Marshall Plan, 237, 238, 242
Mauritania, 150n.89, 155n.104
Menzies, Robert, 67
Mexico, 82, 95–99, 107, 110, 111, 114, 159, 262, 272
middle east, 24n.9, 63, 65, 66, 79, 145
military currencies, 58–59, 60, 139
Millerand, Alexandre, 224
Mollet, Guy, 68
monetary dependence, 8, 12–17, 27, 280–81; benefits to core state from, 13; benefits to members from, 14, 256; costs of exit from, 17; difference between dependency and, 12–13, 115, 117n.5, 268; forms of, 116–19; lessons regarding, 267–69; opportunities for 119–21, 247–49, 260–61, 274–75, 276–77; theory of, 116–21, 166–69, 244–47; viability of, 39–41; vulnerability of target to, 13. *See also* expulsion; enforcement; entrapment; extraction
money, psychology of, 8, 10, 11, 12, 87, 194
Monroe Doctrine, 244
Moreau, Emile, 176, 180, 181, 183, 185–86, 190
Moret, Clément, 191
Morgan, J. P., 86, 224
Morocco, 83–84
Morgenthau, Henry, 32, 52–53, 55, 60, 94, 96, 97, 98, 260
Morrison, Van, 220n.2
Mozambique, 205, 208
Mussolini, Benito, 12, 229, 230, 231, 233,

234, 235, 243, 271–72; Pesaro declaration of, 12, 230–31

Napoleon Bonaparte, 149
Napoleon, Louis, 149
Nasser, Gamal Abdel, 64, 65, 66, 67, 68, 70, 71
Nègre, Louis, 153
New Zealand, 142
Nicaragua, 164, 245
Niemeyer, Otto, 226
Nigeria, 102–6, 204, 207, 267
Nixon, Richard, 30n.22
Nkrumah, Kwame, 206, 207, 207n.99, 258n.106
Noriega, Manuel, 160, 161, 162, 163, 164, 272
Norman, Montagu, 180, 181, 182, 185, 186, 187, 251
Norway, 139, 185
Nurkse, Rangar, 36n.43
Nutting, Anthony, 73n.79, 74
Nyerere, Julius, 206n.95

Ojukwu, Chukwuemeka Odumegwu, 102, 105–6
Organization of African Unity, 203, 206

Palma, Manuel, 160
Pakistan, 64
Panama, 159–66, 167, 268, 272, 277
Pappen, Franz, von, 129
passive currency manipulation, 46, 47–48, 50, 81, 112–13, 262, 265, 266; between the U.S. and Mexico, 95, 97–98, 99
Peloponnesian War, 4n.4, 48n.5
permissive currency manipulation, 46–7, 49, 50, 81, 87, 113, 157, 262, 265, 266; and the tripartite monetary agreement, 92, 94–95
Plato, 6n.7
Pineau, Christian, 68
Poincaré, Raymond, 11, 176, 186, 221, 222, 223
Poland, 10–11, 132, 139, 183, 189, 246
Portugal, 142, 185, 205, 208, 245
pound (British) 15, 51, 80n.98, 100–101, 142, 145, 180, 190, 191, 239; convertibility of, 11, 63, 146, 147, 176; weakness of, 23, 86, 204. See also sterling area

predatory currency manipulation, 46–48, 49, 50, 81, 88, 97, 100, 230, 265, 266; against China, 51, 58–61,
protective currency manipulation 46–47, 49, 81, 87n.117, 91, 95, 96–97, 99, 208, 223n.12, 241, 265, 266; for China, 52–58; self-protection, 47, 50, 86, 88, 89, 265
publicity, and economic coercion, 28, 37, 199
purchasing power parity, 34–5

Quesnay, Pierre, 182

Reagan Administration, 160
Reichsbank, 128, 222, 224
reparations, 181, 188, 220, 226
reserves 7, 9n14, 10, 33, 40, 41, 48–49, 50, 113, 208, 255, 275; adequacy of, 17, 40; British, 73, 76–78, 143, 144, 176; Chinese, 52, 56; French, 76–78, 200; German, 84, 128; Italian, 229, 231, 232, 233; Mexican, 96, 97, 98; pooling of, 14, 16. See also gold; silver
Rhineland, German remilitarization of, 92–93
Rhodesia, 203, 205, 206, 207, 208, 209, 210, 212
Rist, Charles, 181, 185, 191, 195, 195n.60
Robinson, Joan, 35–36, 37
Romania, 125n.17, 134, 183, 186, 246
Roosevelt, Franklin D., 11, 32, 32n.28, 55, 99
ruble, 86, 87, 88, 88nn. 120,121, 279
Rueff, Jacques, 195, 195n.60, 201n.80
Ruhr, 181, French occupation of, 220–28, 243, 247, 262
rumormongering, 40, 47, 53, 89, 91, 187, 266
rupee, 89–91, 276
Russia, 87–88, 278. See also ruble

Schacht, Hjalmar, 130, 130n.28, 181, 182, 185, 222
Schelling, Thomas, 79, 172
Schlesinger, Arthur Jr., 194
Schott, Jeffrey J., 7, 28
Schumpeter, Joseph, 258n.107
security studies, integration with political economy, 4, 263
seigniorage, 6n.9, 195n.62

Senegal, 155n.104
Signaling, 8, 28, 111, 267
silver, 3, 4n.4, 49, 51, 52, 53, 55, 60, 112,
    173, 232, 276; and India, 89–91,
    142n.57; interests in U.S., 55, 55n.20,
    96, 99, 111; and Mexico, 95–97; purchase
    act of 1934, 51, 55; 1918 Pittman act and,
    90. *See also* reserves
Simon, John, 234
Smith, Ian, 203, 208, 209
South Africa, 141, 142, 143n.61, 143n.64,
    148, 205, 208, 210, 270, 275; absence of
    disruption by 249–57, 258, 261
South African reserve bank, 208, 255, 257
Soviet Union, 26, 152, 157 235, 248, 278,
    280; apparent absence of subversive
    disruption by, 258–59, 278, 280; and Suez
    Crisis 64, 72–73
Spain, 93, 141, 245
speculation, 16, 17, 33, 36, 87, 88, 215,
    223, 252, 252n.88, 253, 253n.91, 223,
    223n.15, 224, 264
Sterling Area, 13, 15, 64, 140–48, 166,
    167, 248; South Africa and 252, 255–57;
    sterling balances and 63, 64, 145;
    Zambian disruption of 203–12. *See also*
    pound (British)
Stockholm monetary conference (1968),
    199–200
Strange, Susan, 194
strategic disruption, 171–73, 175, 212–15,
    258, 261, 264, 269–70, 277; French inter-
    war, 190–92; French post-war, 201–2,
    203; Zambian, 210–12
Strong, Benjamin, 181, 182, 185, 187
Suarez, Eduardo, 96
subversive disruption, 18, 171, 173, 175,
    190–92, 201, 203, 261; absence of, 213,
    258–60, 269
Sudan, 65
Suez crisis, 3, 107, 111, 113, 163, 197,
    267; competing explanations of outcome
    of, 70–74; lessons from, 81–83; monetary
    power and, 67–70; oil and, 74–80; origins
    of, 63–65
Sweden, 11, 22, 88
Switzerland, 123, 125n.17, 149
systemic disruption, 8, 18–19, 23, 27; costs
    of defense from, 19; costs to target, 18–
    19, 170; difficulty of, 18, 213, 257, 259;
    French efforts at, 192–203; in interwar

period, 183–92; lessons regarding, 269–
    71; opportunities for, 261, 275, 277;
    South African opportunities for 252–57;
    theory of, 170–75, 212–15; viability of,
    41–42; vulnerabilities to, 18; Zambian
    attempts at, 203–12. *See also* strategic
    disruption; subversive disruption
Sze, Sao-ke, 52

Tanzania, 206n.95
Tobin, James, 173, 198, 201n.80
trade sanctions 4, 21, 22, 24, 206; attributes
    of, 26, 27, 28; compared with monetary
    power, 31, 81, 112, 164, 263, 264; league
    of nations and, 228–30, 232, 234–35
Treaty of Versailles, 181, 189
Triffin dilemma, 193
tripartite monetary agreement, 91–95, 111,
    265
Truman Doctrine, 237
Turkey, 64, 134

United Nations, 236, 237, 242; and Rhodesia
    203, 206; and Suez crisis 67, 68
United States, 15, 23, 28, 29, 177, 189,
    190, 208, 209, 213, 260, 263, 278, 279;
    failure of to extend monetary influence in
    the Caribbean, 244–46, 249; and China,
    51–58, 62, 267; and French occupation of
    Ruhr, 224–28, 243; and stabilization of
    lira, 235–43; and Mexico, 95–99, 262,
    267, 272; and enforcement against
    Panama, 159–66; and Suez crisis, 64–65,
    66, 68, 69–70, 72, 75, 79–82, 277; and
    support for rupee, 90–91; and tripartite
    monetary agreement, 92–95; and World
    War I, 86–87, 87n.117. *See also* dollar
    (U.S.); dollar system

Vargas, Getulio, 97
Venezuela, 159
Vietnam War, 158, 196n.63
Vissering, Gerard, 251
Volcker, Paul, 11
Volpi, Giuseppe, 230

West Germany, 6n.9
White, Harry, 60
Wilson, Harold, 12, 209, 210, 210n.110,
    211
Wina, Arthur, 210

World Bank, 65

World War I, 11, 110, 114, 154n.103, 176, 220, 244, 250, 267, 272, 276; monetary diplomacy during, 85–91

World War II, 6, 57, 58, 63, 149, 154n.103, 157, 204, 254, 257, 276; monetary diplomacy during 91, 100–102, 139, 140, 143–44; monetary reconstruction following, 156, 192

Wu, Yuan-Li, 7, 11

yen, 30, 36, 61, 279

Young, Arthur N., 54, 57, 58

Young Plan, 182, 188

Yugoslavia, 123, 134, 134n.39, 182, 183, 186, 189, 246

Zambia, 203–12, 261, 270